STANLEY GIBBONS

Postcard Catalogue

Fourth Edition, 1985

Stanley Gibbons Publications Ltd

By Appointment to Her Majesty The Queen
Stanley Gibbons Ltd, London Philatelists

399 Strand, London WC2R 0LX

Compiled by
TONIE and VALMAI HOLT

1st edition—September 1980
2nd edition—July 1981
3rd edition—September 1982
4th edition—September 1984

ISSN 0144-249X ISBN 0 85259 084 9

Item No. 2829

Phototypeset by Input Typesetting Ltd, London
Printed in Great Britain by Whitefriars Press,
Tonbridge

CONTENTS

SECTION INDEX

THE COMPILERS

Tonie and Valmai Holt wrote their first picture postcard book in 1971. Over the years, *Picture Postcards of the Golden Age—A Collectors Guide* has become accepted as one of the standard works on the hobby. Their subsequent books have used postcards as source material, their efforts contributing greatly to the growing appreciation of the postcard as a document of historical record and value. Their widely acclaimed *Till the Boys Come Home—The Picture Postcards of the First World War* (1977) was followed by *Best of Fragments from France* (1978)—a collection of Bruce Bairnsfather's cartoons. *Picture Postcard Artists* (1984) covers the postcard work of the artists who produced landscapes, animals and characters. Scheduled for publication in 1985 is *Deutschland Erwache!* (Germany Awake!) an historical account of the rise of National Socialism in Germany again illustrated by postcards. Their writings about postcards have appeared in magazines published on both sides of the Atlantic and they have talked about postcards on both radio and television. However, their most vivid memory is the creation of the first *Stanley Gibbons Postcard Catalogue*, particularly the last 72 hours before they delivered the manuscript, when they didn't go to bed at all!

ACKNOWLEDGEMENTS

We would like to extend our grateful thanks to all the people whom we acknowledged in the third edition of this catalogue, and whose information is published in this fourth edition. For new material we thank:

Brian Asquith (*Aviation*); Lt. Cdr. M. A. Board, R.N. (*Modern*); Mike Clarke (*Artists, Modern*); R. E. Collier (*Publishers*); Fred Foley ('FAGA') (*Modern*); Ron Griffiths (*Modern*); Mark Haddon (*Entertainment*); C. M. Hernon, (*Competitions, etc.*); Conway A. Longworth-Dames (*Aviation*); Brian Lund (*Sport*); Cindy Morris (*Royalty*); David Parkes (*Collections*); Nils Y. Stenstad, (*Artists*) and Dr. Antonio Dell'Aquila (*Artists*).

Tonie & Valmai Holt

PREFACE

The Stanley Gibbons stamp catalogues are not just a dealers price list, they are acknowledged throughout the world as works of reference containing detailed information collected and analysed by Gibbons staff and specialist collectors. It has been our aim since commissioning the first edition of this *Postcard Catalogue* to produce a similar reference work that will be held in high esteem throughout the postcard world. Judging by the letters we receive we have achieved this aim—you tell us that the Gibbons catalogue is more like a postcard encyclopaedia than a catalogue and that the background information—especially that on individual artists—is welcomed and referred to. However it is also evident from your comments that the size of the catalogue (growing with every edition) is becoming a problem—it is difficult to carry round to postcard exhibitions, fairs and shops—and costs perhaps a little more than many of you want to pay. At first sight then we face an impossible situation—to produce a highly informative catalogue which is not too bulky and modestly priced. After consultation with your compilers, Tonie and Valmai Holt, we have devised this new-look catalogue—a more convenient size, at a lower retail price and we hope still containing the important background information you seem to be seeking. We look forward to hearing your reactions.

In redesigning the catalogue we have amalgamated some sections and renamed others. There is one entirely new section—Maps. In the Artists section, some 17 new artists are listed together with the usual biographical notes. The checklists of cards are proving popular but it would not be feasible to continue the listings from one edition to the next—we would soon have a catalogue the size of the London telephone directory! Thus checklists will usually appear in one edition only but will be referred back to in subsequent editions. In this edition checklists are given for Shurey Insert cards, David Allen Theatre cards, Hildesheimer 5000 series, the Judges London series and of course further listings of the LL London cards—this time dealing with cards of outer London areas such as Hampstead and Clapham.

All sections have been revised and in particular additions made to the Aviation, Comic, Children, Glamour, Modern, Political and Royalty sections. We have retained the list of British postcard clubs which we feel is useful to readers who want to join a local or specialist society and so find out more about their chosen postcard collecting subject. However we have cut down one some of the general information about postcard history although have retained the glossary and bibliography which we hope will be of particular use to the new collector.

Prices have been revised by Mr. and Mrs. Holt and by Mr. Richard Iles (of J. A. L. Franks Ltd, a major London stamp and postcard dealer) to whom we extend our thanks.

Considerable numbers of letters addressed to Tonie and Valmai Holt continue to arrive at Gibbons offices—mostly asking for information about single cards not found listed in the catalogue and asking for valuations of cards and help in buying and selling cards. Whenever time permits, Mr. and Mrs. Holt will try to answer genuine enquiries about cards if return postage is enclosed. However under no circumstances can they give valuations for cards or help in selling them and letters requesting such valuations or advice will, regrettably, go unanswered. Users of this catalogue who have cards for sale should contact the Postcard Dept. of Stanley Gibbons Ltd or one of the dealers advertising in this catalogue.

Mr. and Mrs. Holt acknowledge elsewhere in this catalogue the assistance they have received from postcard collectors and dealers in compiling this work. It would be impossible to include here all the new information sent them since the last edition and we hope that collectors who find that details they sent in have not been used will be patient. All information is kept on file for use at an appropriate time. We are proud of the 'team effort' that has developed between ourselves as publisher, Mr. and Mrs. Holt as compilers and you the collector in producing this catalogue and look forward to a long continuation of this happy arrangement. Your comments on this fourth edition of our catalogue will be most welcome and will be carefully considered.

SZ
JRH

The valuations given in this catalogue are for the postcard only and do not take account of stamp, cachet or cancellation unless specifically stated.

The prices are market valuations current at the time of going to press.

The postcard stocks of Stanley Gibbons Ltd., 399 Strand, London WC2R 0LX are priced broadly on the valuations given in this catalogue.

HOW TO USE THIS CATALOGUE

Unlike coins and postage stamps which, because of their accountability, are carefully recorded on issue, picture postcards have few birth records. Collectors have therefore created their own descriptive language in order to name and hence identify their cards. This language is explained in the GLOSSARY.

But a single picture postcard may have many names. To one collector it may be 'Comic'; to another a 'McGill'; to another, 'World War 1'; to another, 'Inter-Art', and to yet one more, 'Ethnic'.

Thus in order to consult the INDEX for a particular card, the card must first be named, and this process will be made much easier if the reader is familiar with the major collecting themes. These themes constitute the framework of this catalogue and are set out in the SECTION INDEX. The process then is simple:

1. **Name the card.**

2. **Locate that name in the index and follow the references.**

NAMING A CARD

There are three descriptive bands within which a name may be found:

1. *Artist's Name*, the signature on the card, e.g. Cassiers.

2. *Publisher*, e.g. Dietrich of Brussels.

3. *Thematic*, based upon the reason for issue or picture content of the card, e.g. COMIC, EXHIBITIONS, RAILWAYS, etc.

For this edition indexes to Artists and Themes are given.

Example 1
Name—by artist—'Tom Browne'. Consult 'Browne' in index and refer to page quoted for listing and value.

Example 2
Name—by theme—'Zeppelin'. Consult 'Zeppelin' in index and refer to page quoted for listing and value.

Where a card has a value because of its thematic content, that value will be increased if the picture is the work of a collected artist or publisher.

The Index

The index is the key to the whole catalogue. It contains, in alphabetical order, all the major references to Artists and Themes and is placed at the back of the catalogue.

The Illustrations

Each illustration is referred to in the text. Cross-reference is indicated by the sign ■. Illustrations are shown reduced size and are intended for identification purposes only.

Artist Information

The major portrait artists are listed in the Artists section with a brief biographical account.

Where appropriate, however, lists of artists occur throughout as sub-divisions of the main sections. Those individuals with a biographical entry under Artists are marked with the † sign, e.g. Barribal, W.†

THE SEVEN POSTCARD PERIODS

In the past the collecting of old picture postcards was confined to the years from about 1890 to 1918—'The Golden Age'.

Now, the extraordinary growth in popularity of the hobby has widened collecting horizons, and a cataloguing system capable of dealing with all the years from 1869 has become necessary. The 'Seven Postcard Period' system has been developed with this in view. It is now widely used by auction cataloguers, dealers and authors on postcard topics.

Period 1. 1869–1899. The first day of issue of the postcard (1 October 1869) to the last day of the 1800s (31 December 1899).

Period 2. 1900–1914. The first day of the 1900s (1 January 1900) to the last day of peace for Britain (3 August 1914).

Period 3. 1914–1918. The first day of war (4 August 1914) to the cessation of hostilities (11 November 1918).

Period 4. 1918–1939. The first day of peace (12 November 1918) to the last day of peace (2 September 1939).

Period 5. 1939–1945. The first day of war for Britain (3 September 1939) to the day of German unconditional surrender (7 May 1945).

Period 6. 1945–1969. The first day of peace (8 May 1945, VE Day) to the 100th Anniversary of the postcard (1 October 1969).

Period 7. 1969–today. From 2 October 1969 onwards.

A detailed account of each of the seven postcard periods was published in the three earlier editions of this catalogue.

PRICING

Intensive research into the question of postcard prices by the compilers has convinced them of the wisdom of continuing the Three-Band Pricing system used since the inception of this catalogue.

There are often considerable diversities in the retail price of any given card, due to a number of factors:

(*1*) *Geographic.* Certain types are more prized in different countries, or even different parts of the same country. For instance: the fine British comic cards are little collected in France, very popular in the UK. Fairly featureless postcards of Canterbury are eagerly sought after, and dearly bought, by collectors in the Canterbury area but would have virtually no value in Edinburgh. The classic *Art Nouveau* cards of the turn of the century have almost no price ceiling in the United States where there is a strong contingent of wealthy 'investor' collectors, yet they often sell in auction in Britain at well below average catalogue prices.

(*2*) *Fashion.* Interest is sometimes stimulated in certain types of card by a new book or article which features them. Collectors rush to buy these types, which pushes up the price, although it may then settle down again at a lower level.

(*3*) *Condition.* Some collectors will only buy cards in excellent condition. This will always have the effect of placing a premium on cards in virtually mint condition. Other collectors are willing to purchase a card in fairly poor condition in order to have an example of a particular artist's work (to complete a series), but usually in the hope of being able to replace that substandard card with a better example in the future. This means that there *is* a market for poor quality cards, but at a low price. In the middle is the reasonable price for a card in good, collectable condition.

(*4*) *Dealers Stock.* Some dealers do not change the price of cards already in their stock even though the price of those cards is generally accepted to have increased. But as they buy in new cards of the same type they mark them at the new price. Therefore in one dealer's stock collectors often find two examples of the same card, in similar condition, at two very different prices.

(5) *Auctions.* At auction, too, prices vary enormously. If two or more potential purchasers are bidding for a card they each urgently want, an uncharacteristically high price is bound to be paid. On the other hand, normally high-priced postcards, sometimes sell in auction at well below their current average price if no-one bidding is particularly interested in them.

The Three Band Pricing System works as follows:

1. Left Hand Band

This is the lowest price you will probably be asked to pay for this card. It is priced thus because of a combination of the following factors:

a. It is in fairly poor condition
b. It is being sold in an area where such a card is little collected
c. The dealer selling it has had it in stock for a long time
d. The dealer selling it does not know the true value of it
e. It is an inferior example of the artist's work
f. It is poorly printed, or is not a particularly clear photograph, or is a very long distance view of the featured subject (e.g. a tram)
g. The design has been obscured by writing, postmark, etc.
h. It is a modern card

2. Middle Band

This what you will normally be asked to pay for this card. It is the average, reasonable, current market price that is being paid for it because of a combination of the following factors:

a. It is in good, collectable condition
b. The dealer selling it has studied the market and marked it at the current average price being paid for it
c. It is a good example of the artist's work/a good, clear, middle distance photograph/well printed
d. Any writing/postmarks do not detract from the design

3. Right Hand Band

This is the highest price you will probably be asked to pay for this card. It is priced so highly because of a combination of the following factors:

a. It is in virtually perfect condition
b. It is a fine/rare/early example of the artist's work/ perhaps it forms part of one of the classic *Collections*

c. It is a superb, close-up, sharp real photograph of an interesting/unusual event, building or location
d. It is a particularly early example of its type
e. It is unique or special in some way (e.g. signed by subject/artist; only very few were issued; was dropped from a balloon, etc.)

Single Price
Where one price only is printed for a card, this means:
a. It is a modern card, with a standard retail price, or
b. It is in plentiful supply in good condition, cards in poor condition are not worth collecting and would not rate the minimum valuation used in this catalogue—25p.

Prix d'Amateur (P/A)
The card concerned is so rare/attractive that its price has not been sufficiently tested at auction or in dealers' stocks and its price ceiling is only determined by the collector's desire and means.

GLOSSARY

Appliqué. Material attached to a postcard to embellish it, e.g. dried flowers, hair, velvet.

Artist drawn. Cards that originate from an artist's drawing, e.g. Tuck's 'Oilette' series, although that drawing may not have been originally or exclusively drawn for the postcard, but may be reproduced from a poster or magazine etc. They are usually printed by an ink process.

Back. That side of the postcard which carries the address.

Chromo-litho. A term used to describe high quality, lithographically printed coloured picture cards such as early Gruss Aus (*qv*) examples, where up to sixteen different colours were sometimes applied separately. Such cards are almost always from Period 1 or very early Period 2 and were ousted by the introduction of the cheaper three-colour process from around 1900.

Composite. Collective name for a number of individual picture cards that fit together to make a larger picture. Most composites consist of a dozen or less cards which may or may not be pictures in their own right.

Court size. Cards measuring approximately 115 mm × 89 mm, which were officially recognised in Britain on 21 January 1895.

Divided back. Cards where the back has been divided by a line into two sections. One is for the address, and the other for the message. The idea originated in Britain in 1902.

Front. That side of the postcard which does not carry

the address and which normally carries the picture.

Full out. A picture which covers the whole of one side of a postcard and does not share it with either the address or a message space.

Full size. Private postcards in Britain had to be the same size as the official (*qv*) postcards sold at Post Offices. On the Continent much larger cards were permitted by the UPU agreement and these allowed the rapid development of the picture card. The UPU 'full size', 140 by 89 mm (5½ by 3½ inches), became legal in Britain on 1 November 1899.

Gruss Aus. Literally 'Greetings From' in German, the term is used to describe early Continental greetings cards with vignetted pictures.

Hold-to-light. A card which, when held up to the light, displays additional colours or pictures.

Local publisher. A publisher whose premises are located in the area depicted on his picture postcards.

Maximum card. Postcard whose illustration corresponds to that of a postage stamp, usually affixed on the same side and cancelled with a first day of issue postmark.

Name. The identity given to a card by a collector. It may be based upon artist, publisher or theme.

Novelty. A postcard which deviates from the normal rectangular item made of standard board.

Official. A card produced by a Government Post Office. *See also* 'Postal stationery'.

Oversize. Also referred to as 'Continental' size, these are squarer and larger than the UPU full size cards. PHQ cards and German and Italian Period 5 official cards are typically 'oversize', being around 147 mm × 105 mm.

Photo-origin. The pictures found on postcards derive from two main sources—an artist's drawing (*see* 'Artist drawn') or a photograph. Those that originate from photographs are referred to here as 'photo-origin'. They may be printed—photographically (*real photo*), or by some 'normal' printing process involving the transfer of ink, (e.g. Tuck's 'Photochrome' series). Normally 'Real photo' cards have a clearer picture and better detail than other photo-origin cards and are therefore valued more highly. Photo-origin cards as a whole tend to be more valuable than artist drawn varieties, except where the drawings can be attributed to 'collectable' artists.

Postal stationery. Cards carrying pre-printed stamps issued by Government Post Offices. Sometimes designs are added later privately.

Postcard. A card produced with the intention of meeting the regulations concerning the appropriate Postcard Postal Rate.

Poster Ad. A card whose picture is a reproduction of a poster advertisement. The term is often loosely used to describe cards for which there is no firm connection with a known poster, but whose style suggests that an equivalent poster exists.

Printed stamp. The impressed or imprinted postage stamp on official (Post Office) postcards.

Private mailing card. Commercially produced American picture postcard for use with an adhesive stamp. Cards carry the words, 'Private mailing card' on the address side and were introduced on 1 July 1898.

Publisher. A term used to identify the issuing house. Strictly it may not identify the publisher in the dictionary sense of the word, but may also refer to the agent, importer, photographer or printer. The names used for Publishers in this catalogue are those in common usage, e.g. 'Tuck', rather than 'Raphael Tuck & Sons'.

Real photo. A card whose picture originated from a photograph and which has been printed by a photographic process, e.g. Tuck's 'Real photograph' series.

Under size. Applied to cards smaller than UPU 'Full size', but which are not 'Court size' (*qv*).

Undivided back. Cards without a dividing line on the back. The term is generally accepted as denoting an early card.

Vignette. A picture without ruled borders. Typically seen on Gruss Aus (*qv*) cards in twos or threes.

ABBREVIATIONS & SYMBOLS

The following abbreviations are used in this catalogue:

ad	advertisement
art.	artist drawn
Aust	Austrian
Austral	Australian
b & w	black and white
Belg	Belgian
Br	British
Bulg	Bulgarian
Can	Canadian
chromo	chromolithographically printed
chromo-litho	chromolithographically printed postcard
col.	coloured
diff	different
Du	Dutch
Fr	French
GB	Great Britain
Ger	German
HTL	Hold-to-light
Hung	Hungarian
illus	illustrated/illustration
incl.	including
It	Italian
LH	left hand
Maxi	Maximum
nos.	numbers
o/s	oversize
ovp	overprint
PHQ	Postal Headquarters
PMC	Private Mailing Card
PS	Postal Stationery
PU	postally used
Pub.	Publisher
RH	right hand
RP	real photo
Rum	Rumanian
Russ	Russian
UB	undivided back
UK	United Kingdom
UPU	Universal Postal Union
u/s	undersize
USA	American (United States)
WW1	World War 1
WW2	World War 2
†	Biographical entry in ARTISTS section

ADVERTISING

This collecting theme is one of the strongest in the hobby. However, collectors have become more selective in their buying and while once upon a time it was sufficient to describe a card as 'Poster-type' or 'Celebrated Poster' to ensure a high price, that is not now the case.

Poster-type designs remain amongst the more valued of this category, but other factors such as age, printing quality and the signature of a collectable artist, are frequently of equal or greater weight. The Tuck 'Celebrated Poster' series is listed under that publisher and while good prices may still be realised by some of the higher series numbers, the commoner types such as the 'Fry's Five Boys' are now generally well below double figures.

The range of advertising cards is endless and in order to provide a finite framework upon which to build a reference/valuation system, we have divided this section into six parts:

Alcohol/Tobacco
Animal Foods/Foods/Medicines
Books/Magazines/Newspapers
Chocolate & Non-Alcoholic Drinks
Commercial/Household/Industrial
General Poster Type Advertising

An *Art Deco* influence in the design may add a premium value to an otherwise average advertising card.

ALCOHOL/TOBACCO

Dewars, James Buchanan, Thornes & Ogdens all have cards in the Tuck 'Celebrated Posters' series.

Ardite Vermouth
Poster type. Artist I. Stall .. .. £8/**£11**/£12

Bacardi
Comic designs .. .. £1/**£2**/£3

Beer
Pullouts 25p/**50p**/75p

Walker's Lager. Poster types for Warrington & Burton brewery .. .. £10/**£15**/£20

Beer & Baccy
Victoria State (1896) .. .. £20/**£25**/£30

Cavanders Army Mixture
Poster type. Period 3 .. .. £7/**£8**/£10

Chairman Cigarettes
Old English Pottery & Porcelain. 24 cards in series, also issued by other firms .. .. £1/**£2**/£2.50

Champagne
Codorniu. Ten card composite set by artist Lorenzo Brunet. Per set .. .. £30/**£35**/£50
Henriot. Chromo vignettes .. .. £5/**£6**/£8

Kempinski. Chromo 'bon viveur' designs. At least 14 known .. .. £6/**£9**/£10
Kupferberg Gold. Chromo 'bon viveur' and bottle designs .. .. £3/**£6**/£7
Mercier. Chromo vignettes. Bottles and leisure activities .. .. £4/**£7**/£10
Moet & Chandon. Mucha vignette .. .. £20/**£50**/£65
Ruinart Pere et Fils. Overprint on a series of at least 6 cards depicting revels at a masked ball. Pub. J. Goffin Fils. Brussels .. .. £5/**£7**/£10

Chateau Loudenne
Lancet ad. Period 2 .. .. £3/**£4**/£5

Chianti
Italian wine bottle design .. .. £2/**£4**/£6

Cider
Schweppes poster type. Glamour. Period 4 .. £15/**£20**/£22
Symons. Devonshire .. .. £2/**£2.50**/£3

Cinzano
Dutch costume studies. UB .. .. £2/**£2.50**/£4
Pub. Rycker & Mendell. Chromos .. .. .. £2/**£3**/£4

Claymore Whisky
Pub. Tuck. Artist Harry Payne. Defenders of the Empire (1924) .. .. £2/**£4**/£6

Cognac Bisquit
Pub. Bru Fils. Poster type .. .. £6/**£7**/£9

Dewars Whisky
Pub. Dewars. Artist Albert Hammond. Gems of Art series. Period 2 .. .. 50p/**£1**/£1.50

Dimitrino Cigarettes
Artist A. Rossi. Chromos .. .. £5/**£6**/£10

Distillers Co.
Joseph Chamberlain silhouette .. .. £7/**£11**/£13

Dubonnet
Grand Prix 1900. Col. UB .. .. £4/**£5**/£6
Period 7. Rare card by artist Cassandre .. £10/**£20**/£40

Fernet Branca
Pub. Chappius Italy. Series of 10 chromolitho fashion studies. Period 2 UB .. .. £40/**£45**/£50
Pub. Coen Milan. Chromo vignettes .. .. .. £3/**£4**/£7

Gallaghers Park Drive
Poster type. Period 3 .. .. £3/**£5**/£6

Gancia
Bottle vignette UB .. .. £3/**£4**/£5

Gitanes Cigarettes
Poster type. *Art Deco.* Artist René Vincent £18/**£25**/£35

Godfrey Phillips
Inserts. Period 5. 127 × 89 mm
Beauty Spots of the Homeland (30 cards), 1938
Coronation of their Majesties (24 cards), 1937
Famous Paintings (26 cards), 1938
Film Stars (24 cards), 1934
Film Stars (24 cards), numbered 25 to 48, 1935
Film Stars (24 cards), vivid background, 1936
Flower Studies (30 cards), 1937
Franco-British Exhibition .. .. £2/**£4**/£5
Garden Studies (30 cards), 1938
Our Dogs (30 cards), 1939
Our Glorious Empire (30 cards), 1939
Our Puppies (30 cards), 1936
Special Jubilee series (12 cards), 1935
Price range (except Franco-British Exhibition) 25p/**50p**/75p

Grapevine Cigarettes
Southend Imperial Lifeboat (1906) .. .. .. £2/**£3**/£4

Guinness
Brewery scenes. Period 4. Photographic .. £1/**£1.50**/£2
Period 6. Oversize .. .. 50p/**£1**/£1.50
Poster ads. Periods 2, 3 .. .. £1/**£2**/£4
Poster ads. Periods 4, 7. Oversize ('Alice', Strength, etc.)
.. .. £1.50/**£2**/£3

Hofbrauhaus, Munich Beer House
Early Period 2. Gruss Aus type vignettes .. £1/**£2**/£2.50
Period 2. Pub. Karl Wittermuller. Comic types £1/**£2**/£2.50
Period 4. Poster type .. .. £2/**£4**/£6
Periods 6, 7 (incl. 'Beer Mat' postcards) .. 25p/**50p**/75p

Job Cigarette Paper
Poster type. Chromo-litho. Pub. Vercasson, Paris £15/**£20**/£22
Vignettes. Artists Leandre, Maxence .. .. .. £5/**£8**/£10

Löwenbrau, Munich Beer
Col. poster type. Period 4 .. .. £6/**£9**/£12

Mitchell's 'Prize Crop' Cigarettes
Chromo-litho vignettes. Glasgow Exhibition 1901 .. ..
.. .. £12/**£15**/£18

Park Drive Cigarettes
Poster type, e.g. stagecoach .. .. .. £12/**£15**/£18

Players Navy Cut
Art with circular ad. Numbered series .. £10/**£12**/£14

'Principe di Piemonte' Cigarettes
Poster type. Artist A. Scorzon .. .. £4/**£6**/£7

Sandorides 'Lucana' Cigarettes
Poster type .. .. £12/**£16**/£20

Taillan Vermouth
Artist Mich. Poster type .. .. £6/**£7**/£9

Vino Aroud
Comic situations .. .. £1.50/**£2**/£3

White Horse Whisky
Pub. Alf. Cooke. Maggs coaching studies. Period 2 .. .. 25p/**50p**/£1

Wills
Poster types for Capstan, Gold Flake, Three Castles, and Westward Ho! .. .. £15/**£26**/£30

ANIMAL FOODS/FOODS/MEDICINES

Colman's Mustard is represented in Tuck's 'Celebrated Poster' series (*see* COLLECTIONS).

Banana Bread & Flour Co.
Bananine poster type .. .. £6/**£8**/£10

Beechams Pills
Blue card. 'Thanks' .. .. £3/**£4**/£6
Artist Tom Browne. Poster type .. .. .. £15/**£21**/£25
Others .. .. 50p/**75p**/£1.50

Birds Custard
Poster type. Ed. VII series .. .. £10/**£12**/£15
Other poster types .. .. £11/**£13**/£16

Buttapat Margarine
Poster type .. .. £10/**£13**/£15

Carnine Lefranc Health Food (1908)
Artist Weal. French Public Figures. (6 cards) .. £3/**£5**/£7

Carters Little Liver Pills
Poster type. Period 3 .. .. £7/**£9**/£10

Cerebos Salt
Poster type. Chromo-litho. Multi-vignettes .. £12/**£24**/£28

Champions Vinegar
Poster type. Chromo-litho .. .. £15/**£20**/£24

Chanteclair Embrocation
Poster type. Artist Mich .. .. £5/**£9**/£11

Chivers & Sons
English fruits .. .. 50p/**75p**/£1
Aerial views of Histon 25p/**50p**/75p

Crawfords Cream Crackers
Russo-Japanese war map (1905) .. .. £1/**£2**/£3
Poster type .. .. £2/**£4**/£6

Ellimans Embrocation
Artist Sturgess. Horse activities .. .. .. 75p/**£1**/£2

Flapper Sardines
Poster type. Period 4 .. .. £4/**£5**/£7

Force Cereal
Special offer cards. Early period 2 .. .. .. £3/**£6**/£9

Glaxo
Various subjects .. .. 75p/**£1**/£1.50

Harrison & Garthwaite Biscuits
VC winners. Action scenes with inset portraits. Set consists of Burt, Dorrel, Holmes, Leefe Robinson, O'Leary and Pollock .. .. £2.50/**£4**/£5.40

Hartley
Production scenes at Aintree. Interior and aerial 50p/**75p**/£1
Poster type. Marmalade .. .. £3/**£5**/£7

Huntley & Palmer Biscuits
Poster type. The Very Best Available .. .. £3/**£5**/£7
Poster type. *Art Deco*. Artist René Vincent £18/**£23**/£35

Jacobs Biscuits
Biscuit production scenes .. .. 50p/**75p**/£1
Cream crackers. Chromo-lithos .. ..£7/**£10**/£12

Jaffa Oranges
Poster type. Jaffa genie .. .. £14/**£22**/£25

Johnston's Corn Flour
Some Methods of Travelling series. Col. court size. Twenty-four numbered cards.
1. Coracle 2. Chariot 3. Stage Coach 4. Sedan Chair 5. Pillion 6. Post-Chaise 7. Hobby Horse 8. Stage Coach 9. Sedan 10. Carriage 11. Wheel Barrow 12. Carriage 21. Irish Jaunting Car 22. Kago 23. Elephant
Per card .. .. £10/**£17**/£20

Lemco
Coronation series .. .. £5/**£8**/£10
Poster type. Artist Hassall. Set of 'Types of Lemco Cattle' (6 cards) .. .. £3/**£4**/£5

Liebig Fray-Bentos
Meat processing scenes .. .. 75p/**£1**/£1.50
Oxo poster types, e.g. My Word! .. .. .. £10/**£15**/£18
Oxo Shackleton Expedition .. .. £3/**£5**/£7

Lustucru Pâtes
Poster type. 1924 Centenary .. .. £3/**£4**/£6

MacFarlane Lang & Co.
Poster type. 'Sultana Sandwich' series .. .. £2/**£4**/£6

Mellins Food
Poster type .. .. £2/**£4**/£5

Melox
Poster types. Animal and poultry food. Numbered sketches .. .. £2/**£3**/£4

Millenium Bread and Flour (1905)
Poster type. Series 2. Artist Cock .. .. .. £2/**£4**/£6
Poster type. Party invitation. Series 3 .. .. £3/**£5**/£7

Molassine Meal Animal Food
Various sketches .. .. £1/**£1.50**/£2

Neaves Baby Food
Poster type .. .. £10/**£12**/£18

New England Maple Syrup Co.
Poster type. 'Uncle John's Golden Tree', 'The Real Flavour from the Maple Grove,' etc. .. ..£7/**£10**/£16

Pan Yan Pickle
Artist G. E. Studdy. Bonzo. Poster type .. .. £3/**£4**/£7

Peark's Butter
Various .. .. 50p/**75p**/£1

Peek Frean
GB views 25p/**50p**/75p

Pitman Health Food Co.
Ideal food series .. .. 75p/**£1.50**/£3

Quaker Oats ■AD 1
Poster type. 'Smiles' Set of 10 (Postman, Grandpa, Sailor, Cook, Tramp) .. ..£8/**£10**/£12
Smiles, text on front .. .. £4/**£5**/£6

■AD 1 Pub. Quaker Oats Ltd. Artist Anon. Period 2 £10

■AD 2 Pub. Coca Cola. Ger. 'The angry tomcat (or, with a German play on words, 'hangover'), flees away only when it sees Coca Cola'. Period 6 £4

Ranks Flour
Poster type. Period 2 .. .. £4/**£6**/£7

St. Ivel
GB views 25p/**50p**/75p

Sainsbury's Margarine
Crelos overprint of Tuck's 'Early days of Sport' 75p/**£1**/£1.50

Scotts Emulsion
Ninety-two cards in series, one for each Department in France, Corsica & Algeria. Period 2 .. .. £2/**£4**/£6

Shippams
Food production scenes .. .. 50p/**75p**/£1

Skipper Sardines
Poster type. Periods 2/3 .. .. £5/**£9**/£11

Spratts Dog Food
Dog studies .. .. 50p/**75p**/£1

Virol
Children of all Nations. Ideal Home Exhibition (1910) .. .. £1/**£1.50**/£2

Walker, Harrison & Garthwaites ■AD 3
City Meat Dog Biscuit. Viscan. Dog studies. Poster type .. .. £2/**£4**/£6
Phoenix Poultry Foods. Poultry studies. Poster type £2/**£4**/£6

■AD 3 Pub. Walker Harrison & Garthwaite Ltd. Artist Anon. PU 1910 £4

BOOKS/MAGAZINES/NEWSPAPERS
Publications of all sorts frequently contained postcards; particularly so in Period 2 and again today. Sometimes the inserted card was intended to be an attractive giveaway that would encourage sales of the publication concerned. On other occasions insert cards advertised quite independent products. Almost all postcards associated with books, magazines and newspapers are insert giveaways, the major exception being the *Daily Mail* scenes (*see* MILITARY). Period 2 inserts are not highly valued and Period 7 varieties are not yet collected.

Answers
Poster type .. .. £1/**£2**/£3

Bazaar, Exchange & Mart
Bazaar, Exchange & Mart series, drawings each side .. .. £2/**£3**/£4

Hutchinson
Period 1. Court size. Ads for novels .. .. £10/**£12**/£14

Inserts
Most insert views are not of good quality. There are some exceptions and it is these that will command the higher prices in the 'view' category. The most valuable Insert remains the facsimile of Grant's *Doré* card which was issued by the *Postcard Connoisseur* in 1904. Unless otherwise stated the following are valued at 50p:

Bretts publications
Canary & Cage Bird Life
Caperns Bird Foods
Captain magazine. Artist Tom Browne .. .. £1/**£2**/£3
Christian Novels
Connoisseur
Daily News Wallet Guide
Dainty Novels
Family Reader
Feathered World
Field. Military sketches .. .. 50p/**£1**/£1.50
Gentlewoman
Girls Own Paper. Hand cut from sheet of 4. UB £1/**£1.50**/£3
Home Words
Idle Moments
Mirror Novels
My Pocket Novels
My Queen & Romance
Postcard Connoisseur
Facsimile of Grants Doré card .. .. .. £30/**£35**/£50
Others .. .. £10/**£12**/£15
Princess Novels
Red Letter
Shureys Publications. *See below.*
Sketchy Bits
Smart Novels
T.A.T. 'The Months' Series .. .. .. 50p/**75p**/£1.25
Others 25p/**50p**/75p
Time Magazine. Period 7
Tiny Tots 25p/**50p**/75p
Ward Lock. Naval .. .. 50p/**75p**/£1
Weekly Tale Teller
Weldon's Bazaar
Yes or No
Other Inserts

■AD 4 Pub. Shurey's Publications. 'A Kentish Village' PU 1910 50p

Shureys Inserts ■AD 4
There are several collective varieties of which the following are the main ones.

1. Christian Novels. Dividing line on back is in thick dots only. 241 examples known.
2. Shureys. 5 line back in red/brown, magazines named. 207 examples known.
3. Shureys. 4 line back in red/brown, magazines named, but no mention of Great Prize Competition. 205 examples known.

Theatricals	25p/**75p**/£1.25
Tube stations	£1/**£2**/£3
Views	25p/**50p**/£1

In the third edition checklists were published of Shurey Theatrical, Tube Station and View cards (places A–G). The listing of view cards is continued in the supplement to this section.

CHOCOLATE/COCOA/COFFEE/TEA/NON-ALCOHOLIC BEVERAGES

Cadbury's, Frys, Rowntrees, Mazawattee, Milkmaid, Idris, Schweppes, Bovril, Appolinaris, Edwards Soup are represented in the Tucks 'Celebrated Posters' series. Price range £15 to £40.

Arlatte Chicory
Pub. Tuck. Periods 1, 2. F › vers UB .. .. .. £3/**£4**/£5

Banania drink
Poster type .. .. £15/**£17**/£20

Bensdorps
Dutch art .. .. £1/**£2**/£3
Dutch artist drawn views UB. Poster type, free sample offers .. .. £3/**£5**/£7
Dutch views. Brightly drawn. PMC backs. 12 cards in set .. .. £4/**£6**/£9
Pierrots UB .. .. £1.50/**£2**/£3

Boon's Cocoa
European views 25p/**50p**/75p

Bovril
Art reproductions . . . . 75p/**£1**/£1.50
Pub. Moss. Famous posters in miniature . . £14/**£16**/£18

Broma Cocoa
Plantation sketches 25p/**50p**/75p

Cadbury
Bourneville village scenes . . . . 50p/**75p**/£1
Cecil Aldin poster type. 'Famous Posters in Miniature' . . . . £4/**£6**/£8

Camp Coffee
Breakfast scenes . . . . £7/**£10**/£12
Poster type. Artist Harry Payne . . . . £25/**£30**/£40
Poster type. Others . . . . £15/**£25**/£32
Write-Away type . . . . £6/**£9**/£12

Chocolat Lombart
Poster type. *Art Deco.* Artist René Vincent £10/**£12**/£15
Scenes of boys, carts, railways, ships. Chromo-litho . . . . £8/**£11**/£15

Coca Cola ■AD 2
Poster types. Periods 6, 7 . . . . £2/**£3**/£5

De Beukelaer's Cocoa
Topographical sketches 25p/**50p**/75p

Epps Milenia Milk Chocolate
Poster type . . . . £12/**£18**/£23

Formosa Ooolong
Japanese types . . . . £2/**£3**/£4
Japanese landscapes . . . . £1/**£1.50**/£2

Fry's Chocolate or Cocoa
Following the detailed breakdown of the publishers of the cards which we gave in the Second Edition, there have been some price changes from publisher to publisher. Valuations are still settling down.
Artists Chas. Pears, Hassall, Maud Fabian. Poster types . . . . £15/**£20**/£35
Artists Reg Carter, Tom B. . . . . £6/**£8**/£12
A. W. Ford 'Celebrated Advertisement' series £17/**£24**/£30
Captain Scott at South Pole. Poster type . . £20/**£30**/£40
G. H. Elliott (the 'Chocolate Coloured Coon') . . £2/**£4**/£6
Hancock & Corfield series . . . . £25/**£30**/£35
Joseph Causton Showcard Replica series . . £6/**£12**/£25
Kingsway Press series . . . . £2/**£3**/£4
Unsigned poster art . . . . £5/**£6**/£8
Views of Somerdale Works . . . . 75p/**£1**/£1.25
Vivian Mansell series. Poster type . . . . £7/**£12**/£25
Woodbury series. Numbered . . . . £10/**£15**/£18

George Payne Tea
GP Government Tea. Poster type .. .. £12/**£14**/£16
Military vignettes .. .. £2/**£3**/£4
Composite set of King at Windsor .. .. **P/A**

Hornimans Tea
Poster type, e.g. Edward VII .. ..£5/**£11**/£15
Views .. .. 75p/**£1**/£1.50

Kathreiner's Kaffee
Artist Henri Meunier. Advertisement tastefully printed, front and back, onto the exquisite 'Girls of 1900' series, e.g. 'Aubépine', 'Iris', etc. .. .. **P/A**

Kohler Chocolate
This Lausanne manufacturer of chocolate and cocoa issued a series of 22 or more col. litho UB cards. Period 1/Early Period 2 .. .. £2/**£3**/£4

Liptons
American UB. Language of flowers .. .. £10/**£12**/£14
Pub. C. W. Faulkner. Estate sketches .. .. £1/**£2**/£3

Maggi
General views .. .. 25p/**50p**/£75p
Pub. Maggi. Artist G. Fraipont. Our Churches series .. .. £1/**£2**/£3

Menier Chocolate
Periods 2, 3. Views of Paris. Numbered. Probably over 100 cards .. .. £1/**£2**/£3

Moxie
Cola type drink. Period 4 .. .. 50p/**75p**/£1

Nestlés
Animals and birds. Series 575. 12 card set .. 75p/**£1**/£1.50
'Famous Posters in Miniature'. Series 4421 ..£7/**£15**/£20
Military vignettes. Poster type .. .. .. £15/**£20**/£22
Pub. Williams. Patriotic Empire designs, incl. New Zealand, Australia, etc. .. .. £2/**£3**/£3.50
Signed artists, e.g. Hassall. Poster types .. £20/**£22**/£24

Ovaltine
Poster type (incl. Phyllis Cooper. Period 4. *Art Deco*) .. .. £12/**£14**/£16

Paul Mairesse Chicory
Chicorée à la française. Period 2 .. .. .. £1/**£3**/£5

Ridgways Tea
Artist John Hayes. Pub. Norman Davy .. .. £2/**£3**/£5
Estate scenes .. .. £1/**£2**/£3

Rowntree
Rowntrees postcard series .. .. 75p/**£1**/£1.50
Various .. .. 50p/**75p**/£1

Salutaris Table Water
Poster type. Artist Hassall, o/s .. .. .. £10/**£14**/£16

Schweppes
Soda Water. Artist FS. Period 4 .. .. .. £17/**£20**/£24
Soda water. Others .. .. £3/**£4**/£7
Table water. Period 3 .. .. £3/**£5**/£7
Tonic water. Poster type. Period 4 .. .. .. £5/**£6**/£8

Suchard Chocolate
There is a wide range of advertising cards from before 1890 until early Period 2. Valuation must take into the account the quality of the design as well as the subject matter and age.

Period 1. Multi-view .. .. £3/**£4**/£8
Period 1. Souvenir—series .. .. £10/**£20**/£24
1900 Paris Exhibition. Numbered chromo vignettes .. .. £10/**£11**/£14
Period 2. UB. Chromo-litho .. .. £5/**£8**/£10
Chromo-litho. PS back .. .. £2/**£3**/£5
Vignettes. Children, etc. .. .. £1/**£2**/£4

Symingtons
Foreign views .. .. 50p/**75p**/£1

Tower Tea
Poster type. Artist John Hassall .. .. £12/**£16**/£18
Proverb series
  Hassall type .. .. £5/**£7**/£8
  Others .. .. 75p/**£1**/£1.50

Van Houten's Cocoa
European views .. .. 50p/**75p**/£1

COMMERCIAL/HOUSEHOLD/INDUSTRIAL

The total number of firms who either issued their own cards or overprinted their message on to already published cards is enormous. Here we list together, in alphabetical order, those companies, products and activities that currently attract collectors.

Allentown Adpostals
Between 1911 and 1913 the Allentown Adpostal Corporation (Pennsylvania) issued seven different advertising cards. They carried a mixture of advertisements (on both sides of Government postal cards) for a number of commercial organisations.
1 cent green printed stamp. 2 cards .. .. £12/**£15**/£30
1 cent red printed stamp. 5 cards .. .. £10/**£14**/£20

Bicycles
Humber Beeston. Self-addressed series (1907) £7/**£10**/£12
Patcho Repair Kit. Art comics. Pub. Sharpe .. £5/**£7**/£10
Rayleigh. Poster type
  Period 2 .. .. £7/**£9**/£10
  Period 4 .. .. £3/**£6**/£8
Regent Cycles. Poster type. Vienna UB .. £16/**£18**/£20

Royal Enfield UB .. .. £2/**£4**/£6
Rudge Whitworth
  Cycling magazine inserts .. .. .. 75p/**£1**/£1.50
  RP personalities. 'Lighting up Times' .. .. £5/**£7**/£10
Sanpene. Artist Pascal Vion .. .. .. £11/**£14**/£15
Singer. Poster type .. .. £16/**£18**/£20
  Others .. .. £6/**£8**/£10

Boot Polish
Berry's Diamond. Poster type. Artist P. Lehmann .. ..
.. .. £12/**£18**/£20
Kiwi. Emblem cut in chalk. Period 3 .. .. 75p/**£1**/£1.50

Candles and Lamps
Bray Gas Burner Poster type .. .. £2/**£4**/£5
Edison Lamps Poster type .. .. £4/**£6**/£7
Philips Lamps
  'Arga' art .. .. £3/**£4**/£7
  Chromo. Dutch style .. .. £2.50/**£4**/£10
  Fr. designs .. .. £1/**£2**/£4
Prices Candles
  Military studies .. .. £2/**£2.50**/£3
  Nursery Rhymes .. .. £7/**£9**/£10
Primus It. Period 4 .. .. £2/**£4**/£6
Tantalum Lamps .. .. £4/**£5**/£8
Veritas Mantles Poster type. Artist Hassall .. £2/**£3**/£5

Carriers and Removers
Carter-Paterson Express Carriers Chromo-litho £15/**£19**/£22
Others
  Photographic .. .. 75p/**£2**/£5
  Artist drawn .. .. 50p/**£1**/£3

China and Pottery
Foley. Pub. E. Brain. Examples of Foley art china £1/**£2**/£3
Goss. Pub. S. Oates. Goss china/Roman vases .. £2/**£4**/£6
Goss. Nantgarw. Pub. R. & J. Lea .. .. .. £1/**£2**/£3
Trent. Pub. Trent Bridge. Trent china/Roman vases
50p/**75p**/£1
Others .. .. 50p/**75p**/£1

Coal
Clay Cross. Mining scenes .. .. £2/**£3**/£4
Haydock. Art reproduction/views .. .. 50p/**75p**/£1
Others .. .. 50p/**75p**/£1

Dentifrice
Erasmic
  Col. poster type. Period 4 .. .. .. £2.50/**£4**/£5
Odol
  Series A112, b & w adverts, recommendations by famous stars—Camille Clifford, Zena Dare, Marie Studholme, etc.
  .. .. £1/**£1.50**/£3

Engineering/General Products
Bell Telephone Co. Series of 12 'Uses' for the telephone ..
.. .. £1.50/**£2**/£2.50
Brasso. Colouring cards .. .. 75p/**£1**/£1.50
Capewell Horse Nails Poster type. b & w .. .. £5/**£8**/£9

Continental Aeroplanstoff (Aircraft fabric) Poster type. Comic .. .. £6/**£10**/£12
Continental Ballonstoff (Balloon fabric) Poster type. Comic .. .. £12/**£20**/£23
Mustad Horse Nails. Poster type. Period 3 .. £10/**£12**/£13
North British Rubber Co. 'Chick' golf balls .. ..
Rules of Golf, Artist Elcock .. .. £2/**£3**/£5
Pelaw Metal Polish. Poster type .. .. £10/**£12**/£20

■AD 5 Pub. Independent Order of Rechabites. Period 2 £8

■AD 6 Pub. Chantecler Motor Oils. Fr. Period 4 £10

Friendly Societies ■AD 5
Grand United Order of Oddfellows .. .. .. £3/**£5**/£8
Hearts of Oak Benefit Society .. .. £3/**£5**/£8
Independent Order of Rechabites .. .. .. £3/**£5**/£8
Order of the Sons of Temperance .. .. .. £3/**£5**/£8
Arms/Crest col. litho .. .. £3/**£5**/£8
Bridges/Cathedrals, etc. .. .. 50p/**75p**/£1
Twentieth Century Equitable Friendly Society .. £3/**£5**/£8
Others .. .. 75p/**£3**/£8

Hotels/Restaurants ■AD 7
Many cards showing hotels and restaurants are photographic in origin or printing. Therefore there is often a street scene or transport item associated with the picture, and this can greatly increase the value of the card (*see also* ROAD TRANSPORT, SOCIAL HISTORY and TOPOGRAPHICAL).

Foreign. Period 2 DB 25p/**50p**/75p
Foreign. 2 UB, not *Gruss Aus* .. .. 50p/**£1**/£1.50
London. Artist drawn. H. M. Bateman/Harold Oakley/T. Stephenson. Periods 2 to 4 .. .. £1/**£3**/£5
London. Artist drawn. Others .. .. 50p/**£1.50**/£2
London. Photographic origin .. .. 25p/**50p**/£1
Poster type .. .. £1/**£3**/£5
Provincial .. .. 50p/**75p**/£1
US. Jack Dempsey Restaurant. Artist Montgomery Flagg. Period 4 .. .. 75p/**£1**/£1.25

■AD 7 Pub. Dühamseuw, Ypres. 'Hotel Continental, Ypres during a post-'14–'18 war Battlefield Tour'. Period 4 £1.50

Industrial Scenes

Cammell Laird. Period 3 .. .. £1/**£1.50**/£2
Harland & Wolff. Pub. Valentine. Period 2 £1/**£1.50**/£2
Others .. .. 25p/**75p**/£1

Insurance Companies

Eagle. Head Office building .. .. £1/**£2**/£3
Illustrated *Sunday Herald.* Period 4. Free Insurance scheme with Lloyds .. .. 50p/**75p**/£1
King Insurance Co. Royalty Sketches .. .. £1/**£2**/£3
Kings of England. Probably 50 in series .. .. £1/**£2**/£3
Norwich Union. Pub. Scott Russell. Motor Fire Engine .. .. £6/**£8**/£10
Ocean Accident. Insurance postcard series .. £1/**£1.50**/£2
'Tit-bits' £1000 Insurance. Poster type .. .. £2/**£3**/£5
Others .. .. 75p/**£3**/£8

Kitchen Equipment

Produits du Lion Noir
Pub. Edition R.D.C., Seine. Artist Beatrice Mallet. Set of 6. Period 4 .. .. £1.50/**£3**/£4
Fonderie Nestor Martin
Pub. Goossens, J. G., Bruxelles. Artist Beatrice Mallet. Set of 6. Period 4 .. .. £1.50/**£3**/£4

■AD 8 Pub. Volkswagen. Ger. PU 1955 £2

Motor Cars ■AD 8

Poster type designs .. .. £3/**£5**/£15
Period 2 .. .. £1.50/**£3**/£5
Period 3, 4 .. .. £2.50/**£5**/£10
Periods 5, 6 .. .. £1/**£1.50**/£2
Period 7 .. .. 25p/50p

Motor Shows

Period 2 .. .. £5/**£10**/£15
Period 4. Berlin (1937–9) .. .. £3/**£5**/£7.50
Period 6. Berlin .. .. £1.50/**£3**/£5
Others .. .. £1/**£2.50**/£4

Oils ■AD 6

Castrol
  Sir Malcolm Campbell in *Bluebird*. Artist Bryan de Grineau .. .. £5/**£6**/£8
  Photo-origin .. .. £1/**£1.50**/£2
Chantecler
  Poster type. Period 4 .. .. £4/**£10**/£15
Mex Motor Spirit (Bowring Petroleum Co.) Poster type .. .. £5/**£12**/£25
Mobiloil
  Period 4. Charles Lindbergh .. .. £7/**£9**/£10
Oilzum Motor Oil
  Poster type .. .. £8/**£12**/£14
Pratts Motor Spirit
  Artist drawn scenes showing use of Anglo-American oil products .. .. £3/**£5**/£7
Shell
  Benzine. HTL. Period 3 .. .. £17/**£20**/£21
  Period 4. Italian design .. .. £16/**£18**/£20
  Poster type. Numbered, e.g. No. 41 'The Spirit of Great Strength' .. .. £12/**£22**/£35
  Poster type suffragette .. .. £12/**£22**/£35
Sternol Oil
  Poster type. Comic. Artist Hassall .. .. .. £12/**£16**/£20
White Rose Kerosene
  Hold to Light .. .. £8/**£10**/£15

Overprints

These are proprietary cards upon which an additional advertising message has been printed. They vary from one line additions, on either side of the card, to full out pictures. They should be valued on the basis of the original card, plus a premium (from 50p) for the advertising overprint according to its rarity or interest.

Phonographs

Edison
  USA. Poster type .. .. £1/**£2**/£4
  Others .. .. 75p/**£1.50**/£3

Schools

Many British schools were, and are, partly or fully supported by the fees paid by their pupils. Schools, therefore, had a need to advertise their facilities to the parents of potential pupils.

This was often done by picture postcards, particularly in Period 4.

Commercial schools, e.g. Pitmans .. .. .. £1/**£3**/£4
General views .. .. £1/**£1.50**/£2
Science laboratories with pupils .. .. £2/**£3**/£4

Shampoo/Soaps
Amami shampoo .. .. 50p/**75p**/£1
Colleen Shampoo. Poster type .. .. .. £1.50/**£3**/£8
CWS soaps .. .. 75p/**£1**/£1.50
Fields Toilet Soap. Childhood series .. .. .. £1/**£2**/£3
Gossages. 'The Right Sort'. Royalty and others .. £4/**£6**/£8
Hudsons: Queen Victoria .. .. £3/**£4**/£5
Vignette studies .. .. £10/**£15**/£19
Knights' Family Soap. Poster type .. .. .. £5/**£9**/£16
Lever Bros. Art views Port Sunlight 25p/**50p**/75p
Lux: Ger. Period 4. Poster type .. .. £2/**£3**/£5
Pears: 'Bubbles' 25p/**50p**/75p
Poster types general .. .. £5/**£7**/£10
Prices. Art nursery rhymes .. .. £4/**£5**/£7
Wrights Coal Tar Soap. Wan-Tang-Fee. Chinaman series.
Numbered .. .. £1.50/**£2**/£3
'The Wright Sort' Poster type .. .. .. £12/**£13**/£16
Others .. .. £1/**£2**/£3

Shops and Stores
Throughout Europe interest has grown in recent years in pictures showing the way that things used to be. Shop fronts, showing goods displayed for sale, are a popular collecting category; photographic cards have added value.

London stores. Artist drawn .. .. £1/**£2**/£3
Photographic origin .. .. 75p/**£1.50**/£2
Provincial stores .. .. £1/**£2**/£3
Shop fronts. British or foreign. Close-ups .. .. £6/**£8**/£10
Shop interiors. Particularly collected in the USA £3/**£5**/£8

Singer Sewing Machines
Aviation studies .. .. £2/**£3**/£4
French. Periods 4/5 .. .. £1.50/**£2**/£4
Battleships .. .. £1/**£1.50**/£2
Others .. .. 50p/**75p**/£1

Starch
Colmans. GB sketches .. .. 50p/**75p**/£1
Postmen of the Empire .. .. £3/**£4**/£5
Remy
Maps with vignette views .. .. £1/**£2**/£2.50

Sutton Seeds
Flowers and vegetables 25p/**50p**/75p

Swan Fountain Pens
Artist Harrison (1906). Comic Historical types 50p/**75p**/£1

Thomas Cook
Periods 1, 2. UB Chromo-litho multi-vignettes £20/**£25**/£30

(Madame) Tussauds
Pub. Tuck .. .. £2/**£3**/£5

Typewriters
Oliver. Writing through the Ages .. .. .. £1/**£2**/£3
Remington. Poster types .. .. £3/**£5**/£7
Vignettes .. .. £4/**£5**/£5.50
Royal. Edward VII caricature .. .. £8/**£9**/£15
Underwood. Poster types. Period 3 .. .. .. £3/**£5**/£7

Tyres
Chaussures Raoul. Artist Caputi. Early motor cars .. .. £10/**£15**/£17
Colonial. Poster type .. .. £7/**£8**/£10
Continental Pneumatique
Periods 2, 3. Col. litho/*Gruss Aus* types .. .. £6/**£8**/£12
Pub. Edler & Krische—Chromo art. Over 30 designs .. .. £1.50/**£2**/£3
Dunlop
Periods 2, 3. Litho .. .. £5/**£7**/£8
Pub. Doring & Huning. UB. Art .. .. £13/**£15**/£17
Engelbert. Poster type. Period 4 .. .. .. £5/**£9**/£11
Excelsior. Period 4 .. .. £3/**£4**/£5
Goodyear. Blimp. Pub. Tichnor USA. Period 6 .. £1/**£2**/£3
Poster type .. .. £7/**£9**/£12
Grammont. Poster type .. .. £6/**£8**/£9
John Bull 1910 First International Cycle Show, Olympia .. .. £5/**£8**/£10
Palmer. Poster type. Period 2 .. .. £14/**£15**/£18
Others .. .. £1/**£7**/£15

Wood-Milne Rubber Heel
Artist Sager. Period 3 pin-up types .. .. .. £2/**£3**/£4
GB views. 40 numbered cards 25p/50p
Poster ads. Unnumbered .. .. £1/**£2**/£3

SECTION SUPPLEMENT—ADVERTISING

Shurey Insert View Cards (Places H—L) ■AD 4

Haddon Hall
Hadley Church, showing Old Beacon
Hall Barn (Lord Burnham's Seat)
Hamilton Sq. Birkenhead (v)
Hampton Court Palace. East Front
Hampton Court. West Gate
Hampton in Arden, Warwickshire
Hampton, Middlesex
The Harbour, Folkestone
Harbour, Margate
Harbour Scene by Moonlight (v)
Harrow Old School
Harrow Old School & Chapel
Hastings
Hastings Castle (*2 types*)
Haughmond Abbey, Wellington
Hawarden Church

Hawes
Hawkesbury River, N.S.W.
Hayes Village, Kent
Haymaking
Haymaking in Hampshire
Head of Bantry Bay, Ireland
Healesville, Victoria
Hedsor (Bucks.) Lord Boston's Seat
Hedsor Church. View & Portrait
Helmond Castle, (Holland)
Helmsley
Helmsley, Yorks
Hemstead Church, Kent
Hengrave Church, near Bury St. Edmunds
Hengrave Hall, near Bury St. Edmunds
Henshaw, Bardon Mill
Hermitage Caves, Bridgnorth
Hertford Bridge & Cathedral (*mis-spelling for Hereford*)
Hesketh Park, Southport
Heysham Village (*2 types*)
Heysham Village Church
High Force, Middleton in Teesdale (v)
Highland Hut
High Rocks, Cheddar (v)
High Street, Swanage
High Street, Tunbridge Wells
Hill Climb, Westerham, Kent
Hindu Temple, Cawnpore (India) (v)
H.M. the Queen arriving in Portsmouth Harbour
H.M.S. *Victory* Flying Nelson's famous Signal
Hoe, Plymouth
Holbrook Church, Ipswich
Holy Trinity Church, Guildford
Holy Trinity Church, Stratford on Avon
Horse & Groom Inn, Merrow, Surrey
Hoseinabad, Lucknow (India)
House at Corston, Bath (Where Southey lived)
The house of Dürer, Nurnberg
8th Hussars Drum Horse (v)
Ice Cutting, Upper Glacier, Grindelwald (v)
Ice Trees at Niagara
Ickworth Church, (Suffolk)
Ilkeston Church, Derby
In a Kentish Lane (v)
Interior of New St. Station, Birmingham
Interior Walsoken Church (v)
Inundation near the Pyramids, (Egypt)
Iona Cathedral, Oban
The Isle of Philae (Egypt)
Isleworth Church
Italian Riviera
Jacob's Ladder, Falmouth (v)
Jesmond Dene (v)
Jew's House, Lincoln
Jezreels Temple, Gillingham
Karnak (Egypt)
Karnak (Egypt) (v)
Kashmir Gate, Dehli (India)

Kenilworth Castle
Kenilworth (from the Castle)
Kenmare Rd. Tunnel, Killarney
Kent Farm
A Kentish Village
Kenwyn Old Church
Kerrara Sound, Oban
Kilburn, near Coxwold, Yorks
Kildrummy Castle
Killarney House, Killarney
King Alfred's Statue, Winchester (v)
King Charles' Bedroom at Holyrood Palace
King Charles' House, Worcester (v)
King Charles' Tower, Chester (v)
The King: God bless him!
King John's Castle, Limerick, Ireland
King's Gate & St. Swithin's Church, Winchester
King's Lynn
King Street, Huddersfield (*2 types*)
King Street, Reading
Kingswear Castle, on the Dart
King William's Obelisk, Drogheda, Ireland (v)
Kiosk of Phylae, (Egypt)
Kirkham Priory
Kirkham, Yorks
Kirk Maughold
Kirkstall Abbey
Kirkstall Abbey, Leeds
Kit's Coity House, Kent
Knaresborough Castle (*2 types*)
Knaresborough from Castle
The Knights' Hall The Hague, (Holland)
Kursaal, Southend (v)
Laatefos near Odde, (Norway)
Lake of Geneva
Lambeth Palace & Church
The Landing Party
Landing Stage, Liverpool
Lands End
Lanercost Priory, Brampton
Langstrath Valley
The Last Load
Laxey Wheel, Isle of Man
Leamington Church
Leamington Parish Church (v)
Leaning Tower of Pisa (v)
Leather Bottle Inn, Cobham
The Lees, Folkestone
Leigh, Essex
Lewes Castle
Lichfield Cathedral (v)
The Lift at Bridgnorth (v)
The Lighthouse and Bathing Place. Douglas I.O.M.
Lighthouse, Genoa (Italy) (v)
Lighthouse, Gt. Ormes' Head (*Llandudno*)
Lime Str & St. Georges Hall, Liverpool (*2 types*)

(v) = *vertical format to be continued*

ANIMALS/BIRDS/FISH/INSECTS/ FLOWERS/FRUIT/VEGETABLES

BEARS

Novelty Bears

Leather bears. Various USA Pubs .. .. £1.50/**£5**/£8
Pub. E. T. W. Dennis. Pull out designs .. 50p/**75p**/£1.50

Performing Bears

Real Photo. Period 2 .. .. £3/**£5**/£8

'Roosevelt' or 'Teddy' Bears

These are highly collected in the USA, the country of their origin (named after President Theodore Roosevelt, who purportedly saved the life of a bear cub on one of his hunting expeditions). They were popularised as a symbol for Roosevelt in the 1907/8 Presidential campaign as opposed to Taft's animal representative, Billy Possum. The craze spread to Europe and many Period 2, 3 and 4 bears are to be found on cards by continental and British publishers.

American Bears

Publishers

J. L. Austin
'Busy Bears' Nos. 427–432 (Days of Week) .. £2/**£3**£5
Bears at School Nos. 433, 436 .. .. £2/**£3**/£5
Collins Baking Co. Advert .. .. £2/**£3**/£5
E. P. Dett & Co. Comic Valentines .. .. .. £1/**£2**/£3
Albert Hahn Various .. .. 75p/**£1.50**/£2
William S. Heal 1907
Days of Week Bears (7) .. .. £2/**£3**/£5
D. Hillson Days of Week Bears (7) .. .. .. £2/**£3**/£5
Illus. P.C. Co. Embossed bears .. .. £2/**£3**/£5
Inter-Art (in USA) No. 791
Artist Magnus Griener. Set of 6
Molly & Teddy .. .. £2/**£3**/£5
Kaiser Co. Various .. .. £1/**£2**/£3
Nat. Art Co. Various .. .. 75p/**£1**/£1.50
Reinthal & Newman Various .. .. .. 75p/**£1.50**/£2
Rotograph Artist Rose Clark .. .. .. 75p/**£1.50**/£2
Thomas F. Schweitzr Period 7. Reproductions of Period 2.
Stern Roosevelt bears 25p/50p
M. T. Sheahan Various .. .. 75p/**£1**/£2
E. Stern
Roosevelt Bears (most famous of all)
Several series of worldwide travels of Teddy B & Teddy G
Cracker Jack Bears (adverts) .. .. £4/**£8**/£12
Tower Various .. .. 75p/**£1**/£1.50
Tuck (in USA)
Series 118 'Little Bears' (12 cards) .. .. .. £3/**£6**/£8
Ullman
'Busy Bears' No. 79. Artist Bernhardt Wall (Days of Weeks)
'Sporty Bears' No. 83 (set of 6) .. .. .. £3/**£6**/£8

Western News Co.
Set of 'Seasons'. Artist St. John .. .. £1.50/**£3**/£4
Others .. .. 75p/**£1.50**/£5

European Bears

Publishers include: Alpha Pub. Co.; Bamforth; Birn Bros.; E. T. W. Dennis; J. Arthur Dixon (Modern); C. W. Faulkner; Harrap; E. J. Hey; Inter-Art (Artistique, Comique, etc.); E. Mack; Vivian Mansell; Medici Soc. (Periods 5, 6, 7); Millar & Lang; Photochrom; Regent Pub. Co.; J. Salmon; Stewart & Woolf; Tuck; A. & G. Taylor; Valentines and Wildt & Kray.

Price range .. .. 75p/**£2.50**/£5

BIRDS

Artists

Scrivener, Maud
Pub. Tuck. Oilette, e.g. 'British Birds' (at least three series). Period 2 .. .. 50p/**75p**/£1.50
Pub. Wrench. Period 2 .. .. 50p/**75p**/£1

West, A. L.
Pub. Tuck. Oilette, e.g. 'Birds and Blossoms', No. 3191. Period 2 .. .. 25p/**50p**/75p

British Museum of Natural History
Several series of British Game Birds, British Resident birds, Summer Visitors, Artist Grunewald. Period 4 25p/**50p**/75p
Add a premium of £1 per series if the original descriptive leaflets still exist.

Canary and Cage Bird Life Series and Capern's Bird Foods Series
See ADVERTISING

Doves/Love Birds
Often found on highly embossed cards, usually of Continental origin, in the GREETINGS category. Publishers include: Stewart & Woolf, Tuck, Wildt & Kray.
Periods 2 to 4 .. .. 50p/**£1**/£2

Parrots
A highly collectable category.
Artist Lawson Wood. Parrots. Period 4 .. £1/**£1.50**/£2
Photographic or lesser known artist drawn 25p/**50p**/75p
Pub. Tuck. 'Pretty Polly' series. Period 2 .. 50p/**75p**/£1
Educational series .. .. 75p/**£1**/£1.50
Other miscellaneous, anonymous artist drawn, photographic studies, etc. .. .. 25p/**50p**/£1.50

Real Feathers: *see* NOVELTY

Swans
Often featured in photographic view cards to add interest to a static scene, and much collected. Publishers include Frith, Valentine, Wildt & Kray and many local publishers. Periods 2 to 4. Value varies according to whether the swans are in the foreground or in the distance.

Price range 25p/**50p**/75p

CATS ■AN 1, A 28, GR 3
Interest in this appealing category has continued to grow during the past year. In the Second Edition a detailed listing of some of the most sought after cat artists was published, thanks to the work of Anne Mobbs. Their names are listed below.

Cat Artists

Barnes, G. L.	£1/**£3**/£6
Boulanger, Maurice	£1.50/**£4**/£8
Butcher, Arthur	£1/**£2**/£3
Carter, Reg.†	£1/**£2**/£4
Cobbe, B.	£1/**£1.50**/£2
Ellam, W. H.	£1.50/**£3**/£6
Kennedy, A. E. (A.E.K.)	£1/**£3**/£5
Knight, M. & Kennedy, A. E.	75p/**£1.50**/£3
Kennedy, Charles	£1/**£2**/£4
Kennedy, T.	£1/**£2**/£3
Lydon, A. F.	£1.50/**£3**/£6
Maguire, Helena	£1.50/**£4**/£6
Roberts, Violet (VR)	£2/**£4**/£6
Schropler, L.	£1.50/**£3**/£4
Thiele, Arthur†	£4/**£6**/£8
Travers Pope, Dorothy	£1.50/**£3**/£5
Wain, Louis†	£4/**£11**/£14

■AN 1 Pub. Theo Stroefer, Nuremberg (T.S.N.). Artist Arthur Thiele. PU 1927 £5

Black Cats
A common and popular theme in Periods 2 to 4. Many series were published by Inter-Art, and often re-printed with greetings overprints or French captions in WW1. Most catland artists produced some postcards of this genre, in particular

Boulanger, Roberts, Thiele and Wain, whose cards command a premium of up to £5. Values according to artist and period.

Pub. Dennis, E. T. W. Periods 2, 3 .. .. £1.50/**£2**/£3
Pub. Inter-Art Comic Periods 2, 3 .. .. £1.50/**£2**/£3

Comic Cats
Cats in humorous situations were featured by many of the well known postcard artists, such as Tom Browne, G. F. Christie, Donald McGill and Lawson Wood. Unfortunately many of the best cards of this type produced by the popular publishers were drawn by artists who will perhaps forever remain anonymous. Typical of the anonymous humour of this genre of card are those produced by the Scottish publishers Millar & Lang who reproduced their famous series 'When Father Says Turn' depicting cats.

Price range .. .. £1.50/**£3.50**/£6

Felix the Cat—*see* ENTERTAINMENT: CINEMA

Photographic Studies

Frees, Harry Whittier (1879–1953)
Born in Reading, Pennsylvania, he soon specialised in animal photography and became famous for his cats, often kittens, in human dress and situations. Published in New York by the Rotograph Co. and in Britain by the Rotary Co. Periods 2–4.

Price range .. .. £1.50/**£2.50**/£3

Landor
Cat studies (also dogs). Periods 2–4. Publishers include Hildesheimer, Tuck and Wrench, incl. b & w, col. and sepia.

Price range .. .. £1.50/**£2**/£3

Other Photographic Studies
Periods 2 to 7 .. .. £1/**£2**/£3

Taber Bas Relief Co.
Photographic studies .. .. £2/**£3**/£4

Publishers
Faulkner, Hildesheimer, Stewart & Woolf, Tuck, Wrench and others all produced countless 'cat' cards, incl. some fine, early chromo-litho cards, often embossed. Periods 1, 2 .. .. ..
Price range .. .. £1.50/**£3.50**/£6

Davidson Bros., Ettlinger, Inter-Art, Rotary, Tuck, Wildt & Kray and others produced many amusing, sentimental cards, many photographic, often on greetings cards. Periods 2 to 7
Price range .. .. £1/**£2**/£3

DOGS ■AN 2

Artists

Aldin, Cecil†
Intelligent, characterful dogs, hunting scenes. Tuck and other publishers.
Period 2 .. .. £1/**£2**/£4

Daws, F. T.
Spratts 'Champion Dog' series. Period 2 .. 75p/**£1.25**/£1.75
Series for Birn Bros. High gloss finish. Periods 2 to 4 .. .. 25p/**50p**/75p

Drummond, Norah
Researcher Linda Cowell has identified the following Tuck Oilette sets of dogs by this highly competent artist of country scenes and animals; 3046, 3184 Favourite Dogs, 3219, 3366, 8669, 9105 Sporting Dogs, 3294, 9273 With Dog and Gun, 9381 The Friend of Man, 9560 Scotch Collies, 9639 Pet Dogs

Price range .. .. 50p/**£1**/£1.50

Muller, Augustus
Worked in Munich. Specialised in Dachsunds.
Pub. Hildesheimer. Periods 1, 2 .. .. .. 50p/**£1**/£1.50

Pope, Dorothy Travers
Fine chromo-litho series, e.g. Misch & Co. Series 806. 'Our Dogs'. Period 2 .. .. £1/**£2**/£3

Stokes, Vernon
Superb, early chromo-litho series on fine board (incl. Bulldog, Husky). Series 11825. Pub. Anon. Periods 1, 2 .. £1/**£2**/£4

Studdy, George†
The famous Bonzo dog. Publishers include Valentine's and 'RPS' Series. Period 4 .. .. £1/**£1.50**/£2

Wardle, Arthur
'Dog' series J1. 'Sporting Dogs & Birds', series J2. Pub. James Henderson. Period 2 .. .. 75p/**£1**/£2

Watson, Maud West
Tuck. Oilette, e.g. Sketches of Dogs, No. 9681. Period 2 .. .. 75p/**£1**/£1.50

Comic Dogs
Dogs in humorous situations were featured by many fine artists, like Tom Browne, Hassall, etc.: *see* ARTISTS.

Famous Dogs
See also MILITARY and Working Dogs below
Beddgelert's Grave RP
Edith Cavell's dog, *Jack* (now stuffed, in the Imperial War Museum)

Edward VII's dog, *Ceasar*
Napoleon's dog on Elba (now stuffed, in *Les Invalides*)
Snowball, gassed in WW1

Price range 25p/**50p**/75p

Publishers
Eyre & Spottiswoode, Hildesheimer, Wrench, etc., produced many early b & w series of photographic and art productions of dogs and other animals by artists like Stanley Berkeley and photographers like Reid. Periods 1, 2 .. 25p/**50p**/£1

Tuck produced countless series of Oilette and photographic studies of varying worth. Periods 2 to 4 .. 50p/**75p**/£1

There are also many Periods 2 to 4 series and single cards of photographic studies of animals in a sentimental vein, often with actresses and pretty girls, often on greetings cards, by Ettlinger, Rotary, Valentine, etc. 25p/**50p**/75p

---

■AN 2 Pub. Tuck. Artist Norah Drummond. Oilette No. 9923. 'The Hunt Day'. Period 2 £1.50

Working Dogs
Swiss St. Bernards. Period 2 .. .. .. 50p/**75p**/£1.50

Dog Carts
Belgian milk carts .. .. £1.50/**£3.50**/£5
Belgian military carts .. .. £2.50/**£4**/£6
Belgian other carts .. .. £1.50/**£3.50**/£5
French milk carts .. .. £4/**£7.50**/£12
French other carts .. .. £6/**£8**/£12
Dutch, German, Russian, Swiss carts .. .. .. £2/**£4**/£6

Military Dogs
Red Cross/Transport Dogs in WW1 .. .. £1/**£1.50**/£3

FISH
Angling Cards
Photographic studies, many local publishers. Periods 2 to 4 .. .. 25p/**£1**/£1.50
Tuck Oilette. Various series. Period 2 .. 50p/**75p**/£1

Poisson d'Avril:

Pub. Hawaii & South Seas Curio Co., Honolulu Chromo-litho tropical fish. Large, colourful series .. 75p/**£1**/£1.50

Pub. Hawaii Jas. Steiner series Probably over 30 in series .. .. 75p/**£1**/£1.50

Stranded Whales and Other Fish Curiosities

Many local photographers and publishers. Periods 2 to 4 .. .. 50p/**75p**/£1

Tuck Oilette/Connoisseur series, e.g. 'British Fresh Water Fish', 'British Fish'. Period 2 .. .. .. 50p/**£1**/£1.50

FLOWERS/FRUIT/VEGETABLES ■AN 3

A very attractive collecting theme, in which fine artist-drawn and photographic examples can be found. The best known artist of this genre is C. Klein (see Artists). Flowers abound on greetings cards (see GREETINGS) and on novelty cards (see NOVELTY).

Artist-drawn cards

Billing, M.	50p/**75p**/£2
Gieste, A.	25p/**50p**/75p
Hedley (later Taylor), Nora	25p/**50p**/£1
Hildebrandt, Fritz	25p/**50p**/£1
Klein, C.	50p/**£1**/£5
Lohmann, F.	25p/**50p**/£1
Walker, Winifred	25p/**50p**/75p
Others	25p/**75p**/£1.50

■AN 3 Pub. Wildt & Kray. Artist C. Klein. Series 927. Period 2 £1.50

'Language of' (*see* GLAMOUR)

Flowers	50p/**75p**/£1.50
Fruit	75p/**£1**/£2.50
Vegetables	50p/**£1**/£3

Novelty

Appliquéd dried flowers	£1/**£2**/£3
Embossed designs	75p/**£1**/£2.50
Scented flowers	£2/**£3**/£4
Others	50p/**£2**/£6

Photographic (*see* SOCIAL HISTORY)
This section includes some beautiful coloured still-lives and pictures of growing, harvesting, etc.

Price range .. .. 25p/**£1**/£4

FROGS

Adverts. Much collected in the USA, especially for throat pastilles (e.g. 'Frog in Your Throat Co.') .. .. £1/**£2**/£4
Alice in Wonderland frogs—*see* 'LITERARY'
Frog Bands .. .. 50p/**75p**/£1
Pub. Meissner & Buch. Series 170 and 283 50p/**75p**/£1
Others .. .. 25p/**50p**/£1

HORSES ■AN 2

The most collectable cards in this sub-section are undoubtedly race horses and allied cards.

Ancient White Horses
An interesting category—early British White Horses carved in chalk on hillsides.
Publishers Wilkinson & Co., Trowbridge and many other local publishers.

Price range .. .. 50p/**75p**/£1

Artists' Impressions of Horses
Periods 2 to 5. Various publishers 25p/**50p**/75p

Horse Studies
Pub. B.K.W. Artist Ludwic Koch. Series. Period 2 £1/**£2**/£4
Pub. 'P.F.' Artist Kocj (signed 'G.K.'). Embossed heads .. .. £1/**£2**/£4
Others .. .. 75p/**£1.50**/£2

Harry Payne Horses
Pub. Tuck. Oilette series. Period 2 .. .. .. £2/**£3**/£4
Pub. Tuck early chromolithographed heads. Period 2 .. .. £1.50/**£2**/£3
Pub. Tuck Oilette, e.g. 'Horse Studies', 'Man's Best Friend'. Period 2 .. .. 75p/**£1.50**/£2

Horse Fairs
In Britain and Eire (e.g. Buttevant) Periods 2 to 4 .. .. £1/**£2.50**/£4

Hunting Scenes

Artists' Impressions
Many Tuck Oilette series, e.g. 'A Hunting We Will Go'. Also E. T. W. Dennis 'Dainty' series. Periods 2 to 4 75p/**£1**/£1.50

Invitations to Meets
All Periods. Price according to Period .. 75p/**£1.50**/£3

Photographic Studies
Specified hunts, e.g. Compiègne (LL), Surrey Union. Period 2 .. .. 75p/**£1**/£2

Military Horses

Boer War
Artists Caton Woodville, Harry Payne. Periods 1, 2 £1/**£2**/£4
Photographic. Periods 1, 2 .. .. £1/**£2**/£4

WW1
Artist Matania, Frederick .. .. 75p/**£1**/£2
Cavalry horses, Officers' horses, pulling gun limbers, military transport .. .. 50p/**75p**/£1.50

General Military
Pub. Gale & Polden type, etc. Period 2 .. 75p/**£1**/£1.50

Named Race Horses—*see* SPORTS
Pub. Tuck. Derby Winners. UB. Periods 1, 2 £1.50/**£2.50**/£3
Pub. Walker & Co. 'Celebrated Racers' series. Period 2 .. .. £1/**£2**/£3
Pub. Wrench series. Period 2 .. .. .. 75p/**£1**/£1.50

Point to Point Races
Periods 2 to 4. Artist drawn .. .. .. 50p/**75p**/£1
Real photographic .. .. 50p/**£1**/£3

Races and Race Courses (British)
Photographic studies. Publishers Frith, Valentines and Wrench and many local publishers. Value varies according to clarity and detail. Periods 2 to 4. Artists' Impressions .. .. 50p/**£1**/£1.50

Races and Race Courses (Foreign)
Chantilly, Le Havre, Ostende, etc. Period 2 50p/**75p**/£1

Royalty at the Races
Photographic. Various Publishers. Periods 2 to 4 £1/**£2**/£3

Spanish Riding School, Vienna
Period 4. Photographer H. Schuhmann .. 75p/**£1**/£1.50

Working Horses
Ploughing, Drawing Cabs, Fire Engines, etc. Various Publishers. Value increases according to rarity of occupation/vehicle and whether the picture is close-up or distant. Periods 2 to 5 .. .. 75p/**£1.50**/£2

As it is difficult to date a card precisely, a period system has been used in this catalogue.
For a full explanation of the system see page viii.

INSECTS
Many early Continental chromo-litho cards, often embossed, featured beetles, ladybirds, etc. Periods 1, 2 75p/**£1.50**/£2

Butterflies

British Museum of Natural History
'British Butterflies'. Probably 100 cards. Printed by Waterlow/Henry Stone & Sons. Period 4 .. .. .. 25p/**50p**/75p

Tuck Oilette
'Butterflies', 'British Butterflies & Moths'. Period 2 .. .. 75p/**£1.50**/£2

Tuck 'Butterflies on the Wing' .. .. £3/**£4**/£5

Fleas
Fleas were the subject of countless humorous cards of Periods 2 to 4, by artists like 'FS', Donald McGill, and many unnamed artists. Value varies according to artist.

Artist drawn .. .. 25p/**75p**/£1.50

Performing Fleas/Circuses
Period 2 .. .. £1/**£3**/£5

PIGS
Pigs were regarded as good luck symbols on the Continent and often appeared on greetings cards.
Early chromo-litho, artist drawn pigs. Periods 1, 2 .. .. 75p/**£1.50**/£3
British humorous cards of pigs. Periods 2 to 5 25p/**75p**/£1.25
Modern French cards with 'dubious' captions. Period 7 .. 25p/50p

MISCELLANEOUS ■AN 4, 5

Animals on Greetings Cards
Greetings cards are, perhaps, the most prolific source for animal card collectors (bunnies and chicks on easter cards, robins on christmas cards, kittens, puppies, horses, etc. on birthday cards, fish on April Fool cards): see GREETINGS.

Circus and Performing Animals

Dogs, Elephants, Fleas, etc.
Barnum & Bailey and other named Circuses: *see* ENTERTAINMENT: Circus

Domestic/Farmyard Animals
Pub. Tuck. Educational series No. 4. Embossed. Late Period 2 .. .. £3/**£4**/£5

■AN 4 Pub. Axel Eliassons, Stockholm. Artist Curt Nystrom 75p

■AN 5 Pub. Tuck. Embossed 'Art' Series 1019. PU 1903 £2

Mickey Mouse, Donald Duck: *see* ENTERTAINMENT Cinema

Monkeys on Barrel Organs
British and Continental. Period 2 .. .. £1.50/**£2.50**/£4

Nursery Animals
Many artist drawn cards, often published by the Medici Society in the 1920s–1950s, feature animals. This is a small selection of some of the named artists. See also CHILDREN.

Folkard, Charles
Periods 4, 5 .. .. 75p/**£1**/£1.50

Tempest, Margaret
Periods 4 to 6 .. .. £1/**£1.50**/£2

Thompson, G. H.
Publisher Nister. Period 2 .. .. 75p/**£1.50**/£2

Others .. .. 25p/**75p**/£1.50

Other Animals
Cows, Donkeys, Mice, Monkeys, Oxen, Rabbits, Squirrels, Stags, etc. often appear on cards. Some fine early Continental chromo-litho cards (often imported by C. W. Faulkner) some embossed, are well worth collecting. Later photographic designs are of little interest or worth. Value increases with age, quality of reproduction.

Price range .. .. 25p/**50p**/£1

Wild Animals

Pub. Tuck's Oilette series, e.g. 'Wild Animals'. Period 2 .. .. 50p/**75p**/£1.50

Pub. Wrench and other b & w photographic series of lions, polar bears, etc. Period 2 .. .. 25p/50p

Artist Rankin, George
Studies of lions, tigers, etc. Tuck's Oilette series, e.g. 'Wild Animal' series. Period 2 .. .. 50p/**75p**/£1.50

Artist Scrivener, Maud
Tuck's Oilette series, e.g. 'In the Jungle'. Period 2 .. .. 50p/**75p**/£1.50

Zoo Animals

Many 'Zoological' cards exist in long series.

Berlin Zoo
Col. chromo-litho set 1900 .. .. £1/**£3**/£4

Cologne Zoo
Various issues. Period 2 .. .. 50p/**£1**/£1.50

London Zoo
'From the Gardens of the Zoological Society Regents Park', b & w photographic studies by W. S. Berridge, Henry Irving, etc. Period 2 .. .. 25p/**50p**/75p

Zoo Buildings and Keepers

Dresden Zoo
Col. chromo-litho series. Vignettes. 1896 .. .. £2/**£4**/£5
Other types through to Period 7 .. .. 25p/**50p**/£1

Other Zoos
Photographic studies of zoos and their keepers were produced by popular publishers of most of the famous zoos in Britain and on the Continent. Value increases with age and rarity of subject as well as clarity of photograph.

Price range .. .. 25p/**£1**/£1.50

Three Band Pricing System

Left Hand Band: The lowest price you will probably be asked to pay for this card.
Middle Band: What you will normally be asked to pay for this card: its average, reasonable price.
Right Hand Band: The highest price you will probably be asked to pay for this card.
For a full explanation of the system see page ix.

ART

ART DECO

Art Deco (from *Art Decoratif*) derived from the more austere and abstract forms of *Art Nouveau* and was a reaction against its more florid aspects. The movement was characterised by the love of the symmetry in design that recalled the classic style. After an early emphasis on stylised garlands, roses and fruit, the style was more and more inspired by cubism and the geometric form. As with *Art Nouveau*, the style was applied to many branches of the arts, both useful and decorative—for example the 'streamlining' of racing cars, architecture, fashion, furniture and interior design.

Art Deco reached its apogee in 1925 with the Paris Exposition des Arts Decoratifs et Modernes, and died out in the mid-1930s.

To a lesser extent than with *Art Nouveau*, *Art Deco* influences can be seen in the borders and decorations of post-cards in several general categories, such as Greetings cards and Adverts. Interesting examples of the *Art Deco* architectural style are to be found on postcards for example the Chrysler Building.

Art Deco styling adds about £2 to the value of cards collectable for other reasons. As the genre becomes more and more popular, the virtuoso exponents of the art command ever higher prices for signed examples of their work.

ADVERTISING/GENERAL/GLAMOUR

NAMED ARTISTS

■ART 1–3, G 3

Anichini, E.
Bakst, L.†
Barbier, P.
Bentivoglio
Bertelli, P.
Bianchi, V.
Birgo
Boccasile, G.
Bompard, S.
Brunelleschi, U.†
Bruno, A.
Busi, A.
Calderara, C.†
Cappiello, L.
Carrere, R.
Chiostri, C.†
Corbella, T.†
Cramer, R.
Degani
Delorme, R.
Dudovich, M.†
Garry, C.
Gesmar, C.
Giles, J.
Gobbi, D.
Gobbo, C.
Graf, M.
Grassi, V.
Grosze, M.
Guillaume, A.
Guitry, S.
Hardy
Hoffmann, J.†
Iribe, P.
Jung, M.
Koehler, M.†
Kokoschka, O.†
Larcombe, E.
Lendecke, O.
Likartz, M.
Loffler, B.†
Longley, C.
Lupa
Marty, A.
Mauzan, A. L.†
Meschini, G.
Metlicovitz, L.

Monier, M.
Montassier, H.
Montedoro, M.
Moser, K.†
Nanni, G.†
Nashnyekov
Pinochi
Sborgi
Scattina
Singer, S.
Sironi, M.
Solanges
Tofi
Vincent, R.
Willoughby, H.
Witt, M.

Price range (if unlisted elsewhere) £3/**£8**/£35

UN-NAMED ARTISTS

Many unsigned, or undecipherable artist signed Art Deco postcards are now emerging. In particular there are some fine advertising designs of Period 4, many of them French or Italian.

Price range .. .. £2/**£5**/£7.50

■ART 1 Pub. Braun et Cie, Salons de Paris. Artist R. Delorme, 'Synchronisme' No. 7508. Period 4 £5

■ART 2 Pub. Braun et Cie, Salons de Paris. Artist A. Guillaume 'Au Fumoir' (in the Smoker). No. 0177. Period 4 £6

'NURSERY' ARTISTS ■CH 2–3, GR 4

In some cases these artists went through an Art Deco phase in a more general artistic career. These are the principal artists recognised by British collectors. Many more are listed and collected on the Continent.

Attwell, M. L.†
Bertiglia, A.†
Cooper, P.
Cramer, R.
Ebner, P.
Folkard, C.†
French, A.
Jacobs, H.
King, J. M.
Mallett, B.
Mercer, J.
Miller, H.
Outhwaite, I. R.
Parkinson, E.

Pearse, S. B.
Pinochi
Preston, C.
Richardson, A.†
Rickard, J.
Shand, C. E.
Smith, J. W.
Sowerby, M.
Wanke, A.
Wheeler, D.
Willebeeke le Mair, H.†

Price range .. .. £2/£4/£8

■ART 3 Pub. E. W. Savory. Artist Ethel Larcombe. 'The Sonnet'. Period 4 £15

■ART 4 Pub. 'E.P.' Artist B. Patella. Period 2 £10

ART NOUVEAU

Now perhaps reaching 'over-exposure', this has since the mid-1970s been the most prized style of design illustrated on the postcard. The style which emerged almost simultaneously in the mid-1880s in Glasgow and Brussels (where it was known as *le style belge*) is characterised by lyrical, flowing, complex, curvilinear designs, often with floral, ivy and clover leaf and peacock feather symbols. The art form spread to Germany and France where it got its name from S. Bing's Paris shop, founded in 1895, *L'Art Nouveau*. It is immortalised in Hector Guimard's entrances to the Paris *Métro* and in Glasgow in the form of stained glass and copper work—notably in the superb building that housed Millar & Lang the postcard publishers. Reaching its apogee in 1900–1902, the style faded out about 1910.

Many of the sought after *Art Nouveau* postcards were originally designed for the poster, but the influence of the style is seen strongly in borders and decorations of advertising/photographic/view and many other types of postcards.

All cards in this category are Periods 1 and 2.

NAMED ARTISTS ■ART 4, A 1, 7, 13, 14, 15, 16, 18, CH 2, L 4

Abeille, J.†
Abbéma, L.
Basch, A.†
Beardsley, A.
Bianchi, V.
Bilibine, I.†
Bompard, L.
Bonnet, G.
Boutet, H.†
Busi, A.
Capiello, L.†
Casas
Chéret, J.†
Christiansen, H.†
Combaz, G.†
Conrad, G.
Dannenberg
Diez, J.
Faivre, A.
De Feure, G.†
'Fidus'†
Fredillo
Géraud
Grasset, E.
Grün, J.
Guillaume, A.
Helleu, P.
Henrida, C.
Hoffmann, J.†
Hohenstein, A.
Iribe, P.
Jossot, H.†
Jozsa, C.†
Kandinsky, W.
Kienerk, G.†
Kieskow
Kirchner, R.†
Klimt, G.
Kosa
Kuhn-Regnier
Laskoff, F.
Léandre, C.
Lélée, L.†
Lessieux, L.
Macdonald, A. K.†
Martini, A.†
Mataloni, G.
Maurice, D.
Mazza, A.
Melina, C. L.
Metlicovitz, L.
Meunier, H.†
Mignot, V.†
Moser, K.†
Mucha, A.†
Noury, G.†
Patella, B.†
Péan, R.
Rau, L.
Riviere, J.
Sem, J.
Sonrel, E.
Steinlen, T.†
Tempestini
Toulouse-Lautrec, H. de
Utrillo, M.

Valloton, F.	Villon, J.†	
Villa, A.	Wanke, A.	
Price range	..	£5/**£15**/£60

UN-NAMED ARTISTS

Some extremely beautiful unsigned, or undecipherable artist signed *Art Nouveau* cards exist. They are highly prized and often fetch high prices. Publishers include: 'A & M, B.' (series of fine heads, printed in Saxony. UB); Davidson's 'Artistic Series' (printed in Saxony. UB); *Femmes Modernes* series and Tuck 'Art' Postcards (UB).

Price range .. .. £4/**£8**/£15

ART NOUVEAU BORDERS/DECORATION

B & w	50p/**75p**/£1
Coloured	£1/**£3**/£5
Russo-Japanese War	£3/**£4**/£5

ART NOUVEAU BUILDINGS/FURNITURE

Paris Métro in *Paris Vécu* series	£1/**£3**/£5
Others	75p/**£1.50**/£3

ART NOUVEAU FANTASY

Large Letter	£1/**£1.50**/£2
Others	50p/**75p**/£1

ART REPRODUCTIONS

One of the most under-estimated categories, which can yield some of the very finest colour printing to be found on the postcard. The section includes reproductions of friezes, heraldic devices, mosaics, paintings, sculpture and tapestries.

FRIEZES

Pub. Gaddis & Sief, Luxor
Mortuary chapels of the Nobles, Thebes. Period 2 (premium of 25% for complete set of at least 30) .. 25p/**50p**/75p

Pub. Luca Gentile & Co., Naples
Pompeii scenes with red border. Period 2 .. 50p/**75p**/£1

CLAN TARTANS/HERALDIC DEVICES

The intricate designs and bold colours of heraldic devices and Scottish tartans were natural for transfer to the picture post-card as the rotary printing processes came into full production early in Period 2. Most Period 1 examples are of foreign designs often used on commemorative issues. Here we are concerned with British designs only, of which there are vast numbers. For example, Stoddard & Co. issued over 1000 different versions of their well known Ja-Ja series. The listing is by publisher.

Brown & Rawcliffe (B. & R.)
Heraldic/view. Camera series 25p/**50p**/75p

Byers, W. E. (W.E.B. & Co.)
'Favourite' series. Heraldic/multi-view .. 50p/**£1**/£1.25

Cambridge Picture Postcard Co.
Cambridge colleges .. .. 50p/**£1**/£1.25
Oxford colleges .. .. 50p/**£1**/£1.25
Public schools .. .. 50p/**£1**/£1.25

Davis, A. M.
Heraldic .. .. 50p/**75p**/£1

Faulkner
Crests .. .. 50p/**£1**/£1.50
Heraldic. Framed .. .. £5/**£1.50**/£2
Heraldic. Unframed .. .. £1.50/**£2**/£2.50

Highland Clan Postcard
Scottish Clans 25p/**50p**/75p

Jarrold
Heraldic .. .. 50p/**£1**/£1.25

Johnston, W. & A. K.
Scottish Clans (about 100 cards) .. .. 50p/**£1**/£1.25

Millar & Lang
Heraldic. National series .. .. 50p/**75p**/£1

Peel, Robert
Cambridge colleges .. .. 50p/**£1**/£1.25
Oxford colleges .. .. 50p/**£1**/£1.25
Public schools .. .. 50p/**£1**/£1.25

Ritchie, William (W. R. & S.)
City Arms. Reliable series .. .. 50p/**75p**/£1

Stoddart (Ja-Ja)
Heraldic series (about 1000 cards) .. .. 75p/**£1**/£1.25

Tuck
Heraldic. Embossed. View. Unframed. UB .. .. £5/**£6**/£8
Heraldic. Framed. UB .. .. £4/**£5**/£6
Scottish clans .. .. £1/**£1.50**/£2

Valentine
Multi-shields .. .. 50p/**75p**/£1

MOSAICS

Pub. A. Reber, Palermo
Mosaic from the Palatine Chapel, gold & silver print. Cards form a type of 'composite'. Period 2 (a large premium would be attached to a complete picture) .. .. 50p/**75p**/£1

PAINTINGS

Pub. Fine Arts Publishing Co.
Royal Exchange paintings. Period 4. Two sets of 6 in original packets with explanatory leaflet.
Set with packet .. .. £2/**£4**/£6
Set without packet .. .. £1/**£3**/£4

Pub. Misch & Co.
World's Galleries series, bearing a Stengel number, as well as a Misch number. Brilliant colours on heavy board. From 1905 .. .. 50p/**75p**/£1

Pub. Misch & Stock/Other Misch & Co. series/Stengel. From the National Gallery
Rembrandt series 25p/**50p**/75p
Millet's masterpieces. Period 2 .. .. .. 25p/**50p**/75p

Pub. Tuck
Many series throughout Periods 2 to 4 in a variety of presentations 25p/**50p**/75p

Other British publishers
Alpha, Boots, Cassell's, Ettlinger, Eyre & Spottiswoode 'Woodbury' series, C. W. Faulkner & Co., S. Hildesheimer, W. MacKenzie, Medici Society, Ernest Nister, Photochrom, Celesque 'Famous Picture' series, Rotary, Schwerdtfeger, Valentine, J. Welch, Wildt & Kray, Wrench.
Period 1 .. .. 25p/**50p**/75p
Periods 2 to 4 .. .. 25p/50p
Periods 5 to 7 .. .. **25p**

Foreign publishers
Period 1 .. .. 25p/**50p**/75p
Periods 2 to 4 .. .. 25p/50p
Carlo Bestetti, Rome, Toulouse-Lautrec reproductions. Period 6 .. .. £2/**£3**/£5

Reproductions from Art Galleries
Birmingham, Lady Lever Art Gallery, Louvre, Manchester, National Gallery, Prado, etc.
Period 1 .. .. 25p/50p
Periods 2–7 .. .. **25p**

SCULPTURES

Alpha/Paris Salon/Others
Period 1 .. .. 25p/50p
Periods 2–7 .. .. **25p**
Pub. Anon. Artist Giris. Personalities like Farman and the Kaiser. Periods 2, 3 .. .. £1.50/**£3**/£6
Pub. D.M. Italy. Artist L. Rizzi. WW1 satire Tzar, Emperor of Austria, Poincaré, etc. .. .. £1.50/**£3**/£6
Pub. A. Noyer, Paris. Artist Mastroianni. Photographs of sculptured military scenes. Periods 2, 3 .. 50p/**75p**/£1

ARTISTS

This section gives general information about the work of the better-known postcard artists, together with some biographical background. It also refers to the sections where more details and specific valuations of the artists' work are to be found. Valuations in this section indicate the price range of the artists' general work.

ABEILLE, JACK ■A 1

One of the earliest French artists to design for the postcard (from about 1898) with delightful vignettes, often featuring lovely ladies (see Social History*). He also designed for the Paris Exhibition of 1900 (see* Exhibitions*) and went on producing postcards well into Period 3, when he produced some military designs.*

Pre-1900 designs	£15/**£25**/£30
Paris Exhibition	£10/**£15**/£20
Period 2. Flower series/Head-dress styles through the ages/ 'Sins' series	£6/**£10**/£18
Later designs	£5/**£10**/£15

■A 1 Pub. 'J.W.H.' Artist Jack Abeille. 'La Colère' (Anger). 1899 £25

■A 2 Pub. Tuck. Artist Cecil Aldin. 'Christmas' Postcard. Series 8080. Period 2 £4

ALDIN, CECIL (d. 1935) ■A 2

Educated at Solihull Grammar School and then under Calderon in Kensington, he was a popular founder member of the London Sketch Club, of which he was President in 1905. He specialised in dogs, hunting scenes and other animal studies and was a Master of Foxhounds.

Lawrence & Jellicoe .. .. £1/**£2**/£3
Savory, E. W. Ltd., Bristol .. .. 0 .. .. .. £1/**£2**/£3
Tuck 'Celebrated Poster' series No. 1500 (1 card), series No. 1502 (2 cards), Cadbury's Cocoa, Colman's Blue, Colman's Starch .. .. £15/**£17**/£22
Tuck. Other series .. .. £1.50/**£2**/£4
Valentine & Sons. The five senses .. .. £1.50/**£2**/£4

ALLEN, DAPHNE (b. 1899)
Daphne Allen achieved fame as a child artist. Much of her work was published in two books—A Child's Visions and The Birth of the Opal. Some of her drawings were reproduced as postcards for Glaxo adverts. Periods 2 and 3.

Price range .. .. £2.50/**£4**/£5

ANDERSON, MARTIN (Cynicus) (1854–1932) ■A 3
A rare, original vein of unconventional humour and satire characterised this prolific artist's work. A Scot by birth and breeding, Anderson moved to London to establish himself as an artist. He set up his own company which produced hundreds of designs, some of them hand-tinted, which dealt with many facets of Edwardian life bicycling, courtship, marriage, parenthood, the railway, Scottish life, and the seaside. See COMIC.

Blum & Degen (1899). Three court-sized sets .. £1/**£3**/£5
Cynicus Pub. Co. (1902–1916). .. .. .. 50p/**75p**/£1.50
Tuck (1914). Set of 'By and Bye' Darby & Joan types .. .. 75p/**£1**/£2

ANDERSON, V. C.
Period 2. American artist. Subjects include children and comic.
Publishers include: Charles Scribner's Sons, Reinthal & Newman, Wildt & Kray.

Price range .. .. 75p/**£1**/£1.50

ARDIZZONE, EDWARD (b. 1900)
Born in Haiphong, China, he came to England to be educated in 1905. He studied at the Westminster School of Art. He is best known as an official War Artist of WW2.

Price range .. .. 50p/**£1**/£1.50

ARMITAGE, WILLIAM (1856–1941)
Son of a Nottingham Quaker family, he worked in the family corn merchant business for some years before taking up painting becoming a proficient landscape artist and animal painter. His famous WW1 patriotic design of the lion and its mane is the only Armstrong postcard so far identified. Other information would be welcomed by the compilers.

Period 3. Pub. Boots. WW1 design 25p/**50p**/75p

ASTI, ANGELO (1847–1903)

Italian artist who mostly worked in France. He was born in Paris and died in Mantua. His work was exhibited in the Paris Salon between 1890 and 1901. He was mostly known for his bosomy beauties (see GLAMOUR*) but his most famous design was for the Collection Job (see* COLLECTIONS*).*

Collection Job

1903	£20/**£25**/£30
1905/07/11/14	£10/**£15**/£20
Pub. H. J. Smith of Brighton 1902	£1/**£1.50**/£2
Pub. Tuck. Several series of girls' heads, many designs reversed	£1/**£1.50**/£2

ATTWELL, MABEL LUCIE (1879–1964)

The Queen of the 'cute' child type of illustration, her postcard career spanned at least four decades. Wife of Harold Earnshaw (qv). Her first postcards appeared before WW1 and she continued drawing through the Great War (with many patriotic and morale-raising designs). Her most prolific output was between the two wars. During WW2 her kiddies donned uniforms and gas masks and queued for their rations. In Period 6 they commented gently on current fashions and mores. See CHILDREN *and* MILITARY*. Her main publishers were Tuck and Valentine.*

Periods 2, 3	75p/**£1**/£1.50
Period 4	25p/**50p**/75p
Period 5	75p/**£1**/£1.50
Period 6	25p/**50p**/75p

■A 3 Pub. Cynicus Pub. Co. Artist Martin Anderson. 'King Lear'. 1906 £1.50

■A 4 Pub. Tuck. Artist F. Aveline. 'Aquarette' Postcard 3602. 'My Fancy'. Period 3 £2

AVELINE, F. ■A 4

Portrayer of elegant ladies, often in period dress.

Pub. James Henderson & Sons. Periods 3, 4. Head studies/In Hoops & Furbelows, etc. Others .. .. .. 75p/**£1**/£2

BANTOCK

Stylised Art Deco designs. Period 4.

'Bantock' series .. .. £1/**£2**/£3

BAIRNSFATHER, BRUCE (1887–1959) ■A 5

Best known for his 'Fragments from France' series of postcards (see MILITARY*). Bairnsfather, who trained at the John Hassall Art School, also did comic strips on postcards between the wars (see* COMIC*) and some fine theatre advertising postcards.*

Period 3.

British Red Cross Society. Surrey Branch fund raiser .. .. £3/**£5**/£8
The Follies. Four Div. .. .. £1/**£3**/£5
Pub. Beagles. Photographic portrait .. .. .. £3/**£5**/£8
Pub. *The Bystander* 'Fragments from France' Nine series of 6 cards (*see* the Second Edition for complete list)
Per card .. .. 75p/**£1**/£1.50
Pub. 'Red Letter' Midget Message miniature versions of 'Fragments from France' series .. .. .. £1.25/**£2.50**/£3
Pub. Tuck. Oilette No. 3189. 'Better 'Ole' series 75p/**£1**/£1.50
Theatre advertising (poster types). Pub. David Allen. C. E. Cochran's 'The Better 'Ole' .. .. .. £10/**£15**/£30
Theatre advertising (poster types). Pub. Waddington. 'Flying Colours' .. .. £10/**£15**/£30
Theatre advertising. Pub. Anon. 'Old Bill M.P.' £8/**£10**/£12

Period 4

British Legion fund raiser .. .. £1/**£1.50**/£3
Pub. Tuck. Comic strips of Old Bill and Bert from *The Passing Show* .. .. 75p/**£1**/£1.50

Period 5

Pub. Valentine. 'Old Bill Again' from *The Bystander* .. .. 75p/**£1**/£1.50

BAKST, LEON NIKOLAEVICH (1866–1924)

Bakst grew up in St. Petersburg, attended the Imperial Academy of Arts and became a member of the Society of Painters in Water Colours and a theatrical designer. In 1906 he exhibited in the Russian section of the Salon d'Automne in Paris and in 1908 designed scenery and costumes for Diaghilev's fabulous Ballet Russe. The seeds of Art Deco *were born. He later became both producer and designer for theatrical and balletic productions in Paris and London. Recently postcards have been discovered of Bakst's revolutionary designs for the* Ballet Russe *in 1908.*

Se of 12 characters from *La Fée des Poupées c.* 1903. Per set	£50/**£80**/£120
Carnaval de Schouman. Per card	£10/**£20**/£30
Other designs. Per card	..£5/**£15**/£40

■A 5 Pub. Anon. Artist Bruce Bairnsfather. Theatre advert for *Old Bill M.P.!* Period 4 £10

■A 6 Pub. Anon. Artist W. Barribal. Period 4 £4

BARHAM, SYBIL

Sybil Barham was one of the artists commissioned by C. W. Faulkner to design their charming 'nursery' postcards (see CHILDREN*). Series include a particularly charming 'Peter Pan' set. Periods 2, 3, 4.*

Price range	75p/**£2**/£4

BARRIBAL, W. ■A 6

Known as 'Barri', he was best known for his glamorous girls—all based on his wife, Babs. He was a very successful commercial artist and drew advertisements for many products, designed playing cards and contributed to numerous magazines. His postcard output spanned both World Wars. See CHILDREN *and* GLAMOUR.

Advertising cards	£16/**£18**/£20
Theatre poster cards	£2/**£3**/£4
Others	£2/**£3**/£4

Barribal Advertising and Theatre Poster Cards were listed in the third edition (p. 39), also some of his General Designs.

BASCH, ARPAD ■A 7

A Hungarian by birth, he was one of the most spectacular Art Nouveau artists producing in Paris around the turn of the century. He worked with Bonnard, mainly for the many illustrated reviews then being published.

Set of 6 'International Girls' (1900)	£40/**£60**/£75
Town Portrait series	£20/**£25**/£35
WW1 Military Scenes, b & w. Pub. Hungary	£2.50/**£5**/£10
Others	£15/**£20**/£30

BATEMAN, H. M.

British cartoonist of the first rank, an admirer of Caran D'Ache (qv) and Aubrey Beardsley, his work appeared all too rarely on the postcard. A contributor to a host of magazines and journals, including Punch, *he specialised in the social 'gaffe'.*

Price range	£1/**£2**/£3

■A 7 Pub. Anon. Artist Arpad Basch. PU 1901 £25

■A 8 Pub. British Art. Co. Artist Marjorie C. Bates. 'Rosalind', from Shakespeare's *As You Like It.* Period 4 £1.50

BATES, MARJORIE CHRISTINE (1883–1962) ■A 8

Born in Derbyshire, she studied at the Nottingham School of Art and later in Paris. In a working style similar to that of 'Jotter' (Hayward Young) she travelled the British Isles, sketching, mostly in her distinctive style of pencil and crayon. During Periods 4, 5 her work was published by the British Art Co. (trademark initials 'B.A.C.' later changed to 'F.A.C.'). Bates also illustrated books and her work was reproduced as prints and trade cards.

Pub. British Art Co. (B.A.C., later F.A.C.)
Period 4 Series of distinctive but delicate pastel/pencil sketches of rural and town scenes: Cambridge; Canterbury; Chester; Edinburgh; London; Oxford; Salisbury; Scarborough; Shrewsbury; Stratford-on-Avon; Whitby; Windsor and Worcestershire.

Period 4. Series of Characters from Shakespeare. So far identified are: 1. Lady Macbeth; 2. Romeo & Juliet; 3. Hamlet; 4. Rosalind (*As You Like It*); 5. Clown (*Twelfth Night*); 6. Malvolio (*Twelfth Night*); 7. Falstaff & the Merry Wives of Windsor; 8. Portia (*Merchant of Venice*); 9. Titania & Bottom (*Midsummer Night's Dream*); 10. Katharina (*The Taming of the Shrew*).

Pub. P. R. Series
Period 4. Princess Royal Hotel Whitby, and other adverts for Princess Royal Hotels.

Pub. Phillipson & Golder of Chester
Period 4 Chester designs.

Others

Price range (highest price for Shakespeare set and the ad.) .. .. 50p/**75p**/£1.50

BEECROFT, HERBERT

Australian artist, whose work is also seen in the UK. He drew portraits and views.

Pub. NSW Bookstall Co. 'Art Series'
Australian Coast (6 cards) .. .. £2/**£2.50**/£3
Sydney Views (6 cards) .. .. £3/**£3.50**/£4
Women: Portraits. Series 1 and 2 each of 6 cards .. .. £3.50/**£4.50**/£6

BEIRNE, F. O.

Superb early UB *chromo-litho military vignettes reminiscent of Harry Payne.*

Pub. Anon. .. .. £6/**£7**/£8

BELCHER, GEORGE

Royal Academician who specialised in analytical charcoal character studies of cockney life. He contributed to Punch, The Tatler *and many books, working from live, authentic models. Sadly few of his designs were reproduced on the postcard. See also* COMIC.

Pub. Tuck 'Celebrated Posters', Ogden's Guinea Gold. No. 1501 .. .. £12/**£15**/£22
Pub. Tuck. Period 2. Two humorous sets .. .. £3/**£5**/£6

BERTIGLIA, A.
Italian artist whose work spanned Periods 2 to 5. Subjects include children, glamour and military subjects for WW1 and WW2.

Price range .. .. £2/**£3**/£6

BILIBINE, IVAN (1876–1942) ■A 9
A much-travelled Russian, who, trained as a lawyer, Bilibine soon started to draw and became highly successful as a theatrical designer. He worked for Diaghilev and the Theatre des Champs-Elysees. *His postcard work, captured the everyday working life and spirit of his countrymen. His local scenes and characters are often surrounded by attractive decorative borders. During WW1 he also drew some designs for the Red Cross. Periods 2, 3.*

Price range .. .. £5/**£10**/£15

BIRD, CYRIL KENNETH (1887–1965)
Postcards signed Fougasse. Studied at the Percy Bradshaw Art School. During WW1 he was wounded in the spine at Gallipoli, leaving him bed-ridden for a while. Fighting back to fitness he became a contributor to Punch, *eventually becoming art editor. His* nom de plume *comes from a small explosive mine! He is best remembered for his WW2 propaganda posters, many of which were reproduced as postcards. See also* MILITARY.

Price range .. .. £1/**£1.25**/£2

BISHOP
American artist who drew appealing children, comic, glamour and greetings cards. One of his best known sets is the 'What do you know about that?' series, with a picture and a verse. Another attractive set is the colourful red, green and yellow Valentine set for A. H. & Co.

Pub. A. H. Co. Valentine set .. .. .. 50p/**£75p**/£1.50
Pub. Anon.
'What do you know about that?' set .. 50p/**75p**/£1.25
Other miscellaneous designs .. .. .. 25p/**75p**/£1

BOETIUS, J. O. ■A 9
Comic artist whose postcard work was reproduced by the prolific British publisher, S. Hildesheimer in their important '5000 series' (see Edition 3 for a full listing). He often signed his designs with his initials, 'J.O.B.' only. Period 2.

Price range .. .. 50p/**75p**/£1

BOILEAU, PHILIP (1864–1917) ■A 10

Born in Quebec to a French diplomat and an American society beauty, Philip studied art and music in Milan. Eventually he settled in the USA where his second wife—Emily Gilbert became his model and inspiration. Success came with his drawings of the 'American Girl'—the transatlantic rival to the 'Gibson Girl', which appeared in newspapers, on posters, prints and calendars as well as on postcards. See GLAMOUR *and* MILITARY.

Advertising work. Contrary Mary Book, Flood & Conklin, Metropolitan Life Ins. Co., Nat. Suit and Cloak Co. Period 2 .. .. £2/**£3.50**/£6

For a listing of cards published by Reinthal & Newman, see Second Edition, pp. 39–40.

Other Pubs. (incl. National Art Co., Wildt & Kray)
Original designs and re-issues of Reinthal titles.

Price range .. .. £2/**£3**/£5

BOMPARD, LUIGI (1873–1953)

Italian Artist, best known for his Period 2 glamour designs. He also drew some attractive adverts for various commemorative events. Periods 2/3.

Price range .. .. £2/**£4**/£8

■A 9 Pub. Hildesheimer. Artist J. O. Boetius. 'The Broken Melody'. 5000 Series No. 5175. PU 1905 £1

■A 10 Pub. Reinthal & Newman, New York. Artist Philip Boileau. 'Be Prepared'. Period 3 £5

BONZAGNI, AROLDO (1887–1918)

Italian artist who drew both glamorous girls en déshabillé *and fund-raising designs. These included anti-Austrian caricatures. Periods 2 to 4.*

Price range .. .. £3/**£6**/£10

BOUTET, HENRI (1851–1921)

An important French postcard artist of Period 1/early Period 2. The 1979 Neudin Argus *lists nearly three hundred cards. His inspiration was in Paris night life, the* midinettes *and artists' models. His 'Corsets' series created a moral furore in England in 1901. Main publishers include Motot, A. D., La Librairie Charles, L'Atelier d'Art, and in England, Southwood. He contributed card No. 8 of the 'Collection des Cent' (see* COLLECTIONS*) and apart from his glamorous art designs, produced some cards with a military theme.*

Price range (highest value for the 'Cent' card) £5/**£20**/£60

BRADSHAW, PERCY V.

Bradshaw always had the desire to draw. At age 18 he became a freelance artist gradually getting work with a number of magazines. He also started writing and eventually started the correspondence art school that made him famous. During his long productive years, many of his clever and humorous drawings were reproduced as postcards. Over one hundred and fifty designs have been recognised, some signed only with his initials, 'P.V.B.'

Pub. Misch & Co. (Early Period 2)
Series No. 947 Excentricity .. .. £2/**£4**/£5
948 Smiles .. .. £2/**£4**/£5
Others .. .. £1.50/**£2**/£4

Pub. Moss & Co. (Early Period 2)
Series No. 4415 Musical Terms up to Date .. .. £2/**£4**/£6
Others .. .. £1.50/**£3**/£5

Pub. Tuck
22 known series—for details of which *see* Second Edition, p. 41.
Price range .. .. £2/**£4**/£6

Pub. Wrench
Nos. 18043–18048 Shakespeare Illustrated by 'Toasts' .. .. £3/**£4**/£6

Others
Various .. .. £2/**£2**/£4

BRETT, MOLLY

Subjects include animals and fairies.

Pub. Faulkner, C. W. .. .. 75p/**£1**/£1.25
Pub. Medici Society .. .. 75p/**£1**/£1.25

BROWNE, TOM (1870–1910)

Born and educated in Nottingham where he attended the local art school. Later in London his comic style developed. He created 'Weary Willie and Tired Tim', joined the Langham Sketching Club and was published in Punch. *A co-founder with his friend, Dudley Hardy, of the rip-roaring London Sketch Club (of which he was President in 1907), his work was first exhibited at the Royal Academy in 1897. His acute but sympathetic observation made him the recorder* par excellence *of the Edwardian working classes at play and at home. On the serious side, his Dutch themes, the result of cycling tours in Holland, are sensitively executed. Two visits to the USA produced some amusing American postcard comments. To date his known postcard output is more than 1300 designs. See* COMIC.

Pub. Baird, Alexander

Two series of Dutch themes on deep brown mounts; among his finest postcard work .. .. £2/**£4**/£6

Commercial work

See also ADVERTISING, ARTISTS and ENTERTAINMENT: Theatre

Arcadians, The	£4/**£6**/£8
Beechams pills	£10/**£15**/£20
Eucryl soap	£4/**£6**/£8
Fry's chocolate & cocoa	£10/**£15**/£20
Peak Frean biscuits	£4/**£6**/£8
Raleigh bicycles	£10/**£15**/£20
Weekly Telegraph	£2/**£4**/£6
Others	£2/**£4**/£6

Pub. Davidson Bros.

Comic series. 2500–2648 (excl. the serious sets below). Subjects include: billiards, boating, cats, Mrs. Caudle's lectures, chicks, courting, cricket, cycling, dogs, fishing, football, golfing, holidays, hunting, Ma & Pa, Military, Naval, Uncle Podger, Weary Willie & Tired Tim. Many were overprinted as greetings cards.

Price range .. .. £1.50/**£3**/£5

Serious series. 2529, 2531–2533, 2542–2543. Castles, Cathedrals, Dutch and London views.

Price range .. .. £1/**£2**/£4

Pub. Hartmann

About five series. Subjects include 'Celebrities' and 'Eminent Men in the Days of Their Youth' .. .. £2.50/**£5**/£10

Pub. Landeker & Brown

'Ellanbee Aquasimile' series .. .. £2/**£4**/£6

Pub. Tuck

Many Oilette series, unsigned, subjects include Jokes from *Punch*, Seaside Humour, Dutch Studies, etc. Periods 2, 3 .. .. £2/**£4**/£6

Pub. Valentine
About ten series, of which about half are signed. Subjects include 'Christmas Humour', 'London Studies', 'Proverbs' .. .. £2/**£4**/£6

Pub. Wrench
Three known series. Dutch themes, Humour of Life, *Punch* Illustrations .. .. £2/**£4**/£6

BRUNDAGE, FRANCES (1854–1937)
Born in New Jersey, USA, she started illustrating books for Tuck in their New York offices, progressing to postcard designs for them and for Sam Gabriel. She travelled to England, working for Tuck there. Nearly three hundred signed designs have been identified. She specialised in CHILDREN *and* GREETINGS *(qv).*

Pub. Gabriel, Sam (from 1910)
Nineteen sets of 10 cards have been identified, including Halloween and Thanksgiving .. .. £1.50/**£2.50**/£3.50

Pub. Tuck (from 1900)
About 25 sets, some unsigned, including 'coons', Dutch children, greetings .. .. £2/**£3**/£5

Others .. .. £1/**£1.50**/£2

BRUNELLESCHI, UMBERTO (1886–1949) ■A 11
Italian artist whose finest work was a series of imaginative girls as birds, butterflies, etc. published c. 1920 in the Art Deco style. He also did strong patriotic and military designs and some commercial work, incl. illustrations for the French fashion magazine, Journal des Dames et des Modes *and the* Guirlande des Mois.

Price range .. .. £30/**£50**/£60

BUCHANAN, FRED
Comic artist, Periods 2 to 4.

Pub. Tuck
Taking the Waters, etc. .. .. 75p/**£1.50**/£2.50

Pub. Woolstone Bros.
Comic series .. .. 50p/**75p**/£1

Others 25p/**50p**/75p

BULL, RENE
Period 2 comic artist, whose humour often had a political flavour. Publishers include Davidson Bros., C. W. Faulkner, Landeker & Brown (Ellanbee)—Humorous & Fiscal series, Chas. Voisey—Humours of Billiards, and others.

Price range .. .. £2/**£3**/£4

BUXTON, DUDLEY

Period 2 comic artist. Publishers include Inter-Art 'Comique' series, A. V. N. Jones and others.

Price range .. .. 50p/**75p**/£1.50

CALDECOTT, RANDOLPH (1846–1886)

Born the son of a Cheshire accountant who forced him to stifle his love of art in order to train in a 'sound profession', Caldecott became a bank clerk. Later he studied in the evenings at the Manchester Art School and had drawings published in a local paper. Befriended and encouraged by Thomas Armstrong of the South Kensington Museum, he became a regular contributor to London Society, The Graphic *and* Punch *and an illustrator of children's books—drawings from which were reproduced in postcard form by Frederick Warne & Co. in 1929/30.*

Pub. Frederick Warne & Co. Period 4

Eight sets of six cards on Nursery Rhyme themes—*see* listing in Second Edition, p. 44.

Price range 25p/**50p**/75p

CALDERARA, C.

Italian artist of fashion and glamour with a distinct Art Deco flavour, often featuring motor cars in the design. See also GLAMOUR *and* MILITARY.

Price range .. .. £2/**£4**/£6

■A 11 Pub. Ricordi, Milan. Artist Umberto Brunelleschi. PU 1919 £30

■A 12 Pub. Anon. Artist Léal de Camara. Fr. UB £9

CAMARA, LEAL de (1877–1948) ■A 12

Spanish artist, most of whose best postcard work was done in Paris. Most famous for his limited edition political caricatures (see also POLITICAL*). He also contributed many illustrations which were reproduced as postcards for the satirical magazine* L'Assiette au Beurre. *Bicycles and motor cars were favourite subjects (Period 2).*

Bicycle themes	£8/**£10**/£15
Motor car themes	£10/**£15**/£20
Others	£7/**£9**/£12

CAMPBELL, B.

Australian artist who portrayed the enduringly popular Australian subjects of country and cattle stations.

Pub. NSW Bookstall Co.	
Series of 6 cards	£3/**£3.50**/£5

CANTLE, J. M.

Australian artist who specialized in bird studies.

Pub. NSW Bookstall Co. 'Art Series'	
New Zealand and Tasmanian scenes (6 cards)	£1.50/**£2**/£3
Pub. Samuel Wood	
Bird Studies (6 cards)	£1/**£1.50**/£2
Pub. Anon.	
38 identified bird paintings	£3/**£4**/£6

CAPIELLO, LEONETTO (1875–1942)

Versatile Italian artist whose work spanned Periods 2, 3 and 4 with a variety of styles and themes. During Period 2 he did exhibition and advert designs in the Art Nouveau style. Possessing a lively sense of caricature, he contributed to the French publications Le Rire *and* L'Assiette au Beurre, *and to the* Album Mariani *collection in 1910. During WW1 he produced patriotic designs and during Period 4 he drew adverts for drink and toothpaste companies etc.*

Period 2	
Art Nouveau adverts	£15/**£20**/£25
Mariani design	£7.50/**£10**/£15
Period 3	
Patriotic designs	£5/**£7.50**/£10
Period 4	
Adverts	£10/**£15**/£20
Propaganda	£7.50/**£10**/£15

CARAN D'ACHE

See Poiré, Emmanuel.

CARR, GENE (1881–1959)

American artist who captured the spirit of childhood in his series of games, like 'Baseball', 'Hide and Seek', Marbles', etc. He also drew Greetings designs for the postcard. A natural cartoonist with no art training. Carr found success whilst still in his teens, and worked for many famous newspapers and magazines—e.g. New York Herald *and* Saturday Evening Post. *Periods 2, 3, 4.*

Pub. Rotograph and others.
Price range .. .. 75p/**£1.50**/£3

CARTER, REGINALD ARTHUR LEE (1886–1950) ■SP 2
Carter was born, and lived most of his life, in Southwold, Suffolk. A member of the North British Academy, he contributed to magazines like The Sketch *and* The Tatler. *His versatile and prolific output of postcards spanned Periods 2 to 4 and was produced by a variety of publishers, including himself ('The Sorrows of Southwold' printed by the Southwold Press). See* ANIMALS.

Pub. B.P. & Co. (Period 4)
Birthday greetings for 1–8 year olds. The set .. £2/**£3**/£4

Pub. Dennis, E. T. W.
'Southwold' comic card 25p/**50p**/75p

Pub. Ettlinger
John Chinaman's Winter Sports (1905) .. 50p/**75p**/£1
Office humour (1906) .. .. 50p/**75p**/£1
Other series .. .. 50p/**75p**/£1

Pub. Mack, E. (Period 2)
Various designs including some fine political cartoons .. .. 50p/**£1**/£2

Pub. Millar & Lang (Periods 2, 3)
Several series, incl. 'At the Seaside' 1910 .. 25p/**50p**/75p

Pub. Salmon, J. (Period 2)
Several series 25p/**50p**/75p

Pub. Southwold Press and Reg. Carter (Period 4)
'Sorrows of Southwold'. Two series of 6 .. 50p/**75p**/£1.50
Period 7 reprints per set **50p**

Pub. Stiebel, Alfred (Periods 2, 3)
'Modern Humour' series, incl. 'Scouting' .. 50p/**75p**/£1.50

Pub. Valentine (Periods 2 to 4)
Series include motoring and seaside themes 25p/**50p**/75p

Pub. Verdier (1909)
Hints to Aeroplanists, Hints to Roller Skaters, A Labour of Love, Studies of Paradise (some with adverts for Sunlight soap), The Territorials, etc. .. .. .. 50p/**75p**/£2

Pub. Wildt & Kray
Chinamen series (1904) .. .. 50p/**75p**/£1.50
Fashion series (1910–1914) for men and for women .. .. 75p/**£1**/£1.50

CARTER, SYDNEY (1874–1945)

Born in Enfield, Middlesex, he moved shortly to Epping Forest, where his lifelong love of trees started. At 15 he went to Walthamstow Art School, was exhibited at the Royal Academy at the age of 20 and went on to the Royal College of Art. He won several art scholarships and was exhibited at the Paris Salon and the British Institute of Watercolours and Oils. After WW1 he emigrated to South Africa. About 170 postcard designs have been identified.

Pub. Birn Bros. (1904)
London views, set of 6 .. .. 50p/**75p**/£1

Pub. Hildesheimer
See also LITERARY.
At least twenty series, including 'How Men Propose' (twelve cards), 'Months of the Year' (twelve cards), Hans Andersen Fairy Tales, sketches from Scott, Shakespeare, Thackeray. (50% premium for complete sets of twelve) .. 50p/**£1**/£1.50

Pub. Smith, W. H. and Ashton, Wm.
Ancient British Halls, set of 6 .. .. .. 50p/**75p**/£1

Pub. Tuck
The Homes of Literary Men, set of 6 .. .. 50p/**75p**/£1

CASCELLA, BASILIO (1860–1950)

Italian artist who drew a range of topics—adverts, commemorative, glamour, peasant types, etc. The early studies show a strong Art Nouveau influence.

Price range .. .. £3/**£6**/£10

CASSIERS, HENRI (b. 1858)

Fine Belgian artist who designed for the postcard from its earliest pictorial days. His distinctive but delicate style found expression in Dutch scenes with figures, landscapes and town scenes. His series for the shipping line 'Red Star' are beautiful examples of how well the art of the poster translates to the smaller medium.

Pub. Dietrich of Brussels from 1900
Bruxelles et Anvers Pittoresque .. .. .. £3/**£4**/£5
Glasgow Exhibition (*see* EXHIBITIONS) .. .. £2/**£3**/£5
La Hollande Pittoresque .. .. £2/**£3**/£5
Le Littoral Belge .. .. £2/**£3**/£5
London views .. .. £2/**£3**/£5
18th-century Characters .. .. £2/**£3**/£5
En Zélande .. .. £2/**£3**/£5

Pub. W. de Haan, Utrecht
Costumes hollondais (12 cards) .. .. £2/**£3**/£5
Various Dutch views .. .. £2/**£3**/£5

Pub. Moss, Henry & Co. (1903–1905)
Several series .. .. £2/**£3**/£5

Pub. Huardel, P. G. & Co. from 1900
Paris views .. .. £2/**£3**/£5

Pub. Southwood, F. C. (1901)
Several series .. .. £1/**£2**/£4

Red Star Liner Advertisements
Thirty cards have been identified .. .. ..£5/**£10**/£15

CATON WOODVILLE, RICHARD (1856–1927)

Born of a German mother and partly educated in Germany, Caton Woodville served under Kitchener in Egypt. He covered the Boer War as a military artist and continued his military work during WW1. See also MILITARY.

Early Period 2
Pub. Collectors' Pub. Co. (1901). Five sets of Boer War cards .. .. £1/**£2**/£4
Pub. Hartmann, Fred. (1901). Famous British Battles .. .. £1/**£1.50**/£3
Pub. 'Imperial Army Series' (1904) Military types .. .. £1/**£1.50**/£3
Pub. Picture Postcard Co. Boer War designs .. £1/**£2**/£4
Pub. Watkins & McCombie. The Gentleman in Khaki .. .. £1/**£1.50**/£2

Period 3
Designs for St. Dunstans .. .. 75p/**£1**/£1.25
Others (tanks, etc.) .. .. 50p/**75p**/£1

CHÉRET, JULES (1836–1932)

French Art Nouveau artist who contributed to many of the important early French series, like the 'Job', Editions Cino, Les Affiches Célèbres, La Collection des Cent *and* Les Cartes Postales Mariani. *From 1856–66 Chéret had studied colour lithography in London and on his return to Paris designed over 1000 theatrical posters.*

Price range .. .. £30/**£50**/£75

CHIOSTRO, CARLO (1863–1939)

Born in Florence, Chiostro became well-known for his illustrations of childrens' books. Subjects of his postcards include comic themes, flower and fruit still-lives. Carlo Chiostri always signed his full name. Cards signed only 'Chiostri' are by his daughter, Sofia (1896–1945) who worked with her sister Eelina.

Price range .. .. £3/**£6**/£12

CHRISTIANSEN, HANS

Art Nouveau artist who contributed to many of the important early French and German series, e.g. 'Les Maîtres de la Carte Postale' *(1898–1900) and* 'Jugend' *(1899).*

Price range .. .. £25/**£50**/£70

CHRISTIE, GEORGE FYFFE

Scottish artist who often signed with his initials 'G.F.C.' and who worked for many Scottish as well as London companies. His work on the postcard spanned Periods 2 to 5. See COMIC.

Pub. Lyon, Wm, Glasgow
Several comic series and some fine early political caricatures (Joseph Chamberlain, etc.) .. .. .. £1/**£1.50**/£2

Pub. Millar & Lang
Periods 2 to 4. Many series, often unsigned 50p/**75p**/£1

Pub. Misch & Co.
Addled Ads (1903) .. .. 75p/**£1**/£2

Pub. Photochrom
Several series. Periods 2, 3 .. .. .. 50p/**75p**/£1
Home Guard Silhouettes. Period 5 .. .. 50p/**75p**/£1

Pub. Ritchie, Wm. & Sons
Several series (*c.* 1907) incl. Diabolo, Our . . . (Evening at Home, Boarding House, etc.) .. .. .. 75p/**£1**/£1.25

CHRISTY, F. EARL (1883–1961)

This American artist (no relation to Howard Christy) was trained at the Pennsylvania Academy of Fine Arts. His specialised version of the American Girl was the 'College Girl' or 'Belle'. He drew for magazines and posters, and the many postcard versions of his designs were produced by a variety of publishers. See GLAMOUR.

Price range .. .. £2.50/**£3**/£12

CHRISTY, HOWARD CHANDLER (1873–1952)

American exponent of a brand of the American Girl known as the 'Christy Girl'. He studied at the National Academy of Design and the Art Students League and became a successful commercial artist, working as a war illustrator in Cuba and for Scribner's Magazine, Harpers, Colliers *and* Cosmopolitan. *During WW1 he did many patriotic designs.* See also GLAMOUR.

Price range .. .. £1/**£2**/£3

CLAPSADDLE, ELLEN (1865–1934) ■GR 1

One of America's most popular artists, specialising in CHILDREN *and* GREETINGS (qv)*—she is credited with 3000 designs. Most of her work was published by the International Art Co. Subjects include Christmas, 'Coons', Easter, Hallowe'en, Patriotics (4 July, Decoration Day, etc.), St. Patrick's Day, Valentines, and some rare and sought after Suffragette designs. Although somewhat stilted and stereotyped, her designs are appealing, and greatly collected in the USA. Periods 2, 3, 4.*

Pub. International Art Co.
  General children, greetings, holidays .. £1/**£2.50**/£4
  Novelty series 1236 (mechanical) .. .. .. £3/**£6**/£10
Pub. Wolf
  2 Suffragette designs on Valentine cards .. £5/**£10**/£15

CLARK, J. CLAYTON (Kyd)

Famous for his representations of characters from Dickens. See LITERARY.

Pub. Faulkner, C. W.
Characters from Dickens. Series 497/8/9

Pub. Hildesheimer
'Heads—And the Tales They Tell' (1903)

Pub. Pictorial Stationery Co.

Pub. Tuck
Characters from Dickens

Pub. Welch, J. & Sons (1905)
Studies from Life by Charles Dickens

Pub. Wrench
About 50 Dickens characters

Price range .. .. £1/**£2**/£4

CLOKE, RENE ■L 1

Still actively working as an illustrator, Rene Cloke had no formal art training other than at school. She had always wanted to draw, and soon found success in greetings cards designs and then as a book illustrator, specialising in fairies and small animals. In the late 1930s the first designs were reproduced as postcards, since when 18 sets have been published, up to 1956.

Pub. C. W. Faulkner
  4 sets
Pub. Medici Society (Periods 6, 7)
  Rabbits and Voles
  Squirrels picking Blackberries
  Mice riding on Tortoise
Pub. J. Salmon
  2 sets
Pub. Valentine (Periods 4, 5, 6)
  12 sets

Price range .. .. 50p/**£1.25**/£2

COMBAZ, GISBERT (1869–1941)

Forced to study law by his father, this versatile Belgian then went on to the Brussels Academy, where he eventually became Professor of Decorative Composition. It was as a poster artist that he gained his reputation as one of the most original exponents of Art Nouveau. *His 1898–1900 series of 12 of 'The Elements', 'The Proverbs', 'The Sins' are particularly sought after. Pub. Dietrich of Brussels.*

Price range .. .. £20/**£40**/£60

COMICUS
See Parlett, Harry.

COPPING, HAROLD (1863–1932)
Artist who drew the famous picture 'The Hope of the World'. In his postcard work he specialised in classical and religious themes, also sentimental designs during Period 3. Pub. Degen & Co. 'England, Home and Beauty'.

Price range .. .. £1/**£2**/£4

CORBELLA, TITO (b. 1885)
Versatile Italian artist, who is best known in the glamour field. Like Barribal, Boileau and Kirchner he used his wife as his model. He also drew powerful propaganda designs. See also GLAMOUR

Glamour designs .. .. £1.50/**£2.50**/£4
Edith Cavell set. Period 3 (*see also* POLITICAL) (up to 50% premium for complete set) .. .. £5/**£7**/£8

COWHAM, HILDA
An artist who specialised in drawing children and cats, her work is becoming increasingly popular. From 1913 to 1922 she produced 24 different designs for Inter-Art and several series for Valentine's.

Price range .. .. 75p/**£1**/£1.50

CYNICUS
See Anderson, Martin.

DAMBLANS, EUGENE (b. 1865)
Born in Montevideo of French parents, Damblans was a pupil of M. G. Buland. A life member of the Salon of French Art, he specialised in etchings and water colours, gaining several silver medals for his work. Damblans drew peasant 'types' (e.g. Bretonne *and* Vieille Béarnaise*) and was the artist of the fine series of postcards* La Poste *en . . .* (qv).

Price range .. .. £3/**£5**/£7.50

DANIELL, EVANGELINE MARY (1880–1902)
Although only about half a dozen postcard designs have been identified because of her tragically early death, this superb Art Nouveau *artist is amongst the most highly regarded exponents*

of the style. She is as highly esteemed on the Continent as in Britain, and even Queen Victoria chose one of her designs for the Royal New Year card in 1901.

Pub. Tuck. Modern Art series 2524/5 .. .. £30/**£40**/£50

DAVEY, GEORGE

Period 2 comic artist whose humour often contained political overtones. See also POLITICAL.

Pub. Mandel, J. & Co.
'Straphangers' and others .. .. 75p/**£1**/£1.50

Pub. Misch & Stock
'The Tourist series' and others .. .. .. £1/**£1.50**/£2

Pub. Valentine
Various designs .. .. 75p/**£1**/£1.50

DAVEY, L. H.

Australian artist who specialised in Northern Tasmanian scenes.

Pubs: Osboldstone & Co./W. T. Pater
 Bush homes (6 cards) .. .. £2.50/**£3**/£4
 Scenery (6 cards) .. .. £2.25/**£3**/£3.50

DEDINA, JEAN (b. 1870) ■G 2

Born in Strak, Czechoslovakia, Dedina was a pupil of Zenisek at the Prague Academy of Beaux Arts. He also studied under Bresnard in Paris where his work was exhibited in 1895. He also painted murals for the Comédie Francaise *and contributed illustrations and philosophical articles to the paper* Fliegende Blätter. *His elegant beauties were reproduced in postcard form by J. Otty, Prague, and include a delightful 'Months of the Year' set. Early Period 2.*

Price range .. .. £2.50/**£5**/£8

DE FEURE, GEORGES (1868–1928)

Highly sought after French artist of the Art Nouveau *genre who contributed to the rare* Cocorico *series* (qv). *A pupil of Chéret, he also produced theatrical designs and adverts. Periods 1/2.*

Cocorico .. .. £100/**£150**/£350
Others .. .. £40/**£60**/£80

DENIZARD

See Orens.

DEXTER, MARJORIE MAY (b. *c.* 1900)

Born in Wellingborough, she attended the Northampton School of Arts & Crafts. Most of her designs were for folded greetings cards and she also illustrated books. The small number of postcards so far identified by this attractive children's artist were for Salmon and Valentine's during Periods 4, 5.

Pub. Salmon. Nos. 3765, 3766, 3769, others.
Pub. Valentine's. Hand-painted effect, others.
Price range 25p/**50p**/75p

DUDE
See Larsen, L. H.

DUDOVICH MARCELLO (1878–1962)
Italian artist whose postcard work spanned from 1900 to 1950. His subject matter raged from commemorative (e.g. exhibitions, festivals) to adverts for theatrical productions, products like Vermouth, Tyres, Fernet-Branca, etc. to patriotic propaganda during WW1, to glamour in Period 4.

Price range .. ..£4/**£20**/£30

DUNCAN, COWAN
Specialist in comic heads and Scottish themes in Period 4.

Pub. Millar & Lang, Series 2616/7 and others 75p/**£1**/£1.50

DUNCAN, JAMES ALLAN (Hamish)
Comic artist, usually on Scottish themes, who drew under the name 'Hamish' or 'Hamish Duncan'. He used his real name for his more serious work.

Pub. Davidson Bros.
Period 2. Several series of Scottish humour (signed Hamish Duncan) .. .. 50p/**75p**/£1

Pub. Monson Bros., Glasgow
Glasgow views (1901) 25p/50p

Pub. Tuck
Period 2. Several series of Scottish humour (signed Hamish) .. .. 50p/**75p**/£1

DWIGGINS, CLARE VICTOR (Dwig) (1873–1958)
Born in Wilmington, Ohio, Dwiggins became a self-taught, self-appointed professor of freehand drawing, who contributed to various newspapers and journals. His first postcard was designed in 1903 for Tuck and he went on to design well over 350 identified cards, some unsigned, for a variety of publishers. He often used his wife as his model. Even his girlie cards bear an unmistakeable touch of humour. See also Comic.

Pub. Kaplan, R.
How Can You Do It? Two series.

Newspaper Cartoon Series (Period 4)
Huck Finn, Nipper & Bill's Diary, Tom Sawyer.

Pub. Rose, Charles
Baby, Frankfurter Girl, Moon, Moving, New York Series, Oyster Girl, Sandwich, Superstition, What are the Wild Waves Saying?

Pub. Tuck
Cheer Up, Everytime, Facts & Fancies, Jollies & Follies, Knocks Witty & Wise, Love Potions, Love's Reveries, Never, Pipe Dreams, School Days, Smiles, Toasts for Occasions, Toasts for Today, Zodiac.

Other Publishers include:
Anderson, W. P.; Blue, A.; Cardinell, Vincent; Gabriel, Sam; Gross, Eric.

Price range for all Dwiggins postcards .. .. £2/**£4**/£6

EARNSHAW, HAROLD (d. 1937)

Member of the London Sketch Club and Chelsea Arts Club, he married Mabel Lucie Attwell (qv) *and they had two sons and a daughter. During WW1 he lost his right arm but he learnt to draw with his left and went on to contribute to* Punch, *illustrate books for Blackie, etc. His postcard work is mostly of a comic nature. Publishers include Gottschalk, Dreyfus & Davis and George Pulman & Sons.*

Price range 25p/**50p**/75p

EDMONDS, MABELLE B.

Australian artist with a versatile range of subjects in both colour and black and white—from children to glamour (in a style reminiscent of Dana Gibson) to 'Large Letter' designs, by a variety of publishers.

Pub. Harding & Billings
Children's Alphabet series (24 cards). Series 121–124 .. .. £3/**£4**/£5
Pub. NSW Bookstall Co. 'Art series'
Glamorous ladies (6 cards) .. .. £5/**£6**/£7
'Large Letter' .. .. £2.50/**£3**/£3.50
Smoke Memories (6 cards) .. .. £5/**£6**/£7
Pub. Anon
Glamorous ladies (b & w sketches *à la* Gibson) .. .. £2.50/**£3**/£3.50

ELLAM, WILLIAM HENRY

Versatile and competent Period 2 artist, whose work includes a variety of general and humorous subjects.

Pub. Excelsior Fine Art Pub. Co.
Famous personages in their cars (e.g. Joseph Chamberlain in his Dixi, Duke of Connaught in his Daimler) .. 75p/**£1**/£2

Pub. Faulkner, C. W.
Several series of Teddy Bears .. .. .. £1/**£1.50**/£2

Pub. Hildesheimer
Various designs, incl. 'Hard Workers' .. 50p/**75p**/£1

Pub. Stewart & Woolf
Seaside themes .. .. 50p/**75p**/£1

Pub. Tuck
Breakfast in Bed, Gentle Art of Angling and other series .. .. £1/**£1.50**/£2
'Japanese' series .. .. £1.50/**£2**/£2.50

ENDACOTT, LILLIE

Wife of Sidney Endacott (see below).

15 cards for the publisher, Worth .. .. £1/**£1.50**/£2

ENDACOTT, SIDNEY (1873–1918)

Born in Devon, Endacott worked for several years in the USA and after establishing a reputation as a wood carver, he returned to Devon and worked at painting for Worth's Gallery in Exeter, as well as continuing to sculpt. He married Lillie Haydon and when his health began to fail, he taught her to paint in his style (see above). *More biographical details, and a full check list of Endacott's postcard work, supplied by Joan Humphreys, were published in the Second Edition (pp. 51–53).*

Pub. Frith's of Reigate .. .. £1/**£1.50**/£1.75
Pub. Worth & Co.
'Devon Worthies' Series .. .. £1.50/**£2**/£3
Others .. .. £1/**£1.75**/£2
Pub. Unknown .. .. £1/**£1.50**/£1.75

ENGLISH, ARCHIBALD ('A.E.')

Prolific comic artist of Periods 2 and 3 whose work was usually signed with his initials only. Publishers include: Mitchell & Watkins, William Ritchie & Sons, Thridgould & Co.

Price range .. .. 50p/**75p**/£1

FELLER, FRANK

An illustrator for journals like Boys Own Paper, *Feller produced some of the most thrilling action scenes reproduced in the postcard. Several series were published in the Tuck 'Oilette' range and those that have been identified are listed below.*

Series 9255. 'In the Alps' (Climbing, daring rescues . . .)
Series 9263. 'Life in Russia'. Series 1 (Hunts, raids . . .)
Series 9296. 'Life in Russia'. Series 2 (Hunts, raids . . .)
Series 9312. 'In the Tyrol' (Avalanches, etc . . .)
Series 9324. 'Life in China' (Devils and Pirates . . .)
Series 9363. 'Life in Spain' (Gypsies and Smugglers . . .)

Price range .. .. £1/**£1.50**/£2

FERNAND, FERNEL

*French artist, best known for his racing car series (*see ROAD TRANSPORT*) with black background and manic-looking drivers. A regular contributor to the satirical magazine,* Le Rire, *from 1898 to 1908, and to the 'Collection des Cent'* (qv)

Courses Automobile (10 cards)
Various sporting series
Others

Price range for the above (highest valuation for the 'Cent' cards) .. .. £3/**£5**/£50

FIDUS

See Höppener, Hugo.

FISHER, HARRISON (1877–1934) ■G 1

American artist born to an artistic family who, from an early age, had success as a commercial artist. He worked for the San Francisco Call & Examiner, *and on moving to New York, for* Puck, Scribner's, Cosmopolitan, Life, The Saturday Evening Post *and* McLure's. *He drew the archetypal American Girl and many of his magazine covers and illustrations were reproduced on the postcard.* See GLAMOUR.

Price range .. .. £1.50/**£3**/£4

FLAGG, JAMES MONTGOMERY (1877–1960)

Best known for his poster of Uncle Sam in WW1, 'I Want You for the US Army', Flagg was born in New York. He was a member of the Arts Students League and studied in England and France. He sold work from the age of 12 and was particularly successful with his female studies. See GLAMOUR.

Price range .. .. 75p/**£1**/£2

FLOWER, CHARLES E. (1871–1951) ■T 5

Watercolour artist who exhibited at the Royal Academy. Most of his postcard work was for Tuck in their Oilette series. Best known for his London series, he also drew cards from other parts of the UK, Germany, North and South America. Between 600 and 700 designs have so far been identified.

Price range .. .. 50p/**75p**/£2

FOLKARD, CHARLES (1878–1963)

Creator of the 'Teddy Tail' strip in the Daily Mail, *Folkard was one of the best loved 'Nursery Artists' of Period 4.* See also CHILDREN.

Pub. Black, A. C.

Series of Mother Goose Nursery Rhymes .. £2/**£2.50**/£3
Songs from *Alice in Wonderland* (Period 4) £2/**£2.50**/£3
Period 7 reprint **50p**

FOUGASSE
See Bird, Cyril Kenneth.

FULLER, EDMUND G.
Competent general artist, often with a touch of humour, whose best postcard work was in early Period 2.

Pub. Moss, Henry & Co. (before 1905)
Horse Racing
Hunting

Pub. Stewart & Woolf
London Types
Others
Price range for all Fuller cards .. .. .. £1/**£1.50**/£2

FULLEYLOVE, JOHN R. I. (1847–1908)
Born in Leicester, he was apprenticed to an architect. Travelling widely throughout Britain, Europe and the Near East, he drew town scenes and landscapes. As well as drawing for the postcard, he also illustrated books. Publishers include Regal Art Co., Robert Peel, Tuck (many 'Oilette' series)

Price range 50p/75p

FULLWOOD, A. H.
Australian artist whose postcards were all published by Raphael Tuck in their 'Wide-Wide-World' series. The originals were probably first published in The Illustrated Atlas of Australasie, *an instalment publication, later published in book form between 1886 and 1888. The series vary in rarity and, hence, in value.*

Pub. Tuck. 'Wide-Wide-World' series
Australian series .. .. £3.50/**£5**/£7
New Zealand series .. .. £2/**£2.50**/£3

GIBBS, MAY
Australian illustrator of 'Gumnut babies', scenes and W. Australian events.

Pub. Osboldstone & Co.
Periods 4/5 designs .. .. £6/**£9**/£12
Pub. Anon
'Gumnut Series' (12 cards) .. ..£9/**£12**/£15
W. Australia mining disaster/local scenes in b & w .. .. £3.50/**£5**/£6

GIBSON, CHARLES DANA
American artist now mostly remembered for his fashionable, glamorous creation, 'The Gibson Girl' (thought to be modelled on the artiste Camille Clifford, and on his wife, Irene Langhorne, sister of the future Lady Astor). During WW1 he

was President of the Society of Illustrators and directed propaganda designs for the US war effort. After the war he became owner and editor of Life *magazine.*

Most of his postcard work is gentle, acutely observed situation humour of the mores and pastimes of the Edwardian middle classes—especially their courtship rituals. At least seventy-two designs have been identified. See GLAMOUR.

Price range .. .. £1/**£1.50**/£2

GILBERT, CHARLES ALLAN (b. 1873)

Born in Hartford, Connecticut, USA he studied in New York and Paris. He illustrated Women of Fiction *and* A Message from Mars *and, on the postcard, typical 'American Girls'* (see GLAMOUR).

Price range .. .. 75p/**£1**/£2

GILL, ARTHUR

Much under-rated artist with a light comic touch. Period 2.

Pub. Tuck. Seaside Sketches. Humorous series 6077 £1/**£2**/£3
Pub. Tuck. Others .. .. £1/**£2**/£3

GILSON, T.

Little is known about this amusing postcard artist whose 'Kute Kids' type of comic cards helped to lighten the years 1914–1918. He drew postcard designs for J. Salmon between 1922 and 1928 but the bulk of his output was for E. J. Hey & Co., who added the trade name 'Ludgate'. Cards were also published by 'Alphalsa', Marcuse Day, 'N.P.G./R.P.A.', and J. Salmon. Some postcards bear the legend 'This is a genuine 'Gilson' Post Card', implying that his style (like so many other successful artists) was being copied, and indeed some very 'Gilson-like', but unsigned postcards exist. It has been suggested that cards signed 'Ludgate' are also by Gilson, although no proof has been found. Most of his postcards portray children, often in adult situations, sometimes 'coons', sometimes Chinese, frequently Scottish. Through their small eyes, many of the hardships and dangers of WW1 were portrayed.

Price range
Pre-WW1 Glamour .. .. £1/**£1.50**/£2
Pre-WW1 Children .. .. 50p/**75p**/£1.50
Period 3 designs .. .. 25p/**75p**/£1.50
Period 4 designs .. .. 50p/**75p**/£1.50

A checklist of Gilson cards was published in the second edition (pp. 59–60).

GODILLOT

See Orens.

GOTHARD, FREDERICK (Spatz) (1882–1971)
Fred Gothard was born in Holmfirth, a town best known for its Bamforth connexions. He started drawing postcards whilst working as a bank clerk and used the pseudonym 'SPATZ' to protect his identity from his employers. Later he used his initials 'F.G.'. Period 2 comic designs examine all aspects of contemporary life, Period 3 designs have a military theme. His cards were published by Thomas Hind (a local Huddersfield printer), E. Mack, Salmon, Tollit & Harvey and Tuck.

Price range .. .. 25p/**50p**/£1

GUNN, ARCHIE (b. 1863)
Born in Taunton, Somerset, he found fame in the USA for his portrayals of 'The American Girl' (see GLAMOUR) *and for his patriotic designs during WW1* (see MILITARY).

Price range .. .. £1/**£1.50**/£2

GWENNET, GUNN
He produced some highly coloured, comic designs for Philco, e.g. Series 4001—'Some British Workmen', 4002—'London Antiquities Up-to-Date', 4009—'Abbreviations'. Also floral design for Johnston's Patent Corn Flour, chromo vignette UB.

Price range (highest price for the Johnston ad.) .. £5/**£8**/£12

HAMISH
See Duncan, James Allen.

HAMPEL, WALTER (sometimes seen as HAMPL)
Austrian artist, much of whose fine work was published by Philipp & Kramer soon after the turn of the century. Series include 'Carnaval', 'Variété'.

Price range .. .. £15/**£25**/£35

HANSEN
See Nolde, Emil.

HANSI
See Waltz, J. J.

HARBOUR, JENNIE
Delicate artist of lovely ladies, etc., often in Period dress. Her main output was for Tuck (Oilette de Luxe). Some designs show an Art Deco *flavour.*

Price range .. .. £2/**£4**/£6

HARDY, DUDLEY (1867–1922)

Born in Sheffield, son of the marine painter, T. B. Hardy, he was sent at the age of 15 to Düsseldorf to study under Crola and Lowenstein, but irked by the constricting tuition he rebelled and was dismissed but was later re-admitted to the Academy. He exhibited in the Royal Academy in 1885 and at the Paris Salon in 1888. His humorous work (which accounts for most of his 125 postcard designs) was also published in Punch. *He designed theatrical posters as well.* See ADVERTISING *and* COMIC.

Advertising work
Tuck 'Celebrated Posters' No. 1502 Liebig
The Pearl Girl
Egyptian Mail Steamship Co.
Royal Naval Tournament
Others

Price range .. ..£5/**£10**/£20

Other work
Price range .. .. £1/**£3**/£6

HARDY, FLORENCE

She produced delightful studies of children, often in a Dutch setting, and attractive scenes with figures in period dress. Her main output was for C. W. Faulkner in Period 2.

Price range .. .. £1/**£2**/£3

HARE, J. KNOWLES (b. 1882)

Born in Montclair, New Jersey, USA, he designed covers for the Saturday Evening Post *and* American Magazine. *His postcard work was in the 'American Girl' genre* (see GLAMOUR). *Periods 2 to 4.*

Price range .. .. 75p/**£1**/£2.50

HASSALL, JOHN (1868–1948)

Hassall came from Walmer, Kent, and was educated at Newton Abbot College and Neuenheim College, Heidelberg. His association with the theatrical publisher David Allen led to the prolific commercial output that gave him the title 'The Poster King'. His postcard work is also vast—over 300 designs have been positively identified. A natural clown, Hassall was a leading light in the artistic and entertainment activities of the London Sketch Club. See ADVERTISING *and* COMIC.
Advertising work .. ..£7/**£18**/£25
Comic & General work .. .. £1/**£3**/£5

HAYES, FREDERICK WILLIAM (1848–1918)

Born in Cheshire, he trained as an architect in Ipswich and studied painting in Liverpool and London. A man of many talents, he was a musician, song writer and author as well as painting well enough to be exhibited at the Royal Academy. His postcard work was of the scenic 'Oilette' variety for Meissner & Buch, Tuck and others. Period 2.

Price range 25p/**50p**/75p

HEARTFIELD, JOHN (1891–1968)

Heartfield's real name was Helmut Herzfelde. He took his English sounding pseudonym as a protest against German xenophobia during WW1. In 1917 he founded the publishing house of Malik Verlag *with his brother, Wieland. Heartfield perfected the technique of photomontage, of which he is often credited with being 'the father'. During the 1920s and 1930s Heartfield produced aggressive and satirical photomontage designs, many with virulent anti-National Socialist, anti-Capitalist, anti-Militarist themes. In 1933 he fled Berlin and continued his anti-Nazi agitation from Prague and later London. He returned to Germany in 1950.*

Period 4 postcards .. ..£5/**£10**/£15
Period 7 reproductions—*see* MODERN.

HEATH-ROBINSON, WILLIAM (1872–1944)

Born to an artistic family, he left school at 15 to go to the Royal Academy and from an early age showed great artistic ability and enjoyed commercial success. He is now best remembered for his pictures of almost surrealist inventions that made him a household name.

Advertising work
Dr. Barnado's Homes. 'To the Rescue'
Ideal Home (1934) Set of 6
Izal. Pub. Newton Chambers & Co. (1920) (10)
Proctor Bros. Wireworks. Mouse Trap
Yorkshire Relish. Poster advertisement

Price range .. ..£3/**£10**/£15

Comic and General work
Pub. Harrap, J. Cherub/Cupid series .. .. 75p/**£1**/£1.50
Pub. Valentine. The Gentle Art of Catching Things (1909). Set of 6 .. .. £1/**£2**/£4

'HERGÉ'

See Remi, Georges.

HOFFMAN, JOSEF (1870–1956)

Austrian artist, much of whose early work was published by Philipp and Kramer He also contributed to the 'Wiener Werkstätte' (see COLLECTIONS) *and the 'Ver Sacrum' series.*

Price range .. .. £20/**£35**/£60

■A 13 Pub. Rommler & Jonas. Artist Hugo Höppener ('Fidus'). 'Weihnacht II' (Christmas II). Period 2 £10

■A 14 Pub. 'V.H.M.'. Artist Carl Jozsa. 'Carneval'. UB. PU 1900 £25

HÖPPENER, HUGO (Fidus) (1868–1948) ■A 13
German artist who created a distinctive genre of Art Nouveau *symbolic and fantasy designs, many in black and white, often erotic. A number of his postcards are reproduced from his work for the magazines* Jugend *and* Pan. *Periods 1 and 2.*

Black and white designs	£3/**£5**/£8
Coloured designs	£5/**£8**/£12
Portrait (phot.) of artist/his studio	£3/**£6**/£10

HORRELL, CHARLES
Artist of sentimental glamour, mostly known for his WW1 designs for James Henderson. His wholesome pretty girls often pose with their pets.

Price range .. .. 75p/**£1**/£2.50

HORSFALL, MARY
Portrayer of delicate female beauties in glowing colours, also children and the occasional women's suffrage theme. Publishers include Carlton Publishing Co., Wm. Ritchie and Tuck. Periods 2, 3.

Price range .. .. £1/**£1.50**/£2

HOWARD, FRED, S.

His postcard work includes Irish subjects in a comic vein and horse racing. Publishers include Misch and Pictorial Stationery Co. (Peacock). Period 2.

Price range .. .. 50p/**75p**/£1

HUBER, G.

Continental comic artist, with a most distinctive style. He specialised in caricatures of rotund, earthy, peasant types, often in courting scenes. Different language versions appear of many of his designs—English, French and German—with continental style backs. Most cards date from 1906–7. A list of the cards so far identified was printed in the Second Edition, p. 61.

Price range .. .. 50p/**£1**/£1.50

HUTCHINGS, J.

One of the most popular portrayers of Australian life in the bush. His 'Oilette type' views tend to glamorise and romanticise the rugged life of the Pioneer. The 36 identified titles are well sought after, although some are slightly 'fuzzy'.

Pub. NSW Bookstall Co. 'Art series'
Australian series .. .. £3/**£3.50**/£4

IBBETSON, ERNEST

Best known for his Military work (see MILITARY), *he also drew general subjects for Faulkner, showing a light and humorous touch.*

Pub. Faulkner, C. W.

Several fine sets, including Always Merry & Bright, The Lilliputian Coronation, The London Police, The Simple Life .. .. 75p/**£1**/£1.50

Several series with Military and Naval themes, e.g. The Boy Army, The Boy Navy .. .. £1/**£1.50**/£2

Pub. Gale & Polden

Periods 2, 3. He was the main artist for their famous 'History & Tradition' series .. .. .. £1/**£2.50**/£3

Period 5. Commandos in Action, 14th Army in Burma (1945), etc. .. .. £1/**£2.50**/£3

ILLINGWORTH, LESLIE

Popular cartoonist with a distinctive and pleasing style who, during WW2, succeeded in capturing the Axis leaders' features and mannerisms in unmistakeable fashion. He worked for the Daily Mail, *his cartoons doing much for morale to a populace beset by bombs, blackout and rationing. Illingworth was amongst the cartoonists whose work was chosen by the British wartime propaganda machine to be reprinted as postcards and distributed through the British Embassy in Lisbon, Portugal.*

Period 5. Propaganda .. .. 75p/**£1.25**/£1.50

INNES, JOHN (1864–1941)
Sought after Canadian artist of 'Western' subjects.

The following designs have been identified, all published by W. G. MacFarlane.
Animal Series (6 cards)
Indian Series (8 cards)
NWM Police Series (5 cards)
Primitive Transportation in the West (10 cards)
Ranching Series (10 cards)
Western Type Series (12 cards)

Price range .. .. £1/**£1.50**/£3

JACOBS, HELEN (1888–1970)
Sister of author W. W. Jacobs. Subjects of her postcard work include elves and fairies and most of her output was published by C. W. Faulkner. See CHILDREN.

Price range .. .. £2/**£3**/£4

JAMES, IVY MILLICENT (1879–1965)
Born in Weston-super-Mare, she studied at the Western School of Art and had additional art tuition in London. Both Ivy and her sister Maud drew greetings cards and calendars for Delgado, Faulkner, Hills, Tuck and Valentine's from 1901 to 1904 but only Faulkner published her postcard work, (1907–19). 19 sets have been identified. The designs are mostly of appealing children in the style of Florence Hardy and Ethel Parkinson, many in the popular 'Dutch' style.

Periods 2, 3, early period 4. Sets of 6 .. .. .. £1/**£2**/£3
Perforated Painting Books of 12 cards. Per card 75p/**£1**/£1.50

JOSSOT, HENRI (b. 1866)
One of the group of sought-after early French postcard artists who contributed to many of the great series like the Collection des Cent, Maîtres de la Carte Postale (see COLLECTIONS). *He also drew advertisements and political designs including Dreyfus.*

Price range .. .. £50/**£70**/£100

JOTTER
See Young, Walter Hayward.

JOZSA, KARL (b. 1872) ■A 14
Sought after artist of the Vienna Secessionist School. His famous series include 'Heart Ladies', Sirens and Circes', 'Smoke Rings' and 'World of Fairy Tales'

Price range .. .. £15/**£25**/£40

KEM

Cartoonist who produced 3000 political cartoons during WW2. They were printed in magazines in London (e.g. Cartoon Comment*), in China, Greece, Morocco and in Portugal, where many of them were reproduced as postcards and distributed through the British Embassy in Lisbon.*

Period 5. Propaganda .. .. 50p/**£1**/£1.25

KIENERK, GEORGIO (1869–1948)

Powerful Italian artist, best known for his portrayals of Dante's Divine Comedy *and his 'Cocorico' designs.*

Period 1 (incl. Cocorico) .. .. £75/**£100**/£150
Period 2 .. ..£5/**£15**/£30

KIMBALL, ALONZO MYRON (1874–1923)

Born in Green Bay, Wisconsin, USA, he studied in New York and Paris (under Lefebre and Whistler). He was a member of the Society of Illustrators and is best known on the postcard for his 'American Girls' (see GLAMOUR).

Price range .. .. £1/**£1.50**/£2

KING, HAMILTON (b. 1871)

Born in Lewiston, Maine, USA, he studied in Paris and was a member of the Society of Illustrators. He is best known in the postcard world for his female studies.

Price range .. .. £2/**£3**/£4

KING, JESSIE MARION (1876–1949)

One of the most prized of the children's artists, who produced beautiful nursery rhyme illustrations in the Art Nouveau *style, but with strong hints of the* Art Deco *style to come. Publishers include Millar & Lang.*

Price range .. .. £20/**£40**/£50

KINSELLA, EDWARD PATRICK

Irish artist, usually known as Pat, he specialised in sporting children and theatre posters.

Pub. David Allen (Theatre Poster Ads.)
Blue Moon
A Chinese Honeymoon
The Duchess of Dantzic
The Female Swindler (2)
Wildflower
The Worst Women in London (9)

Price range .. .. £5/**£8**/£10

Pub. Langsdorff & Co. (1905)
Sporting series featuring children playing cricket, tennis, etc. .. .. 75p/**£1**/£2

KIRCHNER, RAPHAEL (1876–1917)

Born in Vienna, Kirchner moved to Paris in 1905 following his enormous early success in the postcard field. He also became well known in the fields of magazine illustration, portrait painting and theatrical design. Probably the best known Art Nouveau/*Glamour artist, designed some 630 cards—some of which became the subject of poems, sketches in stage revues, etc. They were avidly collected by young officers during WW1 and pinned up in the trenches. His girls were all based on his wife, Nina. After her husband's tragic early death she took to drugs and died in a mental hospital.*

Kirchner's work divides into three sections:

Period 1
The rare pre-1900 designs (many published by Philipp & Kramer) including the 'Leda' series of 10 .. £25/**£40**/£50

Early Period 2 (1900–1903)
Beautiful chromo-litho UB's with a strong *Art Nouveau* flavour.

Price range .. .. £15/**£25**/£50

Later Period 2 and Period 3
These later designs move away from the *Art Nouveau* style and into the 'Glamour' category. *See* GLAMOUR and MILITARY. Designs include The *Maude* series, the *Riquette* series, the *Montmartre* series, *Les Zeppelins à Paris*, *Peinte par elle-même*, *Lolotte*, etc.

Price range .. ..£8/**£12**/£15

KLEE, PAUL (1879–1940)

Born in Munchenbuchsee bei Bern, Switzerland, Klee studied art in Munich. He travelled extensively in Italy and Tunisia and served in the Great War from 1916–1918. In 1920 he joined the Bauhaus group of Walter Gropius in Weimar, becoming an instructor. In 1931 he moved to the Dusseldorf Academy, but was dismissed in 1933 by the Nazis. He died in Locarno.

Bauhaus Postcards Nos. 4 and 5 (only 25 examples of each are thought to have been printed) .. .. £250/**£400**/£550

KLEIN, CATHERINA (b. 1861) ■AN 5

Born in Prussia, she attended the Berlin Academy of Art and also studied in Dresden and Munich. Specialising in flower studies and still-life (fruits, etc.) her superbly coloured postcard work was published by Douglass Post Card Co., Philadelphia and Berlin; Max Ettlinger; C. W. Faulkner; Hildesheimer; International Art Pub. Co. New York and Berlin; 'K. F.' Paris; Meissner and Buch; Miller & Lang; Stenli of Zurich; Stiebel (Alpha); Stecher Litho Co., New York; Theo Stroefer,

Nuremberg; Tuck and Wildt & Kray. Many of her designs were 'pirated'.

Price range .. .. 50p/**£1.50**/£5

Novelty
Several of Klein's designs were issued as 'painting books', (*see* NOVELTY), with perforations to tear out the postcards when coloured, e.g. Tuck No. 4078 'In Garden Ways', with 16 postcards and hard cover.

Per complete booklet .. .. £5/**£8**/£10

KOEHLER, MELA
Elegant designs for the Wiener Werkstätte (see COLLECTIONS) *for which she designed about 90 cards and other fashion and glamour designs with an* Art Deco *flavour.*

Wiener Werkstätte .. .. £40/**£50**/£70
Others .. .. £10/**£15**/£20

KOKOSCHKA, OSKAR (1886–1980)
The son of a goldsmith, the young Oskar wanted to become a chemist. He studied at the School of Arts and Crafts in Vienna, intending to become a teacher. Impressed by painters as contrasting as Klimt and Van Gogh, he drifted into art. In 1907 he worked with the Wiener Werkstätte (see COLLECTIONS) *drawing 13 designs for a series of postcards. These are amongst the most highly prized—and priced—of all postcards. After this initial success, he become a portrait painter, but his distorted, tormented style found little acclaim. Gradually he won renown as an Expressionist, and member of the Vienna Secession. He gained recognition for his original and powerful style between the wars, but it was condemned as 'decadent' by the National Socialist regime, who destroyed 400 of his works during the late 1930s.*

Price range .. .. £50/**£150**/£500

KYD
See Clark, J. Clayton.

LARSEN, L. H. (Dude)
American artist whose droll sense of humour shone through his 'Western' pictures, reproduced as postcards in the late 1930s and early 1940s. A product of the 1930s Depression, the 'Dude' moved from the ranching business in Utah to seek his fortune as an artist. He found success in Washington—his cards portray a variety of ranching activities, cowboys, Indians, horses, steers, and landscapes. His wife, Dot, also drew the occasional (difficult to find nowadays) postcard design. Periods 4, 5.

Price range .. .. 75p/**£1.50**/£2

LEETE, ALFRED (b. 1882)
Most famous for his WW1 recruiting poster, 'Your King and Country Need You', he contributed to The Passing Show *and other magazines and was President of the London Sketch Club in 1925. His postcard work includes several comic designs.*

Price range .. .. £1/**£1.50**/£2

LELEE, LEOPOLD (b. 1872)
French artist of the Art Nouveau *school who studied at the School of Decorative Arts in Paris but who settled in Arles in Provence, which had a local influence on his work. Some of his work contained elements of surrealism.*

Girls' Eyes (10) .. .. £10/**£15**/£30
Mid-day and Midnight .. .. £10/**£15**/£30
Others .. ..£5/**£10**/£15

LINDSAY, NORMAN
Australia's most sought after, best loved and most easily recognised artist. A versatile painter, he was equally at home with pen and ink, oil and etchings.

Bulletin Series
Australian types (10 cards) .. .. .. £30/**£40**/£50
Other sets .. .. £25/**£30**/£50
NSW Bookstall Co. 'Art Series'
Australian Native Series (6 cards) .. .. £20/**£25**/£30

LOIR, LUIGI
French artist who did many fine UB *chromo-litho scenes and town types, notably Paris. His work was published in Britian by P. G. Huardel 1900–1904.*

Price range .. .. £1/**£3**/£5

LUDOVICI, ANTHONY
An accomplished general and comic artist, he is best known for his satirical political caricatures of Joseph Chamberlain, Roseberry, etc. See COMIC, POLITICAL.

Pub. Davidson Bros. (Period 2)
Series 6054 'Mrs. Caudle' types, signed 'AL'
Series 6087 Mr. Chamberlain at Glasgow
Series 6089 as 6054
Series 6093 Female occupations
Series 6098 Political Dances
Series 6100 Home Comforts
Series 6102 London Life
Series 6103 Fiscal Games
Series 6104 Boys' School
Series 6105 Girls' School
Price range .. .. £2/**£3**/£4

Pub. Valentine's
'Write Away' series, signed 'AL' .. .. £2/**£3**/£4
Others .. .. £1/**£2**/£3

Others .. .. £1/**£1.50**/£2

LYNEN, AMEDEE (b. 1852)

A proficient Belgian typographer and stone mason, who became better known for his poster, newspaper and book illustrations. His acute observations of everyday life inspired his great series of over 200 postcards known as De-ci, de-là, à Bruxelles et en Brabant *(Here and there in Brussels and Brabant). Period 2.*

Price range .. .. £4/**£6**/£8.50

MACDONALD, A. K.

An elegant artist, about whom little seems known.

Various Publishers (Early Period 2)
Coloured *Art Nouveau* designs .. .. .. £10/**£25**/£30

Pub. Henderson, James (1909)
Gibson-like pen and ink designs .. .. .. £1/**£2**/£3

Pub. Valentine (1908–1910)
Designs for Franco-British and Japanese-British exhibitions (more for signed examples) .. ..£5/**£10**/£15

MAILICK, A.

Versatile German artist whose work includes charming views/ Faith, Hope, Charity, etc. and other greetings, WW1 sentiment and propaganda.

Early Period 2 and Period 3 .. .. £1/**£2**/£3

MARTINI, ALBERTO (1876–1954)

Italian artist who drew some powerful propaganda surrealist designs during WW1, also adverts and pretty girls, e.g. 'Venetia Antiqua'—medieval maidens (1903).

Price range .. ..£5/**£15**/£30

MARTY, ANDRÉ

French artist of the Art Deco *school, he trained at the Paris Ecole des Beaux Arts. He had a witty and highly original approach and was well known for his fashion illustrations in magazines such as the* Gazette du Bon Ton, Modes et Manières d'Aujourd'hui *etc. Period 4.*

range .. ..£5/**£10**/£15

■A 15 Pub. G. Ricordi, Milan. Artist Giovanni Mataloni. 'Iris' (the Opera). 1898 £20

MATALONI, GIOVANNI ■A 15

Italian artist whose attractive Art Nouveau *designs were used in Period 2 to publicise political events (for the Italian Socialist Party, etc.) products, hotels, exhibitions and operas, e.g. Puccini's* Madame Butterfly *and Mascagni's* Iris. *Mataloni also illustrated the* Divine Comedy *published by Alterocca-Terni. During Period 3 he drew wartime propaganda .*

Periods 1 and 2 designs .. .. £7.50/**£15**/£20
Period 3 WW1 .. .. £1.50/**£3**/£5

MATANIA, FORTUNINO (1881–1963)

A child prodigy born in Naples, he first exhibited at the Naples Academy in 1892. His news pictures for L'Illustrazione *led to an invitation to come to London to cover the coronation of Edward VII for* The Graphic. *Later he worked for* The Sphere *covering every royal event until the coronation of Elizabeth II. During WW1 he was appointed an official war artist and drew his most famous postcard design 'Goodbye Old Man'* (see MILITARY).

Pub. *The Sphere*. Reproductions of his illustrations for the magazine. Periods 2 to 4

Others, including advertising cards, WW1 themes (incl. Italian military scenes/War Bond issues)

Price range .. .. 75p/**£1**/£1.50

MAURICE, REG. ■M 4

A popular comic artist, much of whose work appeared during Period 3 (as military humour) and in Period 4 (general humour). Most cards published by Regent Pub. Co.

Chaplin Humour .. .. 75p/**£1.50**/£2.50
General or WW1 Humour .. .. 75p/**£1.50**/£2.50

MAUZAN, ACHILLE (1886–1940)

This under-estimated Italian artist is mostly collected for his blander, 'glamour' designs. In fact he was a most versatile and original artist. His work includes wartime propaganda and patriotism during WW1, advertisements, both in France and Italy, for a variety of famous products in Period 4. His best work has a distinct Art Deco *flavour, amongst which is a most attractive 'Months of the Year' series.*

Period 3
- Glamour .. £1/**£3**/£5
- Propaganda/Patriotism .. £1.50/**£5**/£7.50

Period 4
- Adverts .. £3/**£7**/£10
- Glamour .. £2/**£5**/£8

Others .. £1/**£3**/£5

MAY, PHIL (1864–1903) ■COM 1

Born near Leeds, Phil May soon gravitated to London. He had a well-developed sense of humour that led him easily into the company of Whistler, Wilde and, inevitably, the other founder members of the London Sketch Club. He lived for 3 years in Australia and worked on the Sydney Bulletin. *Back in London he worked for* Punch, The Graphic *and joined the Chelsea Arts Club. His tragically early death curtailed a prolific output of brilliantly observed sketches of London Life and other types. Ninety postcard designs have been identified to date.* See COMIC.

Advertising work

Dewar's Whisky .. £15/**£20**/£25
Tuck's Celebrated Posters 1506. Appolinaris £15/**£20**/£25

Comic and General work

Pub. Davidson Bros. Nos. 6073–6 (1904/5). Several series of 'Write-Aways', Humour of Life Series .. £1/**£3**/£5
Pub. Landerer & Brown (Ellanbee) (1904/5). Phil May Aquasimile. Series 106–7 .. £1/**£3**/£5
Pub. Tuck. Humour of Life 9266 .. £2/**£4**/£6
Pub. Tuck. Medieval Characters 1258–9, 5259 .. £1/**£3**/£5
Pub. Tuck. Newspaper Headlines 764 .. £1/**£3**/£5
Pub. Tuck. Oilette series 1771–8 .. £1/**£3**/£5
Pub. Tuck. Phil May series 1294–6 .. £1/**£3**/£5
Pub. Tuck. 'Proof' sets (qv) Nos. 1008, 1294–6 .. £4/**£6**/£8
Pub. Tuck. Write-Away series .. £2/**£4**/£6
Pub. Valentine. Comic Sketches (1903). No. 1903 £1/**£3**/£5
Pub. Wrench. Cartoons from *Punch* UB (20+); Humour of Life; Newspaper Headings .. £2/**£4**/£6

McCUTCHEON, JOHN T. (1870–1949)

Described as 'The Dean of American Cartoonists . . .' in his obituary in the New York Times. *McCutcheon captured the carefree innocence of boyhood in many of his designs—always with a gentle touch of humour. His 'Boy in . . .' (Spring-Time, Summer-Time, Fall-Time, Winter-Time) series is particularly fine. His first postcards appeared in 1903 and production continued until after WW2. McCutcheon worked as a war artist and correspondent in many campaigns—from 1896 to 1945, notching up many reporting 'firsts'. Periods 2–5.*

Price range .. .. £1.50/**£3**/£5

McGILL, DONALD (1875–1962)

Donald McGill started designing postcards in 1904 for a sick nephew. He continued pouring out designs for most of the rest of his long life and is, without doubt, Britain's most prolific postcard artist. McGill himself claimed 10,000 designs and experts believe this cannot be too inaccurate a figure (nearly 9000 have been positively identified). Chiefly known for his rumbustious, often vulgar, seaside comics, McGill also drew pungent social and political comments during both World Wars, as well as military humour and patriotic designs. McGill's output is usually classified into 4 periods and, generally speaking, the earlier the card, the higher the value.

Early Period (1904–1906)

About 650 designs. Publishers include Eyre & Spottiswoode, Hudson Bros. and Pictorial P.C. Co. .. .. .. £1/**£2**/£3

Second Period (1907–1914)

About 1750 designs. Publishers include Joseph Asher, Thridgould & Co., Woolstone Bros. and others 75p/**£1**/£1.50

Inter-Art Period (1914–1935)

About 3500 designs. The most prolific period of all, which included some designs for Woolstone Bros. and for Thridgould & Co. .. .. 50p/**75p**/£1

Modern Period (1935–1952)

About 2500 designs. Asher now formed a new company under the name of D. Constance Ltd. which produced the 'New Donald McGill Comics'—greatly inferior printing on poor quality board. Nevertheless the WW2 designs have some interest—*see* MILITARY. At the beginning of this period McGill also drew for Birn Bros. and McCrum (Inter-Art) 25p/**50p**/75p

MENPES, MORTIMER

Water-colorist who is best remembered for his Boer War sketches of Churchill, Conan Doyle, Kipling, Rhodes, Roberts, etc. and scenes at Ladysmith, Modder River, etc. His postcard work includes a delightful series of 'The World's Children' published by Wrench and souvenir postcards for the Japan-British Exhibition of 1910. (See EXHIBITIONS).

Price range .. .. 50p/**75p**/£2

MERCER, JOYCE (1896–1965)

One of the 'Nursery Artists' (see CHILDREN) *whose subjects include children, fairy stories and nursery rhymes, with an* Art Deco *flavour. Most of her work was published by C. W. Faulkner.*

Price range .. .. £2/**£3**/£4

METLICOVITZ, LEOPOLDO (1864–1944) ■L 4
Italian artist whose work spanned the periods of Art Nouveau *and* Art Deco. *His versatile designs covered the themes of Adverts, Glamour, Landscapes and Propaganda. Metlicovitz is perhaps best known for his opera studies, published by G. Ricordi of Milan.*

Period 1/Early Period 2
Adverts for Italian Distilleries
Opera designs (Madame Butterfly, etc.)
Automobile and Cycle Show
Period 3
Italian propaganda designs
Period 4
Glamour
Propaganda
Others

Price range .. .. £3/**£7.50**/£15

MEUNIER, HENRI (1873–1922)
Born in Ixelles in Belgium, Meunier was a highly competent engraver, painter, book illustrator as well as a postcard designer. Many of his beautiful Art Nouveau *designs were published by the fine publishing house of Dietrich in Brussels. Meunier also contributed to the famous* Editions Cinos *series and the* Collection Job (qv). *His glorious series of* 12 Girls, 1900, *is particularly sought after, as are the series* Girls, Flowers, Signs of the Zodiac *and* Le Chic de Paris.

Price range .. .. £30/**£50**/£65

MIGNOT, VICTOR (1872–1944)
Belgian Art Nouveau *artist, best known for his beautiful series of* Sports *(Bicycling, Horse Racing, Ice Skating, Mountaineering, etc.) Pub. Dietrich.*

Price range .. ..£5/**£12**/£15

MILLIÈRE, MAURICE (b. 1871)
Born in Le Havre, Millière studied under Bonnat at L'Ecole des Beaux Arts. He contributed to La Vie Parisienne *and was exhibited in Paris, London and New York. His postcard work is mainly known for 'glamour' subjects during WW1, although there are fine examples of his work during Period 2.* See MILITARY.

Early Period 2
M. Munk Vienna series .. .. £3/**£5**/£10

Period 3
La Vie dans La Campe Indienne à Rouen .. .. £2/**£3**/£5
Petites Femmes de Paris .. .. £2/**£3**/£5
Others .. .. £2/**£3**/£5

MORELAND, ARTHUR

One of Britain's most under-estimated comic artists, who was also capable of making political comments (see POLITICAL). *Over 160 designs have been identified from early Period 2. The 'Humours of History' series were originally published in* The Morning Leader *and also appeared in book form.*

Pub. Faulkner, C. W.
25 series known—listed in Second Edition, p. 69.

Price range .. .. £1/**£2**/£3

Pub. Eyre & Spottiswoode: Woodbury Series
Humours of History .. .. £1/**£2**/£3

Publisher Unknown
Boer War (1904) .. .. £3/**£4**/£5

Others .. .. £1/**£2**/£4

MOSER, KOLOMAN (1868–1918)

Austrian artist, co-founder of the Secessionist Movement in Vienna and a member of the Wiener Werkstätte *(though none of his postcards appeared in that collection). His best postcard work was published by Philipp & Kramer and is in a restrained* Art Nouveau *style. He also contributed to the great German series* Meggendorfer Blätter.

Price range .. .. £15/**£30**/£50

MUCHA, ALPHONSE (1860–1939) ■A 16

Czech artist who came to Paris at the age of 26 in 1887. His first success,which assured his future career, was with a poster of Sarah Bernhardt in 1894. His poster work was published by M. Champenois of Paris, who reproduced the designs on postcards. The most reproduced of all the Art Nouveau *artists, Mucha contributed to many of the important early French series* (see COLLECTIONS). *Mucha returned to his native Czechoslovakia for the last years of his life and died in Prague. His work falls into five categories:*

Period 1
The glorious pre-1900 era. Sarah Bernhardt Posters (1898): Dame aux Camélias, Gismonda, Lorenzaccio, La Samaritaine; Cocorico (1899) .. .. £50/**£65**/£100

Early Period 2
Collection des Cent (2 designs); *Champenois* series, incl. The Four Seasons, The Months of the Year, Precious Stones; Moet et Chandon (10 designs) .. .. £40/**£60**/£75

Later Period 2
Postcard reproductions of 1897, 1898 *Job* Calendars in 1911; Album Mariani; Others .. .. £20/**£30**/£50

Nearly 110 cards have been identified for these three 'French' periods.

Late Period 2/Periods 3, 4 (The Czechoslovakian Period)

Mucha's output from about 1909 was mostly produced in Prague, often with Czech themes, moving away from the stylised *Art Nouveau* influence of the French period. Nearly 60 designs have been identified for this period £15/**£20**/£30

The *Champenois* designs were republished in Britain by Huardel, Pascalis Moss, Henry Moss, H. J. Smith and F. C. Southwood from 1900 to about 1905. Dietrich of Belgium also published many early Period 2 designs .. £10/**£20**/£40

Period 4

Advertisements for the YWCA .. .. .. £10/**£15**/£25

MUTTER, K.

German landscape artist. Publishers include Schmidt, Staub & Co., with many fine UB *chromo-litho.*

Price range .. .. £1/**£2**/£3

■A 16 Pub. L. Novotný, Prague. Artist A. Mucha. Period 2 £25

■A 17 Pub. 'Lampo' gasoline. Artist G. Nanni. Advert for Italo-American Society of Petrol. PU 1929 £15

Three Band Pricing System

Left Hand Band: The lowest price you will probably be asked to pay for this card.
Middle Band: What you will normally be asked to pay for this card: its average, reasonable price.
Right Hand Band: The highest price you will probably be asked to pay for this card.
For a full explanation of the system see page ix.

NANNI, GIOVANNI (1888–1969) ■A 17

Italian artist best known for his elegant, fashionable girls, notably a superb series of behatted heads, Periods 3, 4. He also drew patriotic, propagandist designs in the 1920s and 1930s and commercial work for products like Pirelli. During this period his work was strongly influenced by the Art Deco *style and included some beautiful film posters* (see CINEMA *and* GLAMOUR).

Price range (higher price for *Art Deco* posters) .. £3/**£5**/£18

NASH, ADRIENNE, A.

Subjects include children, patriotic and suffragettes etc. in Periods 2 and 3.

Pub. Henderson

Children's Birthdays (7 cards) .. .. .. 50p/**75p**/£1.50
Others .. .. 50p/**75p**/£2.50

Pub. Inter-Art

25 series between 1913–1918 (*see also* PUBLISHERS, Inter-Art) .. .. 50p/**75p**/£2.50

NIXON, KATHLEEN (b. 1895)

Children's artist (see CHILDREN). *To date 18 postcards only have been recognised, published by C. W. Faulkner, including animals and* Alice in Wonderland *series.*

Price range .. .. £1/**£2**/£3

NOLDE, EMIL (1867–1956)

Christened Emil Hansen, he changed his name to Nolde after his birthplace. Brought up on his father's farm, he became a wood carver and in 1890 moved to Berlin as a furniture designer. In 1894 he drew the personifications of the Swiss mountains which, reproduced on postcards, were such a financial success that he became an independent painter. His frenetic, excited, brightly coloured style emerged as he experimented with Impressionism. He became a member of the Dresden group, Die Brucke *(the Bridge) from about 1905. His religiously inspired paintings were extremely controversial. In 1918, established as an expressionist, he joined the* Novembergruppe. *His work was regarded as 'degenerate' by the National Socialist regime and over 1000 examples of it were destroyed during the 1930s.*

Fantasy mountain designs. Pub. F. Killinger. Period 2 .. .. £5/**£8**/£12

NOURY, GASTON (b. 1866) ■A 18

French artist, born at Elboeuf, he was one of the great Art Nouveau *artists. A poster designer and book illustrator, his postcards show great imagination, with designs that often border on 'fantasy'. Noury contributed to the famous* Editions

Cinos (q.v.) *collection. Some of his designs were in black and white, while others were highly coloured. Periods 1 and 2.*

Price range (lowest for b & w, highest for the *Cinos*) .. .. £10/**£30**/£70

NYSTROM, JENNY (1854–1946) ■A 19

Born in 1854 in Kalmar, Sweden, Jenny attended Art school, and in 1871 illustrated 'Little Vig's Fairy Tales on Christmas Eve' in the Gothenborg newspaper. In 1873 she became a member of the Academy of Independent Artists and in 1882 moved to Paris. In 1886 she moved back to Stockholm and married in 1887. In the 1890s she started to design postcards to support her ailing husband, Dr. Daniel Stoopendaal. Their son Curt was also a postcard artist (see ANIMALS). *She specialised in folklore, fairy tales, greetings cards and 'glamour' and often used her father's face to illustrate her gnomes. Some of her work was distinctly* Art Deco *in flavour and her greetings cards were sometimes produced in 'miniature' form. Periods 2–5.*

Price range .. .. £2/**£4**/£6

■A 18 Pub. Anon. Artist G. Noury. PU 1906 £30

■A 19 Pub. Axel Eliassons, Stockholm. Artist Jenny Nystrom. 'Happy New Year'. PU 1923 £4

O'NEILL, ROSE (1874–1944) ■CH 1

American artist, renowned as the inventor of the 'Kewpie' (corruption of Cupid) doll in 1909. She also wrote rhyming stories and verse (some of which appear on her cards). Over 200 postcards have been identified, mostly published by the Gibson Art Co. Periods 2, 3, 4.

Advertising designs for Victory Cream (Rare)	£15/**£25**/£35
Novelty designs ('Klever Kards'—mechanical)	£5/**£10**/£15
Pub. Gibson Art Co.	
General Kewpie designs	£2/**£5**/£8
Santas and other sought after themes	£3/**£5**/£8
Women's Suffrage	
Campbell Art Co. 1915	£10/**£12**/£15
National Woman Suffrage Pub. Co. 1915	£10/**£12**/£15

ORENS (Denizard *or* Godillot)

French satirical caricaturist, many of whose designs were produced in small limited editions (of 75 to 250 only). He also drew under the names 'Denizard' and 'Godillot', and contributed to the Collection des Cent. See POLITICAL.

Price range (highest valuation for the *Cent* cards) £5/**£10**/£40

OST, ALFRED (1884–1945)

One of Belgium's most popular postcard artists, he studied at the School of Fine Arts at Anvers, specialising in animal studies. Ost's work, which encompassed styles from traditional Flemish baroque to modernism, made strong social comment. More than 300 designs have been identified, many of them in black and white.

Price range .. ..£5/**£10**/£20

OUTCAULT, RICHARD F. (b. 1863)

Born in Lancaster, Ohio, USA, his creation in 1896 in 'The New York World' of the 'Yellow Kid' comic strip was a sensation. He followed its success with 'Buster Brown' in The New York Herald *in 1902. Newspapers vied for his services and many of his comical drawings appeared on postcards* (see CHILDREN *and* COMIC).

Price range .. .. 50p/**75p**/£1

OUTHWAITE, IDA RENTOUL (1889–1961)

Australian artist of the nursery genre (see CHILDREN). *A. & C. Black produced postcard reproductions of the illustrations she drew for their books. Period 4.*

Price range .. .. £1/**£1.50**/£2

OWEN, WILL (d. 1957)

Member of the London Sketch Club, most famous for his 'Aah, Bisto' advertisement, he contributed to Punch, *illustrated books, drew posters and also published books.*

Pub. David Allen (Theatre Poster Adverts)

A Little Bit of Fluff; When Knights were Bold .. £3/**£7**/£10

Pub. Davidson Bros.

Illustrated Songs series .. .. £2/**£3**/£4

Pub. Meissner & Buch
'K-nuts' .. .. £2/**£3**/£4
Fishing series .. .. £2/**£3**/£4

Pub. Tuck
Write-Away series .. .. £2/**£3**/£4

Pub. Wrench
Illustrated Songs and other series .. .. .. £2/**£3**/£4

Others
Various .. .. £1/**£2**/£4

PARKINSON, ETHEL

Several series of charming wintry scenes and children, mainly published by C. W. Faulkner.

Price range .. .. £1/**£2**/£3

PARLETT, HARRY (Comicus)

Many of Parlett's comic cards are signed by his pseudonym, 'Comicus', and others bear only his initials, 'H.P.'

Pub. Gottschalk, Dreyfus & Davis, Star series
Several series of 'How to behave . . .' .. .. 50p/**75p**/£1

Pub. H. B. Series
Several series of comic cards .. .. .. 50p/**75p**/£1

Pub. Midland Pictorial Postcard Co.
Several series of comic cards .. .. .. 50p/**75p**/£1

Others (incl. 'Rinking' themes)
Price range .. .. 50p/**75p**/£1

PARTRIDGE, SIR BERNARD (1861–1945)

Encouraged by his traditionally artistic family to pursue that tradition, Partridge expressed his independence by going into the theatre—working for a while with such illustrious names as Henry Irving and Forbes-Robertson. Later he became a cartoonist, joining the staff of Punch *in 1909. He worked for that magazine until his death. Wrench reproduced some of his early* Punch *cartoons as postcards.*

Pub. Wrench. 'Pictures from Punch' .. .. .. £2/**£3**/£4
Others .. .. £1/**£2**/£3

PATELLA, B. ■ART 4

French Art Nouveau *artist, often confused with Raphael Kirchner. His most famous series are the* Femmes Voilées.

Price range .. ..£5/**£10**/£15

PAYNE, ARTHUR CHARLES (1856–1933) ■A 20

Brother of the more famous Harry (q.v.) *with whom he occasionally did joint work. Arthur painted the background and architectural detail while Harry did the foreground figures. Although Arthur also drew many military designs, his postcard work mainly comprised cathedrals, views and river scenes.*

Pub. De Little, Fenwick & Co.
Several designs .. .. 50p/**75p**/£1

Pub. Hildesheimer
Series include 15th-century London, Cathedrals, London on Thames .. .. 50p/**75p**/£1.50

Pub. Ruddock
'Artist' series .. .. 50p/**75p**/£1

Pub. Tuck
Early chromolithographed vignettes of Cathedrals £3/**£4**/£5

Various Oilette series, incl. 'English Cathedrals', interior and exterior views, churches and Thames views 75p/**£1**/£1.50

PAYNE, G. M.

A highly competent, somewhat under-estimated artist of comic and general subjects during Period 2. Subjects include Bathing, 'Before our Time', sporting, etc. He did many series for Gale & Polden and other publishers. Period 3.

Price range .. .. 50p/**75p**/£1.50

PAYNE, HARRY (1858–1927) ■M 1

Though his drawings now seem somewhat stereotyped and wooden, Harry Payne is undoubtedly the most famous of all the military postcard artists. He had only a sketchy art training at evening school, but his splendid, colourful pictures, with an attention to detail of uniform and horses' trappings, had an early success. He and his brother Arthur (q.v.) *with whom he had a long artistic collaboration, were fascinated as boys by all things military. He was engaged by Tuck (for whom he had been designing 'scraps' and books for several years), to design postcards for them and produced some of their earliest picture postcards. The association was to last until 1918. Then Gale & Polden commissioned 67 designs, of which 22 are estimated to have been published, including his last postcard. It is estimated he prepared about 700 postcard designs.* See MILITARY.

Pub. Davis, A. M. & Co.
Period 3 War Bond poster .. .. £2.50/**£4**/£6

Pub. Gale & Polden (1918/1919)
Twenty-two known military designs .. .. £2/**£3.50**/£4.50

Pub. Hildesheimer
At least 2 Rural series .. .. £1.50/**£3**/£4

Pub. Stewart & Woolf
At least 4 series of military designs .. .. .. £2/**£3**/£4

Pub. Tuck
Chromo-litho UBS. *Period 1/early Period 2*
British Army series Nos. 100–124; Empire series (Baden-Powell, CIV's, Wiping Something off the Slate, etc.); Animal Life series; Types of the British Army .. .. £8/**£10**/£12
Military Oilettes. Periods 2/3
About 40 sets and many single designs on Ceremonial, Regimental, Uniforms, etc. .. .. £2/**£3**/£4
Badges and their Wearers (30 identified) .. .. £3/**£5**/£8
Boy Scouts/Red Cross/US Army .. .. £2/**£4**/£6
Defenders of the Empire. Period 3 .. .. .. £1/**£3**/£5
Defenders of the Empire with whisky advert (1924) £3/**£5**/£7
King George V series 9877 .. .. £2/**£4**/£6
Period 3 Patriotics incl. 'Wake up England' .. £2/**£3**/£5
Rural Oilettes
About 40 series, including 'County' series, Country Life, Man's Best Friend, Seasonal .. .. £1/**£2**/£4
Wild West, USA (1907)
Two series and single designs .. .. £2/**£4**/£6

■A 20 Pub. Hildesheimer. Artist Arthur Payne. 'Fifteenth Century London. St. Bartholomew the Great, Smithfield'. Period 2 £1.50

■A 21 Pub. Rommler and Jonas, Dresden. Artist F. Perlberg. 'Ramses Colossus at Abou Simnel'. Period 2 £2

PERLBERG, F. ■A 21
Prolific, globe-trotting German artist of attractive landscapes, views, historic sites and 'types'. Little is known of the man. The following checklist of the known work of this colourful and pleasing artist has been compiled by New York collector, Paul Silverstone. Details of the undescribed numbers will be appreciated. Period 2.

Pub. C. A. & Co.
Egypt
Series 672/I, 672/II, 764/II, 765/IV, 795
Levant
Series 744, 750
Mediterranean
Series 752, 756, 757, 761
Palestine
Series 709, 763, 766, 774, 781, 782, 783, 787, 790

A full listing of these Series was given in the third edition of this catalogue (pp. 82–84).

Price range .. .. 50p/**£1**/£2

Pub. Rommler & Jonas, Dresden
All prefixed with 'R'
101. On the Terrace
102. Cafe arabe
103. Rue et minaret
104. Ecole de coran
105. Rue au clair de lune
106. Caravanserai
107. Noces juives
108. Promenade de Juifs
109. Cabinet de toilette dans un bain Arabe
110. Tombeau d'un saint
111. Marchand de sucrerie
112. Rue et porte maure
113. Porte maure
114. Juifs à un jour de fête
115. Femmes maures
116. Entrée d'un mosquee
117. Bain au harem
118. Oasis avec foret de dattiers
119. Café arabe et mosquee
120. Entrée d'un palais du Bey
121. Au Bazar
122. Scène de rue
123. Au Bazar
124. Magazin d'un tailleur
125. Cairo
126. The Pyramids of Gizeh
137. Sphinx in Simoom
138. Scene of Harem
143. Cairo in Evening
144. Ascension of the Great Pyramid
145. Statue of Ramses at Memphis
146. Temple at Karnak
147. The Obelisks of Karnak
148. Temple at Luxor
149. The Colossos at Thebes
150. Court of the Temple of Medeenet Haboo
151. Temple of Edfu
152. Pharoah's Bed, Philae
153. Ramses' Colossos at Abou Simbel
154. 2nd Cataract near Wady Haifa

Price range .. .. 50p/**£1**/£2

PHILLIMORE, REGINALD (1855–1941)

Born the son of a Nottingham doctor, Reginald graduated from Oxford University in the early 1870s and went on to teach at a private school in Lancashire. Over the next twenty years he enjoyed sketching in the Manchester area and his interest in history grew. When the picture postcard, became popular in the 1890s, he saw a way of combining his two interests commercially. In 1894 Phillimore went into the business of designing, printing and publishing postcards, many of them being hand tinted by his assistant, Mary Pearson. Phillimore postcards are characterised by their fascinating historical and architectural detail, often combining several designs on a single card. Typical, too, are the small pictures which continue the story on the reverse. Peak production was from 1900 to 1910. Nearly 700 different designs have so far been identified.

A full listing of Phillimore cards was given in the second edition of this catalogue, pp. 75–81.

Price range .. .. £1/**£2**/£3

PINKAWA, ANTON

Art Nouveau *artist, particularly highly regarded for his delicate* Seasons *Series. Early Period 2.*

Price range .. .. £5/**£10**/£15

PIRKIS, ALBERT GEORGE

Amusing and skilful artist, best known for his series showing accident-prone cyclists and motorists for Hildesheimer, many of them 'Write-Aways'. He also did views and London scenes.

Price range .. .. £1/**£2**/£3

POIRE, EMMANUEL (Caran d'Ache) (1859–1909)

French artist of Russian extraction ('Caran D'Ache' is a gallicised version of the Russian for pencil) he contributed to some of the great early French series (see COLLECTIONS) *and is most famous for his military designs.*

Price range (highest valuation for the 'Cent' cards) .. .. £10/**£25**/£100

POULBOT, FRANCISQUE

French artist who came to the public eye in WW1 with his pitiful but spirited urchins ('gosses') orphaned and made homeless by the horror of war. C. B. Cochran introduced a Poulbot sketch into his Bairnsfather 'Better 'Ole' play. Poulbot also drew advertisements and political cards, notably of the famous 'Landru' trial. See POLITICS.

Adverts. Period 4 .. .. £1/**£1.50**/£4
Specials (Landru, Novelty, *Lusitania*, etc.) .. .. £3/**£6**/£12
Various 'Good Causes' Periods 3/4 .. .. £1/**£1.50**/£3
WW1 'Gosses' .. .. 75p/**£1.25**/£2

'PYP'

Comic artist of Period 2, many of whose designs were published by Davidson Bros., e.g. UB *Illustrated Songs, credited as 'Originals by PYP'.*

Price range .. .. 75p/**£1.50**/£3

QUINTON, ALFRED ROBERT (1853–1934) ■T 2

Born in Peckham and educated at Hornsey School and Heatherley Arts School, he excelled in oils, exhibiting at the Royal Academy, the Royal Society of British Artists, etc. He travelled extensively through the British Isles on his bicycle, sketching, and illustrated several books with his watercolours. His most productive association was with J. Salmon, the postcard publishers of Sevenoaks, and he worked for the firm from 1911 until his death.

Pub. Faulkner, C. W.
Several series of views.

Pub. McKenzie, W. & Co.
Artistic series.

Pub. Tuck
Picturesque Coaching Inns and other Town series.

Pub. Salmon, J.
Many series of village, small town, country views. Periods 2 to 4, some signed 'A.R.Q.'

Price range for all above .. .. 75p/**£1.50**/£3

RAEMAEKERS, LOUIS (1869–1956)

Dutch artist whose bitter, anti-German cartoons, published as 'Drawings of a Neutral' did much for the Allied Propaganda machine in WW1 see MILITARY). *They were published for the Amsterdam paper* De Telegraaf *and reprinted in booklet form in aid of British and French wounded and published by Geo. Pulman & Sons.*

Price range .. .. £1/**£2**/£2.50

RAVEN-HILL, LEONARD (1876–1942)

Raven-Hill studied art in London and Paris, where his work was exhibited in the Salon *in 1886. Finding success as an illustrator, he worked for a variety of magazines, notably* Punch. *He commented in his cartoons on politics, social life and wars. Perhaps his best known postcards are in the fine WW1 'Out for Victory' series, and in the reproduction of some of his early* Punch *cartoons by Wrench.*

Pub. Wrench. (1901)
'Pictures from Punch' .. .. £1.50/**£2**/£3

Pub. Anon
'Out for Victory' WW1 series .. .. 50p/**£1**/£2

RÉMI, GEORGES ('Hergé') (1907–1983) ■L 3
Creator of the universally popular children's book character 'Tintin', Rémi was born near Brussels. He was a keen scouter in his youth, and early cards often reflect the scouting theme and the American Indian theme he was fascinated by. In the late 1920s he developed his distinctive strip cartoon style and 'Tintin' went on to star in 23 books, which were translated into 30 languages. The colourful covers of these books have appeared recently in postcard form, but postcards of Tintin's adventures and other 'Hergé' designs appeared from c. 1928.

Period 4 .. .. £2/**£4**/£8
Periods 5, 6 .. .. 50p/**£1.50**/£3
Period 7 .. .. **25p**

REMINGTON, FREDERIC (1861–1909)
Perhaps the most sought after of all the American 'Western' artists, Remington became a cowboy after studying art at Yale. 2700 of his paintings have been identified, and those reproduced as postcards are highly prized. The majority were printed in magazines like Collier's, *and* Harper's *and in books on the American West. Period 2.*

Price range .. .. £2.50/**£5**/£7.50

REYNOLDS, FRANK (b. 1876)
Art editor of Punch *for 10 years, he also worked for* The Sketch *and was a member of the London Sketch Club of which he was President in 1909 and 1922. His 'Characters from Dickens' were reproduced as postcards by A. V. N. Jones & Co.*

Price range .. .. £1/**£1.50**/£2

RICHARDSON, AGNES (1884–1951) ■GR 4
Popular artist, whose postcard work spanned Periods 2 to 4. Subjects include children and patriotic designs. Publishers include: Birn Bros; Davidson Bros; Faulkner, C. W.; Geographia Ltd.; Hauff, Charles; Inter-Art.; Millar & Lang; Photochrom; Regent Pub. Co.; Tuck; Valentine's; Vivian Mansell.

Price range .. .. £1/**£2**/£3

ROBIDA, A.
French artist who did many charming landscapes and town scenes in early Period 2 and who contributed to many of the important French series e.g. Collection des Cent, The Gala Henri Monnier, *Album Mariani* (see Collections).

Price range (highest valuation for the 'Monnier') £2/**£5**/£50+

As it is difficult to date a card precisely, a period system has been used in this catalogue.
For a full explanation of the system see page viii.

ROBINSON, ROBERT (1886–1952)
American artist in the genre of Norman Rockwell, who drew covers for Saturday Evening Post *and illustrations for* Colliers, Harpers, *etc. His postcards depict ordinary Americans and ordinary American life for Edmund Gross. Period 4.*

Price range .. .. £1/**£2.50**/£4

RUBINO, ANTONIO (1880–1964)
Italian artist who drew some fine Period 3 caricatures, also advertisements.

Price range .. .. £3/**£5**/£8

■A 22 Pub. W. T. Ridgley Calendar Co. Pub., Great Falls, Mont. Artist Chas M. Russell. 'Roping a Grizzly'. Period 2 £4

RUSSELL, CHARLES M. (1865–1926) ■A 22
American artist of lively and dramatic Western scenes—cowboys and indians, buffalos and bears, etc.—often with a humorous touch. His authentic atmosphere comes from his years of working as a rancher in Montana. Russell used this experience in his paintings and achieved great success. His work was published in Harper's, *in portfolio form and as book illustrations. At the height of his fame, the Prince of Wales bought one of his pictures. Periods 2, 3, 4.*

Pub. Charles E. Morris .. .. £1/**£2**/£4
Pub. W. T. Ridgley Press
Calendar Co. designs .. .. £2/**£4**/£6
Others .. .. £1/**£2**/£4

SAGER, XAVIER ■M 5
Most prolific of all French postcard artists (Neudin has identified 3000 designs), Sager is best known for his risqué glamour designs. He also produced commercial work and during WW1 his designs had a distinct propaganda message. Sager drew under several pseudonyms, including 'Leger' and 'Salt Lake'. All his work shows a light and humorous touch.

Early Period 2 from 1900	£3/**£6**/£10
Mid period 2	£2/**£4**/£5
Period 3 (*see also* MILITARY)	£2/**£4**/£6
Period 4	£2/**£4**/£5
Ads for 'Welcome' heels/chocolate	£3/**£5**/£8
Pseudonyms/Kirchner copies	£6/**£8**/£10

SAUBER, ROBERT (1865–1936)
One of the founder members of the London Sketch Club in 1898, Sauber spent much of his working life in Northampton. He is chiefly known for his 'London Types' series.

Pub. Pictorial Stationery Co. (from 1901)
Set of 12 'Familiar Figures of London' (*see* SOCIAL HISTORY). At least four different printings have been identified, some with white borders and some without. The borderless cards are UB.

Per card	£4/**£5**/£6
Complete set	£50/**£65**/£80

Pub. Tuck

Works of literary figures (1900)	£4/**£5**/£6
Tuck Celebrated Posters No. 1502 Tatcho ..	£15/**£20**/£25

SCHIELE, EGON (1890–1918)
Recognising his talent while at secondary school, his teachers, against his family's wishes, sent him to study at the Vienna Academy in 1906. The following year he set up his own studio and developed his harsh, disturbing, expressionist style. The erotic element in some of his drawings led to his detention for indecency. Schiele became part of the Vienna Secessionist Group and also worked with the 'Sema' group and for the Wiener Werkstätte, *designing some fine postcards in a gentler style. In 1916 he contributed a special issue of the political Berlin review* Aktion. *His brilliant career was tragically cut short in 1918 when both he and his wife died in the great influenza epidemic.*

Aktion/Wiener Werkstätte	£75/**£250**/£500
Others	£10/**£20**/£40

SCHMUCKER, SAMUEL, L. ■A 23
Schmucker was perhaps America's most accomplished postcard artist, working mostly for the fine publishing company of Winsch, for whom he created the 'Winsch Girl', and for the Detroit Pub. Co. He often signed cards with his initials—S.L.S.—only. Schmucker's designs were imaginative, and his glamour pictures often pure Art Nouveau *in concept. Period 2.*

Pub. Detroit Pub. Co. Art Series (some signed SLS)
Butterfly Girls, Childhood Days, Drinks, Gnomes, International Girls, Mermaids, Smokes .. .. £5/**£9**/£30

Pub. John Winsch
1911 onwards: Greetings, incl. Christmas, Easter, Hallowe'en, New Year, St. Patrick's Day, Thanksgiving, Valentine, etc. .. .. £2.50/**£7.50**/£15

SHINN. COBB X. (1887–1951)
Cobb Shinn was a WW1 'Doughboy' and served in France with the Camouflage Division. During the War he drew cartoons of his fellow soldiers and on his return to civilian life he started drawing a daily newspaper strip cartoon and soon achieved national fame. His postcard output is large, and varies in quality. Sometimes Shinn signed his full name, sometimes his initials only, and the pseudonym 'Tom Yad' is also attributed to him. Periods 2, 3, 4.

Pub. Commercial Colortype Co.
Charlie Chaplin comic set .. .. 75p/**£1.50**/£2.50
Ford Motor car ('Tin Lizzie') comics .. .. 50p/**£2**/£2.50

Pub. E. B. Scofield
Riley Roses .. .. 50p/**75p**/£1.50

Pub. T. P. & Co.
Suffragette design. Series 895 .. .. .. £1/**£1.50**/£2.50

Various
Children, Dutch humour, glamour, greetings, romance .. .. 50p/**75p**/£1.50

SCHÖNPFLUG, FRITZ (1873–1951)
Born in Vienna, son of a prosperous solicitor, Schönpflug was a 'natural', untaught artist, with a sharply observant eye. He recorded with benign accuracy the life and leisure pursuits of fashionable Austrian society and the Austrian army—from personal experience gained during his military service. He had a distinctly humorous touch. His output was prolific, well over 500 designs are estimated and the majority of his postcards were published by Brüder Köhn.

Pub. Köhn, Brüder (Periods 2 to 4)
Many sets of 6 .. .. £2/**£3**/£5

Pub. Munk, M. (Period 2)
Glamour and caricatures .. .. £2.50/**£4**/£6

Period 5
Designs with Nazi interest, e.g. *Tag der Wehrmacht fur das K.W.H.W.* (Winter Relief Campaign. Army Day) £3/**£5**/£10

SEVERN, WALTER (1830–1904)
Born in Rome, he was educated at Westminster. After a short spell as a civil servant he became a landscape artist and designer, founding the Dudley Art Gallery. Pub. Tuck ('Oilette') and others.

Price range 25p/**50p**/75p

SHEPHEARD, GEORGE EDWARD

Talented caricaturist, many of whose designs were reproduced on, or drawn for, the postcard. He is perhaps most famous for his caricature of Rudyard Kipling.

Pub. Avenue Pub. Co. (1906)
Doctor set .. .. 75p/**£1**/£2

Pub. Faulkner, C. W.
Several sets, of which many 'horsy' designs have been remaindered 25p/**50p**/75p

Pub. Photochrom Co. (Period 3)
Silhouette series .. .. 75p/**£1**/£1.50

Pub. Tuck
Cricket, Dutch and Seaside themes .. .. 75p/**£1**/£1.50
'Egg-cellent' series (1918) .. .. 75p/**£1**/£1.50

SMITH, JESSIE WILLCOX (1863–1935)

Born in Philadelphia, Jessie trained as a teacher before she discovered her drawing ability. After studying at the Pennsylvania Academy of Fine Arts, she went on to become one of America's most successful women artists of Periods 2, 3. Children are her favourite subjects and her work often shows a strong, and beautiful Art Deco *influence. Much of her postcard work was published by Reinthal & Newman.*

Price range .. .. £3/**£5.50**/£15

SOWERBY, MILLICENT (1878–1967)

Millicent was born to a well-to-do Tyneside family who supported and encouraged her artistic ambitions. Her natural love of children led her to express her art in illustrating for and about the younger generation. She became the first illustrator of Alice in Wonderland *after the copyright on Tenniel's pictures expired. Her postcard work started in 1905 for C. W. Faulkner and was an instant success. Her career reached its apogée in the 1920s and 1930s when it had a charming* Art Deco *flavour. The bulk of her colourful postcards, featuring children, fairies, flowers and nursery tales were published by Humphrey Milford. During the Great War she drew a few patriotic designs, and afterwards many of her most popular designs were repeatedly reprinted.*

Price range .. .. £1.50/**£3**/£5

SPATZ

See Gothard, Fred.

SPURGIN, FRED (also 'F.S.') (1882–1968) ■CCH 1

Of Latvian origin, born Izydor Spungin, Fred Spurgin came to Britain with his parents at the turn of the century and became a naturalised British subject in 1925. Success came soon, with postcard designs, magazine and book illustrations and advertisements (notably for Rothmans—he married Lilly Rothman). One of the postcard's most versatile artists, he drew humour (from the vulgar seaside type to the political), glamour and many patriotic designs during WW1. His output was enormous, over 2000 designs have been identified, through Periods 2 to 4. In his twilight years he did many 'hack' designs for folded greetings cards. He used many pseudonyms, 'F.S.', collected by many, being the most famous.

Pub. Anon (many printed in Germany) ..	75p/**£1**/£1.50
Pub. Art & Humour/Inter-Art	50p/**£1**/£2
Pub. Bamforth.	£1/**£2**/£4
Pub. Blum & Degen.	75p/**£1**/£1.50
Pub. Ettlinger	75p/**£1**/£1.50
Pub. Gale & Polden	75p/**£1**/£1.50
Pub. Garner, H.	75p/**£1**/£1.50
Pub. J.W.A. & Co.	75p/**£1**/£1.50
Pub. London View Card Co.	50p/**75p**/£1
Pub. Paternoster	£1/**£1.50**/£2
Pub. Regent Pub. Co.	75p/**£1**/£1.50
Pub. Tuck	
Oilette series No. 3032 'In Fairyland' ..	£1/**£1.50**/£2
Others	75p/**£1**/£1.50
Pub. Vertigen	75p/**£1**/£1.50
Pub. Wildt & Kray	50p/**75p**/£1

Theatre advertisements

Princess Charming; Take your Girl Friend to See the Girl Friend .. .. £3/**£5**/£10

Best known Series

'Khaki' (12 cards) per set	£15/**£20**/£30
'Leap Year' (12 cards) per set	£15/**£20**/£30

SPY

See Ward, Sir Leslie.

STANNARD, HENRY JOHN SYLVESTER (1870–1951)

Born in London, the son of the sporting painter, Henry Stannard, he studied at South Kensington and painted rustic and garden studies. In 1922 he held a joint exhibition with his daughter Theresa in the Brook Street Galleries. Publishers of his postcard work include Boots and Tuck ('Oilettes')

Price range .. .. 50p/**75p**/£1

STARR-WOOD, H. ('S.W.')

A self-taught artist, his first exhibition was in 1903. He was a member of the London Sketch Club, where he played an active role in the clowning escapades. He produced few postcards, mainly for Valentine, during Period 2.

Price range .. .. £1/**£1.50**/£2

STEINLEN, ALEXANDRE THEOPHILE (1859–1923)

A Swiss artist who became one of the brilliant group working in Paris around the turn of the century. He was a contributor to many of the important early French series (see COLLECTIONS) *and to magazines and poster designs. Many of his designs show the* Art Nouveau *influence and were published by M. F. Champenois. Neudin 1980 identifies 50 postcard designs.*

Price range .. .. £25/**£50**/£100+

STUDDY, GEORGE (1878–1948) ■COM 2

Born in Devonshire, educated at Newton and Dulwich and Heatherley Art School, Studdy contributed to The Sketch, Titbits *and other publications and became a member of the Savage, Chelsea Arts and London Sketch clubs. His most famous creation was 'Bonzo', a cheeky, cuddly puppy with a distinct personality. Bonzo emerged in the 1920s and like 'Old Bill' appeared on all manner of toys, pottery items, car mascots, etc.*

Advertising work

Excelsior Reisen. Ger. .. .. £3/**£8**/£15
Pascall Butter Almonds .. .. £7.50/**£15**/£20
Sandeman, Stanley. Cotton Belting Co. .. .. £3/**£8**/£15
Wolseley 10 Motor .. .. £7.50/**£15**/£20

Pub. Deans

Various designs .. .. £2/**£3**/£4

Pub. Inter-Art

12 different designs. Early Period 4 .. .. .. £2/**£3**/£4

Pub. Photochrom

Celesque Series. Pre-Bonzo WW1 Patriotics .. £2/**£3**/£4

Pub. 'R.P.S.'

Period 4. Nos. 1002–1072, possibly more .. .. £2/**£3**/£4

Pub. Valentine

Period 4. The Bonzo Series .. .. £2/**£3**/£4
Period 5. Anti-Hitler designs .. .. £3/**£4**/£5

Pub. Warne

Various designs .. .. £2/**£3**/£4

SZYK, ARTHUR

A Polish Jew who fled the Nazi régime and moved to London in 1937, Szyk gained acclaim for his illustrations for a book called The Haggadah *in 1940. His powerful designs and technical brilliance make Szyk (pronounced 'SHICK') one of the greatest WW2 propaganda artists. One of his designs, 'Death in an SS Uniform', was used by the Japanese as aerial dropped propaganda to frighten the defenders of Bataan.* See MILITARY.

Pub. Esquire Magazine. Period 5. Set of 6 oversize cards of anti-Axis leaders cartoons. Highly coloured. Rare. The set .. .. £75/**£100**/£125
Others. Per card .. ..£5/**£10**/£15

TARRANT, MARGARET (1888–1959)
Artist who specialised in children and flower designs during Periods 2 to 5. Publishers include C. W. Faulkner, Humphrey Milford, The Medici Society and Ward Lock. See CHILDREN.

Price range .. .. 50p/**75p**/£1

TAYLER, LAURIE
Australian comic artist with a light and sympathetic touch, whose work was also published in the UK during WW2

Pub. 'Anzac Series'
B & w comics .. .. £1.50/**£2.50**/£3
Prince's Court Advertising cards .. .. ..£8/**£10**/£12
Pub. Tuck/Others
Various comic designs .. .. .. £1.50/**£2.50**/£3.50

TEMPEST, MARGARET (b. 1892)
After studying at art school in Ipswich, Westminster and Chelsea, she became a founder member of the Chelsea Illustrators' Club. She was most famous for her illustrations of Alison Uttley's Little Grey Rabbit. *The Medici Society published postcards of some of her animal designs.*

Price range .. .. 50p/**75p**/£1

THACKERAY, LANCE (d. 1916)
Born in Yorkshire, Thackeray was a founder member of the London Sketch Club in 1898. Thackeray was Tuck's leading comic artist, and the grand master of the 'Write-Away' genre. He worked for Tuck from 1900 to his death in 1916. He produced nearly 1000 postcard designs. A great traveller, Thackeray's Egyptian scenes and types are comparable to Tom Browne's Dutch work. Where Browne portrayed the working classes in a multiplicity of social situations, Thackeray's types were generally middle to upper class. A Thackeray trademark was the small sketch in the border of the design that was a continuation of the main joke. Most of his work was comic in nature, but a couple of advertising cards have been identified.

Pub. David Allen. Theatre Poster Adverts
The Earl and the Girl .. .. £5/**£8**/£10

Pub. Black, A. & C.
People of Egypt. Series 12/13 .. .. £2/**£3**/£4

Pub. Faulkner, C. W.
Series 181 .. .. £3/**£5**/£8

Pub. Hills
'For the Empire' horse pictures .. .. £2/**£3**/£4

Pub. Nestlé's
Advert for Swiss Milk .. .. £5/**£8**/£10

Pub. Tuck
Early chromographed series (over 30). Subjects include Cricket, Golf, Journals Illustrated, Motoring, Popular Plays, Greetings cards (re-issues—over 30). Write-Away designs, incl. Boer War .. .. £1.50/**£4**/£8

Oilette series. Subjects include Bridge, Golf, Egypt, Leap Year, Motoring, Roller Skating, Sea & Riverside, Varsity .. .. £1.50/**£3**/£5

Proof Limited Editions. Series 955, 983, 984 .. £3/**£5**/£8

THIELE, ARTHUR ■AN 1

Much confusion surrounds this increasingly popular artist. It is now felt by several researchers that recently published biographical information about Thiele refers to another, earlier artist of the same name. Thiele's signed production spans the years 1899–1930s—clearly impossible for an artist thought to have died in 1919. There is also doubt as to his nationality. One school of thought is that he was Belgian, not German. Whatever his history, Thiele is an artist whose work becomes increasingly appreciated as even more and varied examples are discovered; prices for good Thiele cards are rising fast. Confusion arises in cataloguing his cards. As he was collected throughout Europe, Britain and the USA, many series were reproduced by several publishers in a variety of qualities; and few of his many series are named. As research is still continuing and no definitive check list has appeared we list here only the most important series or famous sets. Publishers include: Bürger, Bruno & Ottillie, Leipzig; Faulkner, C. W.; 'F.E.D.'; Gebrüder Dietrich, Leipzig; Klaus, Adolf & Co., Leipzig; Kunzli, Carl, Zurich; Stroefer; 'T.S.N.'; Tuck; Ziehar, Ottmar, Munich.

Animals
Cats—*see* ANIMALS.
Chicken/cockerels/hens .. .. £2/**£4**/£5
Chimpanzees .. .. £4/**£6**/£8
Dogs' heads .. .. £4/**£5**/£7
Dogs—Others .. .. £3/**£4**/£5
Monkeys (in school etc.) .. .. £3/**£5**/£7

Dusky Belles/Braves .. .. £4/**£6**/£8

Motoring
'Horse Power Series'—Rare .. .. £6/**£8**/£10
Others .. .. £3/**£5**/£7

Period 1
Gruss aus Moorbad (Mudbath) Chromo-litho vignettes 1899 .. .. £6/**£8**/£10

Others .. .. £4/**£6**/£8

Period 4
Poorer quality designs, e.g. bathing scenes, cats .. £1/**£2**/£3

Propaganda (*See* MILITARY)
Anti-British—Boer War .. .. £6/**£10**/£15
Anti-British—WW1 (incl. Zeppelin Kommt) .. £4/**£6**/£8
Hamster Erlebnisse (post-War Black Market) .. £3/**£5**/£7
Red Cross .. .. £4/**£5**/£6
Wir Barbaren (WW1) .. .. £3/**£4**/£5

Romantic Scenes
Couples, dancing, etc. .. .. £3/**£4**/£5

Sporting Scenes
Billiards, bowling, football, horseracing, hunting, roller-skating, tennis, and tobogganing .. .. .. £3/**£5**/£7

Topical Themes
Komet Kommt (Halley's Comet, 1910) .. .. £6/**£8**/£10
Zeppelin Kommt (Peacetime) .. .. £4/**£6**/£8

Others .. .. £2/**£5**/£12

THOMAS, HERBERT SAMUEL (BERT) (1883–1966) ■A 24

Born in Newport, Wales, the son of a sculptor, he started work in London for a small advertising agency. He also contributed to comics and magazines like London Opinion *and* Punch. *During WW1 he served as a private in the Artists' Rifles and during the War did the picture that was to bring him fame—' 'Arf A Mo, Kaiser!', for the* Weekly Despatch *Tobacco Fund for Troops (Pub. Gale & Polden)—which raised £250,000. After the War he continued to contribute to magazines and newspapers (like the* Evening News*) and re-emerged mainly for Tuck in WW2 with ITMA jokes and other timely humour. Mainly comic, his work also includes some striking caricatures and theatre adverts between the Wars (Pub. Odhams).* See COMIC *and* MILITARY.

Price range .. .. 75p/**£2.50**/£8

TURNER, J. A.

One of Australia's most popular and sought-after artists, who specialised in portraying bush scenes, similar in style to J. Hutchings, but of greater clarity. He was little regarded in the general art world until one of his oil paintings recently fetched a record price in Australian auction. Period 2.

Pub. Robert Jolley
Various designs .. .. £3.50/**£5**/£7
'Panel' cards with gilt edges and greetings messages .. .. £3.50/**£5**/£9

Pub. 'P.S. & Co.'
Swallow and Ariell's adverts .. .. .. £2.50/**£3.50**/£6

A 23 Pub. John Winsch. Artist Samuel Schmucker. Embossed and gilded 'Thanksgiving' card. 1911 £12

A 24 Pub. David Allen & Sons. Artist Bert Thomas. Theatre Poster advert for *Mr. Wu* at the Savoy Theatre £6

TWELVETREES, CHARLES H.

Prolific American artist of babies and cute kids, crosspatches and comic animals, fatties and teddy bears. His work spanned from about 1907 until well into the 1930s. Many cards are signed with the initials 'C.T.' only, some are unsigned but instantly recognisable (although many attempts were made to fake his popular style). The snappy captions are an integral part of the design.

Twelvetrees also drew some glamour, seasonal greetings and WW1 patriotics. In the USA the majority of his work was published by Edward Gross, the House of Art and Reinthal and Newman; in the UK by 'Alpha'.

U.S. Publishers

Edward Gross, N.Y.	75p/**£1**/£1.50
House of Art, N.Y.	50p/**75p**/£1
Illustrated Postal Card & Nov. Co.	50p/**75p**/£1
Reinthal & Newman	50p/**75p**/£1

Cards Distributed in UK

Pub. Alpha. Entitled 'Comic', 'Smile Messengers' or 'Twelvetrees'. Printed Ed. Gross, NY.

A list of these cards was given in the third edition of this catalogue, pp. 95–96.

Price range .. .. 75p/**£1.25**/£2.50

Pub. Alpha. Smile Messengers with no 'Edward Gross' markings.

Price range .. .. 50p/**£1**/£1.50

Pub. Ullman Co.
National Cupids, 1906. incl. England, France, Germany, Holland, Italy, Scotland, United States .. £2.50/**£4**/£5

UPTON, FLORENCE (1873–1922)
Creator of the golliwog in 1893, Florence Upton illustrated a children's book using her original character called The Adventures of Two Dutch Dolls; *it was an instant success. In 1903 Tuck bought the rights to the book and reproduced the illustrations as postcards. Sadly Florence Upton was too naïve about business to profit much from the international success of her creation.*

Pub. Tuck (from 1903). About 15 sets of 6, many overprinted with Christmas Greetings .. .. £5/**£6**/£7

VILLON, JACQUES (Gaston Duchamp) (1875–1963)
French artist who contributed to many satirical publications, like Le Rire, L'Assiette au Beurre, *etc. His postcard output was small and therefore much sought after. First and foremost a poster artist he contributed 7 cards to the Gala Henri Monnier series and his design for the* Collection des Cent (see COLLECTIONS) *is the most highly rated of all.*

Price range .. .. £50/**£100**/£250

■A 25 Pub. Tuck. Artist Louis Wain. 'Write Away' Postcard No. 957. UB. PU 1903 £12

WAIN, LOUIS (1860–1939) ■A 25
Louis Wain is known as 'The Cat Man' par excellence. *His cats which remain typically feline while displaying uncannily human characteristics, first brought fame to their creator as illustrations for children's books. He also drew dogs, birds and other animals with equal competence. His postcard output, for a variety of publishers, was large—500–600 designs have been identified; his most successful association was with Tuck, especially in the 'Amewsing Write-Away' series. Most of his*

work bears at least a trace of almost zany humour and his cards are popular with collectors in several fields—animals, humour, or themes like diabolo, ping-pong, etc. See ANIMALS: Cats.

Price range .. .. £4/**£8**/£20

WALL, BERNHARDT (1872–1956)

Born in Buffalo, N.Y., Wall studied at the Art Students League but soon outgrew his teachers and opened his own art school. He enlisted in the Spanish-American war and on his return took a job with the Ullman Publishing Co. He was reputed to have started the company's postcard production and he went on to publish most of his cards with them. Over 15 identified publishing companies printed his cards, as well as many unnamed companies. Wall went on to become a proficient etcher, illustrating many historical biographies. During WW1 he designed many patriotic cards.

Pub. Ullman
- Busy Bears (*No. 79*), In Holland (*87*), Little Coons (*59*). Overall Boys, Sunbonnets (perhaps his most famous design) .. .. 75p/**£1.50**/£4
- Greetings designs, incl. April Fool (*156*). Hallowe'en (*143*), Independence Day (*124*) .. .. 75p/**£1.50**/£3
- North Pole Series (*2564–2567*) celebrating Peary's feats (1909) .. .. £1.50/**£3**/£5

Pub. Valentine
- Hudson-Fulton Celebration set of 6. 300th Anniv. of discovery of Hudson River (1909) 3 versions, 1 embossed *per card* .. .. £1.50/**£3**/£4

Other Pubs.
- Various designs .. .. 75p/**£1.50**/£3

WALTZ, J. J. (Hansi)

Waltz was an Alsace-Lorrainer, who had fled to France in the summer of 1914 to escape punishment at the hands of the German authorities for his 'seditious' propaganda. He then organised the French propaganda machine against the Germans. Waltz, or 'Hansi', as he preferred to be known, used the popular folk art of the postcard as part of his campaign. Periods 2/3.

Price range .. .. £3/**£7.50**/£15

WARD, SIR LESLIE (Spy) (1851–1922)

Amongst the most reproduced of all caricatures are those drawn by 'Spy', the pseudonym of Sir Leslie Ward, for the satirical magazine Vanity Fair. *It was launched in 1868 as a rival to* Punch, *but did not survive long. 48 of the cartoons were reproduced as postcards by Stewart and Woolf in 4 sets of 12 in 1902.*

Price range .. .. £2/**£3**/£4

WENNERBURG, BRYNOLF
Versatile German artist, whose work ranged from early UB *chromo-litho bathing beauties* (see SOCIAL HISTORY) *through comic tennis players to sentimental WW1 scenes of lovers/ nurses* (see MILITARY) *He also contributed to the famous* Lustigen Blätter *series.*

Price range .. .. £1.50/**£8**/£15

WHEELER, DOROTHY (1891–1966)
From an artistic family and trained at Blackheath Art School, Dorothy was a successful illustrator of magazines and books (incl. Enid Blyton stories).

Pub. Black, A. & C. (*c.* 1926). English Nursery Rhymes .. .. £1/**£1.50**/£3
Pub. Milford, Humphrey. Day at the Fair series £1/**£1.50**/£3
Pub. Salmon, J. Several series .. .. .. 75p/**£1**/£1.50

WHITE, FLORA
Best known for her patriotic children designs during WW1 (see MILITARY) *mostly published by Photochrom.*

Price range .. .. 50p/**75p**/£1

WIEDERSEIM, GRACE (1877–1936)
American artist best known for her chubby, pop-eyed children. She also signed cards by her married name, Grace Drayton. Most of her designs were published by Reinthal & Newman and Tuck in Period 2. She was also famous for being the creator of the 'Campbell's Kids'.

Comic children, general .. .. £2/**£4**/£8
Campbell's soup ads. .. .. £3/**£5**/£10

WIELANDT, MANUEL (1863–1922)
German artist who studied at Karlsruhe and Stuttgart. His love of travel (to Capri, France, Italy, Malta, etc.), resulted in some fine water-colour views. Over 100 designs have now been identified of the French and Italian Rivieras, Lakes, Gulf of Venice, Germany and Switzerland, many UB. *Publishers include Moser, Nister, Schmidt-Staub and Velten.*

Price range .. .. £2/**£3**/£4

WILLEBEEK le MAIR, HENRIETTE (1889–1966)
Dutch-born artist of a wealthy family. She enjoyed a privileged upbringing but found her own commercial success at an early age. Augener Ltd., the music publishers, soon recognised her talents and published her drawings to illustrate a series of children's books, reproducing some of them as postcards. Two

of her finest series were: Schumann's Children's Pieces *and* Little Songs of Long Ago.

Price range .. .. £1.50/**£2.50**/£4

■A 26 Pub. J. Salmon. Artist Madge Williams. Period 5 75p

WILLIAMS, MADGE ■A 26
Daughter of a Suffolk rector, she illustrated several children's books. Her WW2 postcards for J. Salmon epitomised British 'pluck' through the medium of appealing children.

Price range .. .. 50p/**75p**/£1

WILLRICH, WOLF
In Hitler's campaign against 'degenerate art', Willrich was one of the few artists approved by the National Socialist Regime. His work depicted idealistic, sturdy, Aryan, thoroughly approved, Germanic characters—soldiers, sailors, airmen, mothers, fathers, Hitler Youth types, etc. His fine line-drawing portraits are reminiscent of the work of Albrecht Durer as is his spindly, distinctive signature, a 'W' interspersed with the date of the drawing.

Deutscher Blutadel in Aller Welt (German Aristocracy of Blood Throughout the World incl. 'Carinthian Farmer's Wife; Lower Saxony Maiden; Old Bavarian Countryman; Westphalian Country Girl. Periods 4, 5.
b & w .. .. £1.50/**£2**/£2.50
col. .. .. £2/**£2.50**/£3

Fallschirmjager (Parachutists). Fine col. series, incl. Sgt. Arpke, Col. Brauer, Capt. Delicia, Maj. Koch. Period 5 .. .. £6/**£8**/£15

Fundraising cards for National Socialist causes, e.g. V.D.A.—Volksbund fur das Deutschtum in Ausland (League of Expatriate Germans). Subjects similar to 'Deutscher Blutadel'. Periods 4, 5.
b & w .. .. £1.50/**£2**/£2.50
col. .. .. £2/**£2.50**/£3

Heer und Panzer (Army and Tanks) Period 5. Fine series of portraits, incl. Oberst Brauer, Obltn. Brenner, Dietl, Fulda, Goricke, Guderian, von Lutzow, Rommel, von Rundstedt .. .. £5/**£8**/£15

Luftwaffe (Airforce) Period 5. Airborne personalities, incl. Graf Kageneck, Hanna Reitsch .. .. £6/**£9**/£14

Marine (Navy) Period 5. Similar series of naval portraits incl. Donitz, Endrass, Kretschmer, Prien, Raeder, Schepke, Schuhart .. .. £6/**£9**/£11

WIMBUSH, HENRY B.

An accomplished landscape artist, his most productive period was from 1881 to 1908. He painted views of the British Isles and the Channel Isles, illustrating books as well as designing postcards. Most of his postcard work was reproduced by Tuck in the 'Oilette' range and by A. & C. Black. Period 2.

Price range .. .. 50p/**£1**/£1.50

WOOD, CLARENCE LAWSON (1878–1957)

Coming from a distinguished artistic family, he studied at the Slade School of Fine Art and Calderon's School of Animal Painting. He was a member of the London Sketch Club and a friend of Tom Browne. His postcard production spanned from Period 2 to Period 4. The early work is characterised by 'stock' characters—the cheeky boy, the rotund policeman, etc. Also famous were his 'Prehistoric' series. After the war his greatest success came with the creation of 'Gran'pop', an engaging chimpanzee. Parrots were another favourite theme.

Pub. Allen, David. Theatre Poster Advert (1903). Beauty and the Barge .. .. £3/**£6**/£8
Pub. Brown & Bigelow (B & B), USA. Period 4, 'Gran'pop' Calendar cards for the J. E. Fricke Co. .. .. £2/**£3**/£4
Pub. Carlton Pub. Co. Period 2 Comics .. 75p/**£1**/£1.50
Pub. Davidson Bros. Period 2. 'Prehistoric' series .. .. 75p/**£1**/£1.50
Pub. Dobson, Molle & Co. Period 3. Patriotics £1/**£1.50**/£2
Pub. Henderson. Weather Forecasts .. .. 75p/**£1**/£1.50
Pub. Inter-Art. 'Artistique' series/'Comique' series (children) .. .. 50p/**75p**/£1
Pub. Lawrence & Jellicoe. Period 2. London Opinion series .. .. £1/**£1.50**/£2
Pub. Pictorial Stationery Co. 'Prehistoric' series 75p/**£1**/£1.50
Pub. Salmon, J. Period 3 designs .. .. 75p/**£1**/£1.50
Pub. Stiebel, Alfred. Modern Humour series 75p/**£1**/£1.50
Pub. Valentine. Periods 2, 3. Several series; Period 4. Gran'pop/Parrots .. .. 75p/**£1**/£1.50

WOOD, STANLEY L. (1866–1928)
Best known for his WW1, dashing military pictures (see MILITARY) *he exhibited at the Royal Academy and his paintings fetched £100 in his heyday.*

Price range .. .. 50p/**£1**/£1.50

■A 27 Pub. Tuck. Artist Hayward Young ('Jotter'). 'Picturesque Counties. Kent'. No. 7116 'Old House' and Mill, Upper Deal, Kent. PU 1909 £1

YOUNG, WALTER HAYWARD (Jotter) (1868–1920) ■A27
Much research has been done on the life and works of this popular, prolific postcard artist by, among others, Brian Lund, Marjorie Nielson-Jones (Young's daughter) and Hewson Osborne (see Picture Postcard Annual 1982). *Over 800 postcard designs have so far been identified, probably starting with the Tuck Oilette series that made him so well known.*

Price range:
Children/comic/glamour (often signed 'Hayward Young')
.. .. 50p/**£1.25**/£2
Oilette-type scenes (usually signed 'Jotter') 25p/**75p**/£1.50
Hotel/Railway ads. .. .. 75p/**£1.50**/£3

ZEC, PHILIP
Powerful cartoonist, whose WW2 Daily Mirror *cartoons were often controversial and anti-Establishment. However, many of them were reproduced as postcards for propaganda purposes and distributed through the Lisbon British Embassy in neutral Portugal.* See MILITARY.

Period 5 Propaganda .. .. 75p/**£1**/£1.25

ZILLE, H.
The Berlin artist par excellence, *whose output includes finely observed Berlin types—prostitutes, traders, urchins, etc. He was described by the rightwing newspaper* Fridericus *as 'The Berlin portrayer of toilets and pregnancy'. He contributed to the famous German series,* Lustigen Blätter.

Price range .. .. £3/**£5**/£8

AVIATION

Postcards were carried aloft during the siege of Paris in 1870. They and their modern equivalents, like those transported by Concorde, attract a specialist range of collectors. Frequently postal history attributes such as time and place of posting, cancellation, etc. are the decisive factors in assessing the value of a card. Some examples are given under the heading 'Flown' below. Real photographic cards tend to be the most highly valued. Interest also remains strong in cards depicting balloons or Zeppelins and they usually deserve a high valuation. However, collectors and dealers should beware of b & w photo-origin Period 2 German cards showing early Zeppelins; many have been reprinted in recent years and can mislead the unwary. Artistic impressions should not be ignored, however, and the early Tuck series such as 'British higher-than-Air-Craft' are prized.

Cards of WW1 and WW2 are listed under MILITARY.

Accidents

Aircraft. Blackpool, 7 September 1935	£6/**£8**/£10
Aircraft. Period 2	£5/**£8**/£10
Aircraft. Others	£2.50/**£4**/£5
Airships	£6/**£8**/£10

Aircraft (Photographic Types) ■AV 1

Period 2	£3/**£5**/£8
LL 'Nos Aeroplanes' series	£2/**£4**/£4.50
Period 4	£3/**£4**/£5
Periods 6, 7	25p/**50p**/£1

■AV 1 Pub. A. V. Fry. R.P. 'BOAC Constellation with Alcock and Brown Memorial'. PU 1959 £1

Airfields (Photographic Types)
Period 2. General view .. .. £1/**£1.50**/£2
Period 2. With aircraft .. .. £3/**£4**/£7

Airships (Photographic Types)
British. Period 2 .. .. £3/**£6**/£8
British. Period 4 .. .. £6/**£8**/£10
British. Other periods .. .. £4/**£5**/£6
Foreign. Period 2 .. .. £4/**£7**/£8
Foreign. Other periods .. .. £3/**£5**/£6

Artist Drawn ■AV 2

Bannister, Derek
Pub. J. Salmon. Faithful drawings of contemporary aircraft. Periods 2, 4 .. .. £1/**£2**/£3
Pub. Tuck. Oilette. 'Famous Aeroplanes' series .. £2/**£3**/£4
'In the Air' series .. .. £2/**£3**/£4

Handville, R.
US National Air & Space Museum Series. Pub. Dexter. Subjects Amelia Earhart, Charles Lindbergh, Wright Brothers, etc. 25p/50p

Others .. .. 75p/**£5**/£7

■AV 2 Pub. J. Salmon. Artist A. F. D. Bannister. No. 4844. 'Short "Sunderland" '. Period 4 £1

Balloons (Photographic Types)
Period 1 .. .. £4/**£8**/£10
Period 2 .. .. £3/**£6**/£8
Other periods .. .. £3/**£4**/£5

British Commemorative/First Flights/Meetings (in chronological order)

Detailed listings of these cards were given in the third edition of this catalogue, pp. 105–106.

Manchester & Salford, August 1903.
Lifeboat Saturday. Unflown (See also *Flown*) £30/**£50**/£75

Doncaster Meeting, October 1909

Price range .. ..£7/**£12**/£17

Blackpool Meeting, October 1909

Price range .. ..£7/**£12**/£15

Wolverhampton Meeting, June–July 1910

Price range .. .. £5/**£7**/£10

Bournemouth Meeting, July 1910

Price range .. ..£6/**£10**/£12

Blackpool Meeting, July–August 1910

Price range .. ..£6/**£10**/£15

Lanark Meeting, August 1910

Price range .. ..£5/**£10**/£15

Doncaster Meeting, September 1910

Price range .. ..£5/**£12**/£15

Burton-on-Trent Meeting, September–October 1910

Price range .. ..£5/**£10**/£12

First UK Aerial Post (1911). London to Windsor £10/**£12**/£15
First UK Aerial Post (1911). Windsor to London £15/**£25**/£50
Daily Mail circuit. Pictures of competitors with their machines plus facsimile signatures of Salmet, etc. 1912 .. .. £4/**£5**/£6
Daily Mail. Multi-portrait cards. Artist Henry Laussucq .. .. £10/**£12**/£18

British montage cards 1910
Made from agency photographs and sold at aviation meetings, these usually features a pilot, an aircraft and a background view of the meeting location.

Blackpool

Pub. Avis Publishing Co., Birmingham

'The Advance Series'
Views of grounds, with aircraft superimposed
Blackpool Flying Carnival. Grahame-White & Roe flying
Farman flying at Blackpool
Latham flying at Blackpool
Santos Dumont's Demoiselle
Rougier flying at Blackpool
Paulhan flying at Blackpool
Blackpool Flying Carnival. W. H. McArdle flying

Views of Blackpool with pilot inset
Tetard flying over Blackpool

Numbered series. Countryside views and aircraft
104 Latham flying
106 Farman biplane
107 Paulhan in his Voisin biplane
107 Rougier in his Voisin biplane (*same card-change of inscription*)
108 Santos Dumont's Demoiselle
109 Rougier flying at Blackpool

Pub. E. R. Green & Co., Blackpool
Numbered series depicting aircraft and inset pilots. Considerable repetition of aircraft
4 Drexel in flight
6 Grahame-White in flight at Blackpool
8 Cecil Grace in flight
9 Grahame-White. Ready to start at Blackpool
10 Grahame-White in flight at Blackpool
11 Grahame-White in flight
13 Drexel in flight
16 Grahame-White in flight
17 McArdle. Ready to start at Blackpool
19 Lorraine in flight
20 Cecil Grace in flight at Blackpool
21 Aeroplanes at Blackpool
24 Chavez on his new monoplane
25 Chavez in flight
26 A. V. Roe. Ready to start
27 A. V. Roe in flight
38 Grahame-White in flight at Blackpool

Pub. Millar & Lang Ltd., Glasgow
'National' Series
Comic cards (*coloured—series number*)
806 We are enjoying ourselves in the lovely air
939 We are all getting off here
939 It's a very dry climate up here
939 Going the pace
939 We are having a lovely time up here
Aviators and Aircraft (*coloured—cards numbered individually*)
960 Flight of Delagrange
964 M. Latham's Flying Machine
Aviators and Aircraft (*coloured—series numbered*)
1247 Count de Lambert
1247 Curtis
1247 Singer
1265 Mr. Grahame-White
Aviators and Aircraft (*black and white numbered series*)
1367 Grahame-White in flight
1368 Grace in flight
1372 On Bleriot machine—McArdle inset
1373 On Sommer machine—Tetard inset
1375 On Sommer machine—Tetard inset
1376 Cockburn flying—M. Cockburn inset

Aviators and Aircraft (*black and white numbered series*)
50 Morane in flight (Bleriot machine)
51 Audemars in flight (Demoiselle machine)
52 Chavez in flight (Bleriot machine)
53 Audemars (Demoiselle machine)
54 Grahame-White (with passenger)
56 Grahame-White starting a flight
57 Mr Cecil Grace (Farman machine)
58 Captain Bertram Dickson (Farman machine)
59 Radley flying (Bleriot machine)
60 Drexel in flight (Bleriot machine)
61 Cattaneo flying (Bleriot machine)
62 Küller
63 Wagner
64 Roe in flight
65 Gibbs
82 Cody in flight
Price range .. .. £1/**£2.50**/£5

Details of other montage cards will be given in future editions of this catalogue.

Concorde
Some flown *Concorde* cards have been listed in earlier editions; we now include unflown items. *Concorde* cards are very difficult to value—some were produced for promotional purposes in editions as few as 100; none of which have so far appeared on the market. This listing is intended to indicate the range of items available and a possible collecting pattern. *The Concorde Collectors Handbook* by A. J. Asquith (1980) gives more details.

Only one valuation per item is given—this should be considered as the likely maximum price. The listing is chronological.

Pre-First Flight
French prototype 001. Toulouse Dec. 1967 .. .. .. **£1**
Concorde in BOAC livery **50p**
Japan Air Lines **£1**

First Flights, 1969
French prototype 001, March 1969. Maximum card .. **£1**
British prototype 002, April 1969. Maximum card .. **£1**

Test Flights. 1969–1976
There were more than 2500 Test Flights before *Concorde* went into commercial service. Covers and postcards were carried on some of these (unofficially), often in small numbers and are well worth looking for.

British prototype 002, Fairford—Toulouse Blagnac May 1971 .. .. **£10**
British prototype 002. Arctic Flights, May 1973 .. .. **£10**
British prototype 002. Fairford—Madrid, July 1973 .. **£10**
French prototype 001, Total Eclipse of the Sun Flight **£10**
British Concorde 202. Middle and Far East Development Flight **£10**

Commercial Service 1976 onwards
Until January 1976 all *Concorde* flying had been by or under the command of British Aircraft Corporation or Aerospatiale crews. Early that month British Airways and Air France took delivery of their first Concordes. Flown cards only listed.

Air France. Paris—Berlin—Paris. German card Jan. 1976 **£6**
Air France. Paris—Rio de Janeiro & return, inaugural flights Jan. 1976 .. .. **£5**
British Airways, London—Bahrain & return, inaugural flights. Jan. 1976 .. .. **£5**
Air France. Frankfurt—Hamburg—Paris. German card April 1976 .. .. **£6**
British Airways. London—Washington, inaugural flight May 1976 .. .. **£2**
Air France. New York—Paris inaugural flight Nov. 1977 (*Large postcard with special cachet*)
Air France. Paris—Buenos Aires carrying French team to World Cup competition May 1978 .. .. **£3**

The only other airlines to operate *Concorde* were Braniff International and Singapore International Airlines and they only used them for short periods. These are unflown airline cards but in view of the restricted amount of usage they should be worth collecting. The Braniff official postcards depict *Concorde* in their livery although no aircraft was ever painted in this way. Only one *Concorde* carried SIA livery and that on the left-hand side only, BA markings on the other. One of the postcards shows SIA markings on the right-hand side of the aircraft.

Braniff Airlines card **50p**
Singapore Airlines cards *per card* **50p**

Fantasy/Photo-Montage
Artist drawn visions of future air transport 75p/**£1**/£1.50
People photographed in 'Flying Machines' .. £1/**£2**/£2.50
Photographic scenes with superimposed aircraft £1/**£2**/£2.50

Flown
Beckenham, 1902. Pub. Tuck. Edward VII Coronation. Overprinted, 'Despatched from the Clouds', 9 August 1902 (see above) .. .. **P/A**
Daily Graphic Expedition, 1907
Flown .. .. £75/**£125**/£300
Not Flown .. .. £25/**£35**/£40
Friedrichshafen, 1931. Official card. Printed 8pfg stamp. Centenary of the airfield. Flown in the L.S. Graf Zeppelin, 27 August 1931 .. .. £35/**£40**/£50
Johannesburg, 1936. Empire Exhibition Airmail 'Last Day Card'. 18 Jan. 1936. On front RP Rand Airport £5/**£10**/£15
Luxembourg, 1927. International Stamp Exhibition Commemorative. U/S. Flown by balloon, 8 September 1927 .. .. £6/**£8**/£10
Manchester & Salford, 1903. Life-Boat Saturday. Card carried by Balloon Post during fund raising for the Lifeboat Service. Valuation very subject to condition, 29 August 1903 .. .. £500/**£700**/£900

Zeppelin Centenary, 1938. LZ129 Hindenburg. Flight from Frankfurt to Denmark, 8 July 1938 .. .. £8/**£9**/£12

■AV 3 Pub. 'S & F'. Count Zeppelin. Col. Period 2 £5

Personalities ■AV 3
R.P. cards tend to be most highly valued, particularly if both aviator and aeroplane are featured in close-up. Most cards are Period 2.

Alcock & Brown, Period 4	£2/**£4**/£6
Aubrun	£3/**£4**/£5
Audemars	£5/**£7**/£8
Barnes	£3/**£5**/£6
Bielovucie	£3/**£4**/£5
Blackburn, Harold	£3.50/**£4**/£5
Blériot, Louis	
Pub. 'LL'. Landing at Dover	£2/**£3**/£3.50
Others	£2/**£6**/£8
Breguet	£2.50/**£3**/£4
Cody, Col.	£2/**£5**/£6
Drexel	£3/**£5**/£6
Dubonnet	£4/**£7**/£8
Dumont, Santos	£4/**£6**/£9
Earhart, Amelia (Period 4)	£3/**£4**/£5
Farman	£3/**£7**/£9
Ferber	£2/**£4**/£5
Gilmour	£4/**£5**/£6
Godden	£2.50/**£3**/£4
Grace	£1.50/**£2**/£3
Grahame-White	£2/**£3**/£5
Hamel, Gustav	£2/**£4**/£5
Hawker, H. G.	£1.50/**£2**/£3
Hucks, B. C.	£1/**£2.50**/£5
Latham	£2/**£6**/£7
Lindbergh, Charles A.	£1.50/**£2**/£3

McArdle	£3/**£5**/£6
Pangborn, Clyde & Herndon, Hugh (Period 4)	25p/**£1**/£2
Pegoud	£3/**£4**/£5
Prosser	75p/**£1**/£2
Reitsch, Hanna (Period 4)	£5/**£10**/£20
Roe, A. V.	£5/**£7**/£9
Rolls	£2/**£3**/£5
Rougier	£1/**£1.50**/£2
Salmet, H.	£2/**£6**/£7
Sopwith	£2/**£4**/£5
Valentine	£1/**£1.50**/£2
Wright Bros.	75p/**£1.50**/£3
Zeppelin, Count von	£2/**£2.50**/£5

Three Band Pricing System

Left Hand Band: The lowest price you will probably be asked to pay for this card.
Middle Band: What you will normally be asked to pay for this card: its average, reasonable price.
Right Hand Band: The highest price you will probably be asked to pay for this card.
For a full explanation of the system see page ix.

CHILDREN/TOYS

Dutch dolls, golliwogs and teddy bears are much collected. The most important series in this section is Tuck's 'The Queen's Dolls' House'.

ARTISTS

American Artists (Periods 2, 3) ■CH 1, GR 1

Mainly 'Cute Kids', often chubby and wide-eyed (even 'pop'-eyed), 'Kewpie' dolls (a corruption of 'Cupid') and 'Sunbonnet' children. The most brilliant exception is the superb work of Jessie Willcox Smith. Publishers include Gabriel, Sam; Gross, Edward (New York); House of Art (New York); Reinthal & Newman; Rose, Chas.; Rotograph; Tuck; Ullman.

Anderson, V.C.†	50p/**£1**/£1.50
Brundage, Frances†	£2/**£4**/£8
Clapsaddle, Ellen†	£1/**£2.50**/£5
Corbett, Bertha (Sunbonnets)	£1/**£2.50**/£4
Drayton, Grace (*see* Wiederseim)	
Dixon, Dorothy (Sunbonnets)	£1/**£2**/£3
Dwiggins, C. W.† ('Dwig')	£1/**£2**/£3
Gassaway, Kate	75p/**£1.50**/£3
Griggs, H. B. (signed also 'H.B.G.')	50p/**£1**/£2
O'Neill, Rose† (Kewpies)	£2/**£8**/£15
Outcault, Richard Felton†	£1.50/**£3**/£6
Smith, Jessie Willcox† (incl. *Art Deco*)	£2/**£8**/£15
Twelvetrees, Charles†	75p/**£1.50**/£4
Wall, Bernhardt† (incl. Sunbonnets)	£2/**£4**/£6
Weiderseim, Grace†	£1.50/**£3**/£10

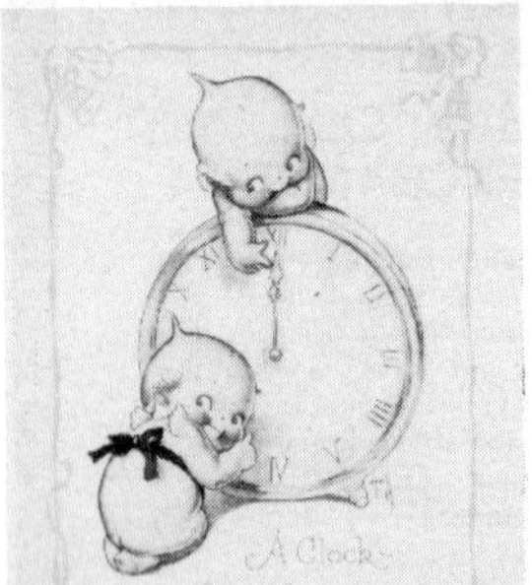

■CH 1 Pub. Gibson Art. Co. Cincinnati. Artist Rose O'Neill. 'Kewpies'. Period 2 £8

■CH 2 Pub. Anon. Artist Alice Wanke. 'Happy Christmas!' Hand coloured. Period 2/3 £5

European Artists (Periods 2, 3) ■CH 2, GR 4

Many of these well-known artists did general designs as well. Publishers include Davidson Bros.; Faulkner, C. W.; Hildesheimer; Inter-Art; Millar & Lang; Tuck.

Barber, C. W.	25p**50p**/75p
Barribal, W.†	£1/**£1.50**/£2
Bertiglia, A.† (It.)	£1/**£2**/£4
Butcher, Arthur (*see* MILITARY)	50p/**75p**/£1
Caldecott, R.†	50p/**75p**/£1
Dexter, Marjorie†	25p/**50p**/75p
Ebner, Pauli	£1/**£2**/£4
Gilson, T.†	50p/**75p**/£1
Goodman, Maude	50p/**£1**/£3
Hardy, Florence†	£1/**£2**/£4
Hassall, John† (Nursery Rhymes)	£1/**£2**/£4
King, Jessie, M.† (incl. *Art Deco*)	£5/**£15**/£40
Kinsella, E.P.† (cricket/tennis)	£1/**£1.50**/£2
Mallet, Beatrice	50p/**75p**/£1
Nash, A. A.†	£1/**£1.50**/£2
Parkinson, Ethel	£2/**£3**/£4
Poulbot, F.† (*see* MILITARY)	75p/**£1.50**/£2
Richardson, Agnes† (*see* MILITARY)	75p/**£1**/£1.50
Upton, Florence†	£5/**£6**/£7
Wanke, Alice	£3/**£5**/£15
White, Flora† (*see* MILITARY)	75p/**£1**/£1.50

Unsigned European Artists (Early Period 2)

Many delightful and beautifully produced early chromo-litho studies (some embossed or silvered) were produced by publishers like Meissner & Buch; M. Munk (Vienna); Nister; Stewart & Woolf; Tuck and many foreign unnamed publishers.

Price range	£1/**£2**/£4

European Artists (Periods 4, 5)

Publishers include Bamforth; Lychgate Ltd. (Worthing); Millar & Lang; Photochrom; Regent Pub. Co.; Salmon; Tuck; Valentine.

Attwell, Mabel Lucie† (also Periods 2 to 4)	£1/**£1.50**/£2
Birch, Norah Annie	25p/**50p**/75p
Broo, Piet (Dutch)	£1/**£2**/£4
Comicus (Harry Parlett)†	25p/**50p**/75p
Cooper, Phyllis	50p/**75p**/£1
Dean, Dora	50p/**75p**/£1
'Dinah'	50p/**75p**/£2
Forres, Kit	50p/**75p**/£1
'Henry' (Belg)	75p/**£1**/£1.50
Mallet, Beatrice	50p/**75p**/£1
Patterson, Vera	50p/**75p**/£1
Richardson, Agnes†	75p/**£1**/£1.50
Taylor, Arnold	50p/**75p**/£1
Tempest, D.	50p/**75p**/£1
White, Brian ('Nipper')	50p/**75p**/£1
Williams, Madge	50p/**75p**/£1
Young, Gwen Hayward	50p/**75p**/£1

Unsigned Belgian, British, Dutch, French and Italian artists .. .. 50p/**£1**/£3

'Nursery' Artists (Period 4) ■CH 3, GR 4, L 1

The popular British children's cards of the 1920s and 1930s depict more ephemeral creations than the robust American children and they often feature elves, fairies, nursery rhymes and whimsical animals. Many of the artists were first and foremost children's book illustrators, and often their postcards were distributed by their publishers to promote books. The best artists of this genre show a distinct Art Deco *influence. Publishers include Augener Ltd.; Black, A. & C.; Faulkner, C. W.; Liberty & Co.; Medici Society; Milford, Humphrey; Millar & Lang; Tuck; Valentine; Vivian Mansell.*

Allen, Daphne†	£2.50/**£4**/£5
Barham, Sybil	£1.25/**£2.50**/£3
Barker, Cecily M.	£1/**£2**/£2.50
Bowden, Doris	75p/**£1**/£1.50
Brett, Mollyw8	75p/**£1**/£1.50
Caldecott, Randulph†	25p/**50p**/75p
Cloke, René†	£1/**£1.50**/£2
Cooper, Phyllis	75p/**£1.50**/£2
Cowham, Hilda†	£1/**£1.50**/£2
Cramer, Rie	£3/**£5**/£10
Folkard, Charles†	£1/**£2**/£3
Jacobs, Helen†	£2/**£3**/£4
King, Jessie M.†	£10/**£15**/£25
Margetson, Hester	75p/**£1.50**/£2
Mercer, Joyce†	£1.50/**£3**/£5
Miller, Hilda T.	£1.50/**£3**/£5
Nixon Kathleen†	£1/**£2**/£3
Outhwaite, Ida Rentoul	£1/**£1.50**/£2
Pearse, Susan Beatrice	£1/**£2**/£3
Preston, Chloë	75p/**£1.50**/£2
Richardson, Agnes†	75p/**£1.50**/£2
Shand, C. E.†	£2/**£4**/£6
Sowerby, Millicent†	£2/**£4**/£5
Tarrant, Margaret†	50p/**£1**/£1.50
Tempest, Margaret T.†	50p/**£1**/£1.50
Wheeler, Dorothy†	£1/**£1.50**/£2

■CH 3 Pub. W. de Haan, Utrecht. Artist Rie Cramer. 'Vieilles Chansons, ill' (Illustrated Old songs). 'Behind my father's house'. Period 4 £5

COONS

A popular theme during Period 2. Artists include:

Burbrook (Coon series)	75p/**£1**/£1.50
Gilson, T.† (Pub. Hey, E. J.)	£1/**£1.50**/£1.75
Hyde, Graham (Pub. Tuck. 1906)	£1/**£1.50**/£2
Sandford, H. Dix (Pub. Tuck 'Happy Little Coons', etc.)	£1/**£1.50**/£2
Twelvetrees, C.† (Pub. Reinthal & Newman)	75p/**£1.15**/£1.75
Wood, Lawson† (Pub. Valentine)	£1/**£1.50**/£2
Unsigned artists	50p/**£1**/£1.50

Pub. Coe—Collotype, Bradford	25p/**75p**/£1
Pub. Davis, A. M. ('Little Darkies') .. 0	25p/**75p**/£1
Pub. Ettlinger (various 'Coon' designs)	75p/**£1**/£1.50
Pub. Inter-Art (Quaint Kids, etc.)	25p/**75p**/£1
Pub. Tuck ('Coon Town Kids', etc.)	£1/**£1.50**/£1.75
Pub. Watkins & McCombie (Coon series)	75p/**£1**/£1.50
Other pubs	75p/**£1**/£1.50

DOLLS/GOLLIWOGS/TEDDY BEARS/OTHER TOYS

Artist drawn Periods 2 to 4

Pauli Ebner—toys with children	£2/**£3**/£4
Rose O'Neill 'Kewpies'	£2/**£3.50**/£5
Florence Upton 'Golliwoggs'	£5/**£6**/£7
Others (value according to calibre of artist and period)	75p/**£2.50**/£5

Mirror Grange, miniature house for Pip, Squeak and Wilfred, Artist A. B. Payne. Pub. Tuck. Period 4.

Sepia	75p/**£1**/£1.50
Col.	£1/**£1.50**/£2

Nudekins (British version of the 'Kewpie' Doll) Pub. Tuck.

Periods 2, 3	50p/**75p**/£1
Posed photographic. Periods 2 to 4	50p/**75p**/£1.50
Teddy Bears—*see* ANIMALS	
Others	50p/**£1.50**/£3

PHOTOGRAPHIC PORTRAITS OF CHILDREN

Thousand of posed portraits of children, ranging from the very appealing to the coyly sentimental, were produced in Periods 2 to 4. Publishers include Birn Bros.; Carlton Pub. Co.; Davidson Bros.; Ettlinger; Hildesheimer; Knight Bros.; Rotary; Schwerdtfeger; Tuck; Wildt & Kray; as well as foreign and other British publishers.

Price range	25p/**50p**/£1

COLLECTIONS: The Great Series

On the Continent there exist several well-documented, artist drawn, 'Classic Collections' of picture postcards—the most prized and sought after cards in existence. Cards from these beautiful series are collected today all over the world, although the prices they command vary from country to country. Both on the Continent and in the USA, fine examples will fetch at least 25% more than the British prices indicated in this catalogue.

The three most famous series of all—the *Collection des Cent, Concours Byrrh,* and *Wiener Werkstätte* were listed in detail in the Second Edition (pp. 105–107).

Austrian ■ C1

Ver Sacrum

1898. Postcards reprinted from the journal of the same name.

Price range (10 cards) .. .. £40/**£60**/£80

Wiener Werkstätte

Literally 'The Vienna Workshop'. Produced in Vienna between 1908 and 1913, this superb collection is the showcase for a style that foreshadowed Art Deco, *Existentialism, Cubism and Surrealism. Like the famous German Bauhaus, the* Wiener Werkstätte *was a workshop with over 100 craftsmen engaged in a variety of arts and crafts—pottery, glass, furniture, architecture, fashion and metal work. The most highly priced examples were drawn by Oskar Kokoscka and Egon Schiele. The elegant ladies of Mela Koehler and Maria Likartz are extremely popular in Britain* (see ARTISTS). *Subjects include Christmas, Easter and New Year Greetings, Months of the Year (Low-Lazar) and illustrated proverbs (Luksch-Lazar). In 1925 a series of designs for silk material were printed for the* Werkstätte *by B.K.W.I. They bear Jewish greetings and were designed by Mlle Arker, Prof. C. O. Czeschka, C. Fochler, E. Hausler, W. Jonas and Pieidl. The postcards from the series can easily be recognised as they all clearly state* Wiener Werkstätte *on the reverse. Some oversize square cards were produced for the series by Mela Koehler, also several 1½ times normal postcard sized examples.*

For a complete listing see Second Edition, p. 107.

Most examples .. .. £20/**£30**/£50
Jung, Koehler, Likarz, Loffier .. .. .. £25/**£35**/£70
Kokoshka, Schiele .. .. £150/**£300**/£450

Philipp & Kramer Early Series

Pub. Philipp & Kramer, Vienna. Over 100 series of 10 cards each have been identified, of which the first 30 are the most sought after, drawn by Hoffman, Kainradl, Kurzweil, Moser and Olbrich. Other superb artists include Gerlach, Hampel, Hedley, and Kirchner.

Price range .. .. £20/**£40**/£60

Austrian/German

Das Grosse Jahrhundert

A vast series of postcards (a total of 612 cards has been suggested, although not authenticated) to chart the achievement of famous men and women of the 19th century as that century drew to a close. Printed in the 1890s, they record international figures of literary, military, musical, political, theatrical and other spheres of fame, e.g. Sarah Bernhardt, Edison, Engels, Marx, Pasteur, etc.

A checklist of this series was given in the third edition of this catalogue, p. 120.

Price range .. .. £3/**£6**/£12

■C 1 Pub. Wiener Werkstätte. Artist Fritzi Low. No. 1000. 1910 £50

■C 2 Pub. David Allen, Harrow. Artist J. Hassall. Theatre poster ad for *The Only Way*. PU 1903 £20

British ■C 2, R 1
Most of the British cards which qualify to be listed under this heading were published by Britain's foremost postcard publishers, Raphael Tuck. Details of the following Tuck series are found under PUBLISHERS: First Dozen Issues; Celebrated Posters; Empire Series; Heraldic Series; Kings and Queens of England and Proof Limited Editions. A listing of Warner Gothard cards was published in the third edition of this catalogue.

David Allen Theatre Postcards
The famous family firm of David Allen celebrated its centenery in 1857 and is still operating in Harrow, Middlesex. Their speciality is the printing of high quality theatre posters. The best commercial artists of the day were commissioned to design the posters, but frustratingly, many of their studies are unsigned. They included: Bruce Bairnsfather, Barribal, John Stuart Browne, (not to be confused with Tom Browne), Buchel, Dennis Dorian Fitzsimmons, John Hassall, Edward Patrick Kinsella, Albert George Morrow, Andrew Murray, Lance Thackeray and Will Owen. Many of the posters were repro-

duced, from c. *1903 onwards, as postcards. They seem, however, to have been considered as of minor importance to the firm. Experts deduce that postcards were probably printed for the majority of titles, some being produced for theatre managers, overprinted with their theatre's name. Postcards were known to have been produced at least to 1927.*

The list in the supplement to this section sets out the names of plays/shows for which postcards have been identified and, where known, the numbers of postcards and their artists.

Price range .. .. £4/**£8**/£20

French

Cocorico
Probably the rarest of all the French series, only 12 cards, of which very few examples exist today. The artists are: Does; Faverot; De Feure; Kienerk; Kupka; Léandre; Michael; Mucha; Popineau; Roubille; Steinlen; Willette.

Price range .. .. £100/**£175**/£300

Collection des Cent
Pub. Greningaire. Literally 'The Collection of the One Hundred'. Actually 99 designs have been identified. They started to appear from 1 Nov. 1901 in packaged sets of 10. It is thought that about 500 examples were printed of each of the early numbers, and less than 100 of the later series. The contributors were amongst the finest illustrators of the day and included Steinlen, Boutet, Mucha, Caran D'Ache, Grasset, Lélée, Villon, Gaston Noury, Chéret, Fernel, Jossot & Orens.

Price range
Most examples .. .. £35/**£45**/£60
Boutet, Capiello, Caran D'Ache, Grasset, Orens, Roubille, Steinlen .. .. £50/**£75**/£100
Mucha, Villon, Vogel .. .. £100/**£200**/£300

Concours Byrrh
French prize competition (1906) for advertisements for the aperitif Byrrh, *a fortified wine with alleged tonic qualities. The competition attracted the very best artists of the day. One hundred and thirteen prizewinning designs were published as postcards. Each design had to incorporate the words,* Byrrh, Tonique, Hygiénique, à base de quinquina et de vins généraux. *Several prize-winners were announced for each prize—two 1st prizes, two 2nd, six 3rd, five 4th, thirty-one 5th and sixty-five 6th. Contributors included Kirchner, Kienerk, Péan, Denis and Valloton.*

Most examples .. .. £20/**£35**/£40
Artists named above .. .. £50/**£100**/£150

Editions Cinos (1898)
Reproductions of posters by the top artists of the day such as Chéret, Mucha, Noury, Redon and Toulouse Lautrec. Thirty-five designs have so far been identified, only the last 9 being numbered.

The cards were listed in the third edition of this catalogue, pp. 120–121.

Price range (highest for the Lautrec) .. .. £55/**£85**/£600

Job
Reproductions of posters/calendars by the cigarette paper manufacturer, 'Job'. Five different series were printed:
1903 (horizontal) Beautiful series of 12 cards
1905 (horizontal) 1 poster, 7 calendar designs
1907 (horizontal) 8 calendar designs
1911 (horizontal) 3 posters, 21 calendar designs
1914 (vertical) 8 posters and 22 calendar designs.
Artists include: Asti, Cheret, Léandre, Mucha.

Price range (highest for earliest series) .. £10/**£25**/£35

Maîtres de la Carte Postale (1898–1900)
Superb postcards, issued in several editions, of designs by some of the most talented current artists, which first appeared in the magazine La Critique.
Artists include: Auburtin; Biais; Bradley; de Caldain; Chapront; Christiansen; Couturier; Delatre; Detouche; Durangel; D'Espagnat; Jordic; Jossot; Lebègue; Lyongrun; Misti; Mouclier; Paraf-Javal; Sloog; Thibaut; Thomen; Valtat and Vibert.

Price range (highest for the Sloog) .. .. £100/**£150**/£200

Germany

Bauhaus
The rarest of all German collections, 20 designs, of which only 25 examples are said to have been printed.

The Bauhaus movement was started by Walter Gropius in Weimar in 1919, incorporating artists of all classes, several nationalities and varying skills and crafts in the fields of pure art, architecture, carving, furniture and interior design, metal work, pottery, etc.

The Bauhaus postcards were produced in 1923. The artists who designed them are: 1 & 2 Feininger; 3 Kandinsky; 4 & 5 Klee; 6 Marcks; 7 Moholynagy; 8 Schlemmer; 9 & 10 Baschant; 11 & 12 Bayer; 13 Haberer; 14 Helm; 15 & 16 Hirschfield-Mack; 17 Molnar; 18 & 19 Schmidt; 20 Teltscher.

Price range (highest for Kandinsky, Klee and Moholynagy) .. .. £50/**£100**/£550

Jugend (1899)
Three series of 25 cards each. Artists include Bernuth, Caspari, Christiansen, Eichler, Hoess, Munzer, Seitz, Weinhold, Zumbach.

Price range .. .. £20/**£40**/£65

Lustigen Blätter
Postcards reproduced from the famous newspaper of the same name in Berlin. Artists include Wennerberg† and Zille† and many of them are anti-British, incl. Kriegs-Karte *during WW1.*

Price range .. ..£5/**£10**/£20

SECTION SUPPLEMENT DAVID ALLEN THEATRE POSTCARDS

Abbreviations
B = Box Office Card
C = Corner Card, Picture is in one corner only
P = Photographic Picture
The naming of an artist does not mean that all cards were by him.

Title	*Number of cards known*	*Artist*
Admirable Crichton	1	
Aladdin	3	A. Morrow, A. Murray
Alice in Wonderland	1	
Alice Sit by the Fire	1 + B	
Aloma	1	
Ambrose Applejohn's Adventure	1	A. Murray
Amorelle	1 (*also photo*)	
Arcadians, The	1	J. Hassall
Arlette	2	
As Good as Gold	1	
Assassin, The	1	
Babes in the Wood	4 + C	Hassall, Hansom, Murray
Baby Bunting	1	
Baby Mine	1	
Beauty and the Beast	2	
Beauty of Bath	2	Hassall
Beside the Bonnie Brier	1	Morrow
Best of Her Sex	1	
Better 'Ole, The	1 + B	B. Bairnsfather
Betty	2	
Bing Boys on Broadway	4	
Bird of Paradise	1	
Blue Beard	2 (+4 *page card*)	
Blue Beard's 8th Wife	1	
Blue Lagoon	1 + B	
Blue Moon	2 + B	E. P. Kinsella
Bohemians	1	
Bo-Peep	1 + C	
Bound to Win	1	

Boy's Best Friend	1	
Breed of the Treshams	2 + B	
Brewster's Millions	2	
Brigadier Gerard	1	J. Cameron
Broadway	1	Hassall
Broadway Jones	1	
Captain of the School	1	
Catch of the Season	2	Hassall
Charley's Aunt	3	Hassall
Chinese Honeymoon	3	Kinsella, Murray
Chocolate Soldier	1	J. S. Browne
Christian, The	1	
Chu Chin Chow	1	
Cinderella	5 + 1C (+*folding card*)	Fitzsimmons
Cingalee, The	3	Kinsella, Morrow
Clancarty	1	
Count of Luxemburg	2	Barribal, Matthews
Country Girl	1	
Country Mouse, A	3 + C	Morrow
Cousin from Nowhere	1	
Cousin Kate	6 + 3C	Morrow
Dancing Girl	2C	
Dandy Doctor	1	
Dante	2	
Daughters of Babylon	1	
Dear Little Denmark	1	Hassall
Dick Whittington	9 + 3C (+1 *folding card*)	Fitzsimmons
Drake	1	Wilkinson
Duchess of Dantzic	3 + B	Fitzsimmons, Hanson, Kinsella
Duke of Killicrankie	1	
Earl and the Girl	2 + B	Browne, L. Thackeray
Eliza Comes to Stay	1	
Emerald Isle	1	
Eternal City	1	A. Morrow
Fairy's Dilemma	2 + B	
False Wife	1	
Farmer's Wife	1	Keens
Faust	1	
Female Swindler, The	10	Kinsella, A. Morgan
Fifinella	1	
Fires of Fate	1	Morrow
Follies, The	1	Hassall
Forty Thieves	4 + C (+4 *page card*)	Murray
Four Just Men	2	
Freedom of Suzanne	2	
Gabrielle	1	
Garden of Lies	B	

Gay Grisette, The	1	
Geisha, The	2	
General Post	1	Kinsella
Gerrard	1	H. Smith
Get-Rich-Quick-Wallingford	1	
Girl Behind the Counter	2	Barribal, C. W. Quinnell
Girl from Kays	3	Murray
Girl From up There	1	
Girl in a Boat	1	
Girl in the Taxi	2	Barribal
Girl on the Stage (or Little Cherub)	3	
Girl who took the Wrong Turning	1	
Glad Eye, The	1	Quinnell
Gypsy Love	2	Barribal, R. Pannett

To be continued

COMIC

This is the type of postcard at which the British excelled during the 'Golden Age' of collecting. It was typically British, as were *Art Nouveau* and topographical French, *Gruss Aus* German and patriotic/political Italian. No other country has such a rich vein of humour in its postcard production. No area of Edwardian life seemed immune from the humorous artist, and the wealth of comic artistic talent was extraordinary.

Cards in most collecting categories were given the humorous treatment. To list them all here would make this section unwieldy. Therefore many 'comic' cards are described under other main headings, notably:

CHILDREN (many artists who did 'general' humour also drew cards on this theme)

MILITARY (for the large and important sections on the humour of WW1 and WW2)

POLITICS (themes like Free Trade, National Insurance Stamps, Suffragettes, etc.)

SOCIAL HISTORY (ethnic and regional humour)

Most comic cards, however, are collected because of their artists, many of whom came to postcard design from the poster, or book and magazine illustration, and have a reputation far beyond their postcard output.

Listed in this COMIC section are many of the minor, but highly collectable, comic artists, examples of whose work can still be found for a modest price. Comic cards are also collected by virtue of their publisher, and some of the main comic publishers are listed here, as are some of the important comic series and the comic 'themes', often drawn by competent but unsigned artists.

N.B. Many of the cards by the following artists may have higher valuations in other sections. The following prices are for their comic designs only.

ARTISTS (Signed)

'A.A.' 25p/**50p**/75p
Adams, Will .. .. 50p/**75p**/£1
'A.E.' *see* English, Archibald
Anderson, Martin (Cynicus)† (*Highest valuation for early Period 2 and 'Court' size*) ■A 3 .. .. £1/**£1.50**/£6
Aris, Ernest .. .. 75p/**£1**/£1.50
Attwell, Mabel Lucie† .. .. F†·£1.50/£3
Austerlitz, E. .. .. 75p/**£1.50**/£2
Bairnsfather, Bruce† ■A 5 .. .. .. 75p/**£1.50**/£3
Bamber, George A. .. .. 50p/**75p**/£1
Barnes, G. L. .. .. 75p/**£1**/£1.50
Bateman, H. M.† .. .. £1/**£2**/£3
Bee, Noah .. .. 50p/**75p**/£1.50
Belcher, George† .. .. £3/**£4**/£5
Biggar, J. L. .. .. 50p/**75p**/£1
'Bob' (*Irish and other humour*) .. .. .. 50p/**£1**/£1.50
Bradshaw, P. V.† (*also signed 'PVB'*), ... £3/**£4**/£6
Browne, Tom† (*also signed 'Tom B.'*) .. .. .. £2/**£3**/£5
Buchanan, Fred† .. .. 50p/**£1**/£1.50

Bull, Rene†	£2/**£3**/£4
Buxton, Dudley†	75p/**£1.25**/£2.50
Cameron, Archie	25p/**75p**/£1
Carter, Reg†	75p/**£1**/£2
Carter, Sydney†	50p/**£1**/£2
Christie, G. F.† (*also signed 'G.F.C.'*)	50p/**£1**/£1.50
Comicus *see* Parlett, Harry	
Cook, Charles K.	75p/**£1.50**/£3
Crombie, Charles	50p/**75p**/£1
Cynicus *see* Anderson, Martin	
'Dauber'	75p/**£1**/£1.50
Davey, George†	75p/**£1.50**/£2
'Dinah'	50p/**75p**/£1.50
Duncan, J. A. ('Hamish')†	50p/**75p**/£1
Dwiggins, C. V. ('Dwig')†	£2/**£3**/£4
Earnshaw, Harold†	50p/**75p**/£1
Ellam, W. H.†	75p/**£1.50**/£3
Elliott, Harry	50p/**£2**/£3
English, Archibald ('A.E.')†	50p/**75p**/£1.50
Esmond (*'Germs', etc.*)	75p/**£1**/£4
'F.S.' *see* Spurgin, Fred	
Fitzpatrick, Brian (*Bamforth*)	25p/50p
Fleury, H.	25p/**50p**/75p
Fuller, Edmund†	£1/**£2**/£2.50
Gibson, Charles Dana†	75p/**£1**/£2
Gill, Arthur†	£1/**£1.50**/£2.50
Gilson, T.†	50p/**£1**/£2
Gothard, Fred ('Spatz')†	25p/**50p**/£1
'Graeff'	50p/**75p**/£1
Greenall, Jack (*'Useless Eustace'*)	50p/**75p**/£1
Grisset, Ernest	75p/**£1**/£1.50
Gunn, Gwennet†	50p/**75p**/£1
'Guy L'	50p/**75p**/£1
Hardy, Dudley†	£2/**£4**/£5
Hassall, John† ■C 2	£2/**£4**/£5
Heath-Robinson, W.†	£2/**£3**/£4
Huber, G.†	50p/**£1**/£2
Hyde, Graham	£1/**£2**/£4
Ibbetson, Ernest†	£1/**£2**/£3
'Karaktakus'	25p/**75p**/£1
'K.S.'	25p/**75p**/£1
Leete, Alfred†	£1/**£1.50**/£2
Ludovici, Anthony†	£2/**£3**/£4
MacBean, L.	50p/**£1**/£1.25
McGill, Donald†	50p/**£1.50**/£3
Martin, Phil	25p/**50p**/75p
Maurice, Reg† ■M 4	75p/**£1**/£2.50
May, Phil† ■COM 1	£2/**£3**/£4
'Mich'	£1.50/**£2.50**/£3.50
Moreland, Arthur†	£1/**£1.50**/£2
Morgan, F. E.	25p/**50p**/75p
Morton, Alfred (*'Imps'*)	£2/**£3**/£4
Noble, Ernest	25p/**50p**/75p
Opper, Frederick Burr	50p/**£1**/£2
Outcault, Richard Felton	75p/**£1.50**/£3
Owen, Will†	£1/**£2**/£3
Parlett, Harry ('Comicus')†	50p/**75p**/£1

Payne, G. M.†	50p/**75p**/£1.50
Pirkis, Albert George†	75p/**£1.50**/£3
'PYP'†	£1.50/**£2**/£2.50
Reynolds, Frank†	75p/**£1.50**/£3
Rob, A.	75p/**£1**/£1.50
Rowland, Ralph	50p/**£1.50**/£3
Rowntree, Harry	£1/**£2**/£3
Schonpflug, Fritz†	£1/**£2**/£3
Shaw, W. Stocker	50p/**75p**/£1
Shepheard, George Edward†	75p/**£1**/£1.50
'Spatz' *see* Gothard, Fred	
Spurgin, Fred† (*also signed 'F.S.'*)	£1/**£1.50**/£3
Starr Wood, H.†	£1/**£1.50**/£2
Studdy, George† ■COM 2	£1.50/**£2**/£3
Taylor, Arnold	25p/**50p**/75p
Tempest, Douglas	50p/**75p**/£1
Thackeray, Lance†	£2/**£3**/£4
Thiele, Arthur† ■AN 1	£2/**£4**/£8
Thomas, Bert† ■A 24	75p/**£1.50**/£3
Wain, Louis† ■A25	£6/**£8**/£15
Ward, Dudley	25p/**50p**/75p
Ward, Sir Leslie†	£2/**£3**/£4
Wilkinson, Gilbert	75p/**£1**/£1.50
Wood, Lawson†	£1/**£2**/£3
Zimmerman, H. G.	75p/**£1.50**/£2

ARTISTS (Unsigned/Minor)

Periods 2 to 6	25p/**50p**/£1.50

■COM 1 Pub. Wrench. (by permission of the Proprietors of *Punch*). Artist Phil May. Series No. 10036, 'Songs and their singers'. 'Drink to Me Only With Thine Eyes'. UB. Early period 2 £5

■COM 2 Pub. Valentine. Artist Geo. Studdy. 'Bonzo Series'. 1925 £2

COMIC PUBLISHERS/SERIES/THEMES

Addled Ads. *see* Misch & Stock

Bamforth & Co.
Many posed humorous song and other series of photographic origin. Periods 2 to 4.
Single cards and sets of 2, 3, 4 .. .. 50p/**75p**/£3
Similar cards by other publishers 25p/**50p**/75p

Couples, Courtship
On of the favourite butts of comic ards.
Artist drawn 25p/**50p**/75p
Photographic in origin (esp. by Pub. 'J.W.S.') 25p/**50p**/75p

'Dam' Family
Pubs. Crockers, Fraser & Jenkinson, others 25p/**50p**/75p

Davidson Bros.
Undoubtedly the 'kings' of the comic card.
Periods 2, 3 .. .. 50p/**75p**/£3

Ethnic/Regional Humour (*see* SOCIAL HISTORY)
Irish humour ('Paddy' jokes, many local pubs.) 25p/**50p**/£1
Jewish humour ('mean' jokes, etc.) .. .. 75p/**£1.50**/£3
Scottish humour (artists like 'Hamish', pubs. like Millar & Lang) 25p/**50p**/75p
Welsh humour ('jawbreaking' placenames, pubs. incl. Valentine) 25p/**50p**/75p
Others **50p**

Marriage
'Is Marriage a Failure?'. Pub. Millar & Lang 25p/**50p**/75p
Mrs. Caudle's Lectures (various pubs.) .. 50p/**75p**/£1.50
Others 25p/**50p**/75p

Military Humour
See MILITARY.
Price range .. .. 50p/**75p**/£1.50

Misch and Stock
This publishing house produced many fine series of comic postcards, using some of the most popular comic artists of the day, in early Period 2.
A listing of these cards was given in the third edition of this catalogue, p. 127.
Price range .. .. 75p/**£1.50**/£4

Punch Cartoons ■COM 1
Early Period 2/Period 3 (various pubs., *see* MILITARY and POLITICAL) .. .. £1/**£1.50**/£2

Sporting Humour
Cricket, Golf, Ping Pong, Skating, etc. (*see* ARTISTS) .. .. 75p/**£1.75**/£3

When Father Said Turn
Pub. Millar & Lang. Series. Period 2 .. .. 50p/**75p**/£2

'Wordy' Humour
The pseudo 'essay' or 'poem' on humorous topics, often in dialect. Various pubs. .. .. 25p/**50p**/£1

Undivided-back Comics
Period 1/Early Period 2, often chromo-lithographs £2/**£3**/£4

Tuck
Many series, many artists, too numerous to list here. Periods 2–6 .. .. 25p/**75p**/£4

Three Band Pricing System

Left Hand Band: The lowest price you will probably be asked to pay for this card.
Middle Band: What you will normally be asked to pay for this card: its average, reasonable price.
Right Hand Band: The highest price you will probably be asked to pay for this card.
For a full explanation of the system see page ix.

COMMEMORATIVE

In its early days the picture postcard evolved to meet the needs of advertisers and to commemorate anniversaries, exhibitions and holidays. There are specialist sections in this catalogue to cover EARLY CARDS, EXHIBITIONS, MILITARY and ROYALTY all of which have a strong commemorative content. However, there are commemorative postcards that do not fit easily into those or any other classifications. This section is for them and we refer to cards commemorating events which are national rather than local. As is normally the case, Period 1 and Period 2 are the most valued, although many interesting official and pictorial commemorative cards have been issued during Periods 4–7 in Germany and the USA. The MODERN cards section should also be consulted.

PERIOD 1

1893. Switzerland. 50th Anniv. of the Postal Service. Limited Edition of 36,000, valid from 25 June–31 December 1893 only .. .. £5/**£8**/£10

1894. Austria. Dr. Hermann pictured on card for 25th Anniv. of the First Postcard. Pub. Friedl.
Signed by Dr. Hermann .. .. **P/A**
Unsigned .. .. £20/**£40**/£55

1894. San Marino. Inauguration of the Palais de Conseil Souverain .. .. £4/**£5**/£7

1895. Italy. 25th Anniv. of the Liberation of Rome £5/**£6**/£10

1895. Port of Spain. 'Dez Reis' (Ten Kings) 1195–1895 .. .. £3/**£4**/£5

1897. Germany. 400th Anniv. of the Leipzig Fair £3/**£4**/£5

1897. Italy. National elections of 27 May .. .. £7/**£9**/£12

1898. Britain. Court size. 'I have done my best for the honour of our country. Goodbye.' Nile Expedition commemorative, showing Gordon & Kitchener **£100**

1898. Canada. USS Maine Memorial .. .. £10/**£15**/£25

1898. Germany. Mourning card for the death of Bismarck .. .. £2/**£3**/£4

1898. Portugal. Official issues. 400th Anniv. of Vasco da Gama's discovery of the route to India .. .. £2/**£3**/£4

1899. Germany and others. 9.9.99 cards. Mint £1.50/**£2**/£2.50
Ditto. Posted with 'all 9's' cancellation .. .. £3/**£4**/£5

PERIOD 2

British

1900. Tuck. Empire series. Embossed with inset photo origin cameos of famous people. 'Souvenir 1900' UB £8/**£12**/£15

1901. Foundation of the Commonwealth of Australia, John Evelyn Wrench issued his first 'Links of the Empire' series to commemorate the Duke and Duchess of Cornwall and York's journey to and from Australia. Twenty cards issued—listed in third edition, p. 130.

Price range *per card* .. ..£9/**£12**/£15

1903. Visit of President Loubet of France/formation of the *Entente Cordiale*. RP and artist drawn, incl. satirical, by artists like Rostro .. .. £2/**£6**/£10
1905. Centenary of Trafalgar. Artistic .. 75p/**£1**/£1.50
Ditto. Photo-origin showing scenes in Trafalgar Square .. .. £1/**£2**/£2.50
1905. Death of Sir Henry Irving .. .. 75p/**£1**/£1.50
1912. Death of General Booth, founder of the Salvation Army .. .. £1/**£3**/£6
1912. London Peace Conference. Albania declared an autonomous state (rare) .. .. £2/**£3**/£6

■COMM 1 Pub. E. le Deley, Paris. Visit of H.M. King Alphonso XIII of Spain to Paris. 'The Queen of Les Halles Market and her entourage'. PU 1905 £4

Foreign ■COMM 1
1900. Germany, Official card with printed stamp welcoming the year 1900 .. .. £1/**£2**/£3
1901. Australia. Foundation of the Commonwealth of Australia .. .. £4/**£5**/£6
1902. USA. Visit of Prince Heinrich .. .. .. £3/**£5**/£6
1904. South Africa. Funeral of ex-President Kruger .. .. £1/**£2**/£2.50
1905. France. Visit of Alphonso XIII to Paris. Pub. E. le Deley .. .. £1/**£2**/£4
1906. Norway. Amundsen and the North West Passage .. .. £1/**£1.50**/£2
1906. USA. The Wedding of the Century. Alice Roosevelt and Nicholas Longworth .. .. £1/**£1.50**/£2
1907. France. Visit of President Fallieres. RP and others .. .. 50p/**£1**/£2.50
1908. Australia. Visit of American Fleet .. .. £5/**£8**/£12
1908. Bulgaria. Declaration of Independence .. £3/**£5**/£8
1908. Canada. Quebec Tercentenary .. .. £2/**£2.50**/£3
1909. USA. Hudson-Fulton Celebration .. .. £1/**£3**/£6
1910. USA. Chicago. 31st Triennial Conclave of Knights Templar.. .. .. £1/**£2**/£2.50
1911. France. Millenaire Normand, celebrated at Rouen. Poster type designs by Baron, Hamelet, Haury, Lalanne, Moise, Motet, Rolland, etc. LL scenes .. 75p/**£1.50**/£4
1911. Italy. Official issues for 50th Anniv. of Kingdom. Twenty cards in series *per card* .. .. £1/**£2**/£2.50

1911. Portugal. First Anniv. of the new Republic £1/**£1.50**/£2
1912. Bulgaria. Official card for Silver Jubilee of Ferdinand the First (father of Prince Boris) .. .. £1/**£1.50**/£2
1912. Germany. 'Postcard Week'. Flown and cancelled by Rhein & Main aerial post .. .. .. £15/**£20**/£25
Unused .. .. £5/**£6**/£8
1914. Switzerland. Official cards for the Centenary of the Reunion of Geneva with Switzerland .. £1/**£1.50**/£2
1914. Austria. Sarajevo. Arrest of Cabrinovic after assassination attempt on Archduke Ferdinand .. .. £3/**£5**/£8
Year Cards. Period 2. Unused .. .. .. 50p/**75p**/£1
Postally used with year cancellation .. .. .. £2/**£3**/£4

PERIOD 4

1924. Canada. Winnipeg. Jubilee Parade .. .. 75p/**£1**/£2
1927. Germany. Hindenburg's 80th Birthday. RP and others .. .. £5/**£8**/£12
1932. Switzerland. International Disarmament Conference, Geneva .. .. £1.50/**£2.50**/£4
1934. Liverpool, UK. Opening of Mersey Tunnel by George V. Pub. Valentine's .. .. 50p/**£1**/£1.50
Various. Germany. Series of official printed stamp issues commemorating the centenaries of the deaths of famous men and carrying a head and shoulders sketch, e.g. 1931 Baron Heinrich von Stein (Prussian Statesman), 1932 Goethe.

Price range .. .. 75p/**£1.50**/£2

PERIOD 6 ■COMM 2

1948. USA. Lincoln card with Gettysburg Address on 85th Anniv. of the Address. PU. Gettysburg 19 Nov. 1948. Limited edition. Pub. Blocher, Gettysburg .. £2/**£3**/£5
1952. Austria. Dr. Hermann picture. 50th Anniv. of his death. Limited edition of 10,000 .. ..£7/**£10**/£12
1954. France. Issues drawn by Raoul Serres for the Bayeux Philatelic Society to commemorate the 10th Anniv. of D Day. Unused .. .. £3/**£4**/£5
Postally used 5/6 June 1954 .. ..£7/**£10**/£15
1958. France. 40th Anniv. of the Armistice. Pub. Committee of 11 November Colmar. Thermographic .. .. £1/**£2**/£3
1963. Germany. Visit of Pres. Kennedy to Berlin. Unused 25p/**50p**/75p
Handstamped with special cachet .. .. .. £1/**£2**/£4
1963. USA. Homage to President John F. Kennedy. President's seal on address side. Col. RP series. Pub. Capsco. 25p/50p
1967. USSR. 50th Anniv. of the Great October Socialist Revolution. .. .. 50p/**75p**/£1
1969. USA. Inauguration of Richard M. Nixon as President. 20 January 1969 .. .. £1.50/**£2**/£2.50

PERIOD 7 ■COMM 3

1972. Norway. Official card commemorating centenary of Norwegian postcard, a reproduction of the first card .. .. £1/**£1.50**/£2

■COMM 2 Foto 'Keystone'. Germany. President Kennedy, with Herr Willi Brandt, during his visit to Berlin, 1963. Special postmark £4

■COMM 3 Pub. Isle of Man Postcard Censoring Committee. Golden Jubilee. Artist David G. Swinton. 1983 50p

---

1973. USA. Official card for the centenary of the postcard with printed stamp. First day cancellation £1/**£1.50**/£2
Unused .. .. 50p/**£1**/£1.50

1974. France. 500th Anniv. of Copernicus's Birth (1973). Issued 1974 by French Post Office to coincide with commemorative stamp **50p**

1974. Italy. Two cards (40L and 55L stamps) commemorating the centenary of the Italian postcard, with miniature reproduction of the first card on address side. Per card .. .. 75p/**£1**/£1.50

1976. USA. Bicentennial of the American Revolution .. **25p**

1979. France. The Egypt/Israel Peace Treaty of 26 March 1979. Card shows Begin, Carter and Sadat **75p**

1980. USSR. Moscow. Olympic Games. *See* SPORT.

1981. UK. Royal Wedding. *See* ROYALTY.

1982. UK. Papal Visit. *See* MODERN.

1983. UK. Golden Jubilee of Isle of Man postcard censorship.
Unused **50p**
Handstamped with special postmark, 5 July 1983 **£1.50**

COMPETITIONS/CRAZES/HOBBIES

BEAUTY COMPETITIONS

Daily Mirror International Beauty Competition (1908)
Pub. C. W. Faulkner
English Beauty Series 847 (incl. paintings by Arthur Hacker) .. .. 75p/**£1**/£1.50
Glossy photographic series .. .. 75p/**£1**/£1.50

Daily Mirror Beauty Competition for Women War Workers (1919)
Pub. *Daily Mirror* and Rotary Photographic Co. 65p/**£1**/£1.50

Daily Express & Seymour Hicks Beauty Competition
Pub. C. W. Faulkner .. .. 75p/**£1**/£1.50

■CCH 1 Pub. Anon. Artist 'F.S. (Fred Spurgin). 'The Pleasures of Cycling'. Period 2 £1.50

BICYCLING ■CCH 1

Bicycling flourished in Victorian and Edwardian times, as well as being a viable means of transport. Advanced young ladies shocked society with their bicycling bloomers; cycling clubs sprang up around the country, rallies, gymkhanas and races regularly took place.

High quality Real Photographic (R.P.) cards attract higher valuations than general photographic origin postcards.

See ADVERTISING.

Artist Drawn

Pub. Pascalis Moss & Co. (1901/1902). Cyclists of All Nations. Series of 12 col. caricatures .. .. .. £1.50/**£2.50**/£4
Pub. Tuck. Period 2. Artist. Leslie Willson. 'The Scorcher's Progress'. Set of 6 witty cycling jokes .. £1/**£1.50**/£2

Most of the well-known comic postcard artists of Period 2 designed series of postcards on cycling themes, notably Browne, F. S. and Pirkis, A. G.

Signed artists .. .. 75p/**£1**/£4
Unsigned artist drawn .. .. 50p/**75p**/£1.50

Cycling Champions
Periods 2, 3 .. .. 75p/**£1.50**/£2.50
Periods 4 to 6 .. .. 50p/**£1**/£1.50

Cycling Clubs
Photographic origin/RP Periods. 2 to 4 .. .. 75p/**£1**/£2

Cycling Gymkhanas
Photographic origin/RP Periods. Periods 2 to 4 .. 75p/**£1**/£2

Cycling Races/Rallies
Artist drawn. Period 2 souvenir cards .. .. £2/**£4**/£6
Artist drawn. Others .. .. £1/**£2**/£4
Milk Race. Periods 6, 7 .. .. 25p/**50p**/75p
Tour de France. Periods 2, 3 .. .. £2/**£4**/£6
Tour de France. Periods 4, 6 .. .. £1/**£2**/£3
Photographic. Edwardian cyclists—posed portraits .. .. 75p/**£1.50**/£3
Others .. .. 50p/**£1.50**/£2

CROSSWORD PUZZLES (Period 4, c. 1924/5)

The last of the great 'crazes' illustrated on the postcard.

'Crosswords' series. Artist Donald McGill .. 75p/**£1.50**/£3
Pub. Tuck. Oilette 3514. 'The Crossword Craze' 1924 .. .. 75p/**£1.50**/£2
Others .. .. 50p/**75p**/£1

DIABOLO (Period 2, from 1906)

The craze boomed from the invention of an aerodynamically efficient 'devil' (and there are many diabolo jokes which play on this word), by Gustave Phillipart in 1906.

Artist drawn
Browne, Tom. Pub. Davidson (Series 2627, 2631) .. .. £1.50/**£2.50**/£3.50
Christie, George Fyffe, Pub. Wm. Ritchie & Sons (W.R. & S.) .. .. 75p/**£1**/£1.50
Cross, J. Pub. Tuck .. .. 50p/**75p**/£1.50
Kinsella, E. P. Pub. Langsdorff .. .. .. 75p/**£1**/£1.50
McGill, Donald .. .. 75p/**£1**/£1.50
Wain, Louis. Pub. Tuck .. .. £4/**£11**/£14
Other artists/publishers, including Birn Bros., H. Vertigen & Co.. .. .. 50p/**£1**/£1.50

Greetings cards featuring Diabolo
Various publishers .. .. 50p/**75p**/£1.50

Photographic Diabolo cards
Various publishers .. .. 75p/**£1**/£2

LIMERICKS (Period 2, mainly 1907/8)

The craze followed the competition in London Opinion *to complete the last line of a limerick. Soon other competitions and even specialist magazines appeared.*

Comic cards
Pub. Davidson Bros. Artist Dudley Hardy. Nos. 3008/9. 'Limericks' .. .. £2/**£4**/£6
Pub. Gottschalk, Dreyfus & Davis (G.D. & D.). Artist 'KS' (c. 1906) .. .. 50p/**75p**/£1
Pub. Hildesheimer. Artist 'Kyd' (1905) .. .. £1/**£2**/£4
Pub. W. & A. K. Johnston. Series 112, 119 (1905) 50p/**75p**/£1
Knight Series. Jingle Cards (1905) .. .. 75p/**£1**/£1.50
Pub. Millar & Lang. 'The Limerick Craze' (1907) .. .. 75p/**£1**/£1.50
Pub. Shamrock & Co. The Limerick Lunatic with appliqué 'noose' .. .. 50p/**75p**/£1.50
Pub. Tuck. Limerick postcards with appliqué checked material. Nos. 9568, 9596/7 .. .. 50p/**75p**/£1.50
Pub. J. Welch & Co. (1907) .. .. .. 75p/**£1**/£1.50
Other pubs. .. .. 50p/**75p**/£1

Competition cards
Palantine Limerick Postcard .. .. .. £1/**£1.50**/£2
Valentine & Sons (1907) .. .. £1/**£1.50**/£2

Novelty cards
Artist Ralph Ruttley. Pub. Shamrock & Co. (Set of 5 views and 1 Limerick card with last line to complete.)

Per set .. .. £3/**£5**/£7.50

POSTCARD COLLECTING

The greatest hobby-cum-craze of the Golden Age of the postcard was, of course, collecting post cards! Many cards alluding to postcard collecting can be found spanning the 7 Periods.

Postcard Clubs (Period 1, Early Period 2)
Period 1. International Poste Carte Club (IPCC). Series of 12 cards designed by artists of the calibre of Jossot, etc. .. .. £50/**£100**/£200
Period 1. Other Clubs .. .. £10/**£20**/£40
Period 2. Various Clubs .. .. £3/**£5**/£15

Postcard Competitions

C. W. Faulkner (Period 2)
611 prizes from 10s. 6d. to £100 for putting in order the best 6 cards from a packet of 12.

Price range .. .. £1/**£2**/£3

St. Paul's Hospital Competition (1924)
To raise funds for a new hospital. Set of 12 sepia view cards of London.

Per set **£1**
Per set complete with detachable entry coupons **£4**

Shurey's Great Prize Competition (Period 2)
Delittle Fenwick & Co. per 6 cards .. .. 50p/**£1.25**/£2

Raphael Tuck & Sons

Postcards advertising Tucks' competitions are popular. The following competitions are known:

1. *July 1900. £100 for largest collections of Tuck postcards. Winner 20,364 cards.*
2. *1902. £2000 prizes. Winner 25,239 cards.*
3. *1 Aug. 1904–31 July 1905. £3000 for placing 300 cards in order of merit.*
4. *1909 in 2 parts, each with 1st prize £100.*
5. *1914. 'The Fourth Competition' for the largest collection of Tuck cards posted after 1 Jan. 1914.*
6. *'Father Tuck's Painting Book Competition' Children's colouring cards in the Postcard Painting Book.*

By well-known artists .. .. £1.50/**£3**/£5
Unsigned artist drawn .. .. £1/**£1.50**/£3
Advertising on reverse only .. .. 75p/**£1**/£2
Sheffield Weekly Telegraph Kodak DIY postcard competition.
Prizes in Tuck postcards) .. .. 75p/**£1.50**/£3
Other Competition .. .. 5p-**£1**/£

Postcard Exhibitions (*see* EXHIBITIONS)

Period 1
Venice 1894, Berlin 1896, Leipzig, Munich, Zürich 1898, Nice, Berlin & others 1899 .. .. £20/**£30**/£75
Period 2
Paris 1900, Paris 1904, Nuremberg 1907 .. ..£5/**£10**/£25
Others .. ..£5/**£10**/£15

Period 7
Century of British Postcards 1970.
With Exhibition Postmark .. .. £3/**£4**/£5
Unused .. .. £1/**£1.50**/£2
Others .. .. £1/**£5**/£10

Postcard 'Inventors' ■CCH 2
Besnardeau (now hotly disputed 'inventor' of the picture card) cards from 1870/71 .. .. £60/**£85**/£100
Besnardeau reprints (1903) .. .. .. £20/**£25**/£30
Dr. Hermann (instigator of the postcard)
Jubilee of the postcard (1894) .. .. .. £75/**£100**/£150
1952 Austrian official issue commemorating Hermann .. ..£8/**£10**/£12

Three Band Pricing System

Left Hand Band: The lowest price you will probably be asked to pay for this card.
Middle Band: What you will normally be asked to pay for this card: its average, reasonable price.
Right Hand Band: The highest price you will probably be asked to pay for this card.
For a full explanation of the system see page ix.

■CCH 2 Pub. Friedl, Vienna. Jubilee of Dr. Emanuel Hermann, 'Inventor of the Correspondence card'. 1894. UB £100

RINKING (Period 2)

The great roller skating craze (which reached its zenith in 1909 as far as postcard production was concerned) swept the United States, Britain and Europe. The great entrepreneur C. B. Cochran opened rinks in Olympia, throughout the UK, in Paris, Berlin, Hanover, Hamburg, Antwerp and Nice. Magazines like The World on Wheels, Roller Skating Record *and* The Rinking World *were published.*

Artist drawn cards

Browne, Tom. Pub. Davidson. Series 2623/1 .. £4/**£5**/£6
Carter, Reg. Pub. Verdier .. .. £1/**£1.50**/£2
'F.S.' .. .. 75p/**£1**/£1.50
Thackeray, Lance. Pub. Tuck. Set No. 9919 .. £2/**£3**/£5
Wiederseim, Grace .. .. £1/**£1.50**/£3
Other signed artists .. .. 75p/**£1**/£1.50

Publishers of comic 'Rinking' cards

Artist drawn. Davidson Bros., Inter-Art, local publishers, McGlennon, Millar & Lang, Wm. Ritchie & Sons, Philco, Tuck .. .. 50p/**75p**/£1.50
Photographic. Bamforth & Co. (premium for complete set) .. .. 50p/**75p**/£1

Skating Rinks

Photographic. Various publishers .. .. .. 75p/**£1**/£2

Skating Rink Managers

Reprinted from *Rinking World*, Artist T. H. Smith £1/**£2**/£3

Skating Champions

Photographic. Various publishers .. .. .. £1/**£2**/£3

CURIOUS/MISCELLANEOUS

In this section are described the odd and the unusual: human freaks, natural phenomena, quaint buildings, record breaking attempts and postcards that do not fit into any of the traditional groupings

CODES/CYPHERS

Many strange devices were used to disguise the messages on postcards to avoid their being read by postmen, servants, etc. If a postcard has its message written in code, in cyphers, in 'mirror writing', in shorthand, in Greek or Latin, or otherwise disguised, add a premium of 50p to £1 to the card, depending on the complexity of the system used.

CURIOSITIES

Animal Curiosities

Cards of photographic origin, usually by local publishers, may show animals with one leg too many or too few; animals with two heads; animals working treadmills; birds' nests in strange places, etc.

Price range .. .. 50p/**75p**/£1.50

■CUR 1 Pub. Anon. 'The Most Mysterious Man in the World'. Hand autographed—'Haddon Charles'. Period 2 75p

■CUR 2 Pub. Ernst Schmidt, Lübeck. 'Rox, the Ventriloquist, with his dogs'. Period 2 £3

Human Curiosities ■CUR 1, 2

Many of these appeared on the stage, or in sideshows at circuses (like Barnum & Bailey) or fairs, or in C. B. Cochran's 'Midget City' at Olympia. The cards carry a premium of 25% if they have been hand autographed by the subject.

Dwarfs/Midgets
Anita the living doll (26 in. high); Asra, 'der lebenden Puppe'; Baron Ernesto Magri; Baron Paucci (62 cm. high); Count Primo Magri; Madame Pauline, the Miniature Comedienne; Major and Mrs. Mite; Major Newell; General Tom Thumb; Mrs. Tom Thumb (née Lavinia Warren, Mrs. Magri by her second marriage); Troupe Lilliputienne Zeynard; Willy Pantzer and his Wonderful Midgets.

Price range .. .. £1/**£1.50**/£3

Freaks
Bearded ladies; Siamese twins; Various physical deformities.

Price range .. .. 50p/**£1**/£2

Giants
Abomah, the Tallest Lady in the World; Hassan Ali, the Egyptian Giant (8 ft. 2 in); Machnow, the Russian Giant; The Nottingham Giant Girl.

Price range .. .. 75p/**£1**/£2

Odd Characters
Bird Charmers of Hyde Park Corner/Tuileries, Paris; Cave dwellers; Others.

Price range .. .. 50p/**£1.50**/£3

Unusual Performers
Conjurers; Contortionists; Escapologists; Hypnotists; Illusionists; Mind Readers; Snake Charmers; Spiritualists and Ventriloquists.

Price range .. .. £1/**£2.50**/£5

Man-made Curiosities ■CUR 3
Mannekin Pis, Brussels: many series, comic and photographic, some in booklet form
Models in icing sugar, made from matchsticks, etc.
Odd-shaped houses, 'smallest' houses and other curious buildings
Ossuaries (e.g. cemetery of Capucin Monks)
Sand sculptures

Price range .. .. 50p/**£1**/£1.50

Natural Curiosities
Crocodile Rock, Millport, USA or other strange rock formations 25p/**50p**/75p
Double trees (e.g. beech and oak joined) .. 25p/**50p**/75p
Giant trees 25p/**50p**/75p
Grottoes/underground caverns 25p/**50p**/75p
Halley's Comet. 1910. German. Set of 6
Col. signed K. Hesse .. .. £2/**£4**/£6
Others .. .. 75p/**£1.50**/£3
Others 25p/**50p**/75p

■CUR 3 Copyright Mrs. E. Williams, Conway. 'The Smallest House in Gr. Britain'. Period 6 50p

FEATS/RECORD-BREAKERS/WAGERS

Allen, W. C.—Walking 2000 miles in 44 days—trained on Bovril (1904)
Belbin, H. W. G.—Riding his land & water cycle
The Crusader walking round the world (£500 reward)
Leach, Bobby—Going over Niagara Falls in a barrel (1911)
Rolling a barrel from Vienna to Paris (1900)
Round Europe. 6 years by Rotorship *Buckau* (1926–32)
Schilling, Geo.—Walking round the world in an airship
Walking round the world in an iron mask (£21,000 wager)
Walking from Vienna to Paris, pushing wife and child (*c.* 1900). Pub. Baumann, pram manufacturer, Vienna

Price range .. .. £1.50/**£2.50**/£4

GAMES OF CHANCE

Playing Cards

Comic postcards of card games by various artists and publishers (*see* Comic).
Pub. Stewart & Woolf. Set of 12 chromo-lithographs of playing cards. Artist J. M. Henman (1903) .. .. .. £1/**£2**/£3
Pub. Welch, J. Col. set of playing cards. Period 2 £1/**£2**/£3
USA. Series of playing card sets. Period 4 .. £1/**£1.50**/£2
Others .. .. 50p/**75p**/£1.50

Roulette and other Gambling Games

For casino buildings *see* Social History.
Croupiers/gamblers. Clear pictures photographic in origin with good detail of people .. .. £1/**£2**/£3
French. Rules of Roulette/other gambling games at Monte Carlo and other Casinos .. .. £2/**£3**/£4
Others .. .. 75p/**£1**/£3

INTERNATIONAL LANGUAGES

Braille

Price range .. .. 50p/**£1**/£2

Deaf and Dumb Sign Language
Price range .. .. 50p/**£1**/£2

Esperanto
For cards with messages written in Esperanto add 50p to £1 to value, the earlier the card the higher the premium.

Esperanto Congresses
Price range .. .. 75p/**£3**/£8

Esperantists
Bourlet .. .. £2/**£3**/£5
Cunningham .. .. £2/**£3**/£5
Zamenhof, Ludwig (1859–1917) (inventor of Esperanto) .. .. £3/**£5**/£8
Others .. .. 75p/**£1.50**/£3

Ido
Revised form of Esperanto, from the initials International Delegation (1907). For cards written in Ido add 50p to £1 to the value of the card, the earlier the card the higher the premium.

Congresses
Price range .. .. 75p/**£1.50**/£5

Ido-ists
Marquis de Beaufront, Louis (Inventor) .. .. £1/**£3**/£5
Others .. .. 75p/**£1.50**/£3

Propaganda cards
Price range .. .. £1/**£3**/£5

MASONIC (and other secret societies)

Artist Drawn
Pub. Millar & Lang. Comic col. series 'Are You a Mason?' 24 cards. Period 2 .. .. £1/**£2**/£3
Other comic series .. .. 75p/**£1**/£1.50

Photographic Origin
Masonic regalia .. .. £1/**£1.50**/£2
People in masonic regalia .. .. £1/**£2**/£3

Other Societies
Price range .. .. 50p/**£1**/£2

MISTAKES ON POSTCARDS
For wrongly printed captions, postcards printed the wrong way round or other mistakes, add 50p to £1 to the value of the card.

'WANTED' CARDS
Pub. USA. with and without stuck on photo of wanted person .. .. **P/A**

EARLY CARDS: Period 1/ Early Period 2

The characteristics of an 'Early Card' are perhaps the most difficult of all to define and to value, yet every collector of any experience can recognise an 'Early' card. The good quality board and high standard of printing which are characteristic of many early cards often makes them recognisable by feel as well as by sight. The recent growth in the popularity of postcard collecting has led to an increase in interest in Period 1 and early Period 2 cards (up to 1902). Cards produced between 1869 and 1902 fall into several main themes, e.g. Advertising, Art, Commemorative, Exhibitions, Royalty, etc. These themes have their own sections in this catalogue and valuations should be sought there. However, there are features, such as the size of the card or its quality of production, which cross the thematic lines between the categories in 'Early' cards. These features, *per se*, make a card collectable. Three of them are considered here: Chromo-litho; Court Size: Gruss Aus.

CHROMO-LITHO CARDS ■EC 1

The majority of these cards were printed on the Continent during Period 1 and early Period 2. They are readily recognised by the excellence of the colour printing (*see* 'Chromo-litho' in the Glossary), are frequently undivided backs and often have vignettes in the design. Some examples were imported by Continental entrepreneurs like Ernest Nister and may appear to have been published in London. Closer examination usually reveals that they were printed elsewhere. We list below the major printers/publishers of chromo-litho cards. Their postcards are listed and valued under the three headings that follow below:

Printers/Publishers

Bechtold, Rudolph (*Wiesbaden*); Berardi, E. (*Milan*); Champenois (*Paris*); Dietrich (*Brussels*); Franzl, L. (*Munich*); Frey & Sons (*Zürich*); Hendelsohn, G. (*Berlin*); Huardel, P. G. (P.G.H. & Co.); Juxberg, F. W. (*Frankfurt*) (F.W.J.); Köhn, Brüder (*Vienna*) (B.K.W.); Meissner & Buch (*Leipzig and London*); Menke-Huber (*Zürich*); Miesler, J. (*Frankfurt*); Moss, Henry (H.M. & Co.); Munk, M. (*Vienna*) (MM); Nister, Ernest (*London and Nuremberg*); Pascalis, Moss & Co.; Philipp & Kramer (*Vienna*); Pictorial Stationery Co. (*London*); Pinkau, Emil (*Leipzig*); Ricordi (*Milan*); Rosenblatt (*Frankfurt*); Roth, Ludwig (*Berlin*); Schmidt, Staub & Co. (*Nuremberg*); Stengel (*Dresden*); Tuck, Raphael & Sons; Winkler & Schorn (*Nuremberg*); Zieher, Ottmar (*Munich*)

General Designs/Views

Period 1	£2/**£3**/£5
Others	£1/**£1.50**/£2

As it is difficult to date a card precisely, a period system has been used in this catalogue. For a full explanation of the system see page viii.

EC 1 Pub. Tuck 'Art' Postcard No. 1687. Chromographed in Saxony. UB. Early period 2 £3

COURT CARDS

The Court Size postcard measures approx. 115 × 89 mm in contrast to the 122 × 75 mm of the normal Periods 1 to 3 cards. Full UPU size in Periods 1 to 3 was 140 × 89 mm. Court cards are indigenous to Britain (though similar size Continental cards exist) and were used from *c.* 1895 until early in Period 2. Court size views of Edinburgh published by George Stewart in 1894 have sometimes been proposed as the first British produced picture postcards, although privately produced court cards were not recognised by the Post Office until the issue of the first official court card (21 January 1895).

Publishers of British Court Cards include:
Beechings (whose views of London and Manchester now command a considerable premium) Blum & Degen; Faulkner; Frith; Photochrom; Pictorial Stationery Co.; Sandle Bros.; Stewart, Geo.; Valentines.

Gruss Aus types

Chromo-litho	£8/**£10**/£12
Col. (not chromo-litho)	£6/**£8**/£10
B & w/sepia	£3/**£5**/£8

Thematic (Advertising, Commemorative, Exhibitions, Royalty, etc.) see the appropriate subject sections in this catalogue. The older the card the higher the value.

General views/vignettes

Chromo-litho	£5/**£12**/£20
Col. (not chromo-litho)	£3/**£5**/£8
B & w/sepia	£1.50/**£3**/£5

GRUSS AUS TYPE ■EC2

Literally 'Greetings from . . .'. A type of card popularised in Germany in the 1880s, showing small, one colour line drawings/vignettes—pictures of a beauty spot or a town and its inhabitants—often in an elaborate border of flowers, scrolls, etc. By the mid-1890s these were also being produced in colour, often chromo-litho. Variations on the German words of greeting (according to the language of the country of origin) are: 'Greetings from . . .' (Britain & Colonies incl. India), *Gruss aus* . . . or *Gruss vom* . . . (Germany and Colonies), *Memorias de* . . . (Spain and Spanish-speaking countries), *Ricordi di* . . . and *Saluti di* . . . (Italy), *Souvenir de* . . . (Belgium, France and Colonies, Switzerland). The type was also produced in Russia! Generally speaking the earlier the card and the more obscure the country of origin (e.g. Heligoland) the more valuable it will be. Ultimately, however, the value of a *Gruss Aus* type card will be determined by its sheer appeal and beauty—and beauty is in the eye of the beholder.

Court Size—*see above*

Period 1 pre-1890

Chromo-litho	£10/**£15**/£25
Col. (not chromo-litho)	£8/**£12**/£18
B & w/sepia	£5/**£8**/£12
Line drawn, letterpress or intaglio black views on buff official cards. Picture occupies a third or less of the card	£13/**£15**/£25

Period 1 post-1890

Chromo-litho	£3/**£6**/£18
Col. (not chromo-litho)	£2/**£5**/£10
B & w-sepia	£1.50/**£3**/£5

Early Period 2

Chromo-litho	£2/**£3**/£6
Col. (not chromo-litho)	£1.50/**£2**/£4
B & w/sepia	£1/**£1.50**/£2

■EC 2 Pub. 'H.C.D.' 'Gruss aus der Bierstadt' (Beertown) Dortmund. Chromolitho. UB. PU 1897 £10

ENTERTAINMENT

CINEMA

CINEMA ADVERTISING

Periods 2 to 4 .. .. £1/**£2**/£3
Periods 5 to 7 .. .. 50p/**£1**/£2
Italian artist Nanni. Superb *Art Deco* poster portraits of stars like Vittorio di Sica, Elsa Merlini .. .. £9/**£12**/£15

CINEMAS/BIOSCOPES (Buildings)

Periods 3 to 5. Sharp photographs .. .. .. £3/**£6**/£10

FILM STARS ■E 1–3

*Many durable stars' careers spanned two or three postcard periods and these are listed in brackets after their name. Those stars whose postcards command a premium (of up to £2 over their Period price) are marked *. Plain backed cards (e.g. 'Red Letter') are not postcards, and are not listed.*

Arbuckle, 'Fatty' (4)
Arthur, Jean (4–6)
Astaire, Fred (4–7)*
Astor, Mary (4–6)
Ayres, Lew (4–7)
Bankhead, Tallulah (4)
Banky, Vilma (4)
Bardot, Brigitte (6, 7)
Bartholomew, Freddie (4–6)
Barrymore, Ethel (4–6)
Barrymore, John (4, 5)
Barrymore, Lionel (4, 5)
Beery, Wallace (4)
Bergman, Ingrid (5–7)
Blondell, Joan (4–6)
Bogarde, Dirk (6, 7)
Bogart, Humphrey (4–6)*
Boles, John (4, 5)
Bow, Clara (4) (*the 'It' girl*)
Boyer, Charles (4–6)
Brando, Marlon (6, 7)
Brynner, Yul (6, 7)
Buchanan, Jack (4, 6)
Cagney, James (4–7)*
Cantor, Eddie (4, 5)
Chaney, Lon Sr. (3, 4)
Chaney, Lon Jr. (4–6)
Chaplin, Charlie (3–6)*
  Artists Donald McGill, Louis Wain/others
  Essanay Film Mfg. Co.
  Imperial Playhouse Series
  Rotary
  Others
Chevalier, Maurice (4–6)
Colbert, Claudette (4–6)
Colman, Ronald (4–6)
Cooper, Gary (4–6)
Coogan, Jackie (4, 6, 7)
Courtneidge, Cecily (4, 5)
Crabbe, Buster (4, 5)
Crain, Jeanne (5–7)
Crawford, Joan (4–7)
Crosby, Bing (4–6)
Curtis, Tony (6, 7)
Davis, Bette (4–7)*
Day, Doris (6)
Dean, James (6)*
Dietrich, Marlene (4–7)*
Donat, Robert (4–6)
Dunne, Irene (4–6)
Durbin, Deanna (4–6)
Eddy, Nelson (4, 5)
Fairbanks, Douglas Sr. (3, 4)
Fairbanks, Douglas Jr. (4–6)
Fields, Gracie (4, 5)*
Fields, W. C. (4, 5)*
Flynn, Errol (4–6)*
Fonda, Henry (4–7)
Fontaine, Joan (4–6)
Gable, Clark (4–6)
Garbo, Greta (4, 5)*

Gardner, Ava (5–7)
Garland, Judy (4–6)*
Gilbert, John (3, 4)
Gish, Dorothy (2–6)
Gish, Lillian (3–7)
Grable, Betty (5, 6)
Grainger, Stewart (5–7)
Grant, Cary (4–6)
Harlow, Jean (4)*
de Haviland, Olivia (4–6)
Hayward, Susan (5, 6)
Henie, Sonja (4–6) (*skating star*)
Hepburn, Audrey (6, 7)
Hepburn, Katherine (4–7)
Holliday, Judy (6)
Hope, Bob (4–6)
Hulbert, Jack (4, 5)
Jones, Jennifer (5–7)
Karloff, Boris (4–6)*
Kaye, Danny (5, 6)
Keaton, Buster (4, 6)*
Kelly, Gene (5–7)
Kelly, Grace (6)
Lamarr, Hedy (4–6)
Lamour, Dorothy (4–6)
Lockwood, Margaret (4–7)
Laurel & Hardy (4, 5)*
Lawford, Peter (6)
Leigh, Vivien (4–6)*
Lloyd, Harold (4)*
Lockwood, Margaret (4–6)
Lombard, Carole (4, 5)*
Loy, Myrna (4–6)
Marx Bros. (4–6)*
MacDonald, Jeanette (4, 5)
March, Fredric (4–6)
Marsh, Mae (2–4)
Mason, James (4–7)
Matthews, Jessie (4, 5)*
Miranda, Carmen (5, 6)
Mitchum, Robert (5–7)
Mix, Tom (2–4)*
Monroe, Marilyn (6)*
Nazimova (4, 5)
Neagle, Anna (4–6)
Negri, Pola (3–6)*
Niven, David (4–7)
Novarro, Ramon (4, 6)*
Oberon, Merle (4–7)
Olivier, Laurence (4–7)*
O'Sullivan, Maureen (4–6)
Pavlova (3) (*see* Theatre)*
Pickford, Mary (3, 4)*
Pilbeam, Nova (4)
Powell, Dick (4–6)
Power, Tyrone (4–6)
Presley, Elvis (6, 7)
Price, Vincent (4–7)
Raft, George (4–6)*
Reagan, Ronald (5, 6)*
Rin-Tin-Tin (4) (*dog star*)*
del Rio, Dolores (4–6)
Robinson, Edward G. (4–6)
Rogers, Ginger (4–6)*
Russell, Jane (5, 6)
Sanders, George (4–6)
Shearer, Norma (4, 5)
Sinatra, Frank (5–7)
Stanwyck, Barbara (4–6)
von Stroheim, Eric (3–6)*
Swanson, Gloria (3, 4, 6, 7)*
Talmadge, Norma (4)*
Taylor, Elizabeth (5, 6, 7)
Taylor, Robert (4, 5, 6)
Temple, Shirley (4, 5, 6)*
Tracey, Spencer (4, 5, 6)
Valentino, Rudolph (3, 4)*
Wayne, John (3, 4)*
Weismuller, Johnny (4, 5)*
Welles, Orson (5, 6)
West, Mae (4, 5, 7)*
White, Pearl (3, 4)*
Wilding, Michael (5, 6)
Wong, Anna May, (5, 6)*
Young, Loretta (5, 6)

B & w/sepia/coloured ,

Periods 2, 3	75p/**£1**/£1.50
Periods 4, 5	£1/**£1.50**/£2
Periods 6, 7	25p/**50p**/£1

Hand autographed cards will always attract a premium.

Animated Film Characters (Periods 4 to 6)

Disney: scenes/characters

Pub. Valentine Period 4	£2.50/**£4**/£7
Published with Fr or Ger text	£2/**£3.50**/£6
Others	£1.50/**£2**/£4
Felix the Cat	£1/**£1.50**/£3
Others	75p/**£1**/£2

■E 1 Pub. Ross. Greta Carbo, courtesy of Metro Goldwyn Mayer. Seal of Davros cigarettes. Period 5 £3

■E 2 Pub. Anon. Fr. Ramon Novarro, with May McAvoy in *Ben-Hur*. Advert for the production at the Cinema Madeleine, Paris, on reverse PU 1927 £2

FILM STILLS (with postcard backs)
Value according to Period and stars .. .. .. £2/**£3**/£4

CIRCUS

The modern circus has its origins in England in the late 18th-century when Philip Astley popularised trick riding. Showmen moved in from the declining fairs with their varying acts. Soon circuses started in America and by the turn of the century had spread throughout Europe and the USA. Permanent buildings housed some European circuses and a theatrical element crept in. By 1900 the circus was thriving throughout the world. Showmen like P. T. Barnum and James A. Bailey in the USA, and C. B. Cochran in Britain put the circus on a more business-like basis. During Periods 1 and 2 the popularity of the circus gave rise to some of the most fascinating and beautiful of postcards. The delicate chromo-litho drawings, the colourful poster type adverts and the intriguing photographs are all to be found in this category.

ACTS
These often have unusual and emotive names, e.g. Madame Alaska and her Performing Seals; Capt. Alphonzo, the Intrepid Lion-Tamer; The Sarrasani; Waldemeer, the Modern Hercules; Zarmah the Wild Animal Trainer.

Period 1/Early Period 2.
Chromo-litho drawings .. .. £2/**£4**/£7.50
Photographs .. .. £2/**£4**/£7.50
Poster type ads. .. .. £2/**£4**/£7.50
Periods 2 to 4 .. .. £1/**£2.50**/£5
Periods 5 to 7 .. .. 75p/**£1**/£1.50

NAMED CIRCUSES

Barnum & Bailey
Illustrations by Courmont and Franzl .. £2/**£3.50**/£5
Poster type ads. Periods 2, 3 .. .. .. £10/**£15**/£20
Various photographic cards of acts .. .. .. £1/**£2**/£4
Wolfgang Holzmour, Lord of the Lions. Period 7 .. .. 50p/**75p**/£1
Buffalo Bill's Wild West Show
Poster type ads .. .. £10/**£15**/£20
Various photographic cards of acts .. .. .. £2/**£4**/£6
Busch Circus
Colourful poster type ads. Period 2 .. .. .. £5/**£7**/£10
Circus Althoff
Early Period 2. 'Gruss Aus' .. .. .. £2/**£3.50**/£5
Circus Cesar Sideli
Colourful poster type ads. Period 2 .. .. .. £3/**£5**/£8
Cirkus Varieté, Copenhagen. Period 2. Acts, etc. £2/**£3**/£5
Hagenbeck's Circus
Various animal and other acts .. .. £1.50/**£2**/£2.50
Ringling Bros. Period 2. Poster ads. .. .. .. £4/**£8**/£10
Royal Netherlands Circus
Early Period 2 vignettes .. .. £2/**£3**/£5
Zirkus Krone, Zirkus Lorch, Zirkus Semsrott. Period 2 .. .. £1.50/**£3**/£6

SITES/TENTS

Artists impressions .. .. £1/**£2**/£3
Photographs .. .. £2.50/**£4.50**/£6

THEATRE

This section describes actors, actresses, advertising, theatre buildings and stills from theatrical productions. It also includes cards dealing with 'fringe theatre' acts like Punch and Judy, etc. Freaks, and other strange phenomena who entertained the public in circus or fair side shows and theatres are described under CURIOUS.

ACTORS AND ACTRESSES

Literally hundreds of thousands of portrait postcards were published. Listed below are the artists most reproduced on the postcard. It is virtually impossible to separate the 'straight' actors/actresses from the musical comedy/music hall/pantomime artistes, as many popular stars performed in several types of theatre (e.g. pantomime during the winter, music hall during the spring and summer; dramatic artistes sometimes played roles that required them to sing or dance, etc.).

Where an artist was predominantly famous in a particular field or fields, the initials D (for Dramatic roles); MC (Musical Comedy); HM (Music Hall) and P (Pantomime) will appear after their name.

Perhaps because they were more photogenic, perhaps because they needed the publicity more, many minor stars (sometimes virtually chorus girls) appeared on a large number of postcards, whereas the great stars often prove more elusive to find on the postcard. This contributes to the fact that their postcard portraits command a premium and they are featured in a separate list.

Female

Allan, Maud (D/MH)
Arundel, Sybil (MC/P)
Ash, Maie (MC)
Ashwell, Lena (D)
Augarde, Adrienne (MC)
Baird, Dorothea (D)
Bateman, Jessie (D)
Braithwaite, Lilian (D)
Brayton, Lily (D)
Boucicault, Nina (D)
Burke, Billie (MC)
Campbell, Mrs. Patrick (D)
Chase, Pauline (MC)
Clifford, Camille (MC)
Compton, Fay
Cooper, Gladys (D/MC)
Courtneidge, Cecily (MC)
Crichton, Madge (MC)
Dainton, Marie (MC)
Dare Sisters (Phyllis and Zena) (MC/P)
Deslys, Gaby (MC)
Elliott, Gertrude (d)
Elsie, Lily (MC)
Fealy, Maude (D)
George, Marie (MC/P)
Gordon, Kitty (MC)
Green, Mabel (MC)
Greene, Evie (MC)
Hare, Winifred (P)
Jay, Isabel (MC)
King, Hettie (MH)
Langtry, Mrs. (D)
Leighton, Queenie (MC/P)
Lessing, Madge (MC)
Love, Mabel (MC)
Loftus, Cissy (D/MH)
May, Edna (MC)
May, Maggie (MC)
Millar, Gertie (MC)
Millard, Evelyn (D)
Monkman, Phyllis (MC)
Moore, Carrie (MC/P)
Moore, Eva (D)
Nielson, Julia (D)
Potter, Mrs. Brown- (D)
Price, Nancy (D)
Ray, Gabrielle (MC)
Ray, Ruby (MC)
Reeve, Ada (MH/P)
Rowlands, Gaynor (MC)
Sevening, Nina (MC)
Studholme, Marie (MC)
Tempest, Marie (D/MC)
Terriss, Ellaline (MC)
Terry, Ellen (D)
Tilly, Vesta (MC/P)
Tree, Viola (D)
Vanbrugh, Dame Irene (D)
Vanbrugh, Violet
Vincent, Madge (MC)
Waller, Mrs. Lewis (D)
Ward, Dorothy (P)

Male

Ainsley, Sir Henry (D)
Alexander, Sir George (D)
Asche, Oscar (D)
Benson, Sir F. R. (D)
Binfield, John (MC)
Bourchier, Arthur (MC)
Bradfield, Louis (MC)
Coffin, Hayden (MC)
Coyne, Joseph (MC)
Farkoa, Maurice (MC)
Forbes-Robertson, Sir Johnston (D)
Gill, Basil (D)
Graves, George (P) (MC)
Hicks, Sir Seymour (D/MC)
Huntley, G. P. (MC)
Irving, H. B. (D)
Lang, Matheson (D)
Martin-Harvey, Sir John (D)
Maurier, Sir Gerald du (MC/D)

Penley, W. S. (MC)
Terry, Fred (D)
Tree, Sir Herbert Beerbohm (D)
Waller, Lewis (D)
Welch, James (D)
Wallis Bertram (MC)
Welchman, Harry (MC)
Wright, Huntley (MC)

Price range .. .. 50p/**75p**/£1.50

The Great Stars ■N 3

Performers whose postcards command a premium for the eminence of the subject and/or the rarity of examples. As well as the straight portraits, many cards depicted the stars in their homes, with their children, parents, pets and spouses.

Baker, Josephine (US col.) (Fr cabaret artist)
Bernhardt, Sarah (D)
Bruant, Aristide (Fr cabaret)
Chevalier, Albert (MH)
Chevalier, Maurice (Fr MH)
'Casque d'Or' (Fr MH clairvoyant)
Chirgwin ('the White-Eyed Kaffir') (MH)
Colette (Fr author with stage act) (*see* LITERARY)
Coward, Noel (D. Cabaret)
Duse, Eleonora (Fr D)
Elliott, G. H. ('The Chocolate-Coloured Coon') (MH)
Ford, Florrie (MH)
Fragson, Harry (P)
Gillette, William (D)
Guilbert, Yvette (MH)
Guitry, Sacha (Fr D)
Irving, Sir Henry (D) (*see* COMMEMORATIVE)
Lauder, Harry (MH)
Leno, Dan (P)
Lloyd, Marie (MH)
Mérode, Cléo de (Fr mistress of Belg King)
Miller, Max (MH)
Mistinguett (Fr MH)
Régane (Fr D)
Robey, Sir George (MH)
Stratton, Eugene (MH)
Tate, Harry (MH)
Tich, Little (MH)
Vernon, Harriet (MH)

Price range .. .. £3/**£6**/£12

The higher band applies to the rare early French cabaret stars, to autographed cards, and to cards of the stars in elusive roles.

Add a premium for hand autographed, Art Nouveau *borders, Large Letters, photomontage, etc., and early* UB*'s.*

ADVERTISING ■A 24

Poster Types

See ARTISTS for details of theatrical work by Tom Browne (the 'Arcadians'), Raphael Kirchner (Geisha, Mikado, San Toy).

Pub. David Allen & Sons Ltd., Belfast & Harrow. *The largest publishers of theatre posters who reproduced many of their full size posters as postcards from about 1903.*
See COLLECTIONS.

Price range .. .. £4/**£8**/£20

Pub. Haycock-Caale Co. Camberley. *Productions include* Mr. Wu; *artists include Bert Thomas.*
Price range .. .. £2/**£4**/£8

Pub. John Waddington. Leeds & London. *A company which produced some fine poster adverts during Periods 2 to 4. Play titles include*:
'Extra Special'; 'Flying Colours' (Artist Bairnsfather); 'Joy Bells'.
Price range .. .. £5/**£15**/£30+

Other Publishers.
Price range .. .. £3/**£8**/£15

Advertising on Reverse/Play Stills

Pub. David Allen
Reproductions for *Answers* magazine .. .. .. £1/**£2**/£4
Photographic scenes from plays (e.g. Bad Girl of the Family, Beggar Girl's Wedding, Girl Who Took the Wrong Turning)
.. .. 75p/**£2**/£4

Pub. James Henderson & Sons
Period 2 Toy Model Series of Pantomimes with 1 card to cut out as theatre: Aladdin, Cinderella, Harlequinade, Red Riding Hood, Robinson Crusoe. Per set .. ..£6/**£10**/£15

Photographer Foulsham & Banfield. Pub. Rotary. Dorothea Baird & H. B. Irving in 'The Bells' and other plays in The Assembly Rooms, Malvern. Period 2 .. .. 50p/**75p**/£1.50

Pub. Rotary: Real Photographic
1903 onwards. Several sets of contemporary productions like Beauty of Bath, Kitty Grey, Mother Goose, Three Little Maids.
1905. Beerbohm Tree's Much Ado About Nothing, Lewis Waller's Henry V.
1907. Antony & Cleopatra, Romeo and Juliet.
Price range .. .. 75p/**£1**/£2

Pub. Tuck
Large number in 'Play Pictorial' series .. .. 75p/**£1**/£2
Others .. .. 50p/**75p**/£1.50

Pub. Victoria & Albert Museum
Period 6 series to commemorate Farewell Performance at the Windmill Theatre 25p/**50p**/75p

Pub. Wrench
Several productions, incl. Country Mouse, Princess of Kensington, by photographer Bassano .. £1/**£1.25**/£2.25

■E 3 Pub. Ross. Photographer Jacobi, Berlin. Anna May Wong. Period 4 £3

■E 4 Pub. Faulkner. Artist Thomas Maybank. 'The Swan'. No. 1345. PU 1914 £2

DANCERS ■E 4

Artist Drawn
Price range .. .. 75p/**£2.50**/£12

Ballet—Real Photographic
Dolin, Anton
Genée, Dame Adeline
Karsavina, Tamara
Markova, Alicia
Massine
Nijinski
Pavlova
Price range .. .. £2.50/**£5**/£10

Other Types of Dancer
Duncan, Isadora
Fuller, Loi
Graham, Martha
Goulue, La
Hari, Mata (Mrs. McLeod)
Price range .. .. £3.50/**£8**/£15

Hand autographed cards will always attract a premium.

PUBLISHERS
Productions vary from matt photographic to highly glossy, ornate borders and frames, photomontages, etc.
Pub. Aristophot; Davidson Bros.; Dennis; Faulkner; Hartmann; Lillywhite; Knight Bros.; Philco; Rapid Photo; Rotary; Tuck; Valentine; Wrench.
Price range .. .. 25p/**50p**/£1.50

Pub. Rotary. Real photo stamp postcards with adhesive backs .. .. £1/**£1.50**/£3
Pub. Silberer & Bros. Leading artists of the American stage .. .. 50p/**75p**/£1.50

THEATRE BUILDINGS

Good close ups of photographic origin of opera houses, theatres on piers and in towns. Publishers include: Excelsior Fine Art Co., Knight Bros., Local Publishers, Rotary, Valentine.
Exteriors .. .. £1/**£3**/£5
Interiors .. .. £1/**£1.50**/£2

WIRELESS

Artist-Drawn Cards With Wireless Interest
Periods 2 to 7; Value according to artist.
Price range .. .. 50p/**£2**/£6

Broadcasters: Groups & Portraits

Periods 2, 3, 4
Often showing groups of musicians from the days of early broadcasting with the station number ('2LO', etc.), some showing good detail of microphones, equipment, etc.
Price range .. .. £1/**£2**/£4

Period 5
Stars from the popular war-time shows, like Arthur Askey, Tommy Handley, etc.
Price range .. .. £1/**£1.50**/£2

Comic Wireless Cards

Periods 2 to 4
Various artists, value according to artist and period .. .. 50p/**75p**/£1.50

Period 5
Incl. 'ITMA' jokes by Bert Thomas (*see* MILITARY) and others .. .. £1/**£1.50**/£2

Other Wireless Subjects
Price range .. .. 75p/**£1**/£1.50

Three Band Pricing System

Left Hand Band: The lowest price you will probably be asked to pay for this card.
Middle Band: What you will normally be asked to pay for this card: its average, reasonable price.
Right Hand Band: The highest price you will probably be asked to pay for this card.
For a full explanation of the system see page ix.

EXHIBITIONS/EXPOSITIONS/ TRADE FESTIVALS/ WORLD FAIRS

The first of the great International Exhibitions was held at the Crystal Palace in Hyde Park in 1851. At the 1882 Nuremberg Exhibition an official commemorative card bearing a photo-litho vignette view was issued—produced by the printer Zrenner who afterwards claimed that it was the first true 'picture' postcard. Whether it was or not, it was at the Paris Exhibition in 1889 that the privately produced picture post-card made the enormous public impact that began the collecting frenzy. After that date every exhibition (or exposition) had its official and privately produced cards. This is a popular collecting theme, particularly for Period 1 and early Period 2 events when the cards produced were often well designed and printed by chromo-lithography. Generally speaking, the higher values relate to especially designed artist drawn cards. Cards bearing Exhibition postmarks will command a premium.

Nuremberg (1882) .. .. £25/**£35**/£40
Turin (1884) .. .. £25/**£30**/£40
Paris (1889) .. .. £15/**£20**/£30
London (1890). Penny Postage Jubilee .. .. £3/**£4**/£5
London (1891). Royal Naval. Eddystone Lighthouse .. .. £30/**£60**/£80
Vienna (1892). International Music. Vignette. Artist Kronstein. PS back .. .. £5/**£9**/£11

Chicago (1893). *The first commercially produced picture post-cards in America were made by Charles W. Goldsmith for the World's Columbian Exposition in Chicago. They are superb chromo-litho prints on an oversize official card. The first set comprised 10 cards all of which are numbered. In a second printing two of the cards, Nos. 6 and 7, had totally new views. These are shown in brackets below.*

1. Government Building .. .. £10/**£12**/£15
2. Administration Building .. .. £8/**£10**/£12
3. Manufacturers & Liberal Arts .. .. .. £8/**£10**/£12
4. The Agricultural Building .. .. £8/**£10**/£12
5. The Electrical Building .. .. .. £8/**£10**/£12
6. Horticultural Building .. .. .. £10/**£12**/£14
   (Fine Art Building). .. .. £6/**£8**/£10
7. Mines Building .. .. £10/**£12**/£14
   (Machinery Building) .. .. £6/**£8**/£10
8. The Fisheries Building .. .. £8/**£10**/£12
9. The Womans Building .. .. £8/**£10**/£12
10. Battle Ship Illinois .. .. £8/**£10**/£12

London (1893). Gardening & Forestry. Eddystone Lighthouse .. .. £50/**£70**/£100
Milan (1894). Philatelic .. .. £6/**£8**/£10
Venice (1894). Postcard Exhibition .. .. .. £15/**£25**/£50
Berlin (1896) .. .. £6/**£8**/£10
Budapest (1896) .. .. £6/**£8**/£10

Nuremberg (1896). Chromo-litho .. .. .. £7/**£8**/£9
Ditto. Photo-origin .. .. £8/**£9**/£10
Brussels (1897) ■EX 1 .. .. £5/**£7**/£10

■EX 1 Pub. Anon. Brussels Universal Exhibition, 1897 £7

Central American (1897) .. .. £5/**£7**/£10
Dresden (1897). Artist drawn. Col. litho .. .. £6/**£9**/£12
Hamburg (1897) .. .. £6/**£8**/£10
Leipzig (1897) .. .. £3/**£4**/£5
London (1897). Victorian Era Exhibition, Earls Court .. .. £35/**£50**/£60
Nuremberg (1897) .. .. £3/**£4**/£5
Toronto (1897). Victorian Era Exposition .. £10/**£25**/£40
Bergen (1898). Artist Carl Dotzler .. .. £16/**£19**/£21
Vienna (1898). Jubilee .. .. £3/**£4**/£5
Ghent (1899) .. .. £5/**£7**/£9
Nice (1899). Exposition de Cartes Postales .. .. £7/**£10**/£12
Period 1. General .. .. £3/**£6**/£10
Paris (1900). Artist Jack Abeille .. .. £10/**£15**/£20
Ditto. Postcard entrance pass .. .. £6/**£8**/£10
Ditto. Meteor transparancies .. .. £8/**£10**/£12
Salzburg (1900). Fishing .. .. £2/**£4**/£5
Berlin (1901). Official cards pub. by Klimoff and Co. At least 3 series of 6 .. .. £2/**£3**/£5
Buffalo NY (1901). Pan American. Over 12 pubs. including Livingston & Strauss .. .. £1/**£4**/£6
Dresden (1901) .. .. £2/**£3**/£5
Glasgow (1901)
Artist Cassiers, pub. Dietrich .. .. £3/**£4**/£5
Other publishers .. .. £1/**£2**/£2.50
Cork (1902) .. .. £1/**£2**/£3
Wolverhampton (1902) .. .. £1/**£2**/£2.50
Bradford (1904) .. .. £1/**£2**/£2.50
St. Louis (1904). Louisiana Purchase World's Fair.
Artist H. Wunderlich .. .. £1/**£3**/£5
Chromo-litho vignettes .. .. 75p/**£1**/£1.50
Hold to Light .. .. £3/**£5**/£6
Monochrome views **50p**
Photo-origin views 25p/**50p**/75p
Silver finish views .. .. 25p/**50p**/£1
Others .. .. 25p/**50p**/£1
Liège (1905) .. .. £1/**£2**/£5

Milan (1906). Gilded cards .. .. £1.50/**£3**/£5
Others .. .. 50p/**75p**/£1.50
Nuremberg (1906) .. .. £1/**£2**/£3
Dublin (1907). Irish International.
General .. .. £1/**£1.50**/£2
Woven silk. Pub. Grant, W. H. .. .. £12/**£15**/£20
Jamestown (1907). 300th Anniv. of first English settlement in America .. .. £2.50/**£5**/£8
Prague (1908). Radiotelegraphic. R. P. cards £1.50/**£3**/£4
White City (1908). Franco-British.
Comic designs by named artists like Crombie, Sarg .. .. 50p/**£1**/£1.50
Designs by artist A. K. Macdonald .. .. ..£5/**£10**/£15
Famous people at the Exhibition .. .. 50p/**75p**/£2
Flip Flop .. .. 50p/**75p**/£1
General views **50p**
Hagenback's Circus .. .. 75p/**£1**/£1.25
Mucha advertisement for Job Cigarettes with Exhibition overprint .. .. £25/**£50**/£75
Ornamental/Patriotic coloured borders .. 75p/**£1**/£1.50
Oversize views .. .. 50p/**75p**/£1
Trade stands .. .. £1/**£1.50**/£2
Unusual designs .. .. £1/**£3**/£8
Frankfurt (1909). Poster type. Artist Correggio .. £5/**£7**/£8
Argentine (1910). Republic Centennial. Poster type £3/**£5**/£7
Vienna (1910). Hunting. Poster type. Artists Kalmsteiner, Lenhard, Puchinger .. .. £2/**£4**/£6
White City (1910). Japan-British. *General categories and valuations as for Franco-British above.*
Artist Fred Spurgin. Pub. Paternoster .. 75p/**£1.50**/£2
Artist Mortimer Menpes. Pub. Tuck .. 75p/**£1.50**/£2
Crystal Palace (1911). Festival of Empire. Rotary Photo Series No. 6799. Over 30 cards in series .. .. 50p/**75p**/£1
Turin (1911). International. Poster type. Artist A. de Karolis .. .. £1.50/**£2**/£3
Chelsea (1912). Royal International Horticultural. Poster type .. .. £4/**£6**/£8
Breslau (1913). Artist drawn .. .. £4/**£5**/£7
Leipzig (1913). International Architecture.
Art Deco poster types .. .. £6/**£9**/£11
Other artist drawn .. .. £1.50/**£2**/£3
Leipzig (1914). Artist drawn .. .. .. £2.50/**£3**/£4

EX 2 Pub. J. P. Bamber, Blackpool. Loos Trenches Exhibition. RP. 1916 £2

San Diego (1915). Panama-Californian. At least 14 different pubs. identified

Pub. Detroit Pub. Co. .. .. 75p/**£1**/£1.50

Pub. Fred Harvey .. .. £1/**£1.25**/£2

Others .. .. 25p/**50p**/£1

San Francisco (1915). Panama-Pacific International. Over 30 different pubs. identified.

Pub. H. S. Crocker. Pre-Exhibition poster .. £2/**£5**/£8

Others .. .. £2/**£5**/£10

Blackpool (1916). Loos Trenches. Recreation of battlefield at Loos. Two different pubs. identified ■EX 2 £1/**£1.75**/£2

Wembley (1924/25). British Empire.

Exhibitors' cards by Tuck included Anglo-Persian Oil Co., Bryant & May, Canadian National Railways, Canadian Pacific Railway, the Catholic Oratory, Idris, Imperial Airways, North British Rubber Co., Schweppes, Sharpe's Toffee and South African Wine .. .. 50p/**£1**/£1.50

General views/art studies, e.g. Artist Ernest Coffin .. .. 25p/**50p**/£1

Named artists e.g. Harry Payne .. .. .. £1/**£3**/£7

Tuck Oilettes .. .. £1/**£2**/£3

Overprints or sepia views for product advertising, incl. Anglo-Persian Oil Co., Eno's Fruit Salts, Express Dairy, Mersey Docks and Pears Soap .. .. 50p/**75p**/£2

'Super Circus' poster ads, pub. Waterlow £18/**£20**/£26

Paris (1925). Decorative Arts. Five different pubs. identified 25p/**50p**/75p

Philadelphia (1926). 150th Anniv. of the founding of the USA. 25p/**50p**/75p

Strasbourg (1927). International Philatelic. Poster type an official, pre-stamped card .. .. £3/**£5**/£6

Newcastle-on-Tyne (1929). North East Coast .. 50p/**£1**/£3

Antwerp (1930). International 25p/50p

Liege (1930). International .. .. .. £1/**£1.50**/£3

Milan (1930). Poster type. Fiat. Artist Mizoli £1/**£2**/£2.50

Vienna (1930). Philatelic. Artist drawn .. £1.50/**£3**/£5

Paris (1931). International Colonial .. .. 25p/**50p**/£1

Chicago (1933). World's Fair .. .. .. 50p/**£1**/£1.25

London (1934). Ideal Home. Photo cards of Heath Robinson exhibits .. .. £1.50/**£2**/£3

Breslau (1935). Col. poster type .. .. £9/**£10**/£12

Dresden (1936). Olympic Year Stamp Show .. £7/**£9**/£10

Paris (1937). International Arts & Crafts .. 25p/**50p**/75p

Glasgow (1938). Empire. Pubs. Valentine's and at least 3 others .. .. 25p/**75p**/£1

Wellington (1939). New Zealand Centennial. Five different pubs. identified .. .. 50p/**£1**/£1.50

San Francisco (1939). Golden Gate. At least seven pubs. identified .. .. –/**25p**/50p

New York (1939). World's Fair 25p/**50p**/75p

New York (1947). Postal Centennial. 'Souvenir Postal Card', Pub. Lee C. Cray Printed stamp. Illus. both sides .. .. £1/**£1.50**/£3

London (1951). Festival of Britain. Pubs. include Salmon, Tuck, Jarrolds & Valentine's. Most cards are photo type ■EX 3 .. .. 25p/**50p**/75p

New York (1964). World's Fair. Most cards pub. by Dexter Color **50p**

Montreal (1967). Expo '67. Various, incl. col. photos, repro. of Exhibition stamp 25p/**50p**/75p

New Orleans (1984). World's Fair. Range of artist drawn/photographic cards. ■EX 4 .. .. **25p**

■EX 3 Pub. Valentine's Festival of Britain. RP. 1951 75p

■EX 4 Pub. Mike Roberts, California. Louisiana World Exposition, New Orleans, 1984 25p

EXPEDITIONS/EXPLORATION

The period covered by the 'Golden Age' of the picture postcard, 1869–1914, was one of intense activity in the field of exploration and adventure. Happily, the course of many of these exciting expeditions was charted on the postcard—from Nansen's 1893 Arctic expedition by sea, to Byrd's historic flight over the North Pole in 1926 and Andrée's exploits in the same area in a hot air balloon, ending with his tragic death in 1930. Other historic characters, like Captain Scott and Amundsen, became postcard heroes too, and expeditions from the Sahara Desert to Victoria Falls were featured on the newsworthy, topical medium of the picture postcard. This is a fascinating area of collection, fast growing in popularity and appreciation.

EVEREST

1922. Gen. the Hon. C. G. Bruce. Everest Expedition. Sepia. RP of named party of 12: Bruce, Crawford, Finch, Longstaff, Mallory, Morris, Morshead, Noel, Norton, Somervell, Strutt, Wakefield .. .. £1/**£1.50**/£2

1924. Gen. the Hon. C. G. Bruce. Everest Expedition. Film ads.

Facsimile signature (unsigned) .. .. .. £5/**£7**/£10
Signed .. .. £10/**£15**/£25

GENERAL ■EXP 1

Pub. Anon. Set of 12 cards. UB. Continental backs. Fine col. and printing.

2. 1492. Découverte de l'Amérique par Christophe Colomb, navigateur genois
2. 1876. Expedition du docteur Crevaux dans les Guyanes
3. 1891. Mission scientifique au Saudan par Français Dybowski
4. 1896. Expedition au Pole Nord par le Norvégien Nansen
5. 1272–1295. Voyage en Asie par Mario (*sic*) Polo
6. 1881. Mission du Colonel Flatters au Nord du Sahara
7. 1900–1903. Expedition du Duèdois Nordenskjold au Pole Sud
8. 1825. Traversée des Andes par la mission anglaise Head
9. 1883–1885. Expedition au Congo de l'explorateur français de Brazza
10. 1805. Mungo-Park, explorateur écossais. Voyage au Soudan
11. 1877. Expedition au Congo par l'explorateur anglais Stanley
12. 1867–1873. David Livingstone, explorateur anglais du centre et du sud de l'Afrique

Despite the doubtful accuracy of some of the captions, this is a fine rare set. Early Period 2.

Per card .. .. £2.50/**£5**/£8
Per complete set .. .. £50/**£75**/£100

■EXP 1 Pub. Anon. Artist Anon. '1492. Discovery of America by Christopher Columbus, Genoan navigator'. Chromo UB. Early period 2 £8

■EXP 2 Photo Beresford. E. H. Shackleton C.V.O. 1908 £4

POLAR ■EXP 2

1893. Nansen's Expedition to the North Pole in *The Fram*

Composite set—*see* NOVELTY

Pub. Aristophot. Period 2. Portrait of Nansen .. £4/**£6**/£8

Pub. Meissner & Buch. (1898). Series 1016 of 12 chromo-litho. *Aus Nansen in Nacht und Eis.* Artist Goldberg.

The cards were listed in the Third edition of this catalogue, p. 162.

Per card .. ..£8/**£12**/£15
Per set .. .. £95/**£195**/£225
Others .. .. £2/**£4**/£6

1897. Adrien de Gerlache (Belg) Antarctic Expedition

Pub. Nels. Series of 10 .. .. £5/**£8**/£10
Return of Expedition (1899) .. ..£8/**£15**/£20
Others .. ..£5/**£10**/£15

1897–1930. Andrée (Fr). Expedition to the North Pole by hot air balloon

Pub. Bergeret, Nancy. Set of 25, showing the expedition ships, the hot air balloon, scenes in Norway, Denmark, etc.
Per card.. .. ..£8/**£10**/£12
Per set .. .. £200/**£250**/P/A

Portraits of Andrée, etc. when his body and diary were found (1930) .. .. £3/**£4**/£5

1899–1900. Duke of Abruzzi/Capt. Cagni (It) Arctic Expedition in the *Stella Polare*
Various expedition cards .. .. £4/**£6**/£8
Rome Conference/Subscription cards (1901) .. £5/**£10**/£15

1901. British National Antarctic Expedition. Capt. Scott and *The Discovery*
Pub. Wrench. 'Links of the Empire'. Series of 4
Posted from ports of call .. .. £75/**£100**/£125
Unposted .. .. £15/**£35**/£50

1901. Otto Sverdrup's Arctic Expedition in the *Fram*
Price range .. .. £3/**£5**/£7

1901. De Drygalski (Ger) South Polar Expedition on the *Gaus*
Price range .. .. £5/**£8**/£10

1903–05. Dr. J. B. Charcot. (Fr) Expedition to Antarctic in the *Français*
Launch of the *Français*. 27 June 1903. St. Malo £8/**£10**/£12
Pub. Tuck. Souvenir card of subscribers .. £15/**£30**/£40
Series of 20 Expedition cards. Per card .. .. £5/**£8**/£10
Others .. .. £3/**£5**/£10

1904. Scottish National Antarctic Expedition
Pub. Wm. Ritchie. Probably 12 cards in set, all numbered
.. .. £4/**£6**/£8

1908–36. Dr. J. B. Charcot (Fr) Expeditions to Antarctic in the *Pourquoi Pas?*
Launch of the *Pourquoi Pas?*. Several versions £8/**£10**/£12
Series of 1908 Expedition. incl. return to Rouen. Pub. E.L.D., N.D. and others .. .. £5/**£8**/£10
Series of 1910 Expedition. Pub. E.L.D., N.D. and others
.. .. £6/**£9**/£19
Shipwreck (1936) .. .. £3/**£5**/£8
Funeral of Charcot (1936) .. .. £10/**£15**/£20

1908. Capt. Robert E. Peary (USA) Expedition to North Pole in the *Roosevelt* and controversy with Dr. Frederick A. Cook in the *John R. Bradley*
Pub. *Hampton's Magazine*
13 Blue/green 'North Pole Gravure Series'. Per card ..
.. .. £2/**£4**/£5
Pub. Kawin & Co. Chicago
Set of 50 b & w photo cards of Cook/Peary Expeditions
.. .. £3/**£5**/£6
Pub. Taggart
Series of sepia photo cards of Cook/Peary Expeditions
.. .. £2/**£4**/£5
Pub. Tuck.
Portrait of Peary by Albert Operti. Oilette 9787 £3/**£5**/£6
Portrait of Cook by Albert Operti. Oilette 9942 £2/**£5**/£6
Three Oilette sets by Albert Operti of the Arctic. Per card
.. .. £3/**£5**/£6
Pub. Ullman
North Pole series 162 (Nos. 2564–2567) by Berardt Wall
.. .. £3/**£4**/£6

Series of 3 official postcards of SS *Roosevelt* with inset Peary portrait. PU. Coastal T.P.O. 12 Sept. 1909. Per card .. .. £50/**£75**/£100

Various comic/satirical designs highlighting the rivalry between Cook and Peary .. .. .. £2/**£3.50**/£4

1908. Shackleton's Expedition to Antarctic with *Nimrod*

Price range .. .. £5/**£8**/£10

1910. Amundsen's Antarctic Expedition

Price range .. .. £8/**£10**/£12

1910. Capt. Scott's Antarctic Expedition (with Bowers, Evans, Oates, Wilson)

Ad. for Fry's Cocoa. Col. Poster type .. .. £30/**£40**/£50
Expedition scenes .. .. £5/**£8**/£10
In Memoriam cards .. .. £6/**£8**/£10
Portraits .. .. £5/**£7**/£8

1911. Australasian Antarctic Expedition with SY *Aurora*

Price range .. .. £1/**£2**/£3

Period 2. Scientific Expedition in the Hot Air Balloon *Princess Alice*

Set of 24, showing Alfonso XIII of Spain and the Prince of Monaco, etc. in Spitzberg
Per card .. .. £5/**£8**/£10
Per set .. .. £160/**£200**/P/A

1914. Shackleton's Antarctic Expedition

Price range .. .. £4/**£6**/£8

1918. Amundsen's attempted drift over N. Pole in the dirigible *Maud*

Price range .. .. £10/**£15**/£20

1925–26. Flights over the N. Pole in airships/dirigibles by Amundsen, Bennett, Byrne, Ellsworth, Nobile

Price range .. .. £12/**£20**/£25

1926. Commander Richard Evelyn Byrd (USA) Flight over North Pole

Series of 18 cards. Per card .. .. £5/**£10**/£15

SAHARA

1921. Captain Angus Buchanan (UK) Expedition to cross the 'Great Sahara'

Set of 12 photo postcards showing Capt. Buchanan, other members of his team, animals, salt cones, oasis, nomads, etc.
Per card .. .. £1/**£2**/£2.25
Per complete set .. .. £13/**£25**/£30

GLAMOUR

The general term 'Glamour' classifies postcards depicting feminine and/or masculine charms, from the nude, through the scantily dressed to the fully clothed. The earliest 'Glamour' postcards are to be found in Period 1 and are usually of bathing beauties (*cf.* Jack Abeille). During Period 2 the pictures became more daring and more popular, with the French the undisputed leaders in the field. The work of Xavier Sager, the most prolific of all the 'Glamour' artists, epitomises the genre. The type blossomed anew during Period 3, when the term 'pin-up' was coined (*see* MILITARY). During Period 4 the best artists survived by adapting to the new decorative art style (*Art Deco*) and the most striking designs in this era are to be found in Italy. Valuations in this section are for the artists' 'Glamour' work only. In some cases their designs in other subjects will rate more or less.

AMERICAN GIRL (THE) ■A 10, 23, G 1

A species unique to that country, of bright, outgoing, athletic, socialite or collegiate types. Her sophistication is tinged with innocence, in direct contrast to the coy, lingerie-clad creations of the European glamour genre. She is slim and active, in contrast to the static, statuesque Asti or Collins beauties. Her heyday was during Periods 2 and 3 and her chief exponents were:

Banks, E. C.	/**£1.50**/£2
Boileau, Philip†	£2/**£4**/£5
Christy, F. Earl†	£2/**£3**/£4
Christy, Howard Chandler†	£1/**£2**/£4
Dewey, Alfred James	£1/**£2**/£3
Elliott, Kathryn	75p/**£1.50**/£2
Farini, May	£1/**£2**/£3
Fidler, Pearle (*married name Le Munyan*)	£1/**£2**/£3
Fidler, Alice Luella	£1/**£2**/£3
Fisher, Harrison†	£2/**£3**/£4
Flagg, James Montgomery†	£1/**£2**/£4
Gilbert, Allen	75p/**£1**/£2
Gunn, Archie†	£1/**£2**/£3
Hare, J. Knowles†	75p/**£1**/£2
Hunter, Lillian Woolsey	£1/**£1.50**/£2
Kimball, Alonzo†	£1.50/**£2.50**/£3.50
King, H.†	75p/**£1**/£2
Kinneys, The	£1/**£2**/£3
McFall, J. V.	75p/**£1**/£2
Mayer, Lou	£2/**£4**/£5
Powell, Lyman C.	75p/**£1.50**/£2
Ralph, Lester	£1/**£2**/£3
Reiter, Brill G.	75p/**£1**/£1.50
Reynolds (*Wild West Flavour*)	£1/**£2**/£3
Schmucker, Samuel†	£3/**£5**/£8
St. John	75p/**£1**/£2
Stanlaws, Penly†	£1/**£2**/£3
Underwood, Clarence†	£1/**£1.50**/£3
Waskow, Edward G.	75p/**£1**/£1.50

EROTIC/PORNOGRAPHIC

Cards in this section vary from the gently titillating to the blatantly erotic.

Deshabille/Lingerie (Periods 2 to 4)

Artist drawn, unsigned/photographic origin 25p/**50p**/£1.50
RP .. .. 50p/**£1**/£2

Erotic

Phallic symbols like asparagus, bananas, flutes, towers, swans, trees, etc. and lesbian interest. The 'suggestive' rather than the explicit.

Artist drawn .. .. 75p/**£1.50**/£3
Photographic origin .. .. 75p/**£1**/£1.50

Eunuchs and Harems

Artist drawn .. .. £1/**£2**/£5
Photographic origin .. .. £2/**£5**/£8

Fantasy

Girls as neckties. French series .. ..£5/**£10**/£15
Heads composed of beauties *en déshabillé* .. .. £4/**£5**/£6
Mechanical incl. Blow-up bosoms and posteriors/ Spanking—*see* NOVELTY .. .. £2/**£4**/£6
Photomontage .. .. £2/**£4**/£6

House of German Art (*see* MILITARY)

Period 5. Hitler-approved Aryan beauties.
B & w .. .. 75p/**£1.50**/£3
Coloured .. .. £2/**£3**/£5

Nudes

Artist drawn .. .. £1/**£3**/£15
Photographic (Paris Salon, etc.) .. .. £1/**£3**/£5
Seldoms and other stage acts .. .. £1/**£2**/£4

Pornographic

Artist drawn .. .. £3/**£5**/£10
Photographic origin .. .. £3/**£5**/£10

Prostitution

Brothels (interior and exterior) .. .. £2/**£4**/£5
Prostitutes .. .. £2/**£4**/£5

EUROPEAN ARTISTS

These fall into three types—the slightly risqué, often scantily clad; the robust, bosomy Asti types; and the elegant Gibson-girl types.

Abeille, Jack (*Fr*)† ■A 1 .. .. £10/**£20**/£25
Asti, Angelo (*It*)† .. .. £1/**£2**/£2.50
Aveline, F.† .. .. 75p/**£1**/£1.50
Balfour-Kerr (*Gibson types*) .. .. .. 75p/**£1**/£1.50
Barribal, W.† ■A 6 .. .. £1.50/**£3**/£4
Bayard-Jones (*Gibson types*) .. .. .. 75p/**£1**/£1.50
Bertiglia, A. (*It*) .. .. £1/**£2**/£3
Bettinelli (*It*) .. .. £1/**£2**/£3

■G 1 Pub. Reinthal & Newman, New York. Artist Harrison Fisher. No. 201. Period 2 £4

■G 2 Pub. Topic. Artist J. Dedina. Months of the Year Series. 'March'. Period 2 £5

Bianchi (*It*)	£1.50/**£2.50**/£4
Blanchard	£1/**£2**/£3
Bompard, Luigi (*It*)†	£1.50/**£2.50**/£4
Bonora (*It*)	75p/**£1**/£2
Bonzagni, Aroldo (*It*)	£1/**£3**/£5
Brunelleschi, Umberto (*It*)† ■A 11	£25/**£50**/£70
Busi, Adolfo (*It*)	£4/**£6**/£8
Butcher, Arthur	75p/**£1.50**/£2
Calderara, C. (*It*)†	£1.50/**£3**/£6
Capiello, Leonetto (*It*)	£1/**£1.50**/£2
Cenni, Elda (*It*)	£1.50/**£3**/£4
Cherubini, M. (*It*)	£1/**£2**/£3
Collins, G. T. (*Asti types*)	75p/**£1**/£1.50
Colombo, E. (*It*)	£1/**£2**/£3
Corbella, Tito (*It*)†	£1.50/**£3**/£5
Dedina, Jean (*Czeck*)† ■G 2	£2.50/**£5**/£8
Dudovich, Marcello (*It*)	£5/**£10**/£15
English, Archibald	50p/**75p**/£1
Fabiano (*Fr*)	£2/**£4**/£5
Fontan, Léo (*Fr*)	£2/**£4**/£6
Gayac (*dancers a speciality*)	£3/**£4**/£6
Gibson, Charles Dana (*American, but with strong European connexions*)†	£1/**£1.50**/£3
Grosze, Manni (*silhouettes*)	£1/**£2**/£4
Guerzoni, C. (*It*)	£1/**£2**/£3
Harbour, Jennie (*crinoline types*)	£2/**£4**/£6
Haviland, Frank	£2/**£3**/£4
Hérouard (*Fr*)	£3/**£5**/£6
Horrell, Charles†	£1/**£1.50**/£2
Horsfall, Mary (*colourful, elegant girls*)†	£1/**£2**/£3
Icart, Louis (*Fr*)	£2/**£4**/£6
Jarasch, A. (*Fr*)	£3/**£5**/£6

Artist	Price
Jozsa, K. (*Aust*) ■A 14	
Kez (*'Simplissimus', etc.*)	£2/**£3**/£4
King, W. R. (*Gibson types*)	75p/**£1**/£1.50
Kirchner, Raphael (*Aust*)†	£7/**£12**/£25
Léonnec (*Fr*)	£3/**£5**/£6
Longley, Chiltern ■G 3	£5/**£10**/£15
Maréchaux, C. (*Fr*)	£1/**£2.50**/£5
Mauzan, Achille (*It*)†	£2/**£3**/£4
Meunier, Suzanne (*Fr*)	£4/**£5**/£6
Millière, Maurice (*Fr*)	£3/**£4**/£5
Monestier, C. (*It*)	£2/**£3**/£4
Montedoro,M. (*It*)	£3/**£8**/£15
Muggiano (*It*)	£1/**£2**/£3
Nanni, Giovanni (*It*) (*Fashion*)† ■A 17	£2/**£4**/£5
Ney (*Fr*)	£4/**£5**/£6
Peltier (*Fr*)	£2/**£3.50**/£5
Pénot, A. (*Fr*)	£2/**£4**/£6
Pépin (*Fr*)	£2/**£4**/£5
Péras (*Fr*)	£1/**£2**/£3
Peraux, Lionel (*Pub. Tuck*)	£1/**£3**/£5
Plum, A.	£1/**£2**/£3
Popini ■G 4	£2.50/**£4**/£6
Rappini (*It*)	£2/**£3**/£4
Sager, Xavier (*Fr*)† ■M 5	£2/**£4**/£10
San Marco (*It*)	£1/**£2.50**/£5
Simonetti, A. M. (*It*)	£2/**£3**/£4
Spurgin, Fred† ■CCH 1	75p/**£1.50**/£2
Tam, Jean	£3/**£5**/£6
Turner (*Gibson types*)	50p/**75p**/£1
Usabal (*Ger*)	£1/**£1.50**/£3
Wennerberg, Brynolf (*Ger*)†	£4/**£6**/£8
Unsigned	50p/**£3**/£10

■G 3 Pub. S. H. & Co., London and Manchester. Artist C. Longley. *Art Deco* style. Period 4 £10

■G 4 Pub. Pascualis Moss. Artist Popini. 'The Barmaid'. 'Some English Girls'. Series 4077. UB. Period 2 £5

LANGUAGE OF . . .

Type of code or message card to convey an amusing/loving/ sexual meaning. Subjects include: *babies, eyes, knots and vegetables. The best known artist seen on this type of card is Maurice Boulanger.*

A list of these subjects was given in the third edition of this catalogue, p. 167.

Price range .. .. 25p/**50p**/£3

MALE GLAMOUR

Boxers/wrestlers in 'beef-cake' or fighting poses—named, e.g. A. Aberg (Russian champ.), Launceston Elliott, Gruhn, Hackenschmidt, Tom Jenkins, Eugen Sandow, others .. .. £1/**£2**/£4

He-man poses, body-builders, boxers, wrestlers, etc.—unnamed .. .. 75p/**£1.50**/£3

Publishers of the above include Beagles. Rapid Photo Co., Rotary.

Homosexual interest .. .. £2/**£3**/£5

ROMANCE/SENTIMENT

Many sentimental wartime postcards exist (notably the embroidered silks) with appropriate verses (see MILITARY). *Pre- and post-war series exist in their thousands, of varying merit and artistic quality. Many with* Art Deco *and* Art Nouveau *interest are well above average quality, accounting for the highest valuations. The romantic theme was often given the comic treatment* (see COMIC).

Anonymous or Minor Artist Drawn

Beauties, courtship, kisses. Periods 1 to 6. Value according to artistic merit and age.

Price range .. .. 50p/**£2**/£5

Photographic in Origin

Posed subjects as above, many hand-tinted, many of Continental origin by anonymous publishers.

Price range .. .. 50p/**75p**/£1.50

Three Band Pricing System

Left Hand Band: The lowest price you will probably be asked to pay for this card.
Middle Band: What you will normally be asked to pay for this card: its average, reasonable price.
Right Hand Band: The highest price you will probably be asked to pay for this card.
For a full explanation of the system see page ix.

GREETINGS/HOLIDAYS

One of the most under-estimated categories of postcard collecting, this section contains examples of some of the printer's finest work.

Some of the best postcard illustrators designed greetings or had their general designs over-printed with seasonal messages.

Because many of the Greetings cards refer to public holidays, the genre is often known as 'Holidays' in the USA, and merges or overlaps with COMMEMORATIVE and 'Patriotic' in many cases. As transatlantic trading increases, more of these colourful, often amusing, postcards are now becoming available and collected in Britian.

See NOVELTY where several types of greetings cards are described.

AMERICAN GREETINGS/HOLIDAYS/PATRIOTICS

Several festivals and holidays are celebrated more in America than in Europe, with resultant appropriate greetings postcards.

Decoration Day/Memorial Day (April)
Ground Hog Day (2 February)
Hallowe'en (31 October)
Independence Day (4 July)
Jewish New Year (September) *(Rosh Hashana)*
Labor Day (September)
Lincoln's Birthday (12 February)
Rally Day
St. Patrick's Day (17 March)
Thanksgiving Day (November)
Washington's Birthday (22 February)

Price range .. .. 75p/**£3**/£6

APRIL FOOL/POISSON D'AVRIL

A day celebrated more on the postcard in France than any other country, with their 'April Fish' jokes.

British publishers 25p/**50p**/75p
French publishers .. .. 50p/**75p**/£1

BIRTHDAY

Cards by well-known artists command a premium.

Period 1/Early Period 2 UB

Chromolitho artist signed, sometimes embossed .. £1/**£3**/£5
Chromolitho unsigned, sometimes embossed .. 75p/**£2**/£4

Periods 2, 3

Artist drawn .. .. 50p/**75p**/£1.50
Appliquéd, embossed, gilded, silvered, tinselled, etc. .. .. 50p/**75p**/£1.50
Others 25p/**50p**/75p

Periods 4, 5
For specified ages/friends/members of family .. 25p/**50p**/75p
Photographic, often with deckle edges or embossed edges, sometimes hand-tinted **50p**
Others 25p/**50p**/75p

CHRISTMAS ■GR 1
Themes include angels, animals, bells, children, food and drink, robins, Santa Claus (qv), *religious subjects, snow scenes, etc.*
Price range .. .. 25p/**£1**/£5

EASTER
Themes include angels, chickens, flowers, rabbits, religious subjects.
Price range .. .. 25p/**75p**/£1.50

FAITH, HOPE & CHARITY
Often known as 'FHC' or 'The Virtues'. Some beautiful series on this theme of Victorian/Edwardian virtues exist, often extending to Innocence, Patience, Prudence, Purity and others.
Artist drawn, signed .. .. 50p/**75p**/£2
Artist drawn, unsigned 25p/**50p**/75p

GENERAL GOOD WISHES
Themes include Forget-me-not, friendship, hearty greetings, kind thoughts, 'sorry', 'write to me', etc.
Price range .. .. 25p/**75p**/£1.50

GREETINGS FROM/GRUSS AUS/SOUVENIR DE *see*
EARLY CARDS

HANDS ACROSS THE SEA
Type of card which came into prominence with the wave of emigrations to the Commonwealth and other countries in early Period 2. They are amongst the most colourful and exuberant postcards printed. They show clasped hands, means of transport and national symbols.
Price range .. .. 75p/**£1.50**/£2

KRAMPUS
Mid-European version of the devil who became the dark alter-ego of Santa Claus. Where Father Christmas rewarded good children, the Krampus beat, or otherwise punished, naughty ones.
Artist drawn, signed .. .. £7/**£15**/£25
Artist drawn unsigned .. .. £3/**£7**/£10

As it is difficult to date a card precisely, a period system has been used in this catalogue. For a full explanation of the system see page viii.

■GR 1 Pub. International Art Pub. Co. New York. Artist Ellen Clapsaddle. Christmas 'Santa'. PU 1912 £5

■GR 2 Pub. Tuck 'Art' Series 6114. 'Cupid's Alphabet'. Embossed. PU 1906 £2

LARGE LETTER

Alphabet Series ■GR 2

Actresses with *Art Nouveau*/Fantasy letters	50p/**75p**/£1.50
German *Art Nouveau* series, incl. children/fantasy/females Period 2 Per set of 26	£35/**£50**/£70
Multi-Baby Alphabets	75p/**£1**/£1.50
Photo Printing & Pub. Co. ABC postcards	£1/**£1.50**/£3
Rotary Photo Co.	50p/**75p**/£1
Tuck. Cupid's Alphabet	75p/**£1.50**/£3
Others	50p/**75p**/£1

Calendar Cards

Various designs, incl. New Year	50p/**75p**/£1.50

Dates

The year, often with New Year greetings. Various designs	75p/**£1**/£1.50
25 December (Premium if posted on that date)	
1 January (Premium if posted on that date)	

Days of Week

Birn Bros. series	75p/**£1**/£1.50
Others (value according to artist or style)	50p/**£1.50**/£5

Many American sets of Teddy Bears, Sunbonnet Children, etc. see ANIMALS, CHILDREN.

Leap Year

Various comic series	50p/**75p**/£1.50

Mizpah
'God be with you till we meet again'. Various designs .. 25p/**50p**/75p

Names
Made up of flowers, photomontages of actresses, etc. Various designs .. 50p/**75p**/£1.50

Numbers (1–10, etc.)
Musterschutz (Ger. Pub.) *Art Nouveau*/Children/Fantasy/Females. Period 2.
Per set of 10 .. £17.50/**£25**/£30
Others .. 50p/**£1**/£2

Towns
Made up of photomontages of views, etc.
Various designs .. 50p/**£1**/£1.50

MONTHS OF THE YEAR ■GR 3

Many well known artists, from Sydney Carter to Mucha, produced sets of 12 of the months, making this a highly desirable type, especially if the set is complete. Value according to the artist.
Per set .. £6/**£24**/P/A

MOURNING/SYMPATHY CARDS

To announce a death, or offer sympathy—rare subjects.
Price range .. 75p/**£1.50**/£5

NEW YEAR ■GR 4

Themes include angels with trumpets, calendars and dates.
Price range .. 25p/**75p**/£10

■GR 3 Pub. Anon. FR. Artist M. Boulanger. Months of the Year Series. 'September'. PU 1907 £6

■GR 4 Pub. Inter-Art. Artist Agnes Richardson. 'Artistique Xmas' Series No. 2220 Period 4 £3

SANTA CLAUS (Father Christmas)

A type much collected in the USA and now being sought after in Britain. The best designs were printed in Germany. Santas come in green and other colours, as well as the traditional red, and US Santas wear a suit rather than the European long robe. Many 'Santas' are given the Novelty *treatment—with appliqué, embossing, H.T.L. Others are by well known artists. All these factors will add a premium to the prices below.*

Tuck were amongst the finest and most prolific of Santa postcard publishers. Other publishers include Langsdorf, Nash, Schwerdtfeger and Winsch.

Period 1/Early Period 2. Highly decorative	£2/**£3**/£5
Later designs	£1/**£2**/£3

SEASONS, THE

Many artists have treated this attractive subject of the 4 Seasons—Spring, Summer, Autumn, Winter. There also exist fine, unsigned sets in distinct Art Deco *or* Art Nouveau *style.*

Artist signed—value according to artist.

Per set	£8/**£30**/P/A

Well-designed, unsigned sets.

Per set	£4/**£12**/£20
Others	50p/**£2**/£3

VALENTINES

Comic Designs

Artist drawn, value according to artist	75p/**£1.50**/£3
Photographic origin	25p/**50p**/75p

Sentimental

Early chromolithographic, embossed, etc.	£1/**£2**/£4
Later designs	50p/**75p**/£1

WEDDING GREETINGS AND CONGRATULATIONS

Rarely seen on postcards, and then usually in Period 4.

Early, good quality productions	£1/**£1.50**/£3
Later designs	25p/**50p**/75p

Three Band Pricing System

Left Hand Band: The lowest price you will probably be asked to pay for this card.
Middle Band: What you will normally be asked to pay for this card: its average, reasonable price.
Right Hand Band: The highest price you will probably be asked to pay for this card.
For a full explanation of the system see page ix.

LITERARY/MUSICAL

LITERARY REPRESENTATIONS

Alice in Wonderland/Through the Looking Glass

Pub. Black, A. & C. Artist Charles Folkard†. Series of Songs from *Alice in Wonderland* and *Through the Looking Glass*. Period 4 .. .. £1.50/**£2**/£2.50

Pub. British PO 1979 Year of the Child 13p stamp—scene from *Alice* (PHQ 37d) **50p**

Pub. Faulkner, C. W. Artist Kathleen Nixon†. Series 1819 set of 6 *Alice* cards. Period 4 .. .. £1/**£2**/£3

Pub. Fuller & Richard. Artist Tenniel. Reproductions of his original illustrations for *Alice*. Set of 8 cards (1910) .. .. £1/**£2**/£3

Pub. King, Gerald M. Twenty-one cards reproduced from his book, *Alice through the Pillar Box*, all hand stamped and designed. Period 7. The set **£20**

Pub. Guinness. Set of advertising cards with re-written episodes from *Alice*. Period 4 .. .. .. 75p/**£1**/£1.50

Pub. Lester, Leslie. Artist Mendoza. Set of 6 *Alice* cards by permission of Walt Disney. Period 6 .. £1/**£1.50**/£2

Pub. Merrimack. Reprints of Tenniel's illustrations for *Alice*. Period 7 .. .. **50p**

Pub. R.P.S. Series. Artist Studdy†. *Alice in Wonderland* dog .. .. £1/**£2**/£3

Pub. Salmon, J. Artist Flora White†. Series No. 1472 .. .. 50p/**75p**/£1.50

Pub. Savory Ltd. Cheshire Cat with *Alice* quotation. Period 2 .. .. 75p/**£1**/£1.25

Andersen, Hans

Pub. Henderson. Illustrated Fairy Tales. Artist Sydney Carter†. Period 2 .. .. 50p/**£1**/£1.50

Burns, Robert

Pub. Art Pub. Co. Burns Souvenir cards. Period 2 .. .. 75p/**£1**/£1.25

Pub. Johnston W. & A. K. Several series of Burns sets from 1902 .. .. 25p/**50p**/75p

Pub. Stoddart & Co. Burns Pictorial series. Period 2 .. **50p**

Pub. Tuck. Oilette series 7703, 7694 (1918) 50p/**75p**/£1

Byron, Lord

Pub. Tuck. Oilette series 2750 (1918) .. .. 50p/**75p**/£1

Dante's Inferno

Artist Ezio Anichini. *Art Deco* studies in red and black, 18 cards recorded. .. .. 75p/**£1.25**/£2

Artist Kienerk—*see* ARTISTS

Dickens, Charles

Pub. Beagles. Centenary of Dickens' birth (1912) £2/**£3**/£4

Pub. Cassell & Co. Character Sketches from Dickens. Artist Frederick Barnard. Three sets of 6 (1904) 50p/**75p**/£1

Pub. Chapman & Hall. Set of 13 cards reproducing monthly parts of Dickens' novels (1905) .. .. 50p/**75p**/£1
Pub. Faulkner, C. W. & Co. 'Pickwick' series No. 244. B & w .. .. 50p/**75p**/£1
Pub. Hildesheimer. B &w Dickens characters. Artist E. F. Manning UB 25p/**50p**/75p
Pub. Jones, A. V. N. Dickens Characters. Artist Frank Reynolds .. .. £1/**£2**/£3
Pub. London Stereoscopic Co. Set of 12 cards illustrating the production of The Only Way (adaptation of *Tale of Two Cities*) 25p/**50p**/75p
Pub. Stewart & Woolf. Dickens' Characters. 3 sets by Artist Alfred Crowquill (1902) .. .. 75p/**£1**/£1.25
Pub. Tuck. At least 15 series of 'In Dickens Land' Oilettes (from 1903) .. .. 50p/**75p**/£1
'With Famous Authors and Painters' (1918). Eight Dickens sets .. .. 50p/**75p**/£1
Pub. Valentine. Several series of Dickens designs. Period 2 .. .. 25p/**50p**/75p

For the many fine series of Dickens characters by Joseph Clayton Clark ('Kyd'), *see* ARTISTS

Fairy Tales/Nursery Rhymes ■L 1

Pub. Anon. (Dutch). Artist Kirchbach. Col. Princess and the Pea .. .. 75p/**£1**/£2
Pub. B.K.W. Col. Series 885, incl. Pied Piper .. 75p/**£1**/£2
Pub. A. & C. Black Ltd. Series No. 91. 'Nursery Rhymes and Tales', illustrated by Charles Folkard. Superb col. set of 6—Cinderella; Tom, the Piper's Son; Beauty and The Beast; Little Bo Peep; Sleeping Beauty; Red Riding Hood.
Price range .. .. £2/**£3**/£5
Pub. Misch & Stock. Series No. 120. Fairy Tales and Pantomime Stories, e.g. Little Red Riding Hood, Blue Beard, etc. .. .. 75p/**£1.50**/£3
Pub. Tuck. 'Art' Nos. 3471/3/5. Cinderella, Puss in Boots, Hansel and Gretel, Little Snowhite, etc. Period 2 .. .. 75p/**£1.50**/£2
Pub. Valentine's. Various artists .. .. 50p/**75p**/£3
Others (incl. Artist Arthur Thiele) .. .. 25p/**£1.50**/£8

Hardy, Thomas

Pub. Tuck. Oilette series 7700, 7755, 7763 (1918) 50p/**75p**/£1

Jerome, Jerome K.

Pub. Blum & Degen. 'Three Men in a Boat' series with Jerome seal of approval on reverse (1907) .. .. 75p/**£1.50**/£2

Lorna Doone

Pub. Photochrom 'Celesque'. Scenes from Lorna Doone. Period 2 .. .. 50p/**75p**/£1
Pub. Valentine. Characters from Lorna Doone. Period 2 .. .. 25p/**50p**/75p
Various scenes from 'Lorna Doone Country', etc. .. **50p**

Milton

Pub. Tuck. Oilette Series 7039, 7420/1 (1918) 50p/**75p**/£1

■L 1 Pub. Valentine's. Rene Cloke Postcards No. 4147. Period 4 75p

■L 2 Pub. A. & C. Black. Artist Gilbert James. 'Rubaiyat of Omar Khayyam'. Series No. 27. Period 2 £3

Omar Khayam ■L 2
Pub. A & C Black. Art studies by Gilbert James. Set of 6. Per card .. .. £1/**£1.50**/£3
Pub. Harrop. Art studies by Willy Pogany. Set of 6. Per card .. .. £1/**£1.50**/£3

One Thousand and One Nights
Kunstlerkarten Series 1102 (Ger). *Marchen aus 1001 Nacht.* Artist Mackott. Beautiful col. series. UB. PU 1900. Titles include Aladin, Sinbad the Sailor, Scheherzerade (*sic*) .. .. £1/**£2**/£4

Pilgrim's Progress
Pub. Religious Tract Soc. Four sets of 6 by Artist Harold Copping† (1911) .. .. 75p/**£1**/£2

Scott, Sir Walter
Pub. Hildesheimer. Sketches from Scott. Artist Sydney Carter†. Period 2 .. .. 50p/**£1**/£1.50
Pub. Ritchie & Sons. Home & Haunts of Sir Walter Scott. Artist J. Douglas (1906) .. .. 50p/**75p**/£1
Pub. Ritchie & Sons. Comic characters from Sir Walter Scott (1907) .. .. 50p/**75p**/£1
Pub. Tuck, Artist J. Finnemore. Nos. 460–5. Vignettes UB .. .. £1/**£1.50**/£2
Pub. Valentine. Scenes from Scott 25p/**50p**/75p

Shakespeare (*see* ENTERTAINMENT: Theatre)
Pub. Ackermann, Munich. Set of 12 silhouettes, various play. Period 2 .. .. 50p/**£1**/£2

Pub. Collins, Wm. Shakespeare characters in sepia by Artist Dudley Hardy†. Period 2 .. .. .. £1/**£1.50**/£2
Pub. Faulkner, C. W. 'Shakespeare Series'. Superb UB chromolithographed .. .. £1/**£2**/£4
Pub. Hildesheimer. Sketches from Shakespeare. Artist Sydney Carter. Period 2 .. .. 50p/**£1**/£1.50
Pub. Lyon, Wm. Set of ping-pong cards with titles from Shakespeare. Period 2 .. .. 50p/**75p**/£1.50
Pub. Nister. Scenes from Shakespeare. Superb col. UB chromolithographs .. .. £1/**£2**/£4
Pub. Nister. Later series divided backs .. 75p/**£1.50**/£3
Pub. Stewart & Woolf. Comic series with Shakespeare quotes UB chromolithographs .. .. £1/**£1.50**/£2
Pub. Tuck. Set of 12 cards from *Hamlet* by Artist Harold Copping† (1901) .. .. £1/**£2**/£4
Pub. Tuck. Merry Wives of Windsor. Vignettes. Nos. 466–477. UB Early Period 2 .. .. 0 .. £2/**£3**/£4
Pub. Valentine. Characters from Shakespeare. Several designs. Period 2 .. .. 25p/**50p**/£1

Thackeray, William Makepeace
Pub. Hildesheimer. Sketches from Thackeray. Artist Sydney Carter. Period .. .. 50p/**£1**/£1.50
Pub. Tuck. *Vanity Fair* Oilette series .. .. 50p/**75p**/£1

Tintin ■L 3
Adventures of Tintin by Hergé
Pub. Anon. Period 4 .. .. £2/**£4**/£8
Pub. Arno. France. Period 7 .. .. **25p**

■L 3 Pub. Editions Arno, France. Artist 'Hergé' (Georges Rémi). 'The Adventures of Tintin. Tintin in America'. Period 7 25p

MUSICAL

Bands

Clear pictures of photographic origin with good detail of people, etc.—Brass bands; Dance bands; Military bands; Pipe bands; Religious groups' bands; School bands.
Price range .. .. 50p/**£1.50**/£3

Bandstands—*see* Social History

Comic Musical Cards

Pub. DeLittle, Fenwick & Co. Songs and Singers. Period 2 .. .. 50p/**75p**/£1
Pub. Moss, Henry & Co. Musical Terms up to Date. Artist P. V. Bradshaw† .. .. £2/**£4**/£6
Pub. Ponajowski, E. Humorous Musical Series in Write-Away style. Period 2 .. .. 75p/**£1**/£1.50
Various publishers. Various artists, signed and unsigned. Value according to artist, period, etc. .. 50p/**75p**/£3

■L 4 Pub. G. Ricordi, Milan. Artist L. Metlicovitz. The Composer, Verdi with his dogs. Chromo. UB. Early period 2 £6

Composers ■L 4

Pub. Ackerman, Munich. Tonkünstler Silhouetten Series (Composers' Silhouettes) Artist W. Bithorn. Period 2 .. .. £1/**£2**/£3
Pub. Blum & Degen. Musical Composers (1899) .. £1/**£2**/£3
Pub. Brüder Köhn. Col. series by Artist Ulreich (1908) .. .. £1/**£2**/£3
Pub. Gerstmayer, J. Col series by Artist O. Elsner of Schubert Lieder. Period 2 .. .. £1/**£2**/£3
Pub. J.B.B. Fantasy Heads of Composers. Period 2 .. .. £10/**£20**/£30
Pub. *La Revue Musicale*. Paris. Portraits of Rimsky Korsakov, etc. by Lebedoff. Period 4 .. .. 75p/**£1**/£2
Pub. Philipp & Kramer. Tondichter (Composer) Series XXVII. Artist Percy N. F. Hedley .. .. £2/**£4**/£5
Pub. Ricordi. Scenes of Verdi's home, showing the composer at leisure. Artist C. Metlicovitz. Early Period 2 UB chromolitho .. .. £1.50/**£3**/£6
Pub. Rotary. Composers and Music 25p/**50p**/75p

Pub. Unknown. Col. series by Artist E. Kutzer of Schubert Lieder. Period 2 .. .. £1/**£2**/£3
Others .. .. 25p/**50p**/£1.50

Concerts
Clear pictures of photographic origin with good detail of people.
Indoor views 25p/**50p**/75p
Exterior views .. .. 50p/**75p**/£1.50

Conductors
Big Band .. .. 50p/**75p**/£1
Classical orchestras **50p**
Famous names .. .. 50p/**75p**/£1

Instruments
Bells/Bell ringing .. .. 75p/**£1.50**/£2
Orchestral instruments 25p/**50p**/75p
Organs—church 25p/**50p**/75p
Organs—cinema .. .. £1/**£2**/£3
Others **50p**

Instrumentalists
Big band bandleaders and musicians (e.g. Count Basie, Bennie Goodman, Glenn Miller, Tommy Dorsey, etc.) Periods 4 to 6 .. .. £1/**£2**/£3

Opera
Gilbert & Sullivan. Pub. Savoy Co. .. .. £1/**£1.50**/£3
Other pubs .. .. 50p/**75p**/£1.50
Opera Heroines. Early Period 2. Artist drawn col. vignettes (Ger) .. .. £2/**£4**/£5
Pub. Breitkoff & Hartel. Series of 60 cards of Wagner operas, incl. portraits of conductors, singers, etc. Period 2 .. .. £1/**£1.50**/£5
Pub. Faulkner, C.W. Series of 12 Wagner operas. Col. Period 2 .. .. 75p/**£1.50**/£2
Pub. Meissner & Buch. Wagner series .. .. £1/**£2**/£3
Pub. Ricordi
Iris by Mascagni (1898). Japanese style chromo-lithos UB .. .. £8/**£10**/£15
Madame Butterfly by Puccini (1898). Japanese style chromo-lithos .. 0 .. .. £8/**£10**/£15
Tosca by Puccini (1898). Chromo-lithos .. .. £8/**£10**/£15
Pub. SA Nazionalie del Grammofono, Milano. Period 4. HMV ads. by Artist Nanni, incl. Toti dal Monte as 'Lucia di Lammermoor' .. .. £6/**£12**/£18
Pub. Tuck. Period 2. Col. chromo-litho Wagner series. Nos. 691, 693, 694 .. .. £1/**£2**/£4
Others 25p/**50p**/75p

Singers
Cabaret/Concert singers (e.g. Dame Clara Butt, Ben Davies, John McCormack, Edith Piaf, Kennerley Rumford, Charles Trenet, etc.) .. .. 50p/**£1**/£2
Jazz singers (e.g. Louis Armstrong) .. .. .. £1/**£2**/£3

Opera singers (e.g. Enrico Caruso*, Feodor Chaliapin*, Geraldine Farrar, Benjamino Gigli, Dame Nelly Melba, Toti dal Monte, Dame Adelina Patti, Luisa Tetrazini, etc.) .. .. 75p/**£2.50**/£5
Other singers 25p/**50p**/75p
(* = commands the highest price)

Song Cards

Pub. Augener. Little Songs of Long Ago. Artist Henriette Willebeek Le Mair† .. .. £1.50/**£2.50**/£4
Pub. Bamforth. Several thousand designs. Periods 2 to 4:
- Per pair .. .. 50p/**75p**/£1.25
- Per set of 3 .. .. 75p/**£1.25**/£2
- Per set of 4 .. .. £1/**£2**/£3
- Single cards 25p/**50p**/75p

Pub. Davidson Bros. *See* Comic. Many series by well known artists .. .. af21.. .. .. 75p/**£1.50**/£4
Pub. Shamrock. Nearly 400 titles (1908) .. 25p/**50p**/75p
Pub. Tuck. Many Oilette series 25p/**50p**/75p
Pub. Valentine. Several series **50p**
Other pubs. .. .. 25p/**50p**/£1
National Anthems 25p/**50p**/75p

Songs with Musical Notations/Words

Pub. Musical Post Card Syndicate. Musical Invitations (1903) .. .. 75p/**£1**/£1.50
Pub. Musical Post Card Syndicate. Popular Songs series 25p/**50p**/75p
Pub. Reid Bros. Six sets of 6 (1906) 25p/**50p**/75p
Others **50p**

Other Musical Series

Price range 25p/**50p**/75p

MAPS

Listed in this section are cards featuring just maps and others including view vignettes, heraldic devices and inset pictures, etc. Non-war map cards were introduced into Britain in *c.* 1903. John Walker, whose map cards were produced by J. Bartholomew, had issued over 400 different cards by 1904 covering places as far away as Australia. Specialist map cards e.g. RAILWAYS, MILITARY, etc. will also be found under those headings. The bulk of the information here was supplied by Barry Gray whose map collection exceeds 3500 cards.

The listing is alphabetical by publisher/series within a number of different countries. The information given covers from Period 2 to Period 7, the cheaper cards being the more recent issues. Most of the overseas cards listed are modern issues.

Australia

Nucolorvue Productions Pty. Ltd.	50p/**75p**/£1
Others. Periods 2–6	£2/**£3**/£4
Others. Period 7	50p/**75p**/£1

Belgium

Congo. Prince Albert's visit, 1909	£2/**£4**/£6
Edit Anciens ets Ern Thill S.A.	50p/**75p**/£1
Others Periods 2–6	£1/**£2**/£3
Others Period 7	50p/**75p**/£1

Britain ■MAP 1–3

Ads. General	£6/**£7**/£8
Antler Series (*O/S heraldic cards*)	50p/**75p**/£1
G. W. Bacon & Co. (incl. Excelsior Series)	£2/**£3**/£4

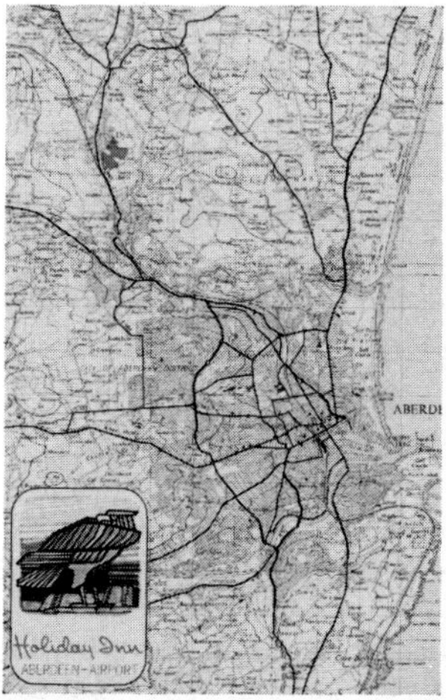

■MAP 1 Pub. Holiday Inn, printed by Ordnance Survey. Aberdeen Airport. Period 7 75p

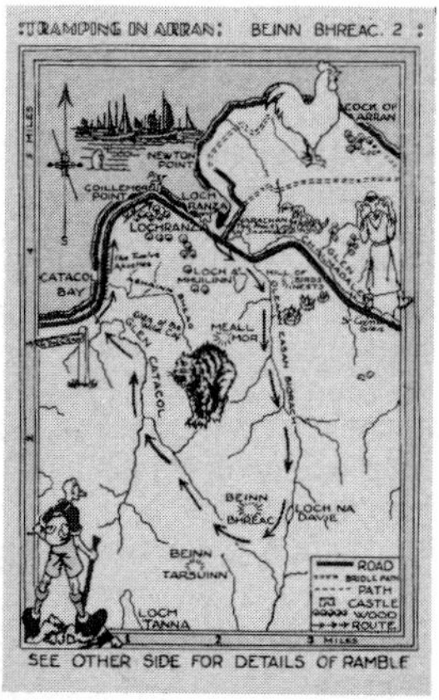

■MAP 2 Pub. Holmes 'Tramping in Arran' Series No. 2. 'Beinn Bhreac'. Period 4 £3

Bamforth/Colin Richardson Printers/Lilywhite Ltd. .. .. 50p/**75p**/£1
Harvey Barton Bristol (*West Country/Wales*) 50p/**75p**/£1
Beer Mats (*Buckley/Badger/Huntsman/Pony—West Country & Channel Is.*) .. .. £1/**£1.50**/£2
Bennett Publications/Shoesmith & Etheridge Ltd. (*South Coast*) .. .. £1/**£1.50**/£2
Braemar Films Ltd. (*Scotland*) .. .. .. 50p/**75p**/£1
A. J. Carter ('This is where I am' series) .. .. £1/**£2**/£3
Colourpicture Pubs. Inc. .. .. 50p/**75p**/£1
Cyclists Touring Club (*All numbered. Probably 20 in set*) .. .. £3/**£4**/£5

Dalkeith Publishing Co. *see* MODERN.
E. T. W. Dennis & Sons Ltd. .. .. 50p/**75p**/£1
Dexter. Canada. For NPO Ltd. (*Channel Is., Ireland, I.O.M., Lake District, Scotland*) .. .. 50p/**75p**/£1
J. Arthur Dixon .. .. 25p/**50p**/£1
Embossed maps .. .. £5/**£6**/£7
Ettlinger .. .. £3/**£4**/£5
Faga O/S. (*see* MODERN) .. .. 50p/**75p**/£2.50
Fisa .. .. 50p/**75p**/£1
F. Frith & Co. Reigate (*3 diff. series*) .. .. .. £1/**£2**/£3
Goodhews Ltd. (Hotel & Rib set) .. .. £1/**£1.50**/£2
Hampton Printing Bristol Ltd (*Mendip Series. O/S*) .. .. 50p/**75p**/£1

John Hinde Ltd .. .. 50p/**75p**/£1
Holiday Inn Hotels (*8 in series, Period 7*) .. 25p/**75p**/£1
Holmes 'Tramping in Arran'. (*At least 6 cards. Numbered. Period 4*) .. .. £2/**£2.50**/£3
Jarrold & Sons Ltd .. .. 50p/**75p**/£1
Jay Em Jay (*Outline map with pics*) .. .. .. £2/**£3**/£4
W. A. K. Johnston Ltd. (*Tartans & clans*) .. .. £2/**£3**/£4
Murray King Studio (*Devon/Cornwall*) .. 50p/**75p**/£1
Pharus (Giesen Bros.) (*12 sections of London*) .. £4/**£5**/£6
G. Philip & Son ('Wrench' series) .. .. .. £2/**£3**/£4
The Photographic Greeting Card Co. .. .. 50p/**75p**/£1
Photo Precision Ltd .. .. 50p/**75p**/£1
A. J. Potts ('Premier' & 'Garden Isle' series) 0 .. £2/**£3**/£4
QSL cards (*see* CURIOUS) .. .. 50p/**75p**/£1
Railways. Metropolitan/Midlands/North Eastern (*see* RAILWAYS) .. .. £20/**£25**/£30
Andrew Reid. Visit of Channel Fleet, 1904 .. £5/**£10**/£12
Remy .. .. £4/**£5**/£6
J. Salmon .. .. 50p/**75p**/£1
Schneider Trophy Course. 1929 .. .. £3/**£6**/£7
Stamp & Map designs .. .. £4/**£5**/£6
Valentine & Sons .. .. 50p/**75p**/£1
John Walker & Co. Geographical series. (About 800 cards) .. .. £4/**£5**/£6

John Walker & Co. Gordon Bennett Race Course. Autocar overprint .. .. £7/**£8**/£9
Wars. General .. .. £6/**£7**/£8
J. B. White Ltd (*Scotland*) .. .. 50p/**75p**/£1
Whiteholme Pubs. Ltd (*Scotland*) .. .. £1/**£1.50**/£2
Others. Periods 2–6 .. .. £1.50/**£4**/£6
  Period 7 .. .. 25p/**75p**/£2

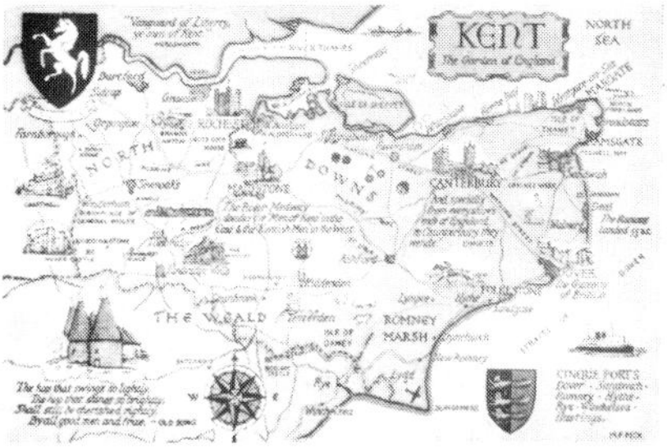

■MAP 3 Pub. J. Salmon. 'Kent' No. 4589. PU 1959 75p

Canada

Natural Color Productions Ltd	50p/**75p**/£1
Others. Periods 2–6	£1/**£2**/£3
Others. Period 7	25p/**50p**/£1

France

Artaud Pere et Fils. Editions 'Gaby'	50p/**£1**/£1.50
As de Coeur	50p/**£1**/£1.50
Cie des Arts Photomecaniques	50p/**£1**/£1.50
Combier Imprimeur. Macon. (*2 diff. sets each about 100 cards*)	50p/**£1**/£1.50
Edit. Blondella la Rougery	50p/**£1**/£1.50
Editions C.A.P.	50p/**£1**/£1.50
Editions D'Art Jos	50p/**£1**/£1.50
Editions 'La Cigogne'	50p/**£1**/£1.50
Editions De L'Est	50p/**£1**/£1.50
Etablissements G. Gandini	50p/**£1**/£1.50
Editions Du Lys	50p/**£1**/£1.50
Editions Lyna	50p/**£1**/£1.50
Editions Mage	£2/**£3**/£4
Editions Rella	50p/**£1**/£1.50
Editions L. Rocher Le Puy	50p/**£1**/£1.50
Emulsion Scott Ads. (*92 cards*)	£2/**£4**/£6
Les Tirages Modernes	£2/**£3**/£4
Others. Periods 2–6	£2/**£3**/£5
Period 7	025p/**75p**/£1

Germany

A. Hoppe	50p/**£1**/£1.50
Isenbeck. Wiesbaden. Gordon-Bennett Circuit	£7/**£8**/£9
Kanis (*E. Germany*)	£1/**£1.50**/£2
Kunstverlag H. Dulberg	50p/**£1**/£1.50
Liebes—Rathsel (Love Puzzle) Men and women concealed in map design (*10 cards in set*)	£5/**£8**/£9
Richter (E. Germany)	£1/**£1.50**/£2
J. P. Jantzen	50p/**£1**/£1.50
J. Alex Klein	50p/**£1**/£1.50
Folo Kohlbauer	50p/**£1**/£1.50
Kunstanstalt Wilhelm Gerling	50p/**£1**/£1.50
Wilh Maul	50p/**£1**/£1.50
Michael & Co.	50p/**£1**/£1.50

Schoning & Co. .. .. 50p/**£1**/£1.50
Others. Periods 2–6 .. .. £1/**£2**/£3
Period 7 .. .. 25p/**75p**/£1

Holland
Hank .. .. 50p/**75p**/£1
Gebr. Spanjersberg .. .. 50p/**75p**/£1
Sleding .. .. 50p/**75p**/£1
Van Gelderen .. .. 50p/**75p**/£1
Others .. .. 25p/**50p**/£1

Hungary
Pub. Hungarian Womens' National Assoc. Mechanical. Trianon Treaty Areas .. .. £6/**£7**/£13

Italy
Italgeo .. .. £3/**£4**/£5
Pub. Colonial Ministry Eritrea, 1929 .. .. £2.50/**£3**/£5
Others .. .. 25p/**£1**/£3

Portugal
Edicao Iberex-Lisboa .. .. 50p/**£1**/£1.50
Ediciones Fisa .. .. 50p/**£1**/£1.50
Others .. .. 25p/**75p**/£1

Switzerland
Mountain charts .. .. 50p/**£1**/£1.50
Pub. Kunzli Zurich (*Boer propaganda*) .. .. £7/**£11**/£20
Others .. .. £1/**£2**/£3

Spain
Alfil. Outline map with girl & stamp .. .. .. £1/**£2**/£3
Others .. .. 25p/**£1**/£1.50

USA
Publishers include: C.T. American Art; C.T. Art-Colortone; Max Basker & Sons; Mike Boyer; Bromley & Co. Inc.; Clem-cards Inc.; Colourpicture Pubs. Inc.; H. S. Crocker Co. Inc.; Dexter Press Inc.; Eastern Illustrating Co.; Florida Natural Color Inc.; Hartman Card Co.; Johnson Printing Inc.; CP. Johnston Company; E. C. Kropp Co.; Manhattan Postcard Pub. Co. Inc.; Mitock Pubs. Inc.; Petty Studios; Scenic Art; The Scheller Co.; Tichnor Bros. Inc.; Tomlin Art Co.; David E. Traub; E. D. West Co.; Western Pub. & Novelty Co.
Price range .. .. £2/**£3**/£4

Jamestown Expo 1907. Pocohontas' Head design £3/**£5**/£6
Others Periods 2–6 .. .. £1.50/**£2**/£4
Period 7 .. .. 25p/**50p**/75p

As it is difficult to date a card precisely, a period system has been used in this catalogue. For a full explanation of the system see page viii.

MILITARY

This section deals with cards whose subject matter is, in the main, historical rather than contemporary. The listing is divided into three main groups: *Artists, Foreign, Publishers* and *Wars*. The last-named section covers 12 conflicts from the Boer War to Vietnam. The major specialist British publisher of military cards was Gale & Polden, although Tucks produced hundreds of titles. Artists who stand out in this field are Richard Caton-Woodville and Harry Payne. Splendid chromo-litho cards were produced in Italy from around 1890 carrying the flags and battle honours of military regiments and these are currently attracting attention.

ARTISTS

Caton-Woodville, Richard† .. .. £1/**£1.50**/£2
Ibbetson, Ernest† (*see* Gale & Polden under 'Publishers' below) .. .. £1.50/**£2**/£4
McNeil, J. (*see* Gale & Polden under 'Publishers' below) .. .. £1.50/**£2**/£4
O'Beirne, F. .. .. £3/**£5**/£8
Payne, Harry† .. .. £2/**£5**/£20
Others .. .. 75p/**£1.50**/£3

FOREIGN

French

Military figures published by L'H (probably L'Hirondelle) of Paris. Cards are numbered and initialled, 'P.K.' At last 40 cards .. .. £1.50/**£2**/£5.50
Others .. .. 50p/**75p**/£1

Italian

Period 1. Chromo-litho. UB. .. .. £4/**£6**/£8
Period 2. Chromo-litho. UB. .. .. £2/**£3**/£4
Others .. .. 50p/**75p**/£1

PUBLISHERS

The major specialist publisher in this field is Gale & Polden.

Gale & Polden

Badge series. Gold border. About 120 cards £1.50/**£2.50**/£3
British Army (History & Traditions) series. UB. 120 cards in Period 2. Welsh Guards added in Period 3. First issues unnumbered. Artists J. McNeil & Ernest Ibbetson.

- No. 1–31 Cavalry .. .. £2/**£3**/£4
- Nos. 32–104 Infantry .. .. £2/**£2.50**/£3
- Nos. 105–117 Corps .. .. £1.50/**£2**/£3
- Lord Kitchener .. .. £1/**£2**/£2.50
- Sir John French .. .. £1/**£1.50**/£2
- Military Mail .. .. £3/**£4**/£5
- Nelson series .. .. 50p/**£1**/£1.50

Recruiting cards. Regimental recruiting offices used G & P cards picturing their Regiment but changed the text to give details of rates of pay. Many such cards were not postcards. We refer only to postcards printed for HMSO.

Price range .. ..£8/**£10**/£12

Wellington series. Inset photo-origin cameo views with surrounding artistic military design. UB .. .. £2/**£3**/£4

Others .. .. 50p/**75p**/£1

Knight Bros.

Chromo-litho Regimental series .. .. .. 75p/**£1**/£1.25

Salmon, J.

Various military artist-drawn designs (incl. A. R. Quinton) .. .. 50p/**75p**/£1

Tuck

Our Army/Our Navy. Oilettes 25p/**50p**/75p

Our Generals. Series 68. UB .. .. £1/**£2**/£3

Valentine

The Kings Army. Artotype series 25p/**50p**/75p

WARS

This section covers cards issued immediately before, during and after each war, i.e. they are *Contemporary* records. This is an important distinction which separates this category from cards depicting warlike activities, uniforms, etc. but issued long after the event.

BOER WAR (Oct. 1899–May 1902)

This is a specialist field in which values may fluctuate widely. All cards are UB.

Anti-British Satire

Dutch Pub. J. G. Vlieger Cartoons UB .. £8/**£10**/£12

French Artist Fredillo UB .. .. £6/**£8**/£10

German Pub. Antiquariat Bremen UB .. .. £6/**£8**/£10

Collectors Publishing Co.

Personalities, photographic origin UB .. .. .. £4/**£6**/£8

Personalities as above plus *The Picture Postcard* magazine title overprint .. .. £7/**£9**/£10

Peace, Memorials and Reconciliation

Divided back all types 25p/**50p**/75p

Joseph Chamberlain Tour Memorial card showing route and full designs both sides UB .. .. .. £12/**£20**/£25

Peace Conference commemorative UB .. .. .. £5/**£8**/£10

Picture Postcard Co.

Artist drawn battle scenes. Caton Woodville, etc. £4/**£6**/£8

Vignettes of army commanders .. .. £3/**£4**/£6

Sieges

Ladysmith (2 November 1899–28 February 1900)

Natal officials printed during the siege, plus line drawn vignettes in red each side.

Used .. .. £100/**£150**/£300
Unused .. .. £25/**£40**/£50
Photo origin views of siege .. .. .. £10/**£15**/£25

Mafeking (12 October 1899–17 May 1900)
Artist drawn .. .. £8/**£10**/£12
Photo origin .. .. £10/**£15**/£20

Tuck Empire Series
Artist drawn. Berkeley, Payne, Teller, etc. .. .. £7/**£9**/£12
Photographic origin .. .. £5/**£8**/£10

BOXER REBELLION (June 1900–Sep. 1901) ■M 1
Allied soldiers: American, British, Christian Chinese, French, German, Italian, Japanese and Russian.
B & w photo origin poses .. .. £4/**£6**/£8
German artist drawn satire .. .. .. £10/**£15**/£20

■M 1 Pub. Anon. Ger. Artist Anon. Boxer Rebellion Satire 'Haute cuisine in the Chinese Menagerie'. UB. 1900 £20

RUSSO-JAPANESE WAR (Feb. 1904–Sep. 1905)

Battle Scenes/Maps/War Portraits
Pub. Hildesheimer
Col. art. Seppings Wright. Ships .. .. £1.50/**£2**/£2.50
War series. Various artists .. .. .. £1.50/**£2**/£3
Pub. J. W. & Co. Russian ships .. .. £2/**£3**/£4
Pub. Knight Bros. Russian navy .. .. £1.50/**£2.50**/£3
Pub. Pictorial Postcard Co. Empire series .. £1/**£2**/£2.50
Pub. Tattimoto, Tsujimoto, etc. Art personalities, ships, etc. .. .. £1.50/**£2.50**/£3
Pub. Tuck. Oilettes .. .. £1/**£1.50**/£2.50
Pub. Tuck. RP .. .. £2/**£2.50**/£3
Pub. A. J. Young, Harlesden. Action scenes £1/**£1.50**/£2
Others .. .. £1/**£1.50**/£3.50

Humour/Satire
Artist Dudley Hardy. Pub. Hildesheimer. Series 3015 .. .. £4/**£5**/£7
French. Artist E. Muller. Pub. P. L. Paris .. .. £2/**£3**/£4
French. Pub. MM, Paris .. .. £2/**£4**/£5

French. 'Le Burin Satirique'. Artist Orens ■POL 2 .. .. £10/**£15**/£20
Others .. .. £1/**£2**/£2.50

Military Review 1906
This was a review to celebrate Japanese success in the war. Special cards with photo montage battle scenes were issued in transparent envelopes in Tokyo and Kobe.

With Tokyo handstamp .. .. £4/**£6**/£8
With Kobe handstamp .. .. £5/**£7**/£10
Without handstamp .. .. £2/**£3**/£5
Transparent envelope .. .. 50p/**£1**/£2

Official Japanese
Communications Department. Post War issue .. £1/**£2**/£3
Post Office 1904 issue. Photo montage. Art borders UB .. .. £3/**£4**/£5
Tuck. Real photographic series no. 5170. 1904 £1/**£1.50**/£2
Tuck. Russo-Japanese series no. 1330 .. £1/**£1.50**/£2

Peace Conference
Pub. Knight Bros. Multi-view .. .. £2/**£3**/£5
Pub. Rotograph Co. New York (1906). 'The Portsmouth Drama' .. .. £3/**£4**/£5

Russian Outrage on Hull Fleet
Anonymous/minor pub. artistic cards .. .. 50p/**75p**/£1
Photographic origin. Damage detail .. .. £1/**£2**/£2.50
Valentines .. .. 75p/**£1**/£1.50

ITALO-TURKISH WAR (Sep. 1911–Oct. 1912)

With the object of seizing Libya, and thus counterbalncing French Colonial influence in north Africa, Italian forces invaded from the sea and captured Tripoli and Tobruk. Turkish military resistance was slight and threatened by the impending Balkan War, Turkey negotiated a peace, ceding Libya to Italy.

General scenes .. .. £1/**£2**/£3
Pub. Traldi, Milan. Numbered. RP. At least 17 known .. .. £4/**£6**/£8
Higher values for RP cards and unposed military scenes.

CHINESE CIVIL WAR (Oct. 1911–Aug. 1917)

Following the Russo-Japanese War, during which most of the fighting had taken place on Chinese soil, the Europeans and Japanese made strong territorial claims upon China. Dissatisfied with the response of their government, Chinese troops mutinied and established the Republic of China. Various internal struggles continued with several changes of President until August 1917 when China joined the Allies and declared war on Germany (WW1).

European and Japanese troops/barracks £1.25/**£1.50**/£1.75
General art impressions of actions, Hankow, Nanking, etc. .. .. £1.50/**£2**/£3

BALKAN WARS (Oct. 1912–July 1913)

In 1912 Bulgaria, Serbia and Greece joined forces in the Balkan League and moved simultaneously into Turkish European territories, hoping to take advantage of Turkey's war with Italy to extend their borders. Anxious for their own colonial ambitions in the area, the Great European Powers imposed a peace on the combatants in the Treaty of London in May 1913.

RP. Battle scenes. Art borders .. .. £2.50/**£4**/£5
Others .. .. £1.50/**£2**/£2.50

WORLD WAR 1 (4 Aug. 1914–11 Nov. 1918) PERIOD 3

Higher valuations generally attach to RP cards. French issues tend to be less valuable than others.

Air Warfare

Aces/Personalities
Highest values for RP well known personalities.
British .. .. £1/**£1.50**/£5
French .. .. 75p/**£1.50**/£6
German .. .. £1.50/**£2**/£7
USA .. .. 75p/**£1.50**/£6
'Air War Personalities' series. Aviators in aeroplanes. Pub. Deley (*Fr.*) .. .. £2/**£3**/£5

Bomb Damage in Britain
Photographic origin only .. .. £1/**£2.50**/£3
Ramsgate 17 May 1917. Zeppelin Raid .. £1/**£1.75**/£2.50

Combat Studies
Artistic .. .. £1.50/**£2.50**/£4
Crashes .. .. £1.50/**£2**/£3.50
Photographic origin .. .. 75p/**£1.50**/£3

Observation Balloons
Price range .. .. 50p/**£1**/£1.50

Zeppelins

Artistic impressions—general .. .. .. 50p/**75p**/£1
German propaganda (incl. Thiele *q.v.*) .. .. £4/**£5**/£6
Zeppelins brought down
- Cuffley. (Sep. 1916) SL 11 .. .. .. 50p/**75p**/£1
- Great Bursted (Sep. 1916) L32 .. .. 50p/**£1**/£1.25
- Hartlepool. (Nov. 1916) L34 .. .. .. 50p/**75p**/£1
- Little Wigborough. (Sep. 1916) L33 .. 50p/**£1**/£1.25
- Potters Bar. (Oct. 1916) L31 .. .. .. 50p/**75p**/£1
- Theberton. (June 1917) .. .. £1/**£1.50**/£2

Pub. I.V. 'Zepp Slayers' .. .. £1/**£1.50**/£2
Pub. Faulkner .. .. 50p/**75p**/£1

Fund Raising/Welfare

'Arf a Mo Kaiser' Pub. Gale & Polden, Artist Bert Thomas .. .. £1/**£2**/£2.50
Bovril, Gladys Storey Fund, etc. 25p/**50p**/75p

Egg Fund 25p/50p
Evening News POW Fund. Attached stamp type 75p/**£1**/£2

Official Organisations

Belgian cards	25p/**50p**/£1
British Ambulance Committee	25p/50p
Church Army	25p/50p
French cards	25p/**50p**/75p
German cards	50p/**75p**/£1.50
Institute for the Blind	25p/**50p**/75p
Italian cards	75p/**£1**/£1.50
Regimental days	25p/**50p**/75p
Relief Fund, Sir John French, etc.	25p/**50p**/75p
St. John Ambulance Association	25p/**50p**/£1
Salvation Army	25p/50p
Star & Garter	£3/**£5**/£7
Submarine banks	50p/**£1**/£2
Tank banks, photographic detail	25p/**50p**/£1
War Bonds Campaign	25p/**50p**/75p
Welsh Troops days	25p/50p
YMCA Hut Fund	25p/50p

Red Cross

Belgian	25p/50p
British	25p/**50p**/75p
Dutch Artist Louis Raemaekers	£1/**£1.25**/£1.50
French	25p/**50p**/75p
Italian	50p/**75p**/£1
German	£1/**£1.25**/£1.50

Tobacco Funds

Performers 25p/**50p**/75p
Weekly Dispatch (*see also* 'Arf a Mo Kaiser' above) .. .. £1/**£2**/£2.50

Heroes/Personalities/Soldiers ■M 2

Particularly at the beginning of WW1 it was believed that 'Great Leaders' would decide the outcome. Thus statesmen, royalty, generals and admirals feature on thousands of cards, sometimes in order to raise funds, sometimes for propaganda and frequently because publishers knew that such cards sold well. As the war progressed, heroic deeds became news, and all nations have cards describing individual actions of gallantry, some drawn by fine artists, e.g. Caton-Woodville and Georges Scott.

Artist drawn
Price range .. .. 25p/**£1**/£3
Boy Scout Movement
'A Hero's Fate' .. .. 25p/**50p**/£1
Churchill, Winston .. .. £1/**£1.50**/£2
George V & Queen Mary
Christmas card 1914, Army & Naval uniforms 25p/**50p**/£1
Heroic Deeds
Artists impressions 25p/**50p**/75p
Photographic origin 25p/50p

Kitchener Memorial cards .. .. £2/**£3**/£4

'L' Battery Pub. ELD 25p/**50p**/75p

Portraits
German cards are valued about 25% higher than others.
Generals, etc. .. .. 50p/**75p**/£1
Politicians/Civilian leaders 25p/**50p**/75p
Soldiers 25p/50p
VC's. Pub. Gale & Polden, Artist Stanley Wood, rounded corners .. .. 75p/**£1**/£1.25

■M 2 Pub. Rotary. Gen. Sir Douglas Haig. RP. PU 1914 75p

■M 3 Pub. P. Coustoulidis, Alexandria. Artist V. Manavian. No. 1. 1916 £2

Humour ■M 3
The ordinary comic card has a base value of around 50p, but those by well-known artists or which include a contemporary reference in the drawing or caption (gas mask, ration book, etc.) will be considerably more valuable. A list of artists was given in the second edition of this catalogue (p. 235).

Sets
Deutschmeister Witwen, etc. 'Action in the Field'. Pub. C. Pietsch. Artist R. Kristen. 75 numbered examples known .. .. 75p/**£1**/£1.50
Egyptian Humour. Pub. P. Coustoulidis. Artist V. Manavian. At least 12 cards .. .. £1/**£1.50**/£2
Fragments from France. Pub. *The Bystander*. Artist Bairnsfather. Nine series each of 6 cards. Fully listed in the Second Edition (pp. 36–38) .. .. £1/**£1.25**/£1.50
'La Journée Du Poilu'. Artist Saul Chambry 25p/**50p**/75p
'More News by Liarless From Berlin. Pub. Jarrold. Artist Hassall (two series) .. .. £3/**£3.50**/£4
'Our Sailors'. Pub. Raffaelli, Toulon. Artist H. Gervèse. At least 30 cards .. .. £1/**£1.50**/£2

Silhouettes. Pub. Photochrom. 'American Silhouettes', 'Camp Silhouettes' & 'Jack Ashore' (each set probably 6 cards) .. .. 75p/**£1**/£1.50

Topics
Conscientious Objectors .. .. £1/**£1.25**/£1.50
DORA (Defence of the Realm Act) .. .. £1/**£1.50**/£2
Rationing .. .. 75p/**£1**/£1.25
Recruiting .. .. 50p/**£1**/£3
Submarines .. .. 50p/**75p**/£1
Women's Suffrage .. .. £2/**£4**/£5
Zeppelins .. .. 25p/**50p**/£1

Land Warfare
The main interest centres upon details of clothing, equipment and general environment. Busy cards of photo-origin are valued most when clear details of motor vehicles, guns and tanks, etc. can be seen. The great mass of French cards showing war damage are little collected. The major British series was published by the Daily Mail.

Combat scenes .. .. 50p/**75p**/£2
Damage (Booklets 20p per card) 25p/50p
Equipment and vehicles .. .. £1/**£1.25**/£2.50
Front line life .. .. 75p/**£1**/£1.25
Irish rebellion May 1916 .. .. 75p/**£1.25**/£2.50
Prisoners of War .. .. £1/**£1.50**/£3
Tanks. Close-up views .. .. 75p/**£1**/£2
Weapons. Artillery, flame-throwers, machine guns, mortars, etc. .. .. 25p/**75p**/£1.75
Wounded. Groups, home or overseas 25p/**50p**/75p

Publishers
Daily Mail 176 cards in 22 series. *See* Second Edition (pp. 236–239) .. .. £1/**£1.25**/£2
Photochrom. 48 cards. *See* Third Edition (p. 284) .. .. 75p/**£1**/£1.50

Official Cards
Church Army 25p/**50p**/75p
Field service postcards. AF2042/W3229 .. 50p/**75p**/£1
French with col. flags .. .. 25p/**50p**/£1
French with col. flags and border .. .. 50p/**£1**/£1.25
German view of captured locality .. .. 75p/**£1.50**/£3
Italian with col. flags 25p/**50p**/75p
Regimental issues .. .. 75p/**£1**/£1.25
YMCA active service .. .. 25p/**75p**/£1
Others 25p/50p

Patriotism/Propaganda/Sentiment ■M 4
National patriotic fervours in 1914 ran very high in every nation. Postcards in their millions carried waving flags and pretty ladies symbolising allies and alliances. As the war progressed propaganda became more thoughtful, more specific.

Artists
Armitage, William† 25p/**50p**/75p
Arus, Raoul (Fr) .. .. 75p/**£1**/£1.50

Averell, Joyce	25p/**50p**/75p
Barribal, W.†	£1.50/**£2**/£3
Beerts, Albert (Fr)	50p/**75p**/£1
Bertl, H. (Aust)	£1/**£1.50**/£2
Biggar, J. L.	25p/**50p**/75p
Boileau, Philip† (USA)	£1.50/**£2**/£2.50
Bone, Muirhead	£1/**£1.25**/£1.50
Boulanger, Maurice (Fr)	75p/**£1**/£1.50
Brinsley, E. C.	50p/**75p**/£1.50
Brunelleschi, Umberto† (It)	£15/**£25**/£30
Butcher, Arthur	25p/**50p**/75p
Canivet, H. (Fr)	25p/**50p**/75p
Cartill, T. (Fr)	**50p**
Corbella, Tito (It)†	£1/**£1.50**/£2
Dupuis, Emile (Fr)	£1/**£1.25**/£1.50
Ellam, William Henry†	25p/**50p**/75p
English, Archibald† (A.E.)	25p/**50p**/75p
Freiertag, F. (Aust)	£1/**£1.50**/£2
Gilson, T.†	25p/**50p**/75p
Gunn, Archie† (USA)	£1/**£1.50**/£2
Hirleman (Belg)	25p/**50p**/£1
Hofer, A. (Fr)	25p/**50p**/75p
Hoffmann, R. J. (Ger)	£2/**£3**/£5
Holland, Frank	£1/**£2**/£2.50
Ibbetson, Ernest†	75p/**£1**/£1.50
Joseph, Karl (Ger)	£3/**£4**/£5
Jung, F. R. (Aust)	£1/**£1.25**/£1.50
Larwin, H. (Aust)	£1/**£1.25**/£1.50
Lenhard (Ger)	£3/**£7**/£10
Mailick, A.† (Ger)	£1/**£1.50**/£2
Martini, Alberto† (It)	£3/**£5**/£8
Maurice, Reg†	75p/**£1.50**/£2.50
Mauzan, Achille† (It)	£2/**£3**/£5
Meschini, G. (It)	£2/**£4**/£5
Pastien, Emil (Belg)	£1/**£1.50**/£2.50
Payne, Harry†	£2/**£3**/£5
Pearse, A.	£1/**£2**/£3
Poulbot, Francisque† (Fr)	50p/**£1**/£1.50
Raemaekers, Louis† (Du)	75p/**£1**/£2.50
Raven-Hill, Leonard†	50p/**£1**/£2
Richardson, Agnes†	75p/**£1**/£1.50
Riss, Th. (Ger)	50p/**75p**/£1
Rubino, Antonio† (It)	£2/**£3**/£5
Sager, X.† (Fr)	£1/**£2**/£3
Scott, Georges (Fr)	£1/**£1.50**/£2
Shepherd, G. E.†	50p/**£1**/£1.50
Tauzin, Louis (Fr)	50p/**£1**/£1.50
Thomas, Bert†	75p/**£1.50**/£2
Wennerburg, Brynolf† (Ger)	£1.50/**£2**/£3
Wilson, Oscar	25p/**50p**/75p
Wood, Lawson†	£1/**£1.50**/£2
Others	25p/**50p**/75p

Publishers

Bamforth song cards 25p/**50p**/75p

Others .. .. 25p/**50p**/£1

Over 30 publishers of this genre were listed in the Second Edition (p. 241).

Sets

See the third edition of this catalogue for details.

Price range .. ..75p/**£5**/£20

Themes

Certain events provided ideal ammunition for propaganda, e.g. the execution of Edith Cavell and the sinking of the *Lusitania*. Slogans such as 'Ils Ne Passeront Pas', 'Gott Mit Uns', 'Are We Downhearted?—No!' provided emotive patriotic rallying themes.

Cavell, Edith .. .. £1/**£1.50**/£2.50

Hatred:

British .. .. £2/**£3**/£5

French .. .. 75p/**£1**/£2.50

German .. .. £1/**£2**/£3

Home Front. Direct references to rationing, national insurance, air raids, etc... .. .. 50p/**£1**/£1.50

King & Country .. .. 25p/**50p**/£1

Kultur:

Allied Cards .. .. 25p/**50p**/£1

German Defence of .. .. 50p/**£1**/£2

Lusitania .. .. £1.50/**£2**/£2.50

Quotations. National leaders, Kitchener, Kaiser, etc. 25p/**50p**/75p

Recruiting:

Artistic references to .. .. 50p/**75p**/£1.25

Photographic origin, rallies, etc. .. .. £1.50/**£2**/£3

Sentiment:

American 25p/**50p**/75p

British 25p/**50p**/75p

French (two cards) 25p/50p

German 25p/**50p**/75p

Italian .. .. 50p/**75p**/£1

Slogans:

Are we downhearted? No! 25p/**50p**/75p

Deutschland Über Alles .. .. 50p/**75p**/£1

Gott Strafe England .. .. 50p/**75p**/£1

Ils Ne Passeront Pas 25p/**50p**/75p

On Les Aura .. .. 25p/**75p**/£1

Poor Little Belgium/Serbia 25p/**50p**/75p

Verdun .. .. 75p/**£1**/£1.50

Others 25p/**50p**/75p

Peace/Victory

There was rejoicing everywhere when the war ended—for a while anyway. Here we are concerned only with the period immediately after the war, when references to it continued. Thus we are now in Period 4. Values are low.

Memorials
Views 25p/50p
Unveilings with crowd details 25p/**50p**/75p

National Thanksgiving Service 1919
Photographic origin with detail .. .. .. £1/**£1.50**/£1.75
Frank O'Salisbury picture .. .. 75p/**£1.50**/£2

Personalities
Fund raising or similar. Value according to personality .. .. 50p/**75p**/£1

Victory Parades (close-up detail only)
British 25p/**50p**/75p
Other 25p/**50p**/75p

■M 4 Pub. Regent Pub. Co. Artist Reg. Maurice. No. 2393. Period 3 £2

■M 5 Pub. Anon. Fr. Artist X. Sager. 'Midnight Thoughts'. Series 61. No. 319. Period 3 £4

Pin-Ups

During WW1 the soldiers pinned up saucy postcards to relieve the horrors of trench life. The ladies became known as pin-ups. Many cards of this type are artists impressions produced in France; the leading exponent being Raphael Kirchner. The most prolific pin-up artist was Xavier Sager. Collecting is mainly centered around artists' signatures and we have listed cards in that way. All cards are Period 3.

Déshabillé ■M 5
Cards showing ladies in various forms of undress. These are generally valued more highly than glamour cards.
Bonzagni, Aroldo† (It) .. .. £3/**£6**/£12
Calderara, C.† (It) .. .. £2/**£4**/£6
Fabiano (Fr) .. .. £2/**£3**/£4
Fontan, Léo (Fr) .. .. £2/**£4**/£5

Hérouard (Fr) .. .. £2/**£3**/£4
Jarach, A. (Fr) .. .. £3/**£5**/£6
Kirchner, Raphael† (Fr domicile) .. .. ..£8/**£12**/£15
Maréchaux, C. .. .. £2/**£3**/£5
Meunier, Suzanne (Fr) .. .. £1/**£3**/£5
Millière, Maurice† (It) .. .. £3/**£5**/£6
Ney (Fr) .. .. £2/**£3**/£6
Peltier (Fr) .. .. £1.50/**£3**/£4.50
Penot, A. (Fr) .. .. £2/**£3**/£5
Pépin, Maurice (Fr) .. .. £1/**£2**/£4
Sager, Xavier† (Fr) .. .. £2/**£4**/£6
San Marco (It) .. .. £1.50/**£3**/£5
Anonymous .. .. 75p/**£1**/£2

Glamour ■A 6, 10
Cards showing attractive ladies but not undressed, undressing or over-exposing.
Barribal, W.† .. .. £2/**£2.50**/£3.50
Bianchi, Alberto (It) .. .. £1.50/**£2**/£3
Boileau, Philip† (USA) .. .. £2/**£2.50**/£3
Bompard, Luigi (It) .. .. £2/**£3**/£4
Busi, Adolfo (It) .. .. £2/**£3**/£5
Colombo, E. (Fr) .. .. £2/**£2.50**/£3
Corbella, Tito† (Fr) .. .. £1.50/**£2.50**/£4
English, Archibald (A.E.)† .. .. 75p/**£1**/£1.50
Fidler, Alice Luella (USA) .. .. 75p/**£1**/£1.50
Fuchs, R. (Ger) .. .. 75p/**£1**/£1.50
Leonnec (Fr) .. .. £2/**£3**/£5
Mauzan, Achille† (It) .. .. £2/**£4**/£6
Nanni, Giovanni† .. .. £2/**£3**/£4
Rappini (It) .. .. £2/**£2.50**/£3.50
Anonymous .. .. 75p/**£1**/£1.50

Queen Mary's Collection

Queen Mary, wife of George V, was presented with a quantity of confiscated picture postcards by a postal censor. They are mostly German and Dutch. The total number of cards in the collection, now housed in Windsor, is about 100. This collection was listed in the Second Edition (p. 244).
Price range .. ..75p to £12

Sea Warfare

The war at sea was a continuous assault by German U-boats upon Allied merchant shipping interspersed by a number of surface actions. In the early months actions were often depicted on postcards, but Germany soon censored these. Britain's best known series by Photochrom showing scenes from the Admiralty film Britain Prepared *was issued in June 1916 the same month as censorship was imposed. Cards produced prior to 1916 tend to be photographic in origin, later cards tend to be artistic impressions. The dates given below are those on which the actions began:*

Photo Origin
Bombardment—Dardanelles. 18 Mar. 1915 £1/**£1.50**/£2
Bombardment—Scarborough. 16 Dec. 1914 75p/**£1**/£1.25
Britain Prepared. 24 cards .. .. £1/**£1.50**/£2
Coronel—1 Nov. 1914 .. .. 75p/**£1**/£1.50

Falkland Islands—8 Dec. 1914 .. .. .. £1.50/**£2**/£3
Heligoland—28 Aug. 1914 .. .. 50p/**75p**/£1
Jutland (Skagerrak)—31 May 1916 .. .. 75p/**£1.50**/£2
Others 25p/**50p**/75p

The Britain Prepared *series was listed in the third edition (p. 288).*

Artist drawn
Most artistic impressions rate less than cards of photographic origin; exceptions are:
Baumgarten, E. V. (Ger) .. .. £3/**£4**/£5
Bohrdt, Professor Hans (Ger). .. .. £2/**£3**/£4
Gribble, Bernard F. .. .. 50p/**75p**/£1

Ships
HMAS *Sydney* (*see* SMS *Emden*) .. .. 50p/**75p**/£1
HMS *Aboukir* (*see* U9) .. .. 75p/**£1.50**/£2
HMS *Cressy* (*see* U9) .. .. 75p/**£1.50**/£2
HMS *Hogue* (*see* U9) .. .. 75p/**£1.50**/£2
Lusitania 7 May 1915. *See* 'Patriotism/Propaganda/ Sentiment' .. .. £1/**£1.50**/£2.50
SMS *Emden* (sunk by HMAS *Sydney* on 9 Nov. 1914) .. .. 50p/**75p**/£1.50
U *Deutschland* (sailed to America in June 1916) £1/**£2**/£3
U9 (sank Aboukir, Cressy & Hogue on 22 Sept. 1914) .. .. 75p/**£1.50**/£2
Others .. .. 25p/**75p**/£1

Silks
We consider three types of cards—embroidered, printed and woven. The majority of silk cards were made in France and Belgium during WW1, although the type originated in Germany late in Period 1.

Embroidered
There is an extraordinary range of embroidered cards but it can be covered by the 5 main classifications below:

Badges:
British Air units including RNAS .. .. ..£8/**£10**/£12
British Corps .. .. £2/**£3**/£4
British Line Regiments .. .. £10/**£12**/£15
British Naval units including ships .. ..£8/**£10**/£12
Other Corps .. .. £1/**£2**/£3
Other Line Regiments .. .. £1/**£2**/£4

Inserts:
Found in embroidered cards with pockets; valuations for sentimental designs
Card .. .. 50p/**£1**/£2
Celluloid .. .. £1/**£2**/£3
Silk hankies .. .. £2/**£3**/£4
Without insert .. .. 75p/**£1**/£1.25

Military Designs:
Air/Land/Sea .. .. £2/**£4**/£6
Barracks .. .. £8/**£12**/£15

Comfort organisations, e.g. Red Cross .. £10/**£12**/£15
Equipment/Weapons .. £3/**£5**/£7
Flames .. £5/**£8**/£10
Men .. £3/**£5**/£7

Personalities:
Inset photographs are often found stuck within an embroidered design. The values below are for single photos. Double photos rate up to 50% above the single valuation.

Albert, King of the Belgians .. £3/**£5**/£10
Cavell, Edith .. £2.50/**£4**/£7
Elisabeth, Queen of the Belgians .. £3/**£5**/£10
Foch, Maréchal .. £4/**£6**/£12
French, Sir John .. £2/**£4**/£8
George V, King .. £2/**£4**/£8
Haig, Sir Douglas .. £3/**£5**/£10
Joffre .. £2.50/**£4**/£7
Kitchener, Lord .. £3/**£5**/£10
Nicholas, Tsar of Russia .. £3/**£5**/£10
Pershing, General .. £4/**£6**/£12
Poincaré, President of France .. £3/**£5**/£10
Sarrail, General .. £2.50/**£4**/£7
Victor Emmanuel .. £2/**£3**/£6

Printed
This is the smallest category of silk cards. A prominent publisher was Editions Gabriel of Paris and their initials may often be found on the silk.

Flames:
Albert .. £3/**£5**/£7.50
Arras .. £4/**£6**/£8
Dixmuide .. £3/**£5**/£7.50
Nieuport .. £5/**£7**/£10
Rheims .. £3/**£5**/£7.50
Ypres .. £2/**£3**/£6

Personalities:
Cavell, Edith .. 75p/**£1.50**/£2
Kitchener, Lord .. 50p/**75p**/£1

Woven

Flames
Pictures depicting French and Belgian towns burning. Pub. Bertrand & Boiran.
Albert .. £8/**£10**/£12
Amiens Cathedral .. £10/**£15**/£20
Arras .. £8/**£10**/£12
Bapaume .. £10/**£15**/£20
Cambrai .. £10/**£15**/£20
Dixmuide .. £8/**£10**/£12
Douai .. £10/**£15**/£20
Dunkerque .. £8/**£10**/£12
Gand .. £10/**£15**/£20
Nieuport .. £8/**£10**/£12
Peronne .. £8/**£10**/£12

Pervyse .. .. £10/**£12**/£15
Rheims .. .. £10/**£12**/£15
Verdun .. ..£8/**£10**/£12
Vimy .. .. £15/**£20**/£25
Ypres .. .. £8/**£10**/£12
Others .. .. £7/**£9**/£15

Personalities:
Pub. Bertrand & Boiran.
Albert, King of the Belgians .. .. .. £20/**£30**/£35
Cavell, Edith .. .. £20/**£30**/£35
Foch, Maréchal .. .. £15/**£25**/£30
George V, King .. .. £15/**£25**/£30
Jellicoe, Admiral .. .. £20/**£30**/£35
Joffre .. .. £15/**£25**/£30
Kitchener, Lord .. .. £15/**£25**/£30
Poincaré, President of France .. .. .. £15/**£25**/£30
Sarrail, General .. .. £20/**£30**/£35
Others .. .. £10/**£20**/£25

Pub. E. Deffrene
Albert, King of the Belgians .. .. .. £10/**£12**/£15
Cavell, Edith, without flower .. ..£8/**£10**/£15
Cavell, Edith, with flower .. .. £20/**£35**/£45
Clemenceau .. .. £15/**£25**/£30
Elisabeth, Queen of the Belgians .. .. £15/**£25**/£30
Foch, Maréchal .. .. £12/**£15**/£18
French, Sir John .. .. £15/**£18**/£20
George V, King .. .. £10/**£12**/£15
Haig, Sir Douglas .. .. £10/**£12**/£15
Joffre .. .. £10/**£12**/£15
Kitchener, Lord .. .. £10/**£12**/£15
Lloyd George, David .. .. £25/**£30**/£40
Pétain .. .. £12/**£15**/£20
Poincaré, President of France .. .. .. £10/**£12**/£15
Wilson, President of America .. .. .. £20/**£30**/£35

Pub. W. H. Grant
French, Sir John .. .. £30/**£35**/£45
George V, King .. .. £25/**£30**/£35
Jellicoe, Admiral .. .. £20/**£25**/£30
Kitchener, Lord .. .. £18/**£20**/£25
Mary, Queen .. .. £25/**£35**/£40
Others .. .. £10/**£20**/£40

Pub. Thomas Stevens
French, Sir John .. .. £40/**£80**/£100
George V, King .. .. £40/**£80**/£100
Kitchener, Lord .. .. £40/**£80**/£100
Mary, Queen .. .. £40/**£80**/£100

Women at War
As the men went to fight so women had to take over their jobs. Interest centres around women performing men's jobs and any reference to female emancipation. Major publishers on this theme include Art & Humour, Inter-Art, Noyer (Fr), Photochrom and Tuck. Nursing is the most common theme.

Artists

Butcher, Arthur	50p/**75p**/£1
Copping, Harold	50p/**75p**/£1
Dupuis, Emile (Fr)	75p/**£1**/£1.50
Edmunds, Kay	25p/**50p**/£2
Horsfall, Mary†	50p/**75p**/£1.50
Leroy (Fr)	£1/**£1.50**/£2
Sager, Xavier† (Fr)	£1/**£2**/£2.50
Skinner, E. F.	50p/**75p**/£2
Spurgin, Fred†	50p/**75p**/£1.50
Wennerburg, B.†	£1.50/**£3**/£4
White, Flora.†	25p/**50p**/75p

Emancipation .. .. £2/**£3**/£5

Men's Jobs

Artist drawn:

British	75p/**£1**/£1.25
German	25p/**£1**/£1.50
Others	25p/**50p**/£1

Photographic:

Clear detail	£2/**£2.50**/£3
French posed (Bamforth type)	25p/**50p**/75p
Ger. Pub. Knackstedt. Set of 6	75p/**£1**/£2

Series

'For the Cause' Pub. Tuck 25p/**50p**/75p

La Femme and La Guerre. Pub. Gallais (Fr). Artist Leroy (at least 10 cards) .. .. 75p/**£1**/£2

Pub. Merval Corp. (US). Unnamed drawn series showing women at war work (at least 10 cards) .. 50p/**75p**/£1

'Our Own Girls' Pub. Inter-Art. Artist Arthur Butcher 25p/**50p**/75p

RUSSIAN CIVIL WAR (Mar. 1917–Dec. 1921)

This is a complicated conflict which began during WW1. At its heart was the struggle between the Red (Bolshevik) and White (Royalist) Russian forces.

Civil strife was triggered by a series of workers' strikes in Petrograd which began in March 1917. Armed conflict spread throughout Russia following the Bolshevik Revolution of November that same year and Russia withdrew from WW1. The Allies intervened in order to prevent war supplies falling into the hands of the Germans. Many other nationalities were involved including Czechs and Poles before Russia signed a peace treaty with the last of its opponents, Italy, in December 1921.

Allied Expeditionary Forces. Photo origin and RP scenes	£3/**£3.50**/£6
Red propaganda. Not RP	75p/**£1**/£1.50
White Russian propaganda. RP	£2/**£2.50**/£3
Others	75p/**£1**/£1.50

Highest valuations for dated RP cards depicting named events.

THE GRAECO-TURKISH WAR (May 1919–July 1923)

At the end of WW1 Turkey was in a state of near anarchy. To preserve their interests the Allies sent a Greek army into Smyrna thus provoking a patriotic national resistance. Fierce fighting characterised the conflict which ended in a Greek defeat. The Turks re-took Smyrna in September 1922 and the war came to an end with the Treaty of Lausanne in July 1923.

RP scenes. Smyrna .. .. £3/**£5**/£8
Others .. .. 75p/**£1**/£3

SPANISH CIVIL WAR (17 July 1936–23 Mar. 1939)

Artist drawn—General .. .. £2/**£7**/£8
General Franco propaganda, e.g. Commissariat of Propaganda, Catalonia .. .. £3/**£5**/£10
Nazi. Col. art .. .. £4/**£5**/£8
Photo-origin. *RP action scenes rate highest* .. .. £6/**£8**/£12
Republican propaganda
Anti-Franco, e.g. Republican Delegation for the defence of Madrid .. .. £2/**£3**/£7
Anti-German .. .. £2/**£4**/£7
Anti-Italian .. .. £6/**£8**/£10

WORLD WAR 2 (3 Sep. 1939–7 May 1945) PERIOD 5

This war was essentially a struggle against National Socialism (Nazism). Therefore we have included in this section, under the sub-heading German Propaganda, *information on Nazi cards even though some issues date from Period 4. Sub-divisions used here are broadly similar to those used for First World War cards.*

Air Warfare/Airborne Forces ■M 6

Aeroplanes
These are classified according to their publisher.

German
Official and other cards drawn by von Axster-Heudtlass .. .. £3/**£7**/£10

Photochrom
'Britain Prepared' photo series. Black and white £1/**£2**/£2.50
'Britain Prepared' photographic origin series. Brown and white .. .. 50p/**£1**/£1.25
'Colour Photograph' series. Prime Minister's slogan on the back .. .. 25p/**50p**/£1

P.C. Parif (Fr)
Aviation Britannique series .. .. .. 50p/**£1**/£1.25

Salmon
Artistic coloured impressions by A. F. D. Bannister, about 100 designs all numbered consecutively from no. 4839.
Full out pictures, details on back .. .. £1.50/**£2**/£3
Details in white strip on the front .. .. £1/**£1.50**/£2

Valentines
'Real Photograph' series, numbered on front, black and white, about 100 cards, action and other scenes .. £1/**£2**/£2.50
'Real Photograph' series with coloured Union Jack overprint .. .. 50p/**75p**/£1

Westland Aircraft Ltd.
Photomontage .. .. £1/**£2**/£4

Other Publishers .. .. 50p/**75p**/£1

Barrage Balloons
Drawn .. .. £1/**£1.50**/£1.75
Photographic origin .. .. £1/**£2**/£2.50

Ground Activity
Valuations given are for cards of photographic origin; drawn pictures command about 30% less.
Airfields .. .. £2/**£3**/£4
Anti-aircraft guns/predictors/searchlights .. £1.50/**£2.50**/£2
Crashes .. .. £2/**£5**/£7
V1. Flying Bomb .. .. .. , ... £5/**£8**/£10
V2. Ballistic Missile .. .. £4/**£6**/£8

Paratroops
Art. Unsigned .. .. £1.50/**£2**/£3
Photo-origin. RP rate highest .. .. .. £1.50/**£2**/£5

■M 6 Pub. Westland Aircraft Ltd. Photomontage 'Westland Lysanders drop supplies to the heroic garrison at Calais. June 1940' £4

■M 7 Pub. 'G.P.D.' (Govt. Propaganda Dept). 'For Freedom'. No. 445/2/5. President Roosevelt. Period 4 £3

Fund Raising/Welfare ■M 7

The British made little use of postcards as fund raisers compared to the Germans who issued many official postcards for that purpose. German and Italian designs are often coloured, dramatic and are oversize (o/s) cards.

British Fund Raisers

Academy Patriotic Publications, photographs of personalities, o/s .. .. £1/**£1.50**/£2
Tuck. 'In a World of Space' series .. .. 50p/**£1**/£1.25
Others .. .. 50p/**75p**/£1

German

'Tag der—' ('Day of—') cards. Official cards and fieldpost, o/s .. .. £3/**£4**/£6
'Wandkalendar' (Wall calendar) artist-drawn action scenes .. .. £6/**£9**/£10
Others .. .. £2/**£2.50**/£3

Italian

Coloured artist war scenes, o/s .. .. £3/**£4**/£5
Coloured other, o/s .. .. £1.50/**£2**/£3

US Treasury Department

'Buy War Bonds' .. .. £2/**£2.50**/£3

Welfare Organisations

NAAFI, Montgomery Club, Red Cross, YMCA, etc. .. .. £1/**£1.50**/£2

Heroes/Personalities/Soldiers

Unless stated valuations are for cards of photo-origin. Higher values for RP.

Belgian

Col. artist drawn portraits .. .. £2/**£3**/£5

British

Chamberlain .. .. £1/**£2**/£2.50
Churchill .. .. £1/**£1.50**/£3
Montgomery .. .. £1/**£1.25**/£2
Pub. G.P.D. 'For Freedom' series .. .. £1.50/**£2.50**/£3
Pub. G.P.D. 'Victory' series .. .. .. £1.50/**£2**/£3
Pub. Gale & Polden. Artist Ernest Ibbetson £1.50/**£2**/£2.50
Pub. Overseas League. VC series .. .. £1.50/**£2**/£2.50
Pub. Photochrom .. .. £1/**£1.50**/£2
Pub. Tuck:
'Real Photograph' series .. .. £1.50/**£2**/£3
'Royal Portrait' series .. .. £1.50/**£2**/£3.50

Others .. .. £1/**£2**/£2.50

Dutch

Col. art. British commanders, e.g. Dempsey £10/**£12**/£13

French

Pub. André Leconte. Artist Paul Barbier. *Armée Française* series .. .. £1.50/**£2**/£3

German

Artist W. Willrich. Col. o/s	£5/**£12**/£15
Pub. Hoffman, photo series	
Eben Emael paratroopers with Hitler	£30/**£35**/£50
Others	£5/**£12**/£15

Italian

Col. Artist drawn o/s	£1.50/**£2**/£4

Studio Portraits

German	50p/**£1**/£3
Others	25p/**75p**/£2

Humour

British cards overwhelm those of every other nation. Here we value cards that have a direct reference to wartime conditions, e.g. gas masks, blackouts, queues, Hitler, the home front, etc. Collecting is normally by artist. Cards depicting Hitler attract the higher values.

Artists

Akki	50p/**75p**/£1
Attwell, Mabel Lucie†	50p/**£1**/£1.50
Bairnsfather, Bruce†	75p/**£1**/£1.50
Barlog (Ger)	£1.50/**£2**/£3
Birch, Norah Annie	50p/**75p**/£1
Bizuth (Belg)	£1/**£2**/£2.50
Boudart, Bob (Belg)	75p/**£1**/£1.25
Breger, Dave (US)	£1/**£1.50**/£2
Carter, Reg.†	50p/**75p**/£1
Cheneval (Belg)	60p/**£1**/£1.20
Cheval, Jean (Fr)	75p/**£1**/£1.50
Christie, G.F.†	£1/**£1.50**/£1.75
Comicus†	**50p**
Cooper, Phyllis†	**50p**
Dean, Dora	**50p**
Delanchy (Fr)	25p/**50p**/£1
Dinah	50p/**75p**/£1
Driscoll	25p/**50p**/75p
Faizant, Jacques (Fr)	£1/**£2**/£2.50
Forres, Kit	75p/**£1**/£1.50
Geesink, Joop (Belg)	£1/**£1.50**/£2
Grimes	75p/**£1**/£1.50
Groth, John	75p/**£1**/£1.50
Havenstein, Bill (US	£1/**£1.50**/£1.75
Hemard, Joseph (Fr)	50p/**75p**/£1
Henry (Belg)	£1/**£1.50**/£1.75
Howe, A. Ian	75p/**£1**/£1.25
Kem	75p/**£1**/£1.50
Kern, L. (Fr)	F†·50p/75p
Leclerc (Fr)	75p/**£1**/£1.50
Licterstein, George (US)	75p/**£1**/£1.50
Long, Wilf (Can)	50p/**£1**/£4
Mallet, Beatrice	£1/**£1.25**/£1.50
Manning, Reg. (US)	£1/**£1.25**/£1.50
Maurice, Reg	25p/**50p**/75p
McGill, Donald† (new comics)	25p/**50p**/75p
Owen, Will	£2.50/**£3**/£4

Paris (US) .. .. £1/**£1.50**/£2
Paterson, Vera .. .. 50p/**75p**/£1
Pearson, J. G. (US) 25p/**50p**/75p
Purser, Phyllis 25p/**50p**/75p
Rémy, P. (Fr) .. .. £1.50/**£2**/£2.50
Richardson, Agnes† .. .. 75p/**£1**/£1.25
Rigby, Cecil T. **50p**
Saroukhan (Egypt) .. .. £1/**£1.50**/£2
Schnebelen, Jean (Fr) .. .. £1.50/**£2**/£3
Shaw, W. Stocker .. .. £1/**£1.50**/£1.75
'Strube' .. .. 75p/**£1**/£1.50
Studdy, George† .. .. £1/**£1.50**/£2
Tayler, Laurie .. .. 60p/**£1**/£1.20
Taylor, Arnold .. .. 25p/**50p**/£1
Tempest, Douglas .. .. 25p/**50p**/£1
Thomas, Bert† (ITMA) .. .. £1/**£1.50**/£1.75
Tobey, Barney (US) .. .. £1/**£1.25**/£1.50
Wellman, Walter (US) .. .. 75p/**£1**/£1.50
White, Brian **50p**
Wilkin, Bob **50p**
Wilkinson, Gilbert .. .. 75p/**£1**/£1.50
Williams, Madge .. .. 50p/**75p**/£1
Zec. Donald .. .. 75p/**£1**/£1.50

Land Warfare

Armoured vehicles. Carriers, self-propelled guns, tanks, etc. .. .. .. £1/**£1.50**/£2
Combat scenes .. .. £1/**£2**/£2.50
Damage. Atomic bomb .. .. £2/**£3**/£4
Damage. Other .. .. 50p/**£1**/£1.50
Débarquement en Normandie. Photo Gaby. Over 20 RP cards .. .. .. £1/**£1.75**/£2.50
Front line life .. .. £1/**£1.50**/£2
Polish Army (Polski Korpus) Sepia o/s, posed battle scenes .. .. .. 50p/**75p**/£1
Prisoners of War. In camp .. .. £1/**£1.50**/£2
Prisoners of War. Under escort .. .. .. £1/**£1.50**/£2
Prisoner of War mail ex-Jap. camps. Value depends upon camp (rarest is Sandakan) and clarity censor mark .. .. .. £7/**£8**/£10
Soft-skinned vehicles. Cars, jeeps, trucks, etc. 50p/**75p**/£1
Weapons .. .. £1/**£1.50**/£2

Munich

Price range .. .. 50p/**£6**/£12

Official Cards

The Germans used their fieldpost cards to carry propaganda pictures and to raise money, thus there are entries in the sections. Otherwise, apart from some American issues, official cards tend to be dull and not highly valued.

Air raid casualty. Card No. G. & S. 704 .. .. .. **50p**
Divisional/Regimental cards .. .. .. 50p/**£1**/£1.50
Fieldpost—German
Artists Hans O. Wendt .. .. £1/**£1.50**/£2

Others .. £2/**£4**/£5
Fieldpost—Others 50p/**75p**/£1
US Army leave sections £1/**£1.50**/£2
US Navy 'V' for Victory cards 25p/**50p**/75p

Patriotism/Propaganda/Sentiment

During WW2, as in WW1, both sides made great use of aerial propaganda. The British dropped leaflets over Germany the day that War was declared, but when the first postcards were used is not certain. The French dropped cards on the Germans during the Phony War of 1940, the Germans on the French, the British and Russians on the Germans. Although hundreds of thousands of cards were dropped, very few have survived; those that have are definitely collectors' items. Country of origin of cards shown in brackets.

Air-Dropped Propaganda

Crete. Probably 1941. Shows Italian assaulting blonde German Fraulein (Br) £3.50/**£4**/£5
Eastern Front. Dec. 1941 onwards. Series of 5 cards. Printed green 5 pfg Hindenburg stamp. *Des Führers Weinachtsbescherung* (The Fuhrer's Christmas Gifts). The gifts are death and destruction (Russ Black Propaganda) .. £20/P/A
North Africa. 1940/42. Pro-Arab anti-British (Ger) £3/**£5**/£6
Southern Germany. 23 March to 8 May 1940. *Bitte Herr Führer*. Line drawing of Hitler and two children (Fr Black Propaganda) .. £4/**£5**/£6
Anti-Bolshevist .. £10/**£25**/£40
Anti-Capitalist .. £10/**£15**/£25
Anti-Nazi .. £3.50/**£5**/£6
Anti-Semitic £25/**£50**/£100
Anti-War .. £3/**£5**/£6

Artists ■M 8

Ardizzone, Edward 50p/**£1**/£1.50
Axster-Heudtlass, von (Ger) .. £3/**£7**/£10
Bartholomaus, H. (Ger) .. £2/**£3**/£5
Bartoli, Guiseppe (It) .. £4/**£7**/£8
Bee, Noah .. £3/**£5**/£6
Bloch, Marcel (Fr) 75p/**£1**/£1.50
Boccasile, Gino (It) £12/**£20**/£25
Brockman, Nico (Du) .. £12/**£20**/£25
Broos, Piet (Du) .. £1/**£1.50**/£2.50
Cass (Fr) .. £2/**£4**/£6
Crali, Tullio (It) .. £7/**£12**/£15
Davis, Marshall (US) .. £1/**£2**/£3
D'Ercoli, Masslio (It) .. £3/**£7**/£9
Eichhorst, Franz (Ger) .. £5/**£8**/£10
Fougasse† .. £1.50/**£2**/£3
Gotschke (Ger) .. £3/**£5**/£9
'Guy' (Belg) .. £5/**£7**/£8
Igert, Paul (Fr) .. £2/**£3**/£5
Klein, Gottfried (Ger) £10/**£15**/£17
Klein, Richard (Ger) .. £18/**£25**/£40
Pisani, Vittorio (It) .. £3/**£5**/£7
Smits (Du) £3/**£10**/£12
Steen (Du) .. £1.50/**£2**/£2.25
Strong, Patience 50p/**£1.50**/£2

Szyk, Arthur (US) .. .. £15/**£20**/£40
Tafuri, R. (It) .. .. £3/**£7**/£9
Thomas, Bert† .. .. £1/**£3**/£4
Willrich, W. (Ger)† .. ..£5/**£12**/£15
Woude, Sikko van de (Du) .. .. £1/**£2**/£3

■M 8 Pub. Sella, Milan. Artist Gino Boccasile. Official Fascist Party Field Postcard. 'Pearl Harbour' Dec. 1941 £25

■M 9 Pub. NSDAP Official Field Postcard for Party Day, Nuremberg. 11 Sep. 1939 £8

British Embassies/Legations Propaganda

B & w reproductions of anti-Axis cartoons from London papers. Artists include Groth, Kem, Strube and Zec. Signed cards rate highest. Produced by Embassy in Lisbon .. .. 75p/**£1**/£1.50

Iranian folk tale of the wicked ruler (Hitler) and the three wise men (Churchill, Stalin and Roosevelt). 5 cards in set. Col. o/s. Produced by Embassy in Teheran £12/**£20**/£25

Dutch

Anti-German .. .. 50p/**£1**/£2

Free Forces (French, Polish, etc.)

Artist designed .. .. £2/**£5**/£10
Photographic origin .. .. £1.50/**£2.50**/£3

French

Photographic posed views of Maginot Line .. £1/**£1.50**/£2

German ■M 9

See also Fund Raising/Welfare and Heroes/Personalities & Soldiers.

Anti-Allies
  B & w art/photo origin .. .. £1/**£2**/£4
  Col. art .. .. £3/**£5**/£7
Commemorative. Col. art .. .. £5/**£7**/£10
Flags/Medals .. .. £2/**£4**/£10
Hitler (*alone*)
  B & w art/photo origin .. .. £2/**£5**/£7
  Col. art .. .. £3/**£6**/£8
House of German Art
  Civilian pictures. B & w .. .. 75p/**£1.50**/£3
  Col. .. .. £2.50/**£4**/£5
  Military pictures. B & w .. .. .. £2.50/**£4**/£5
  Col. .. .. £3/**£6**/£8
Nuremberg Rallies
  B & w art/photo origin .. .. £3/**£8**/£10
  Col. art .. .. £20/**£25**/£50
Official Postal Stationery Cards .. .. .. £1/**£3.50**/£10

Italian
Militaristic scenes .. .. £5/**£10**/£20
Peaceful scenes .. .. £1/**£1.50**/£2

Japanese
Fall of Singapore. Watercolour art .. .. .. £5/**£6**/£8

USA
There is considerable overlapping between propaganda and humour. In this section the listing is by publisher. The higher values relate to cards whose content is more political than humorous, but that can be a fine judgement to make.

Beals. (Des Moines, Iowa)
  'Kick' cards. *Cards featuring Hitler rate the highest value*
.. .. £1/**£2**/£3
  GC (General Comics) series .. .. .. 75p/**£1**/£1.50
Curteich
  USA series (Army) .. .. 75p/**£1**/£1.50
  USN series (Navy) .. .. 75p/**£1**/£1.50
  AS series .. .. 75p/**£1**/£1.50
Graycraft. Artist Dave Breger .. .. .. £1/**£1.50**/£2
Kropp, E. C. (Milwaukee) .. .. £1/**£2**/£2.50
Metrocraft (also 'Photo by Acme') .. .. 50p/**£1**/£1.25
Mid States Press (Chicago) .. .. .. £1/**£1.50**/£2
RHD Corp. Cards on the theme 'The Army's Thinking' ..
.. .. £1/**£1.25**/£2.50
Tichnor Bros. (Boston)
  AP (Airplane series) .. .. 50p/**£1**/£1.25
  Hitler Comics. 5 cards in set .. .. .. £1.50/**£2**/£3
  Jap Comics. 10 cards in set .. .. .. £1/**£2**/£2.50
  M (Military series) .. .. 50p/**£1**/£1.25
  MA (Military Activities) .. .. 50p/**£1**/£1.25

Peace/Victory
As the Western Allies pushed the Germans back so Belgium, Denmark, France and Holland were liberated. They issued cards to celebrate. When the fighting ceased there were victory parades and then the job of restoring Europe to health began. It was called 'Restoration'. There were cards for that too and

also for the return of the fighting man to civilian life—'Demobilisation'. As the date of a man's demobilisation drew near he would count the number of 'days to do'. The French celebrated '100 days to do' with Père Cent *cards.*

Armistice. Photographic cards issued at Rheims on 7 July 1945 showing signing of armistice at Rheims on 7 May 1945. Stamped and date cancelled .. .. £15/**£25**/£30
Demobilisation .. .. £1/**£1.50**/£2
Liberation:
Belgium .. .. 50p/**£1.50**/£3
Denmark .. .. 50p/**£1**/£1.50
France: Liberation of Paris
RP o/s .. .. 75p/**£1.50**/£3
RP o/s. Pub. C.A.P. .. .. £3/**£5**/£6
Art .. .. 75p/**£1**/£1.50
Holland .. .. £1/**£1.50**/£2.50
Marshall Plan. Col. art .. .. £3/**£6**/£10
Père Cent .. .. £1/**£2**/£4
Reconstruction .. .. 75p/**£1**/£1.50
Memorials .. .. 50p/**75p**/£1
Victory parades .. .. 50p/**75p**/£1
VE Day scenes .. .. 75p/**£1.50**/£3
VJ Day scenes .. .. 75p/**£1**/£2

Pin-Ups

Magazines such as the American Yank *provided most of the pin-ups for the forces. Postcard pin-ups are far fewer than in WW1. However, film star photographic cards were very popular.*

Déshabillé
Artist Barribal .. .. £2/**£3**/£5
Artist Hermond (Fr) .. .. £1/**£2**/£3
Pub. Hoffman. 'House of German Art' Nudes £1/**£2**/£2.50
Schönheit der Gymnastik (Beauty of Gymnastics) (Ger) .. .. £2/**£3**/£5
Others .. .. £1/**£1.50**/£2

Glamour
Artist drawn .. .. 60p/**£1**/£1.20
Film star photos .. .. 50p/**75p**/£1

Sea Warfare

Good artistic impressions of ships and battles, or cards showing clear photographic details are most highly valued. Specific actions, such as the sinking of the Graf Spee, *were sometimes recorded by sets of cards.*

Actions
Graf Spee sinking. 12 cards in set .. .. .. £2/**£3**/£5
Narvik .. .. £5/**£7**/£12
Pearl Harbour .. .. £1/**£2**/£5
Scapa Flow *Der Adler* series .. .. £2/**£3**/£4

Artists
Axster-Heudtlass, von (Ger) .. .. £3/**£7**/£10
Bannister, A. F. D. .. .. 75p/**£1**/£1.50

Church, Bernard W. .. .. 75p/**£1**/£1.50
Igert, Paul (Fr) .. .. £2/**£3**/£5
Venturini, Antonio (It) .. .. £3/**£5**/£7
Vicary, P. A. .. .. 75p/**£1**/£1.50
Werner, Carl (Ger) .. .. £1/**£2**/£3

Ships
Bismarck (Ger) .. .. £1/**£2**/£3
FFNF (Free French Naval Forces) .. .. 75p/**£1**/£1.25

HMS *Hood* .. .. £1/**£1.50**/£2
Kriegsopfer-Wandkalender (War victims wall calendar series) .. .. £5/**£7**/£10
Pub. Photochrom. 'Britain Prepared' series. English and French texts .. .. £1/**£1.25**/£1.50
Pub. Salmon .. .. 75p/**£1**/£1.50
Pub. Tuck. 'Our Navy' series .. .. .. 50p/**75p**/£1
Pub. Valentines.. .. .. 75p/**£1**/£1.50

Silks

Few silk cards were produced in Period 5. Some embroidered cards with year dates exist for 1939, 1940 and 1945, those years that Allied armies were on the continent of Europe. A limited range of embroidered and woven cards was produced during the German occupation. Woven, or combined embroidered/woven cards of this type, have gold frames on grey borders.

Combined Embroidered/Woven
Gold frames .. .. £3/**£4**/£5

Embroidered
German occupation .. .. £7/**£10**/£12
Year dates 1939/1940/1945 .. .. .. £1.50/**£2**/£3

Women at War

The Germans used the theme of women's help for the war effort as propaganda, the British and Americans still viewed the idea with amusement.

Men's Jobs
Humorous comment 25p/**50p**/75p
Photographic origin .. .. 75p/**£1.50**/£3

Nursing
Price range 25p/**50p**/75p

Series
Arbeitsmädchen. 'Working Girl' series .. .. £3/**£5**/£8
Bund Deutscher Mädchen. 'League of German Maidens' .. .. £3/**£4**/£5
Frauen schaffen für Euch! 'Women are working for you' .. .. £10/**£12**/£15
Free French photo series .. .. 75p/**£1**/£1.25
Pub. Beals (US). Over 25 cards in series .. £1/**£1.50**/£2
Pub. Tuck. 'With the WAAF'. Over 25 cards in series .. .. 50p/**75p**/£1

■M 10 Pub. Curteich. 'The Screaming Eagles returned to Fort Campbell from Vietnam in 1972'. Period 7 £2

VIETNAM WAR (1965–73) ■M 10

In 1954, following her military defeat at Dienbienphu, France granted her former colonies in Indo-China their independence. America quickly assumed the mantle of the champion of the capitalist system in the area and by 1965 was engaged in a growing war against Chinese supported North Vietnamese forces. Within the USA there was great dissent against the war and public pressure finally forced President Nixon to withdraw US forces in 1973. Picture postcards have recorded the inner turmoil of America during this period as well as conditions in the firing area.

Protest cards	£1/**£1.50**/£3
Others	50p/**£1.50**/£2

MODERN CARDS

The Postcards Produced During Period 7

The trend towards appreciating modern cards, became apparent in 1980–81.

The event which, above all others, inspired the modern post-card producers, was the Royal Wedding. It was an occasion that was like a spark of sunshine on a rainy day to a world depressed by recession, inflation and unemployment. Like many Royal events during the Golden Age of the Postcard, the pageantry and excitement were captured in a variety of ways—photographic, photomontage and artist drawn—by everyone from the large commercial postcard firms (like Dixon and Salmon) to the small specialist producers like FAGA, Carousel, TVH Current Events and Veldale.

After the Battle Postcard Series

3 New Plaistow Road, London E15

A well-printed, highly colourful and attractive series by the publishers of the excellent magazine of the same name, designed for military buffs. All superb colour photographs. Packaged sets of 16 (105 mm × 148 mm) of aircraft, military vehicles and steam trains. See the third edition of this catalogue for further details.

Per set **£1.25**

American Postcard Co. ■MOD 1

Designs employing photomontage techniques to satirise President and Mrs. Reagan. Banned in some American cities.

'Queen Nancy'. Photo by Alfred Gescheidt (1981) .. **55p**
'American Gothic' (President and Mrs Reagan) (1981) **60p**
'Budget Cut' (Bald President and Mrs. Reagan) (1982) **55p**

Bibliophilen Kunstpostkarten ■MOD 2

Stockist and full details, Desiderata, Postfach 5362, D7800 Freiburg, W. Germany. 56 series of 10 cards; superbly coloured art reproductions on numerous themes. Of immediate postcard interest are:

No. 8. Art Nouveau Postcards. Series 1
No. 9. Art Nouveau Postcards. Series 2
No. 23. Advertising postcards of yesterday
No. 32. Hearty Greetings Series I
No. 33. Hearty Greetings Series II
No. 37. 'Smile please', (*photography theme*)
No. 39. Exaggeration Postcards
No. 56. Giants, Midgets and Fat Girls
No. 52. Play girls of yesterday (*Erotic*)
No. 55. 'My goodness, The Love!'
Price, per set **£2**

Carousel Limited Editions

Designed and published by Michael Dummer, 28 Ambleside Road, Kingsway, Bath BA2 2LR. Nos. 1–28 were listed in the second and third editions of this catalogue. Subsequent issues are:

■MOD 1 Pub. American Postcard Co. Photomontage design by Alfred Gescheidt. 'American Gothic'. 1981 60p

■MOD 2 Pub. Marenberg Kommunikation, Dortmund. Bibliophilen Kunst postkarten. Series No. 23 'Poster adverts of yesterday'. Reproduction of Period 2 David Allen tea advert. Period 7. Set of 6 £2

29. Mary Rose
30. Birth of Prince William
31. Christening of Prince William
32. 60th Anniv. of British small car
33. Princess Grace of Monaco
34. Tribute to Falklands Taskforce
35. 150th Anniv. of G.W.R.
36. 30th Anniv. of Coronation
37. The Three Elizabeths
38. Mother Teresa of Calcutta

Price per card **30p**

Collector Cards/Pamlin Prints

73 Temple Road, Croydon, Surrey, CR0 1HW

Checklists of pre-1982 cards were given in the second and third editions of this catalogue (pp. 146–147 and 188–189 respectively).

Price range .. .. 25p/**50p**/£1

Coral Lee

P.O. Box 314, Rancho Cordova, CA 95670. USA

See the third edition of this catalogue for details of cards issued 1976–81.

1983 Royal Baby (comics) per card **30p**
1983 Ronald Reagan (comics) per card **30p**
1983 Paper Doll series—British Royalty and Reagan (comics) per card **30p**

1982 Mrs Thatcher and President Reagan **30p**
1983 President and Mrs Reagan with the Queen and Prince Philip per card **30p**

Dalkeith Publishing Co. ■R 1
Big Four Raiway Museum, 81b Old Christchurch Rd., Bournemouth, BH1 1EW.
Original and most attractive standard-size postcards, well printed on quality board. Each set is packaged in a colourful, printed, hand-numbered envelope describing the contents. In 1982, the new publishing company was formed and it is diversifying into postcard reproductions of old 'classic' posters, and railway-allied topics like tickets.

The first 102 designs were listed in the third edition of this catalogue, pp. 189–190. Nos. 103–192 are listed below.

103–108. Somerset & Dorset Rly.
109–114. North Eastern Rly.
115–120. Corris Rly.
121–126. Leicester & Swannington Rly.
127–132. Railway Paddle Steamer trips.
133–138. Great Western Rly.—Posters 1.
139–144. Great Western Rly.—Posters 2.
145–150. Great Central Rly.
151–156. Weymouth & Portland Rly.
157–162. Flying Scotsman 60th Anniv.
163–168. Padarn & Penrhyn Rlys.
169–174. Tickets.
175–180. Cheshire Lines Rly.
181–186. L.N.E.R. Northern Belle.
187–192. West Highland Rly.
193–198. Severn & Wye Rly./Severn Bridge
199–204. G.W.R. & L.M.S. Posters
205–210. London, Chatham & Dover Rly.
211–216. Pullmans
217–222. Invergarry & Fort Augustus Rly.
223–228. G.W.R. posters
229–234. G.W.R. posters
235–240. Railway Guide covers
241–246. Railway Guide covers
247–252. Manhood/Selsey Tramways

Classic Poster Cards
P1–P6. Early Transport
P7–P12. Toulouse-Lautrec
P13–P18. Alphonse Mucha
P19–P24. Early Aviation meetings
P25–P30. Jules Cheret
P31–P36. Ludwig Hohlwein
P37–P42. Shipping
P43–P48. Automobiles
P49–P54. Early Theatre
P55–P60. Airlines
P61–P66. Orient Express
P67–P72. Circus
P73–P78. Bicycles

P79–P84. First World War
P85–P90. Schweppes
P91–P96. The Beggarstaffs
P97–P102. Publishers
P103–P108. Entertainments

Price Per set **£1.50**

FAGA (Frederick G. Foley)
Stockist: Ron Griffiths, 47 Long Arrotts, Hemel Hempstead, Herts, HP1 4EX.
The first 20 cards and the 1980- mid-1982 cards by this highly collected calligrapher, cartographer and designer were listed in the second and third editions of this catalogue (pp. 149–150 and 191 respectively). Listed below are 1982–84 productions, numbered 345–363. Numbers printed in brackets.

345. 70th Anniv. of sinking of Titanic. Black on white (1000) **£1**
Ditto, black on amber (500) **£1**
346. 21st Birthday of Princess of Wales (1250) **£1**
347. Cutty Sark International Tall Ships Races **65p**
348. Maritime Britain Year 1982. Brown (855) **£1**
Ditto, black (145) **£1.10**
349. Falkland Islands. Blue **40p**
Ditto, brown (500) **60p**
350. Falkland Islands Task Force. Blue **40p**
Ditto, brown **60p**
351. Falklands—150th Anniv. of British Rule **40p**
352. Mrs. Thatcher & the Antarctic possessions inscribed 'ARCTIC CIRCLE' **40p**
Ditto, inscribed 'ANTARCTIC CIRCLE' **50p**
353. First Polar Route Flight **40p**
354. Ascension Island **40p**
355. Falklands—Britannia **40p**
356. 150th Anniv. of Darwin in Falkland Islands .. **40p**
357. 200th Anniv. of Hot Air Balloon **40p**
358. *Athenia*, ship torpedoed by German sub., 1939 .. **40p**
359. Redesigned reprint of un-numbered 'New Forest' card **40p**
360. British Army **40p**
361. Conquest of the Atlantic **40p**
362. Royal Tour of Australia **40p**
363. 40th Anniv. of the liberation of Europe **40p**
364. 70th Anniv. of Battle of Falklands **40p**
365. Airship centenary **40p**
366. 200th Anniv. of Mail Coaches **40p**

Stanley Gibbons Ltd■MOD 3
399 Strand, London WC2R 0LX.
1984 Postcards of the Spanish Royal Family
1. King Juan Carlos in Palma, Majorca
2. Queen Sophie opening the Murillo Exhibition at the Royal Academy London
3. The King and Queen
4. The three Royal children
5. The King and Queen with Crown Prince Felipe

6. The Queen with other members of European Royal families at the christening of the daughter of King Constantine of the Hellenes in London, 1983

Per set of six **£1**

These cards were produced for sale at the International Stamp Exhibition in Madrid, April/May 1984.

■MOD 3 Pub. Stanley Gibbons Ltd. Spanish Royal Family series 1984. King Juan Carlos, Queen Sophie and Prince Felipe. Per set £1

Brian Lund Postcards ■MOD 4

27 Walton Drive, Keyworth, Nottingham, NG12 5FN

1980 Sportsmen—six cards featuring Muhammad Ali, Billy Beaumont (*rugby*), Brian Clough (*football*), Robin Cousins (*ice-skating*), Ilie Nastase (*tennis*) and Derek Randall (*cricket*). Per set **£1**

1983 General Election—12 cards featuring Mrs. Thatcher, Michael Foot, David Steel, Roy Jenkins, Shirley Williams, Norman Tebbitt, Neil Kinnock, Michael Heseltine, David Owen, Denis Healy, Tony Benn and general election results. Per set **£2**

Prescott-Pickup & Co. Ltd. ■MOD 5

Rodwin, Allscott, Telford, Shropshire, TF6 5EQ.

This company specialises in the production of high-quality cards mostly having a topical appeal—Royal events and the like. Normally cards are produced in sets together with a lavishly illustrated album in which they can be mounted. The main sets are as follows:

Queen & People (1977) 60 cards. Per set £7.50
Royal Wedding (1981) 60 cards. Per set £7.50
Royal Family 1982 (1982) 70 cards. Per set £8.25
30 Years EIIR (1982) 60 cards. Per set £7.50
Charles & Diana in the Antipodes (1983) 30 cards. Per set £3.75
Charles & Diana in Canada (1983) 15 cards. Per set £1.85
Papal Visit to Britain (1982) 63 cards. Per set £7.50
Falklands Task Force (1982) 63 cards. Per set .. £7.50
War in the South Atlantic (1983). Per set £7.50

■MOD 4 Pub. Brian Lund Postcards. Artist John Beeton. Series 2 'Election '83' No. 7. 'David Owen (Alliance).' 1983. Set of 6 £2

■MOD 5 Pub. Prescott-Pickup & Co. The Prince & Princess of Wales with Prince William in New Zealand. One of 30 cards in the 'Charles & Diana in the Antipodes' series. 1983. Per set £3.75

Philatelic Anniversary Postcards
Set 1 Victorian & George V stamps 10 cards (1983). Per set £1.20

Many other sets have been issued featuring railway locomotives, trams, cars, etc. Some of these have printed backs and are thus not true postcards.

Rhinoceros
22c Ferndale Road, London SW4.
Reprints of some of the 1930s satirical, anti-national socialist photomontage of John Heartfield (q.v.). *Originally published in the magazine* AIZ, *they are now printed as postcards by arrangement with Gertrude Heartfield, the artist's widow, who maintains the Heartfield Archives in East Berlin. 8 sets.*
Price per set **£2**

SAS (Seasonal Art Series)
Stockist: Ron Griffiths, 47 Long Arrotts, Hemel Hempstead, Hert.
George Orwell and 1984 Calendar **25p**
Greetings from Oceania **25p**

TVH Current Event Postcards ■MOD 6
Oak House, Woodnesborough, Sandwich, Kent, CT13 0NJ.
Limited edition of 500 only. Two col. print, designed by cartoonist Bryan Reading.

1. Teheran, 1979. Red/black. The Ayatollah, Pres. Carter and the hostages
2. Dallas, 1980. Blue/black. 'Who Shot J.R.?'
3. St. Paul's, 1981. Purple/black. Royal Wedding
4. Cairo, 1981. Sand/black. Year of the Assassin/President Sadat
5. Warsaw, 1981/82. Scarlet/black. 'Poland's Anguish'
6. London, 1983. Blue/black. 'Maggie Rides Again' (General Election)

Per card **£1.25**

■MOD 6 Pub. TVH Current Event Cards. No. 6. 'Maggie Rides Again'. Artist Bryan Reading. Limited edition of 500. 1983 £1.25

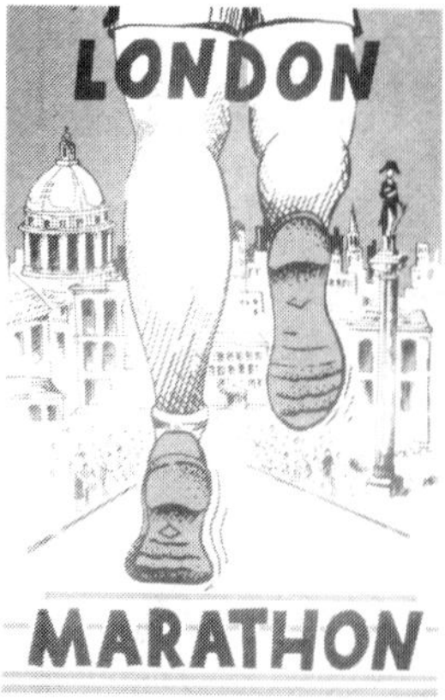

■MOD 7 Pub. Veldale No. SE 17/1. 'London Marathon'. 1983 30p

Veldale Covers ■MOD 7
6 Comberton Park Rd., Kidderminster, Worcs., DY10 3DY.
Limited edition postcards designed to complement Post Office stamp issues and commemorate current events and anniversaries. There are three distinct series—Special Event (SE), Postcards commemorating British Stamps (CBS) and Veldale Series (VS). The cards are well printed on good quality board, and are standard size unless otherwise stated.

Cards issued 1980–early 1982 were listed in the third edition of this catalogue, pp. 196–197.

Subsequent issues are:
SE Series
8/1. Barbican Centre

9/1. Papal visit
10/1. Birth of Prince William
11/1. 21st Birthday of Princess of Wales
12/1. World Cup
13/1. Falklands Crisis
14/1. Commonwealth Games
15/1. 30th Anniv. of *The Mousetrap* play
16/1. Breakfast Television
17/1. London Marathon
18/1. 30th Anniv. of Coronation
19/1. Athletics Championships
20/1. Parcel Post Centenary
21/1. Veteran Car Run
22/1. Kennedy Assassination
23/1. Big Brother is Watching You

CB Series

14/1. British Theatre
15/1. Maritime Heritage
16/1. British Textiles
17/1. Information Technology
18/1. British Cars
19/1. Christmas 1982
20/1. British River Fishes
21/1. Commonwealth Day
22/1. Engineering Achievements
23/1. British Army
24/1. British Gardens
25/1. British Fairs
26/1. Christmas 1983
27/1. Heraldry
28/1. Cattle
29/1. Urban Renewal

VS Series

7/1. Calendarcard 1983
8/1. Calendarcard 1984

Price range .. .. 30p/**50p**/£1

NOVELTY

A novelty postcard is one that deviates from the normal rectangular item made of standard board. It may have something stuck on it, may be made of unusual material or be of an unusual size or shape. It may also *do* something—squeak, smell or move—in which case it is a 'mechanical' postcard. Many novelty cards contravened existing Post Office regulations for postcards because of their irregular size, shape or material. They were then subject to letter or book rate (1*d.* instead of ½*d.* as for normal postcards in Periods 1 to 3). Some, like jewelled or tinselled items, had to be sent through the post in protective envelopes.

APPLIQUED MATERIALS ■N 1

Buttons
Dried flowers
Envelope (to enclose a tiny letter)
Glass (eyes for animals)
Hair (on heads and other parts of the body)
Jewelling/glitter (usually mica)
Lace
Mirror (i.e. metal that reflects an image)
Photographs (inset personal portrait)
Pocket (to enclose a card or tiny hankie)
Pussy willow (to make the bodies of kittens)
'Real Japanese' (Tuck series with linen finish)
Sand paper (to strike matches)
Seeds (shamrock and others)
Velvet and other materials (in the shapes of bloomers, flowers, hats, etc.)
Other materials
Price range .. .. £1/**£2**/£5

BANKNOTES/COINS

In Period 2 cards were printed to represent the banknotes and coins of various countries. Some of the gilded/silvered, embossed versions are most realistic.
Price range .. .. £2/**£4**/£6

BAS RELIEF

A deep form of embossing with a three-dimensional effect, often with 'jewelling'. Subjects are normally important personages. *See* ROYALTY. Publishers include Stengel & Co., and Sutton, Sharpe & Co.
Price range .. .. 75p/**£1**/£1.50

BEER MATS

Period 7 cards produced by brewers in Britain and on the Continent (e.g. Munchner Hofbrau) often o/s.
Price range 25p/50p

COMPOSITE

A composite set is a number of postcards (from 2 upwards) which fit together to make a complete picture. See second edition for listing.

Price range .. .. £3/**£25**/£120

EMBOSSING

Many beautiful early Continental embossed designs exist. *See* GREETINGS. British publishers include DeLittle, Fenwick & Co., Hildesheimer, Ettlinger, Tuck ('Art' and 'Connoisseur' series).

Price range .. .. 75p/**£1.50**/£3

FANTASY

This is an imaginative, frequently surrealist, type of design, often with a *trompe l'oeil* element, sometimes using photomontage. Very popular are cards featuring heads composed of figures. These are known on the Continent as *Arcimboldesque* after the 16th century Italian painter, Arcimboldo, who devised the technique of using the shapes of animals, fish, fruit and other objects to form human portraits.

Girls in Neckties .. .. £10/**£20**/£30

Arcimboldesque Heads

Period 2: Composers
Beethoven, Liszt, Mozart, Strauss, Wagner, etc.

Period 2: Miscellaneous
L'Abbé; L'Amour de Pierrot; Bonjour!; Bon Vivant; Les Buveurs; Cherchez le Viveur; Diabolo; L'Eunuque; Un Faune; Grand Prix; Le Muletier de Taragone; Mylord pince sans rire; Gourmand; Pluton et Proserpine; Quai de la Gare; Au Revoir; Un Beau Sauteur; So ein Narr; Songe d'un Enfant; Source de Jeunesse; Tête Chaude; Tête de Mort; Le Vanqueur

Period 2: Personalities
Abdul Hamid; Albert I; Bismarck; Edward VII; Goethe; Kaiser; Leopold II; Mephistopheles; Napoleon I (b & w); Napoleon I (col.); Schiller; William II.

Price range .. ..£5/**£10**/£15

Period 7: French
Artist Jacques Lardie. Political figures .. 25p/**50p**/£1

HAND PAINTED/TINTED ■N 2

Amateur artists.. .. .. 50p/**75p**/£1.50
Commercially produced hand coloured artist drawn .. .. 50p/**£1**/£2
Continental commercially produced water colours of flowers, etc. .. .. 75p/**£1.50**/£2.50
Japanese oil paintings, miniature works of art which are much underrated .. .. £1/**£2**/£3
Japanese water colours .. .. 75p/**£1**/£1.50

■N 1 'Mirror of Life' Card. Appliquéd mirror. Period 2 £2

■N 2 Pub. 'M.M.' Ger. Handmade Art Card, Series 488. Handpainted. Period 4 £1.50

Photographic origin. Hand tinted .. .. 50p/**75p**/£1.50
Others .. .. 25p/**50p**/£1.50

HOLD TO LIGHT (HTL)/TRANSPARENCIES

These are cards which, as their title implies, reveal a surprise when held to the light. They came in two forms—cards that appear quite standard until held to the light (transparencies) and those that have cut out sections representing a source of light—candles, moons, suns, windows, etc.—(cut outs).

Christmas and other greetings .. .. £4/**£8**/£10
Cupples, Samuel (incl. World's Fair 1904) .. .. £1/**£2**/£3
Hartmann transparency series .. .. £2/**£3**/£4
Meteor transparencies (incl. Paris Exhibition 1900) .. .. .. £6/**£8**/£10
W.H. (Wittagelberg) Berlin (HTL and transparencies) .. .. £1.50/**£2.50**/£3
Others .. .. £1/**£2**/£4

MECHANICAL ■N 3

Postcards demanding some kind of action.

Action Cards
Moved by levers, wheels, etc.

Barometers
Changing colour in the damp.

Blow Up
With rubber inflatable sections.

Cigarette Cards
Pub. Ettlinger. Artist Browne, Tom. 2 cigarettes attached.

Cut Outs
Notably Tuck 'Birds and Butterflies on the Wing', Dolls for Dressing, etc. (*see* CHILDREN).

Deeks Puzzle Cards
USA. Changing pictures.

Girls' Own Paper Postcards
1900. Two sets of 4 postcards printed on one page to cut out. Views from the Editor's window, readers' portraits, signatures, etc.

Gramophone Records
Modern. Melody cards. Series of 8″ × 6″ cards with 45 rpm discs. Titles include: 'Whole Lotta Woman', 'For You', 'April Love', 'Somebody Loves Me', etc.
Pub. Ettlinger, at least 12 designs
Pub. Tuck, at least 40 designs.

Heat-activated Cards
To show hidden pictures.

Jigsaw Cards
Notably Tuck Picture Puzzle Postcards, miniature 'zag-zaw' puzzles in boxes of 6, each of 30 pieces. Thirty sets (1918).

Kaleidoscopes
Pub. Alpha, at least 20 designs.

Reversible Cards
Showing a different picture when turned upside down.

Scented Cards
With impregnated pads to rub to release perfume.

Squeakers
Various publishers.

Windows
Or boxes that open to show another picture.

Wire Coils
Used for 'flying' butterflies, wagging tails, etc.

Price range for all above .. .. £2/**£8**/£15

PULLOUTS

The commonest kind of novelty card where a flap is raised to reveal a concertina of small pictures, usually views. Pullouts exist for most categories of postcards including ADVERTISING, ANIMALS, COMIC, ROYALTY, SOCIAL HISTORY, etc.
Artist drawn, signed .. .. 75p/**£1**/£3
Artist drawn, unsigned .. .. 50p/**75p**/£1.50
Photographic origin 25p/**50p**/75p

SHAPES

Cards were produced in a variety of unusual shapes, e.g. animals, circular, leaf, etc.
Price range .. .. 75p/**£1**/£3

■N 3 Pub. Bendix. 'Charterhouse' Series 444. Music hall artist George Robey, with head that nods. Period 2 £15

■N 4 Pub. Thomas Stevens. Woven Silk 'Ecce Homo'. Period 2 £30

SILK ■N 4

This is the best documented type of novelty postcard (in the booklets of C. Radley). Three main types exist: embroidered, printed and woven. *See* MILITARY.

Embroidered Silks

Period 2. Mostly Floral in Design
Austrian from 1903
British. Pub. Birn Bros. Town Series
French from 1907
German from 1906. Pub. Duroldt, A.
Swiss from 1907 (for Embroidery Exhib.)
Others
Price range .. .. £4/**£6**/£12

Period 4
Continuation of Continental sentimental Period 3 type designs.
British. Pub. Tuck. 'Broderie d'Art series.
Price range .. .. £2/**£3**/£5

Printed on Satin/Silk

The least collectable type of silk card, though some fine Continental *Art Nouveau* designs exist and the British 'Fab' Patchwork series is interesting.
1900–1903. Ger. Pub. Krieger. Four Seasons series. Per set .. .. £20/**£40**/£60

1900–1903. Various Continental designs .. .. £3/**£5**/£10
Period 2. 'Fab' Patchwork. Clan Crests/Flowers/Views .. .. £4/**£6**/£8
'Fab' designs for the USA market of State Capitals (Series 5) .. .. £5/**£6**/£8
Others .. .. 75p/**£1.50**/£3

N.B. Cards with plain backs (e.g. Cinema stars, Edith Cavell, etc.) are *not* postcards and are not listed.

Woven

These are the most artistic, skilfully produced and the most sought after of all the 'Silks'.

Alpha. Flags, greetings, etc. .. .. £9/**£14**/£28
American. St. Louis Exhibition (1904) .. £14/**£28**/£40
Austrian. Periods 2, 4 .. .. £10/**£20**/£28
French. 1900. Pub. Benoiston, Paris Exhibition £20/**£28**/£35
French. Period 2. Pub. Neyret Frères. *Art Nouveau*, Classical, Portraits, Views (the highest value is for col. *Art Nouveau*) .. .. £20/**£35**/£135
German. Periods 1/Early Period 2. Pubs. include Knuffmann and Knieger .. .. £14/**£28**/£40
Grant, W. H. & Co. Exhibitions, Greetings, Hands Across the Sea, Portraits, Ships, Subjects, Views (the highest value is for col. subjects) .. .. £14/**£35**/£50
Japanese. 1908–1910. Admiral Togo, View of Amanohashitate .. .. £6/**£14**/£20
Stevens, Thomas. Exhibitions, Greetings, Hands Across the Sea, Portraits, Religious subjects, Ships, Subjects, Views (the highest valuation is for col. views and rare personalities) .. .. £14/**£35**/£100
Others .. .. £3.50/**£5**/£7.50

UNUSUAL MATERIALS

Postcards were manufactured from the most curious substances, which include aluminium, bark, celluloid, cork, ivory, leather, panel cards (on stout board), peat, wood, others. The highest value is for postally used cards of unusual substances. One of the most original materials ever used was pulped paper currency in the USA—known as 'Macerated Money Cards'. Rare.

Price range .. .. £1/**£3**/£10

Three Band Pricing System

Left Hand Band: The lowest price you will probably be asked to pay for this card.
Middle Band: What you will normally be asked to pay for this card: its average, reasonable price.
Right Hand Band: The highest price you will probably be asked to pay for this card.
For a full explanation of the system see page ix.

POLITICAL/PROPAGANDA/ PUNISHMENT & JUSTICE

The postcard was a medium greatly utilised by civil, military and political commentators. Sometimes this was spontaneous comment by the artist, sometimes it was inspired or commissioned by governments and other bodies for their campaigns. This vehicle flourished in wartime, so consult also MILITARY. This is another section where artists reign supreme, although, sadly, much fine work is unsigned and as yet unidentified. To make the pointed barbs palatable to the collecting public, many political/propaganda drawings appear as cartoons. Therefore a high proportion of designers of political cards will also be found under COMIC. Several themes in this section also overlap with SOCIAL HISTORY.

Listed below are the main causes and themes of importance in this category.

Alsace-Lorraine (Periods 2, 3) .. .. £3/**£4**/£5
Anti-British (*see* MILITARY) .. ..£5/**£15**/£25
Anti-Royalty. Q. Victoria, Boer War, Edward VII debauchery,
George V, WW1 .. .. .. , ... £3/**£10**/£25
Anti-Semitic (*see* Military) .. ..£5/**£15**/£25
Berlin Blockade (1948) .. .. £15/**£25**/£30
Bolshevism/anti-Bolshevism .. .. .. £5/**£10**/£20
Communism (incl. Period 7) .. .. £3/**£8**/£10
Edith Cavell (*see* MILITARY) .. .. £1/**£3**/£4
Fascism .. .. £3/**£5**/£10
Freemasonry .. .. £1/**£3**/£5
Irish Home Rule/Sinn Fein ■POL 1 .. .. .. £1/**£3**/£5
Lusitania (*see* MILITARY) .. .. £1/**£3**/£5
Maternity benefit (1914) .. .. £1/**£2**/£3
National Insurance Acts .. .. 75p/**£1.50**/£3
National Socialism (*see* MILITARY) .. .. £3/**£7.50**/£15
Sidney Street Siege .. .. £1/**£3**/£5
Socialism (throughout Europe) .. .. £2/**£4**/£10
Spartakist uprising (1919) .. .. £3/**£5**/£8
State Visits (e.g. Czar to France 1896) .. ..£7/**£15**/£25
Strikes (*see* SOCIAL HISTORY) .. .. £2/**£4**/£8
Suffragettes .. .. £2/**£4**/£15
Tariff Reform .. .. 75p/**£1.50**/£3

NOTABLE SERIES

American

Pub. Austen, J. I. America's Famous Men. Series of 50. Period 2 .. .. £1/**£3**/£5
Pub. Coral-Lee. Political series, *see* MODERN
Pub. Donaldson, R. M. Famous Americans (1908) £1/**£3**/£5
Pub. Sheehan, M. A. (Topanga, California). The Presidents of the United States from Washington to Truman. Black silhouettes on yellow background, gilded, marked 'Hand-made original Serigraph'. Limited edition of 2000. Period 5.
Per card .. .. £1/**£2**/£3
Per set (32 cards) .. .. /**£75**/£110

British

Pub. Birn Bros. Suffrage series E19, E23. 'This is the House that Man Built'. Per set .. .. £20/**£30**/£45

Pub. Davidson Bros. Fiscal Games, Mr. Chamberlain at . . . , Political Dances, etc. Artist Ludovici† and others £2/**£3**/£4

Pub. Faulkner, C.W. Chamberlain, Fiscal, John Bull, Suffragette series. Artist Arthur Moreland† and others £2/**£3**/£4

Pub. Hartmann

Eminent Men in their Youth. Period 2 .. .. 75p/**£1**/£2

Pub. Inter-Art

'Licker' (National Insurance stamps) series. Period 2 £1/**£2**/£3

Pub. Jarrold

Punch War Cartoons. Period 3 .. .. .. £1.50/**£3**/£4

Pub. Millar & Lang

Freemason series. Period 2 (*see* CURIOUS) £1/**£2**/£3

Pub. Tuck

Aesop's Fables by Sancha (*see* MILITARY). Period 3 £4/**£5**/£7

Empire series. UB chromolithographed Statesmen £3/**£4**/£5

Fiscal series/Game Birds .. .. £2/**£3**/£4

'Political Leaders' .. .. £2/**£3**/£4

Others .. .. £1/**£3**/£5

Pub. Valentine

Various Political series .. .. £1/**£2**/£3

Pub. Wrench

Punch Cartoons (1901) .. .. £2/**£3**/£4

Pub. Anonymous

Many anonymous (as to artist and/or publisher) series exist, with powerful political themes.

Price range .. .. £1/**£3**/£5

French ■POL 2

Many are reproductions from satiric publications like *Le Rire*.

Musée des Sires. Artist Roubille .. .. ..£5/**£10**/£15

Musée des Souverains. Artists E. Cadel, Léal de Camara†, P. Kauffmann, Charles Léandre .. ..£5/**£10**/£15

Le Burin Satirique and other limited edition series by Orens† .. ..£7/**£15**/£20

Les Organisateurs de la Guerre and other limited edition series by Léal de Camara† .. ..£7/**£15**/£20

Les Monstres des Cathédrales. Period 3 caricatures £2/**£3**/£4

Anonymous anti-Establishment series .. £3/**£10**/£15

Italian

Many fine series of propaganda cards exist for Periods 2 to 5 notably 'Edith Cavell' by Corbella (*see* MILITARY).

Price range .. ..£2/**£15**/£20

Portuguese

Series of 14 col. postcards published by the Information Dept. of the Armed Forces Movement showing the political revolution of 1974–75.

Per set **£3.50**

POLITICAL ARTISTS ■POL 2, A 12, M 4

Camara, Léal de, Noel. French. Powerful political satire. Period 1. Usually small limited editions .. ..£5/**£15**/£25

Carter, Reg.† Political cartoons. Pub. E. Mack £1/**£1.50**/£2

Corbella, Tito† Edith Cavell .. .. £2/**£4**/£6

■POL 1 Pub. Valentine, Dublin. Sinn Fein Rebellion. Countess Markiewicz after Court Martial. Period 3 £5

■POL 2 Pub. 'F.J.', Paris, for the publication *Le Burin Satirique*. Artist 'Orens'. 'His Majesty Mutsu Hito, Emperor of the Apaches of Japan'. (Russo-Japanese War comment). Limited edition of 250, No. 77. 1904 £20

Crane, Walter. *Punch* contributor, famous for illustrations of children's books .. .. £2/**£3**/£5
Davey, George†. Valentine's Suffragette series .. £1/**£2**/£4
'Dudley'. Joseph Chamberlain caricature (as Bubbles). Pub. W. McKenzie .. .. 75p/**£1**/£2
Fredillo, Fr. Anti-British Boer War Cartoons .. £5/**£8**/£12
Furniss, Harry. Political cartoons with a humorous slant. Pub. John Walker & Co. .. .. £1/**£2**/£4
Ludovici, Anthony† Pub. Davidson Bros. Several series incl. Rosebery at Sheffield, Jospeh Chamberlain at Glasgow .. .. £2/**£3**/£4
Maurice, Reg.† Signed 'Reg. M.'. Pub. Regent Pub. Co. (1906) .. .. 75p/**£1**/£1.50
Mirko. Italian artist. Fascist propaganda in a distinct *Art Deco* style. Period 4 .. .. £2/**£4**/£8
Moreland, Arthur.† John Bull series. Pub. C. W. Faulkner .. .. £2/**£3**/£4
Orens.† Also signed 'Denizard', 'Godillot'. French. Powerful caricatures of political/war leaders. Often small limited editions .. .. £3/**£7.50**/£20
Partridge, Bernard.† Humour with a political flavour, incl. cartoons from *Punch*. Pub. Wrench (1901) .. £2/**£3**/£4
Raemaekers, Louis.† *See* MILITARY. Period 3 cartoons .. .. £1/**£2**/£2.50
Raven-Hill, Leonard.† Pub. Wrench. Pictures from *Punch* (1901) .. .. £1.50/**£2**/£3
Raven-Hill, Leonard.† Pub. Jarrold. *Punch* war cartoons. Period 3 .. .. 50p/**£1**/£1.50

Retrosi, Virgilio. 1892–. Italian artist. Fascist propaganda. Period 4 .. .. £2/**£4**/£6

Rostro (Fr). Several editions limited to 250 and other political caricatures. Period 2 .. ..£5/**£10**/£15

Roubille, A. (Fr). Anti Militarist. 'Musee des Sires etc. Period 2 .. ..£5/**£10**/£15

Roverini, Mario. Italian artist. Fascist propaganda. Period 4 .. .. £1/**£3**/£5

Sancha, F. Pub. Tuck. Aesop's fables WW1 style (*see* MILITARY) .. .. £4/**£5**/£7

Spurgin, Fred.† (Also under his initials, 'FS'.) Suffragette/ National Insurance themes for several publishers, notably Inter-Art .. .. £2/**£4**/£6

Thiele, Arthur.† Period 3. German propaganda/military .. .. £2/**£4**/£6

POLITICAL LEADERS/PERSONALITIES

Heads of State, Members of Parliament, Presidents, Prime Ministers, Royalty. Favourite subjects are—*Britain*: Balfour, Campbell-Bannerman, Joseph Chamberlain, Churchill, Edward VII, Sir Edward Grey, Lloyd George and Queen Victoria; *France*: Clemenceau, Felix Faure, de Gaulle, Loubet and Poincaré; *Germany*: Bismarck, Hitler and the Kaiser; *USA*: Eisenhower, Kennedy, Lincoln, Nixon and Washington. Period 7 subjects include: Ayatollah Khomeini, Giscard d'Estaing, Elizabeth II, Pope John Paul II and Margaret Thatcher.

Cartoons/Caricatures

Value according to quality of the artist.
Price range .. .. £2/**£5**/£20

Political Campaigns/Candidates/Election Results/ Groups of Cabinets/Governments

Artist drawn .. .. 75p/**£1.50**/£3
Photographic in origin .. .. £1/**£3**/£5

Straight Portraits

Artist drawn. Value according to quality of artist £1/**£2**/£3
Photographic .. .. 75p/**£1.50**/£2

PUNISHMENT & JUSTICE

Famous Trials

Dreyfus Affair. *See below.*
Haarmann the Mass Murderer (1924) .. .. £2/**£4**/£6
Humpert-Crawford affair (1902)
  Artist drawn .. .. £3/**£6**/£10
  Photographic .. .. £3/**£6**/£8
Landru. Period 2. Artist Poulbot.† .. .. .. £6/**£8**/£10
  Other artists .. .. £2/**£3**/£5
Other trials. British and French. Periods 2, 7 .. £2/**£5**/£10

Dreyfus Affair ■POL 3

Alfred Dreyfus was a Jewish Officer in the French Army. On 15 October 1894, on the strength of a letter, known later as le Bordereau, *Dreyfus was arrested, accused of treason. Found guilty, he was deported to Devil's Island for life. As the evidence was scanty and there was obvious antisemitic bias, his cause was taken up by his family and a handful of energetic supporters. Clemenceau denounced the first court martial as irregular and the novelist Emile Zola wrote an open letter to the President of France, entitled* J'Accuse. *A petition signed by 3000 persons, including Anatole France and Marcel Proust, led to a trial of Zola (who was found guilty and sentenced) which focussed public attention on Dreyfus's plight. One of the principal witnesses in the original trial, Major Henry, confessed that* le Bordereau *was a forgery and committed suicide; another fled abroad. The controversy dragged on, and it was not until August 1899 that Dreyfus was accorded a new trial—the* Proces de Rennes. *He was found guilty, but his sentence was reduced. In March 1904, a review of his case was begun, which ended with his re-instatement on 22 July, when he was awarded the* Légion d'Honneur. *The* Affaire *was an important landmark in French history, and its effects reverberated around the world. Postcard comment was made not only in France, but in America, Belgium, Germany and Hungary.*

Artists
Cavelet. Dreyfus procession—satire. B & w
Dangel, Louis. Zola au Pantheon. B & w
Enzo. 'Truth is gagged'. Satire of trial. B & w
'H.T.' B & w series
Hebourgine, L. L'oeuvre de Zola. B & w
Muller, E. *L'enterrement de Général André La Dernière Corvée*. Col.
Orens. Zola *J'accuse*. Satire. B & w (*set of 6*)
Photographic
Various portraits of Zola.
With *Art Nouveau* border, gold background
A. M. Amiot, den Haag:
Photos of Dreyfus, Picquart, Zola
Stuyvesant & Co. N.Y.
Zola portrait/red & blue eagle/stars & stripes

Publishers' Series
Cie Americaine
Series of 24
E. le Deley, Paris
Set of 6, *La Rehabilitation de Dreyfus*
J. Deurwaerder, Bruxelles (Julio)
Set of 36, satirical line drawings. B & w
'E.N.' Series 21
At least 10 b & w cards
Herbut & Frank, Frankfurt
Map Card: *Gruss aus Cayenne/Wo ist Zola*. Blue
J. Jungingers, Stuttgart. No. 403
Dreyfus, Esterhazy, Labon, Zola
S. Krotoschin, Görlitz
Set of 4. B & w
Max Marcus, Berlin
Erinnerung an den Zola Prozess. Paris 1898 (6 cards)
Artist F. Füssner 1897. Blue/b & w (6 cards)
Numbered cards between 512 and 606 b & 2
S. & G. Saulsohn
B & w set

Fritz Schardt, Nurnberg
Various designs, incl. Zola. B & w
Seljenka & Szel, Budapest
Artist signed set. B & w
Societé Ed. Cartes Illustrées, Turin
Various
Sternfeld, Venise
Set of 12. B & w
Anon
Series of *Affaire Dreyfus* documents. Blue on cream
Les deux compères: Dreyfus et Andre. Brown & white
Set of reproductions of Dreyfus's letters to his wife. Blue

Price range .. ..£5/**£10**/£15
Complete sets command a premium.

■POL 3 Pub. Societe Ed. Cartes Illustrées, Turin. 'Affaire Dreyfus For Justice and Truth. "One last Word, M. Zola, and I will be free," says Justice.' UB. Period 1 £15

Punishments
Chain gangs/convicts/prisoners and prisons/slave ships. Clear photographs .. .. £1/**£2**/£4
Decapitation/flogging/hanging/various executions and punishments. Clear photographs .. .. .. £1.50/**£3**/£5
Tottenham Assassins. Privately produced, real photo cards of the siege and the suicides .. .. 75p/**£1**/£3

Unusual Punishments
Fr. Series of comic artist drawn penalties of gossip—hideously enlarged tongues. Period 2 .. .. .. 75p/**£1**/£1.50
Ger. Pub. Nister. col. artist drawn series which includes ducking, muzzling, neck collars, pillories, stocks, etc. Period 2 .. .. 75p/**£1**/£1.50

POST OFFICE

In recent years many philatelists have become more interested in postcards and in particular in those cards which have a postal theme—i.e. illustrations of post offices, posting boxes, mail trains, etc. (*see* SOCIAL HISTORY). To cater for this interest several postal administrations have produced cards having a direct appeal to the stamp collector. The British PO began in 1973 a series of cards reproducing in large size the designs of various commemorative stamps—known as 'PHQ cards'. These are listed in Stanley Gibbons *Collect British Stamps* checklist (published twice a year—in May and November).

In addition other cards have been issued by the National Postal Museum (since 1969) and by the regional headquarters of the various postal regions (since 1971). A simplified listing of those issued to mid 1981 was given in the second edition of this catalogue (pp. 161–163) and cards issued mid 1981–mid 1982 in the third edition (pp. 207–208). Cards issued September 1982 to June 1984 are listed below.

BRITISH PO—NPM & REGIONAL ISSUES ■PO 1

Notes

NPM = National Postal Museum
EPR = Eastern Postal Region
LPR = London Postal Region
MPB = Midlands Postal Board
NEPR = North Eastern Postal Region
NWPB = North Western Postal Board
SEPR = South Eastern Postal Region
SWPR = South Western Postal Region
WMPB = Wales and The Marches Postal Board

Where reference is shown in brackets, reference is not printed on the card.

1982

8 Sep. NPM SS/12 Information Technology Year .. **50p**
13 Sep. SEPR35 Brighton Philatelic Counter Tenth Anniv. (*Bandstand*) **30p**
6 Oct. NPM SS/11 1882 £5 Orange stamp **50p**
11 Oct. LPR1 New style letter box near Albert Hall .. **30p**
25 Oct. LPR2 A Collection of Croydon Postmarks .. **30p**
1 Nov. NPM 9/1 Edward VIII—Essays of a pictorial design for the Coronation issue
1 Nov. NPM 9/2 Edward VIII—Essays for the King's Head designs for the Coronation issue
1 Nov. NPM 9/3 Edward VIII—Essays of the King's Head design for the definitive issue
1 Nov. NPM 9/4 Edward VIII—Essays and colour trials for issued stamps, 1936
Per set of 4 .. .. **£1**

1983

6 Jan. NPM SS/13 London Exhibitions 1851–1951 .. **40p**
30 Mar. NPM A/4 Machin Head advertising card (blue) **30p**
18 Apr. NPM SS/14 Royal Mint Exhibition **40p**
25 Apr. LPR 3 Post Office Railway **30p**

6 May NPM SS/15 National Stamp Day—5s Seahorse **40p**
10 May SWPR 19 Falmouth Packet Boat **30p**
27 Jun. WMPB 18 Castell Coch, Cardiff
.. .. **£1**
27 Jun. WMPB 19 Pembroke Castle
27 Jun. WMPB 20 Rhuddlan Castle
27 Jun. WMPB 21 Ragland Castle
27 Jun. WMPB 22 Beaumaris Castle
27 Jun. WMPB 23 Powis Castle
Per set of 6 .. .. **£1**
5 Jul. MPB 14.1 Nantwich Mural
5 Jul. MPB 14.2 Nantwich Mural
5 Jul. MPB 14.3 Nantwich Mural
Per set of 3 .. .. **75p**
6 Jul. NPM SS/16 P.O. at War—Part 3 .. .. .. **40p**
18 Jul. SEPR 36 Cartoon—Building Site
18 Jul. SEPR 37 Cartoon—Beware of Dog
Per set of 2 .. .. **50p**
1 Aug. LPR 4 Parcel Post Centenary **30p**
3 Aug. SWPR 20 Parcel Post Centenary **30p**
24 Aug. NPM SS/17 1964 6d Roses stamp **40p**
19 Sep. SEPR 38 Cartoon—Armed Dog
19 Sep. SEPR 39 Cartoon—Private Sorting Office
Per set of 2 .. .. **50p**
10 Oct. NPM SS/19 Wyon Medal, 1d black, 2d blue .. **40p**
10 Oct. NWPB 8(a) Mechanised Offices
10 Oct. NWPB 8(b) Philatelic Counters
10 Oct. NWPB 8(c) Sub Post Offices
10 Oct. NWPB 8(d) Rural Postmen
Per set of 4 .. .. **75p**
19 Oct. SWPR 21 GWK Mail Van at Cheltenham .. **30p**
26 Oct. NPM SS/18 Essays of 1958 Regional stamps .. **40p**

■PO 1 National Postal Museum SS/20 'Half Way Round the World' airmails exhibition card, 1984 40p

---

1984

5 Jan. NPM SS/20 Airmail Exhibition **40p**
17 Jan. NPM SS/21 Heraldry Exhibition **40p**
15 Feb. (EPR)1 Great Tew PO, Oxon
15 Feb. (EPR)2 Dorchester-on-Thames PO, Oxon

15 Feb. (EPR)3 Swalecliffe PO, Oxon
15 Feb. (EPR)4 Wytham PO, Oxon
Per set of 4 .. .. **75p**
6 Mar. NPM SS/22 Cattle Stamps Exhibition **40p**
1 May NPM A/5 Postage Label advertising card **£1**
2 May NWPB 9 (a) The Rose Garden
2 May NWPB 9 (b) The Liverpool 'Special' Pillar Box at Herculaneum entrance
2 May NWPB 9 (c) The Pillar Box at Fullwood entrance
2 May NWPB 9 (d) The smallest travelling post office in the world
Per set of 4 .. .. **75p**
2 May NWPB 10 (a) London-Liverpool mail coach 1838
2 May NWPB 10 (b) Liverpool Post Office Canning Dock 1839–1899
2 May NWPB 10 (c) Aquitania loading American mails 1919
2 May NWPB 10 (d) Air mail at Liverpool Aerodrome 1935
Per set of 4 .. .. **75p**
8 May NPM SS/23 National Stamp Day **40p**
30 May SWPR 22 Mail Coach **30p**
5 Jun. NPM SS/24 UPU Monument **40p**
6 Jun. SWPR 23 D-Day Mural **30p**
7 Jun. SEPR 40 Mail Coach at Ostrich Inn, Colnbrook **30p**
26 Jun. NPM SS/25 Navigation & Astronomy **40p**

GUERNSEY POST OFFICE

1. Peter Le Lievre Paintings (Nov. 80) 5 cards Per set **£1**
2. Royal Wedding (Jul. 81) 7 cards Per set **90p**
3. Europa/Historical Events (Apr. 82) 6 cards Per set .. **45p**
4. Renoir Paintings (Sep. 83) 6 cards Per set **40p**

JERSEY POST OFFICE

1. Postal Headquarters (Oct. 79) **25p**
2. Christmas (Sep. 81) 3 cards Per set **20p**
3. RNLI Centenary (Jun. 84) **20p**

ISLE OF MAN POST OFFICE

1 TT Races (May 82) 5 cards Per set **50p**
2. PO 10th Anniversary (Jul. 83) 2 cards Per set .. **25p**

Cards with imprinted stamp

1. San Marino Postal Stationery Centenary (Sep. 82) .. **50p**
2. Tembal Stamp Exhibition (May 83) **50p**
3. Madrid Stamp Exhibition (Apr. 84) **50p**

Three Band Pricing System

Left Hand Band: The lowest price you will probably be asked to pay for this card.
Middle Band: What you will normally be asked to pay for this card: its average, reasonable price.
Right Hand Band: The highest price you will probably be asked to pay for this card.
For a full explanation of the system see page ix.

■PO 2 US Post Office. Artwork for 40c Olympic Games Stamp, 1983. One of set of 4. Per set £2.10

USA POST OFFICE ■PO 2

April 1983. Olympic Games 40c stamps 4 cards Per set	**£3**
June 1983. Reprints of above (with reference numbers) Per set	**£2.10**
June 1983. Olympic Games 28c stamps 4 cards Per set	**£2.10**
July 1983. Olympic Games 13c stamps 4 cards Per set	**£2.10**
Nov. 1983. Olympic Games 35c stamps 4 cards Per set	**£2.10**
Jan. 1984. Olympic Games 20c stamps 4 cards Per set	**£2.10**
May 1984. Olympic Games 20c stamps 4 cards Per set	**£2.10**

PUBLISHERS

We continue here the listing of cards of some of the most famous and important postcard publishers.

ALLEN, DAVID ■P 1, C 2
See COLLECTIONS.

DAVIDSON BROS
Famous for humorous cards by the best British artists. Tom Browne, their main artist, drew about 900 designs for them. Production began around 1902. A listing of the artists who drew for this publisher was given in the Second Edition (p. 168).
Price range .. .. £2/**£4**/£12

■P 1 Pub. David Allen & Sons. 'The Bad Girl of the Family'. B & w. Period 3 £2

■P 2 Pub. Hildesheimer. '5000 series'. Artist Robina. 'In the Trossachs'. No. 5376. PU 1906 £1

S. HILDESHEIMER ■P 2
Hildesheimers began their business in London in 1876 producing greetings cards; their earliest postcards appear to have been sepia, court size, issued in 1899. Business developed rapidly and many artists were used to meet the demand for view cards. Soon a numbering system was introduced, but a

higher number does not necessarily mean a later issue than a lower number. Perhaps the best known of Hildesheimer's work is the '5000 Series', a mixture of British and Foreign views (mostly artist drawn, but some photographic) with the occasional comic design. The series began *c.* 1904 and many cards are similar in concept and execution to the great Tuck *Oilette* series of views and scenes—possibly it was designed to rival the Tuck sets. Production appears to have ceased *c.* 1912.

Cards in the '5000 Series' in the number range 5038–5299 were listed in the third edition of this catalogue (pp. 214–215). This listing is continued in the supplement to this section.

Price range .. .. 50p/**£1.50**/£4

JUDGES ■P 3

In 1902 Fred Judge (*1872–1950*) and his brother Thomas Winn purchased and managed a Hastings photographic store. By August 1903 postcard views of Hastings and District—'The Judge Series'—were published using real photographic, collotype, photogravure and colour photogravure techniques.

By 1906 cards in a consecutively numbered *Main Series*, incorporating some renumbered special event cards, were available. Prior to No. 700 there are different negatives with the same number. By 1909 the *London Series* had appeared, and by 1914 the *Main Series* numbered over 4000. Photogravure, collotype and Fred Judge's sketched and initialed cards were produced as a cheap alternative to sepia in the 1920s and 1930s. In the mid 1950s b & w cards replaced sepia and the new current series of col. cards was introduced.

We have divided Judges output into 4 categories.

1. Early—non-Main Series

Series of local views (some printed in Germany), dated Hastings' events and flowers. Varied photographic and non-photographic cards; some col.

Price range .. .. 50p/**£1.50**/£4

2. Main Series

Consecutively numbered (50–31, 781–) of British Isles topography, animals and floral studies. Mainly sepia (some hand-tinted) but also black/white, photogravure, sketch, collotype and col. Some duplicated numbers. Extensive reprinting; identifiable by back design. Also four-view topographical cards (4-1–4-806).

Price range .. .. 25p/**75p**/£1.50

3. London Series

Similar to Main series, consecutively numbered, L1–L799 (*possibly more*).

Price range .. .. 25p/**75p**/£1.50

A listing of these cards from Nos. 1–152 were given in the third edition of this catalogue (pp. 217–218). The listing is continued in the supplement to this section.

4. Modern Cards
Col., consecutively numbered series, e.g. C6035, including retailers' special orders, e.g. C5573X. Also sketch, monochrome, unnumbered, col. and serrated ex-calendar cards.
Price range 25p/50p

■P 3 Pub. Judges Ltd. Modern series No. C5358X. 'The High Street, Rayleigh'. Period 7 25p

■P 4 Pub. 'LL' London No. 694 'Hampstead Heath—The Viaduct'. Period 2 £2

LL (LOUIS LEVY) ■P 4
In the Second Edition we published a full description of current knowledge and prevailing theories concerning LL together with a check list of London cards, Nos. 1–420. This check list was continued in the third edition (Nos. 499–670) and is continued (Nos. 671–813) in the supplement to this section where we also give additions to the two previous listings.

Valuations: Highest prices apply to *London Types* and then to active street scenes with clear detail of people/transport.
Period 2 pictures, published in Period 2 .. .. £2/**£4**/£8
Period 2 pictures, published in Period 4 .. £1/**£1.50**/£2

REID, ANDREW

Andrew Reid established his printing business in Newcastle in 1845. Much early work was done for railway and shipping companies using both litho and letterpress techniques. His sons and grandsons carried on the business until the 1920s when it passed out of family management. The first postcards were produced in 1902. The shipping and railway cards are generally well printed chromo-litho products, particularly the UB vignettes, but amongst the local subject cards can be found some poorer examples of printing and colouring.

Price range
Railway cards .. ..£2/**£15**/£60
Shipping cards .. .. £1.50/**£8**/£25

Listings of Railway and Shipping cards appeared in the third edition of this catalogue, p. 221.

J. W. RUDDOCK & SONS

J. W. Ruddock was born in New Malton, North Yorkshire in 1852. After apprenticeship he set up his own stationers and bookselling business in Lincoln in the 1880s. Postcard production followed later. The best known of Ruddock's cards are those in the *Artist* series probably begun in 1902. A 1907 catalogue refers to over 400 views in the series.

A listing of Ruddock view cards, arranged by artist was given in the third edition of this catalogue, p. 222.

Price range 25p/**50p**/75p

TUCK ■P 5

Raphael Tuck & Sons Ltd. is probably the most famous of all postcard publishers. Founded in the 1870s by Raphael Tuck and continued by his son Adolph, the company developed such a reputation for the quality of its printing work that in 1893 it received its first Royal Warrant from Queen Victoria. Adolph Tuck led a campaign to persuade Parliament to allow British manufacturers to publish picture cards of the full Continental size. On 1 November 1899 that freedom was granted and the first dozen Tuck cards were quickly issued.
The company continued producing postcards until after the Second World War.

The First Dozen Issues

These are chromo-litho productions. Each card has its own number. No Series number is indicated. All the examples listed here are titled as 'View' cards and are UB. Horizontal format unless marked (V).

1. The Tower of London. A Beefeater
2. St. Paul's from Blackfriars Bridge
3. St. James's Palace (V)
4. London Bridge. The Monument
5. Westminster Abbey. Poet's Corner

6. Royal Horse Guards. First Life-Guards (V)
7. Houses of Parliament and Westminster Bridge
8. Albert Hall. Albert Memorial
9. The Mansion House. The Lord Mayor's Coach (V)
10. The Bank of England, Royal Exchange
11. Trafalgar Square. Gordon Memorial (V)
12. Hyde Park Corner. The Serpentine

Prices:

No. 1	£7/**£11**/£13
Nos. 2–12	£2.50/**£3**/£4

Celebrated Posters

These have been amongst the most collectable of British cards during the last decade. Despite intense interest in them a complete listing has not yet been agreed. The abbreviated titles given below are followed by the artists' name where known.

Series 1500	
Cadburys' Cocoa	Cecil Aldin
Colman's Blue	Aldin
Colman's Mustard. Klondyke	John Hassall
Force Cereal	
Fry's Pure Cocoa	Gordon Browne
Pears' Soap	L. Cobrichon
Pears' Soap	Harry Furniss
Series 1501	
A Country Girl	Howard Forrest
A Country Girl	Hassall
Dewars' Whisky	Charles Jupp
Ogden's Guinea Gold	George Belcher
Rowntree's Elect Cocoa	Beggarstaff Bros.
Rowntree's Elect Cocoa	Walter West
Series 1502	
Colman's Starch	Aldin
Edwards' Soup	Louis Weierter
Fry's Milk Chocolate	
Liebig Meat Extract	Dudley Hardy
Pears; Soap	Rossi
Tatcho	Sauber
Series 1503	
Bovril	Ernest Bertram
Dewar's Whisky	G. Bataille
Nixey's Black Lead	Fred Morgan
Nixey's Blue	William Grove
Rosbach Table Walters	G. Bataille
Schweppes Table Waters	
Series 1504	
Barker & Dobson	Alfred Schwarz
Farola	G. L. Seymour
Force Cereal	
Milkmaid Brand Milk	
Milkmaid Milk	
Oxo	W. H. Caffyn
Thorne's Scotch Whisky	
Series 1505	
Apollinaris	Hal Ludlow
Apollinaris	M. A. Ramsay

Hoe's Sauce	
Idris	
Stower's Lime Juice	
Triscuit	
Series 1506	
Apollinaris	Phil May
James Buchanan & Co.	
Mazawattee Cocoa	
Pat-a-Cake	
Thorne's Whisky	
Union Castle Steamship Co.	Frank Brangwyn
Series 1507	
Bird's Custard	
James Buchanan & Co.	
Red Maid Soap	
Richmond Gas Stoves	
Shredded Wheat	Hassall
Thomson's Scotch Whisky	
Portland China	
Series 1508	
Bluebell Metal Polish	
Jacob's Cream Crackers	
Levant Gold Flake	
Palethorpe's Sausages	Aldin
Scottish Tyres	
Steedman's Powders	
Series 1510	
Milkmaid Brand Milk. Chinese art	
Milkmaid Condensed Milk	
Series 1511	
Milkmaid Brand Milk	

Price range .. ..£8/**£20**/£40

Values fluctuate wildly and are particularly sensitive to the artist concerned and to the condition of the cards. Higher series numbers are less common than lower numbers.

The Empire Series

As the title implies, the subjects of these cards are patriotic—naval vessels, famous generals, etc.

The cards are individually numbered but also form series—e.g. Series 47 The Empire's Navy comprises cards 243–254.

Details of cards in series 47, 48, 49, 50, 55, 68, 69 and 70 were given in the third edition of this catalogue (p. 225).

Price range .. ..£5/**£10**/£12

The Heraldic Series

These are amongst the most beautiful of Tuck postcards. Coloured embossed coats of arms on the left of the card are accompanied on the right by a fine monochrome view. Each series has a common coat of arms with differing monochrome views on its cards. Cards carry individual numbers or series

numbers but apparently not both. It is, therefore, very difficult to correlate card and series numbers.
Details of the cards in series 150 (London), 152 (Glasgow), 153 (Manchester), 154 (Liverpool), 155 (Dublin), 156 (Edinburgh), 157 (Birmingham), 158 (Belfast), 159 (Bristol), 160 (York), 161 (Plymouth), 162 (Leamington), 163 (Brighton), 164 (Oxford), 165 (Cambridge), 166 (Aberdeen) and 167 (Bath) were given in the third edition of this catalogue (pp. 225–226).
Price range .. .. £3/**£6**/£12

Kings and Queens of England
This collection of 3 series (Nos. 614, 615 & 616) each of 12 cards, plus Edward VII (617), was described in the second edition of this catalogue (p. 109). There are 6 versions of Edward VII.

Per card .. .. £5/**£7**/£8
Complete set of 42 .. .. £250/**£300**/£400

Proof Limited Edition Sets
In May 1903 Tuck announced that they would, from time to time, issue special limited editions of their new postcards. Only 1000 copies of each set would be produced. All would have an individual Proof number in gold and would be printed on a special thick board. All purchasers would receive a certificate and be listed in a special register.

Sets numbered I–L were listed in the third editon of this catalogue, p. 226.

Price range .. .. £5/**£6.50**/£12

■P 5 Pub. Tuck 'Proof Limited Edition'. No. 2630. Artist M. Morris. 'Sunset'. Period 2 £6.50

'United Kingdom' Postcard Series
A checklist is invited for this little-researched series, featuring photographic origin scenes on a green background, decorated with embossed, gilded symbols of the counties of the U.K.

Price range .. .. £2/**£4**/£6

SECTION SUPPLEMENT—PUBLISHERS CHECKLISTS
1. Hildesheimer 5000 Series
2. Judges London Series Nos L155–332

3. LL Cards of London Nos 671–813 and additions to earlier listings

1. Hildesheimer '5000 Series'

No.	*Subject*	*Artist*
5300.	Dogs	
5301.	North Country views	
5303.	North Country views	R. Gallon
5304.	Country views	incl. Gallon
5305.	Beauties (*Photographic, b & w*)	
5306.	Children (*Sepia*)	
5307.	Girls (*Sepia*)	
5308.	Glamour (*Photographic, sepia*)	
5309.	Buildings	Arthur C. Payne
5310.	North Country views	R. Gallon
5311.	Scotland	
5312.	Country views	Niemann
5313.	Scotland	
5314.	Various children etc. (*Photographic, sepia*)	
5315.	Musical children (*Photographic, sepia*)	
5316.	Children (*Photographic, b & w*)	
5317.	Paintings	
5318.	Photographic (*B & w*)	
5319.	Scotland	Chas. Mali
5320.	Fruit	N.S.
5321.	Gems of Coed series	
5322.	Views	C. Eilers
5323.	Paintings	
5324.	Fifteenth Century London	Payne
5325.	Bettws-y-Coed series	
5326.	Foreign (*Photographic*)	
5327.	Art repros. (*12 cards*)	Various
5329.	Foreign	
5331.	Italy	
5332.	Foreign	
5333.	Austria	
5334.	Rhine	
5335.	Austria	
5336.	Actresses (*Photographic*)	
5337.	Ireland	
5339.	Actresses	
5340.	Boys (*Photographic*)	
5341.	Ireland	
5342.	Vanished London	Payne
5343.	Children (*Photographic, sepia*)	
5344.	Actresses (*Photographic*)	
5345.	English Lakes (*Photographic*)	
5346.	Surrey views	
5347.	Killarney series	Gallon

5348. Welsh views	Gallon
5349. Fruit	
5350. Sea views	
5351. Welsh series	Gallon
5352. Nuremberg	
5353. Thames views (*12 cards*)	
5354. New York (*Photographic*)	
5355. Paintings	
5356. New Zealand (*Photographic*)	
5357. River scenes	Gallon
5358. Surrey views	
5359. On the Avon series	
5360. Warwick	Gallon
5361. Scottish series	
5362. North Devon Series	
5363. Stratford on Avon series (Shakespeare)	Gallon
5364. Norfolk Broad Series (*Issued 1906 onwards*)	
5365. Devonshire	
5366. Ruined Abbeys	
5367. Norfolk Broads	
5368. Cathedral Interiors	
5369. Lynton & District series	
5370. Scottish Lochs	Robina
5371. Farm Life	
5372. British animals	Maude Scrivener
5373. Yorkshire	
5374. Girl (*Photographic, sepia*)	
5375. Children (*Photographic, sepia*)	
5376. In the Trossachs	Robina
5377. Cornish views	Gallon
5379. Write Away	Pirkis
5380. Write Away	Pirkis
5381. Scottish Series	Robina
5382. Algerian views	
5383. Isle of Wight series (*12 cards*)	
5384. Views of Riviera	
5385. Forest scenes	J. Forsberg
5386. Views from Sunny South	
5387. Cornish views	
5388. Thames views	
5389. Northumberland	
5390. Yorkshire views	
5391. Thames views	Gallon
5392. Bournemouth	
5393. Salisbury views	
5394. Views of Riviera	
5395. Salisbury	
5396. On the Medway	Gallon
5397. On the Severn	
5398. Surrey views	
5399. Surrey views	

To be continued

2. Judges—London Series Nos. L155–332

Cards are prefixed by 'L' and are mainly sepia but some titles appear in sketch form and in photogravure—listed (S) or (P) where known. Postmark dates are included where known. Titles listed (R) were published by the Regent Publishing Co. Ltd., 310 Euston Road, London NW. L1–L450 were photographed entirely by Fred Judge. L451–*c*. L778 were photographed by 1939, mainly by Norman Button. The remainder were photographed by Oliver Butler and Fred Judge. Remaining cards in the series were photographed and published after 1945.

L155 St. Bartholomew's Hospital. The Fountain
L156 St. Bartholomew The Great. Smithfield
L157 St. Bartholomew The Great. The Pillars
L158 St. Bartholomew The Great. Across Chancel
L159 St. Bartholomew The Great. North Aisle
L160 St. Bartholomew The Great. South Door
L161 St. Bartholomew The Great. Across Nave
L162 St. Bartholomew The Great. South Aisle and Founder's Tomb
L163 Rotten Row and Hyde Park Corner
L165 Southwark Cathedral
L166 Southwark Cathedral in North Choir Aisle
L167 In Southwark Cathedral
L168 Southwark Cathedral. Altar Screen
L169 Southwark Cathedral. South Transept
L170 Southwark Cathedral. Entrance to Lady Chapel
L171 Southwark Cathedral. From North Choir Aisle
L172 Southwark Cathedral. Nave Looking West
L173 Southwark Cathedral. North Choir Aisle
L174 Westminster Abbey
L175 Westminster Abbey. Cloisters
L176 Westminster Abbey. In the Cloisters
L178 Westminster Abbey. Entrance to Cloisters
L179 Westminster Abbey. Cloisters
L180 Sunset Over London Bridge
L181 St. Pauls from Bankside
L183 The Dome of St. Pauls
L185 Sunset from Blackfriars Bridge
L186 The Tower Bridge—'Sundown'
L187 St. Pauls from London Bridge
L188 The Old Curiosity Shop
L192 The Lake. Tooting Bec Common (*1918*)
L193 St. Giles'. Cripplegate
L194 St. Giles'. Cripplegate
L196 St. Giles'. Cripplegate
L197 St. Giles'. Cripplegate. Milton's Tomb
L200 St. Botolph's. Aldersgate St.
L201 St. Botolph's Churchyard
L202 Old Roman Bastion in Cripplegate Churchyard
L203 Old Roman City Wall
L205 St. Pauls from Bankside
L207 Westminster Abbey Henry VII's Chapel
L208 The Old Curiosity Shop (*Fred Judge in picture*)
L210 The Thames from London Bridge
L211 Below Blackfriars. Low Tide
L214 Blackfriars Bridge. Sunset
L215 A London Wharf
L216 Whitehall
L217 On Tooting Bec Common

L219 Ludgate Hill from St. Pauls
L220 The Dome of St. Pauls
L221 St. Pauls from Canon Alley
LS221 St. Pauls from Canon Alley (S)
L223 Florence Nightingale's Monument. St. Pauls
L224 Nelson's Tomb. St. Pauls
L226 Chapel of St. Michael and St. George
L227 Amen Court
S227 Amen Court. London (*S*)
L229 Entrance to the Square. St. Bartholomew's Hospital (*1921*)
L231 Nelson's Column. Trafalgar Square
L236 Old Sundial Amen Court
L239 Wellington's Tomb St. Pauls
S241 Westminster Cathedral. London (*S*)
L243 Captured U Boat in London
L245 Captured German Guns in London
L246 Captured German Guns in London
L248 Captured German Guns in London
L250 Captured German Guns in London
L253 Peter Pan London
LS253 Peter Pan (*1922*)
L254 Peter Pan. London
L257 The Cenotaph
L258 The Cenotaph
L260 The Thames from Vauxhall
L263 Blackfriars (*1923*)
L264 Gateway. St. Bartholomew's Church
L265 Victoria Embankment
L266 Cleopatra's Needle (*1925*)
L267 Cleopatra's Needle
L268 Cleopatra's Needle and Whitehall Court
L268 Cleopatra's Needle and Hotel Cecil (*same negative*)
L270 Smithfield
L279 Night Snaps. In Piccadilly Circus
L285 Night Snaps. Hot Chestnuts
L287 Night Snaps. The Bus to Westminster
L291 Night Snaps. The Pavillion
L293 Night Snaps. Piccadilly Circus
L297 Night Snaps. Ludgate Hill
L298 Night Snaps. The Cenotaph
L301 Night Snaps. The Signal
L305 Night Snaps. In Piccadilly Circus
L308 Night Snaps. By Ludgate Bridge
L309 Night Snaps. On Ludgate Hill
L316 Night Snaps. The Jewellers Shop
L320 Night Snaps. In Trafalgar Square
L326 Night Snaps. St. Pauls Bus Stop
L331 Night Snaps. In Ludgate Circus
L332 Night Snaps. Crossing Ludgate Circus

To be continued.

3. LL Cards of London Nos. 671–813

The captions in these checklists have sometimes been slightly abbreviated but are adequate for identification purposes.
(V) = Vertical design
(C) = exists in coloured version only

(+C) = exists in both b & w and coloured
Dates of PU cards are quoted where known

671. Hampstead—Entrance to the Heath (+C) (*1910*)
672. Hampstead Heath—View from Parliament Hill
673. Hampstead Heath—View from Parliament Hill
674. Hampstead Heath—View from Spaniards Road (+C) (*1908*)
675. Hampstead Heath—View from Flag Staff
676. Hampstead Heath—Leg of Mutton Pond
677. Hampstead Heath—Ladies Bathing (+C)
677. Hampstead Heath—Ladies Bathing (*1910*)
678. Hampstead Heath—Bathing Pond (+C)
679. Hampstead Heath—The Pond, Vale of Heath (*1909*)
680. Hampstead Heath—White Stone Pond
681. Hampstead Heath—The Vale of Health
682. Hampstead Heath—View at Vale of Health (*1907*)
683. Hampstead—North End Road
684. Hampstead Heath—At North End
685. Hampstead—The Avenue, North End (+C) (V)
686. Hampstead—The Avenue
687. Hampstead—Wildwood Farm
688. Hampstead Heath. Top of the Drive
689. Hampstead—View on the Heath
690. Hampstead Heath—Viaduct—Looking South
691. Hampstead Heath—The Viaduct
693. Hampstead—The Viaduct
694. Hampstead Heath—The Viaduct (*1910*)
695. Hampstead Heath—Keeper's House and Fountain (+C)
696. Hampstead—Old Houses, North End
697. Hampstead Heath—Flagstaff and Spaniards Road (+C)
698. Hampstead Heath—The Bull and Bush (*1914*)
699. Hampstead Heath—The Spaniards (+C)
700. Hampstead Heath—Jack Straws Castle
701. Hampstead Heath—Kite Flying
702. Hampstead—Golders Hill—The Gardens (+C)
703. Hampstead—Golders Hill—The Gardens (*1908*)
704. Hampstead—Golders Hill—The Mansion
705. Hampstead—Golders Hill—The Mansion S
706. Hampstead—Golders Hill—The Mansion
707. Hampstead—Golders Hill—The Mansion (C)
708. Hampstead—Golders Hill—The Bridge (C)
709. Hampstead—Golders Hill—The Emu (*1908*)
710. Hampstead—Royal Soldiers' Daughters Home—The School
712. Hampstead—General Hospital
715. Hampstead—Mount Vernon Hospital—South Front (*1907*)
716. Hampstead—The Parish Church
717. Hampstead—The Parish Church—Interior
718. Hampstead—The Town Hall
719. Hampstead—High Street
720. Hampstead—High Street, Looking East
721. Hampstead—Church Row
722. Hampstead—Rosslyn Hill (C)
723. Hampstead—South End Road (*1907*)
724. Hampstead—Heath Street
725. The Zoo (London)—The Lion (C)

726. The Zoo (London)—The Lion
727. The Zoo (London)—The Elephant 'Refusing to Bathe' (C)
728. The Zoo (London)—The Elephant 'Obedience' (+C) (*1907*)
729. Hampstead—The Lake. Golders Hill Park
729. The Zoo (London)—The Elephant Ride (*1907*)
730. The Zoo (London)—The Elephant Ride (+C)
731. The Zoo (London)—The Elephant Ride (*1907*)
733. Hampstead—Leg of Mutton Pond
733. The Zoo (London)—The Elephant Ride—'A Busy Day'
734. The Zoo (London)—The Elephant at Work (C) (V)
735. The Zoo (London)—The Camel Ride (+C) (*1910*)
736. Hampstead—Christ Church (+C)
737. The Zoo (London)—Camels (+C) (*1909*)
738. The Zoo (London)—The Elephant. 'Obedience' (*1909*)
738. The Zoo (London)—The Bear (V)
739. The Zoo (London)—The Bear (+C) (V)
741. The Zoo (London)—The Sea Lion
742. The Zoo (London)—Watching the Polar Bears (C)
743. The Zoo (London)-The Polar Bears (+C)
745. The Zoo (London)—Giraffes (V)
747. The Zoo (London)—The Zebras (C)
750. The Zoo (London)—The Rhinoceros. 'More Please' (+C)
751. The Zoo (London)—The Hippopotamus. 'Hungry'
752. The Zoo (London)—Penguins (C)
753. The Zoo (London)—Talking to the Parrots (C)
754. The Zoo (London)—The Sea Eagle (V)
755. The Zoo (London)—Storks (V) (*1907*)
758. The Zoo (London)—Vultures
759. The Zoo (London)—The Lawn (*1907*)
760. The Zoo (London)—The Camel House
761. The Zoo (London)—Persian Deer

770. Croydon—High Street
772. Croydon—London Road (*1920*)
784. Balham Hill

785. Brockwell Park—The Old House (*1907*)
788. Brockwell Park—Ye Olde Garden (+C) (*1907*)
790. Brockwell Park—The Bathing Pond (C)
791. Brockwell Park—The Bandstand (C)

793. Battersea Park—The Aviary
794. Battersea Park—The Sub Tropical Garden (C)

798. Clapham Common—The Mount Pond
799. Clapham Common—The Mount Pond (*1907*)
800. Clapham Common—The Long Road (*1907*)
801. Clapham Common—South Side
802. Clapham Common—North Side

804. Clapham—The Clock Tower
805. Clapham—The Plough
806. Clapham—The Pavement
807. Clapham—Old Parish Church
808. Clapham—St. Mary's Church, Park Road (V)
809. Clapham—Weslyn (*sic*) Chapel, High Street
810. Clapham—The Old Town
811. Clapham—The Public Library
812. Clapham—High Street
813. Clapham—Park Road (*1907*)

Additions to 'LL' London listings published in the second and third editions of this catalogue:

87. The Strand from Trafalgar Square (C)
205. View in Hyde Park
223. Kew Gardens—The Palace
244. Westminster Abbey—The choir—Looking West
286. The Ritz Hotel, Piccadilly
287. Grand Hotel and Strand (*1912*)

RAILWAYS

This is the province of the specialist collector and values fluctuate wildly. Intense competitive interest can focus on particular cards thus pushing up the prices paid for them, but once that limited demand has been satisfied, prices can drop dramatically. Such action and reaction is not exclusive to this category of course but the novice railway collector would do well to look around a little before buying. The highest values in this section attach to poster-type designs and early vignette views. The continuing interest in local history RP cards make views of railway hotels and stations most desirable and map cards retain their popularity.
A more detailed introduction was given in the second edition of this catalogue (p. 177).
The listing here is given under the following headings:
Non-Official Cards. Thematic
Official Cards. Pre-1923 Companies
Official Cards. Post-1923 Companies

Non-Official Cards—Thematic Listing

Accidents
Gothard, W.—photographic series .. .. £15/**£19**/£25
Other photographic/halftone/collotype cards. (Much of the value of these cards depends on their picture content and publisher interest) .. ..£6/**£10**/£12

Advertisements ■R 1
Reproductions of posters (see official cards)
Periods 2–4 .. .. £25/**£35**/£50
Period 7 .. .. 25p/50p
French poster series. With/without references to railways in the British Isles .. ..£6/**£10**/£15

■R 1 Pub. Dalkeith. Classic Poster Series No. P63. 'The Golden Arrow'. Period 7 30p

Poster type advertising (artistic cards from many countries) .. .. £4/**£6**/£10

Artists

Although the railway companies employed many capable and well known artists to design their posters, brochures and holiday literature, very few of the designs were transferred to the medium of the postcard. A small number of notable exceptions occur and some of these are listed under 'official' cards.

Foreign Railways (those other than in the British Isles).
■R 2

Official cards (those issued with company crests or titles), e.g. America & Canada (various), Cape, Japan, Natal, Russia, Tasmania .. .. £4/**£6**/£10
Engines .. .. £1/**£2**/£3
General views of track etc. .. .. £1/**£2**/£3
Rolling stock, inside/external views .. .. £1/**£1.50**/£2
Stations .. .. £2/**£3**/£4

■R 2 Pub. Anon. Fr. 'Paris. Gare Montparnasse'. PU 1910 £4

Funicular & Cliff Railways/Lifts
Great Britain .. .. , ... £1/**£2**/£3
Foreign .. .. 75p/**£1**/£2

Locomotive & Rolling Stock—Pre-1923

Fleury, Paris—a series of many hundred cards of locomotives of French Railways. Two different printings.
Red captions .. .. £2/**£3**/£6
Black captions .. .. £1/**£2**/£3
Hartmann (Series 3061) .. .. £1/**£2**/£3
JWB (Commercial series No. 312–12 No.) .. £1/**£1.50**/£2
Knight series .. .. £1/**£2**/£3
Locomotive magazine .. .. £1/**£1.50**/£2
Locomotive Publishing Co. (Early vignettes, both single and multi-col.) .. .. £15/**£20**/£25
Locomotive Publishing Co.—collotypes/half tone £1/**£1.50**/£2
Locomotive Publishing Co.—photographic issues £1/**£1.50**/£2
Locomotive Publishing Co.—col. series (Goffey 4–291) (F. Moore paintings) .. .. £1/**£1.50**/£2

Misch & Co.—'Noted Trains' series 331 and 332 .. £3/**£4**/£6
Parsons, F. J. .. .. £1/**£2**/£3
Pictorial Centre, Brighton (24 cards) .. .. .. £1/**£2**/£3
Pouteau—half-tone/photographic .. .. £1/**£1.50**/£2
Railway photographs (photographic cards, no specific publishers) .. .. £1/**£1.50**/£3
Smith, G. .. .. £1/**£2**/£3
Smith, W. H.—'Kingsway series' .. .. £1.50/**£2**/£3
Tuck, R. & Sons. 'Oilette' and other similar series (1904–1923). (6493, 9040, 9150, 9226, 9274, 9316, 9329, 9161, 9662, 9972, 9637, 8619, 9715, 9760) .. £2/**£3**/£5
Tuck R. & Sons—Kerr Stuart series (4983, 4984) .. .. £1.50/**£2.50**/£4
By Train (9186) and Villes de France (123, 124) £2/**£4**/£6
LCC Reward cards (12 No.) .. .. £2/**£3**/£4
Valentines series .. .. £1.50/**£2**/£3
Wildt & Kray (Series 1814, 1834) .. .. .. £1/**£2**/£3
Wrench series—uncol. (2280–2291, 4185–4193 & 4500–4512) .. .. £1.50/**£2**/£3
Wrench Red Bordered series (10,089–10,106) .. £2/**£3**/£4

Locomotives & Rolling Stock—1923 Onwards
Allan, Ian—col./photogravure .. .. .. 75p/**£1**/£1.25
Chadwick views .. .. af21 .. 75p/**£1**/£1.25
Dennis, E. T. W. .. .. 75p/**£1**/£1.25
Dixon, J. A. (col.) .. .. 75p/**£1**/£1.25
Judges (col.) .. .. 75p/**£1**/£1.25
Lake, G. H. (Eric Oldham paintings—10 cards) .. £1/**£2**/£3
Locomotive Publishing Co.—col. series (Goffey 292–328) .. .. £2/**£3**/£4
Mack, W. E.—(tinted cards) .. .. .. £1.50/**£2**/£3
Photochrom Co. .. .. £1.50/**£2**/£3
Pike .. .. £1/**£1.50**/£2
Regent—photographic series .. .. .. £1/**£1.50**/£2
Salmon, J. (col.) .. .. £1/**£1.50**/£2
Tuck, R. & Sons. 'Oilette' and other similar series (1923–1936). (3541, 3547, 3569, 3570, 3593, 5303, 5304.)
Model Railway Engines (3404) .. .. .. £2/**£3**/£4
Valentines series .. .. £1/**£2**/£3

Locomotives and rolling stock were also well depicted on 'official' cards. *See below.*

Local Lines (Standard & Narrow Gauge)

Branch lines owned or operated by major railway companies, or small independent companies promoted by Parliament or Light Railway Acts. A number of superb local published cards exist of these railways. Owing to publisher, social history or topographical interest they are often rated even higher in value than for their railway interest alone.

Bridges/Viaducts/Tunnels .. .. 50p/**75p**/£1
Level crossings and general trackside views £2/**£2.50**/£3
Motor buses/road vehicles (railway owned) .. .. £5/**£7**/£10
Official cards. *See below.*
Railway staff. Uniformed/groups .. .. £2/**£2.50**/£3
Rolling stock .. .. £2/**£2.50**/£3

Stations, Town (interior/platform views) .. .. £3/**£5**/£7
Stations, Town (exterior) .. .. £2/**£4**/£6
Stations, Village (interior/platform views) .. .. £5/**£6**/£8
Stations, Village (exterior) .. .. £4/**£5**/£6

■R 3 Pub. Kingsway Real Photo Series. 'Tilbury Station Interior'. PU 1913 £7

■R 4 Pub. Tilley's of Ledbury. Colwall Railway Station. Period 2 £5

Main Lines (Standard Gauge) ■R 3–4

Main trunk railways (Periods 1 to 3) connecting major towns and cities such as London, Liverpool, Manchester & Glasgow. Within the British Isles, these railways became grouped together into four major concerns in 1923 (Periods 4, 5) and became State owned in 1948 (Periods 6, 7).

Bridges/Viaducts/Tunnels .. .. 50p/**75p**/£1
Level crossings/trackside views .. .. .. £2/**£2.50**/£3
Motor buses/road vehicles (railway owned) .. .. £5/**£7**/£16
Official cards. *See below.*
Railway staff. Uniformed/groups .. .. £1.50/**£2**/£3
Rolling stock .. .. £2/**£2.50**/£3
Stations, City (interior) .. .. £2/**£3**/£4
Stations, City (exterior) .. .. £1/**£2**/£3
Stations, Town (interior/platform views) .. .. £5/**£6**/£7
Stations, Town (exterior) .. .. £3/**£5**/£6

Miniature/Pleasure/Beach Railways—(Up to 38 cm Gauge)

Ravenglass & Eskdale. Photographic/col./collotype. Periods 1–5 .. .. £1/**£3**/£5

Periods 6–7 .. .. 25p/**50p**/75p

Romney, Hythe & Dymchurch. Photographic/col. Periods 3–5 .. .. .. , ... £1/**£1.50**/£2

Periods 6–7 .. .. .. af21.. .. .. 25p/**50p**/75p

Various pleasure/Beach railways .. .. .. £1/**£2**/£3

Mountain Railways

Snowdon Mountain railway. Periods 1–5 .. £1/**£2.50**/£4

Periods 6–7 .. .. 25p/**50p**/75p

Foreign locations. Periods 1–5 .. .. £2/**£3**/£4

Official Cards—Pre-1923 Companies

'Official cards' is a term used to describe postcards issued/sold by railway companies to gain revenue and to promote all aspects of their business. Cards advertising railway hotels, ships and buses are excluded from this listing. Official cards have been issued from Periods 1 to 7 and are still being issued, although in ever reducing numbers.

Caledonian

Vignette/multi-view (early Period 2) .. .. £10/**£15**/£25

Views (Glosso) .. .. £3/**£4**/£6

Views (col.) (National, Valentine) .. .. .. £4/**£5**/£6

Engines/Rolling stock (col.) .. .. £4/**£6**/£8

Engines/Rolling stock (Glosso) .. .. £3/**£4**/£5

Poster reproductions (col. photographic) .. £40/**£50**/£60

Tartan-bordered views .. .. £5/**£6**/£8

Ambulance train .. .. £2/**£3**/£4

Sleeping Car—Reservation card .. .. .. £10/**£15**/£20

Cambrian

Vignette-intermediate (Picture Postcard Company) .. .. £15/**£20**/£25

Views—col. (Cambrian railways, Valentine, Photochrom) .. .. £4/**£5**/£6

Correspondence/holiday advertising .. .. .. £6/**£8**/£10

Maps.. .. .. £15/**£20**/£25

Cork, Bandon & South Coast

Views—col. (Tuck 'Oilette', Sunnyside of Ireland) £2/**£4**/£6

Dublin & South Eastern

Correspondence/views .. .. £20/**£25**/£30

Dublin, Wicklow & Wexford

Views—vignetted .. .. £20/**£25**/£30

Celesque series .. .. £15/**£20**/£25

East Coast Route (Great Northern, North Eastern, North British Railways)

'Write-away' type Vignette (Andrew Reid) .. £12/**£15**/£18

Rolling stock/stations/views—col. .. .. £8/**£12**/£16

Flying Scotsman (Hildersheimer) .. .. .. £3/**£4**/£5

Furness

English 'Gruss Aus'—(chromo) (McCorquodale) £10/**£15**/£20
Views—col. (McCorquodale) .. .. £2/**£3**/£4
Views—col. (Heaton-Cooper paintings) (Tuck) £1.50/**£2**/£3
Engines/Rolling stock (photographic) (Tuck) .. £4/**£5**/£6
Poster reproductions—col. .. .. £50/**£55**/£60
Furness Abbey/Hotel (photographic) (Tuck) .. £2/**£3**/£4
Art studies—George Romney paintings (photographic) (James Atkinson) .. .. £4/**£6**/£8

Glasgow & South Western

Vignette—col. (McCorquodale/Maclure MacDonald) .. .. £15/**£20**/£25
Views—col. (Tuck 'Oilette') .. .. £3/**£4**/£5
Ambulances—WW1 .. .. £4/**£6**/£8

Great Central

Vignette—intermediate (Picture Postcard Company) .. .. £15/**£20**/£25
Views—col. (Faulkner series) .. .. £4/**£5**/£6
Views—photographic (HHH series) .. .. .. £6/**£8**/£10
Engines/Rolling stock .. .. £6/**£8**/£10
Poster .. .. £50/**£55**/£60
Perforated engine card—col. (Central Advertising Co.) .. .. £75/**£80**/£100
Restaurant car—'En Route' .. .. £6/**£8**/£15

Great Eastern

Views/correspondence/advertising .. .. .. £6/**£8**/£10
View/correspondence/advertising (col.) .. £10/**£12**/£15
View correspondence/advertising (Jarrolds series col. and plain) .. .. £6/**£8**/£10
Views—col. (Tuck 'Oilette') .. .. £1.50/**£2**/£2.50
Trains/Stations—col. (Locomotive Publishing Co.) £2/**£3**/£4
Poster reproductions—(plain, col. incl. those by J. Hassall) .. .. £50/**£55**/£60
Collotype series with crest—various subjects incl. locomotives, steamers, Southwold bus and views) £2/**£2.50**/£3
Underground Railway Maps of London (incl. GER advertising) .. .. £5/**£8**/£10

Great Northern

Vignette—intermediate (Picture Postcard Company) .. .. £15/**£20**/£25
Vignette—London views (Picture Postcard Company) .. .. £8/**£12**/£16
Views—col. (Photochrom) .. .. £1/**£1.50**/£2
Engines—col. (Photochrom) .. .. £1.50/**£2**/£2.50
Engines/Trains—col. (Locomotive Publishing Co.) .. .. £1.50/**£2**/£2.50
Poster reproductions—col. (including Hassall's 'Skegness is so Bracing') .. .. £50/**£55**/£60
Poster type advertising—Panoramic .. .. £12/**£15**/£18
Correspondence/view cards .. .. £6/**£8**/£10

Great Northern (Ireland)

Views/Correspondence .. .. £10/**£12**/£15
Shamrock—hotel advertising .. .. £15/**£20**/£25

Great North of Scotland
Views (Porter, Aberdeen) .. .. £6/**£7**/£8
Cruden Bay Golf Tournament .. .. £8/**£10**/£12

Great Southern & Western
Views—col. (Tuck 'Oilette', Sunnyside of Ireland) £3/**£4**/£5

Great Western
Vignette—intermediate (Picture Postcard Co.) £15/**£20**/£25
Vignette—London views (court size) .. .. £15/**£20**/£25
Views—sepia collotype/gravure/photographic .. £2/**£3**/£4
Views—col. .. .. £2/**£3**/£4
Engines/Rolling stock—collotype/gravure/photographic .. .. £2/**£3**/£4
'Fishguard Harbour as a Port of Call' .. .. £4/**£5**/£6
Docks series (Autotype Co.) .. .. £4/**£5**/£6
Fishguard route .. .. £4/**£5**/£6
Poster reproductions—Series 3, col. (many are the work of Alec Fraser) .. .. £50/**£55**/£60
Poster reproductions—col. (Acme Press, Andrew Reid) .. .. £45/**£50**/£55
General interest—bridges, tunnels, stations etc. .. £2/**£3**/£4
Restaurant cars—'En Route' .. .. .. £12/**£15**/£20
Correspondence/view cards (single colour) .. .. £4/**£6**/£8
Wyndams series—correspondence cards (4 varieties) £4/**£6**/£8

Highland
Views—Railway title in red (Valentines) .. .. £6/**£7**/£8
Views—Railway crest in colour (Valentines) .. £4/**£5**/£6
Views—col. (Valentines) .. .. £5/**£6**/£7
Views—photographic (Valentines) .. .. .. £4/**£5**/£6

Lancashire & Yorkshire
Vignette (Picture Postcard Co.) .. .. .. £15/**£20**/£25
Views—plain .. .. £2/**£3**/£4
Views—col. .. .. £2/**£3**/£4
Engines/Rolling stock—plain .. .. £2/**£3**/£4
Engines/Rolling stock—col. .. .. £2/**£3**/£4

Note: Many of these cards (probably all) were overprinted in French in 1910 and 1913 with advertisements for holidays in England, Isle of Man and Ireland. Cards having these overprints should have their prices increased to twice the prices given here.

Wyre Dock/correspondence .. .. £15/**£20**/£25

London, Brighton & South Coast
Vignette—including London views (Picture Postcard Co.) .. .. £15/**£20**/£25
Views/general interest (Waterlow) .. .. .. £2/**£3**/£4
Bridges (Waterlow) .. .. £3/**£4**/£5
Poster reproductions—(single colour) .. .. £50/**£55**/£60
Correspondence .. .. £4/**£6**/£8

London, Chatham & Dover
Vignette—col. (court size) (Pictorial Postcard Syndicate) .. .. £20/**£25**/£30

Vignette—single colour (court size) (Pictorial Postcard Syndicate) .. .. £20/**£25**/£30
Vignette—single colour (court size) (Picture Postcard Company) .. .. £20/**£25**/£30

London & North Western
St. Louis exposition .. .. £6/**£7**/£8

Tuck Cards
Engines and Rolling stock .. .. £1/**£2**/£3
Views and others .. .. £1/**£2**/£3

McCorquodale Cards
Views—plain/col. .. .. £1/**£2**/£3
Engines/Rolling stock—plain/col. .. .. .. £1/**£2**/£3
Ships plain/col. .. .. £2/**£3**/£5
Poster reproductions—plain/col. .. .. .. £50/**£55**/£60
Maps—col. .. .. £50/**£55**/£60

For full and detailed listing of all London & North Western Railway postcards see *Official Railway Postcards of the British Isles* Vol. 1 by R. Silvester. (1978)

London & South Western
Vignette—(court size) (single colour) (Pictorial Postcard Syndicate) .. .. £20/**£25**/£30
Vignette—intermediate (col.) (Pictorial Postcard Syndicate) .. .. £15/**£20**/£25
Vignette—intermediate (Picture Postcard Co.) £15/**£20**/£25
Vignette—London views (Picture Postcard Co.) £10/**£15**/£20
Poster reproductions .. .. £50/**£55**/£60
Correspondence/view .. ..£8/**£10**/£12
Orphanage (Locomotive Publishing Co.) .. .. £3/**£4**/£5

Midland
Vignette (Picture Postcard Co., British and Colonial Auto. Trading Co., Automatic General Stores—same views) .. .. £15/**£20**/£25
Vignette—London views (Picture Postcard Co.) £10/**£15**/£20
Vignette—col. (Route to Scotland) (Andrew Reid) .. .. £12/**£15**/£18
'Nearest Station'—views—col. .. .. £6/**£8**/£10
Views—col. (Photochrom, with/without 'bear' trademark) .. .. £2/**£3**/£4
Rolling stock—col. .. .. £2/**£4**/£6
Engines—plain .. .. £1.50/**£2**/£2.50
Poster reproductions—Series (col.) .. .. £50/**£55**/£60
Poster reproductions (col.) .. .. £40/**£45**/£50
Maps (col.) .. .. £10/**£12**/£14
Heysham—Morecambe Electric Train (col.) £20/**£25**/£30
Exhibitions .. .. £15/**£18**/£20

North British
Views—plain with crest on front .. .. .. £6/**£8**/£10
Views—plain, col., tinted .. .. £3/**£4**/£5
Views—Edinburgh (col.) (Caledonian 129 series) £2/**£3**/£4

North Eastern
Views—photo Panoramic (series of 40) .. .. £6/**£7**/£8
Views—photo Panoramic (with map overprints) £10/**£12**/£15
Newcastle Electric trains (col./plain) .. .. .. £4/**£5**/£6
Poster reproductions (series of 20) (col.) (Photochrom) .. .. £50/**£55**/£60
Industrial poster reproduction (series of 4) (col.) £55/**£60**/£75
Riverside Quay, Hull (col.) .. .. £6/**£8**/£10
North Eastern railway houses—(col.) .. .. .. £2/**£4**/£6
Exhibition .. .. £4/**£5**/£6

North Staffordshire
Views—collotype, gravure, col. enamelled, platemarked .. .. £4/**£5**/£6
Views—as above (including scenes on the Leek and Manifold railway) .. .. £4/**£6**/£8

Portpatrick & Wigtownshire Joint
Views—single/multi-view, numbered series £15/**£20**/£25
Correspondence/views .. .. £20/**£25**/£30

South-Eastern & Chatham & Dover
Vignette—intermediate (col.) (Pictorial Postcard Syndicate) .. .. £20/**£25**/£30
Vignette—intermediate (Picture Postcard Co.) £15/**£20**/£25
Vignette—London views (Picture Postcard Co./Automatic General Stores) .. .. £10/**£15**/£20
Engines/Rolling Stock—col. (McCorquodale) .. £2/**£3**/£4
Trains/Stations—col. (McCorquodale) .. .. .. £2/**£3**/£4
Poster reproduction (col.) .. .. £50/**£55**/£60
Maps (col.) .. .. £16/**£18**/£20
Maps/engines and trains (plain) .. .. .. £16/**£18**/£20
Correspondence/views (Photochrom) .. .. £10/**£12**/£15
Exhibition .. .. £4/**£6**/£8
Boulogne views—col. (Stevenard edit with overprints) .. .. £4/**£6**/£8

West Coast Route (Caledonian and London & North Western)
Views—(plain/col.) .. .. £6/**£8**/£10
Rolling Stock (plain/col.) .. .. £12/**£14**/£16

West Highland
Views—col. (National) .. .. £8/**£10**/£12

Wirral
Pictorial route map .. .. £40/**£45**/£50

Official Cards—Post-1923 Companies ■R 5

Great Western Railway
Views—col. (L. Richmond paintings) .. .. .. £2/**£3**/£4
Engines—gravure/photographic .. .. £1/**£2**/£3
Engines—col. .. .. £1/**£2**/£3
Poster reproductions .. .. £45/**£50**/£55
'King George V'—folded col. locomotive card £20/**£25**/£30

London Midland & Scottish Railway
Engines—col. .. .. £1/**£2**/£3

Holiday tickets/views—photographic with overprints .. .. £3/**£4**/£5
Poster reproductions .. .. £30/**£35**/£40
Container services advertising .. .. .. £20/**£25**/£30

London & North Eastern Railway
Engines/Trains—photographic .. .. £2/**£3**/£4
Poster reproductions .. .. £30/**£35**/£40

Southern Railway
Engines—gravure/photographic .. .. .. £1/**£2**/£3
Engines/trains—col. .. .. £1/**£2**/£3
Poster reproductions .. .. £30/**£35**/£40
Correspondence .. .. £2/**£3**/£4
Harbours/West Country scenes (paintings by L. Richmond) .. .. £2/**£3**/£4

British Railways
Trains—col. .. .. £1/**£2**/£3
Poster reproduction (HST Services—Western Region) .. .. £1/**£2**/£3
Poster reproduction (APT London/Glasgow) 1981 .. **50p**
Gleneagles/Turnberry Golf Courses—col. .. 50p/**75p**/£1
Birmingham 'New Street Station'—photographic (London Midland Region) .. .. £1/**£1.50**/£2
Kyle of Lochalsh Station (Scottish Region) .. .. £1/**£2**/£3
Correspondence .. .. £1/**£2**/£3

R 5 Pub. Locomotive Pub. Co. 'Southern Railway'. Mixed Traffic Engine No. B343. Period 4 £3

Three Band Pricing System

Left Hand Band: The lowest price you will probably be asked to pay for this card.
Middle Band: What you will normally be asked to pay for this card: its average, reasonable price.
Right Hand Band: The highest price you will probably be asked to pay for this card.
For a full explanation of the system see page ix.

RELIGION

It is the Roman Catholic countries, especially Italy, which provide the most colourful and the greatest number of postcards—through all the 7 periods. Also included in the section are missions and associations like the YMCA and the Salvation Army. For Jewish cards, *see* SOCIAL HISTORY.

ANGLICAN CHURCH

Cathedrals, churches—*see* 'Buildings' under SOCIAL HISTORY.
Portraits of clergy **50p**
Others **50p**

CHRISTIAN SCIENCE

Churches **50p**
Personalities 25p/**50p**/75p

GENERAL RELIGIOUS THEMES

Angels, Christmas and Easter Themes (*see* GREETINGS), Old Testament Texts, Reproductions of Religious Old Masters (*see* ART) etc. Many of these postcards are beautifully produced, often embossed and/or gilded. Publishers include Birn Bros. (especially 'Guardian Angel' series), Ettlinger, Tuck, Wildt & Kray.

Price range .. .. 50p/**75p**/£2

HINDUISM

Many beautiful coloured series of Indian cards showing Hindu legends exist.

Hindu Myths. Artist Evelyn, Paul .. .. £1/**£1.50**/£2
Pub. Ravi-Varma Press .. .. £1/**£1.50**/£3
Others .. .. 50p/**75p**/£1.50

MISSIONS/SOCIETIES

Church Lads' Brigade .. .. 50p/**75p**/£1.50
Church Mission to Jews. Personalities .. 50p/**75p**/£1
Ditto. Special overpints by Photochrom **50p**
International Society of the Apocrypha. Subscription reminders, etc. **50p**
London Society for Promoting Christianity to the Jews. Personalities .. .. 50p/**75p**/£1
Ditto. Special overprints by Photochrom **50p**
Scripture Gift Mission. Various issues **50p**
St. John's League of Mercy. Outings, etc. .. 25p/**50p**/75p
Society for the Propagation of the Gospel. Photographic origin issues showing good ethnic detail .. .. 50p/**75p**/£1
Others **50p**
South American Missionary Soc. Various issues **50p**
Universities Mission to Central Africa. Various issues **50p**
YMCA/YWCA (*see* MILITARY). Various .. 25p/**50p**/75p

NONCONFORMISM

Chapels—*see* 'Buildings' under SOCIAL HISTORY.
Outings—cards of photographic origin .. 50p/**75p**/£1.50
Personalities 25p/**50p**/75p

PASSION PLAYS

Oberammergau: every ten years incl. 1980.
Photographs of actors/stills .. .. .. 50p/**75p**/£1.50
General views 25p/50p
USA Pubs. Periods 2 to 4 incl. Bruckmann Trant, Commercial Color-type, Conwell, Crocker, Leo Schweyer 50p/**75p**/£1
Others 25p/**50p**/75p

PRAYERS ■REL 1

Lord's Prayer. Ger. series of 6. Period 2. chromo-litho. Per set .. .. £4/**£6**/£8
Lord's Prayer. USA Pub. Taggart. Series of 8. Per set .. .. £3/**£5**/£15
USA Others. Per set .. .. £3/**£5**/£15
Others .. .. 25p/**50p**/£1

■REL 1 Pub. Valentine's. Alphabet card 'L', with religious message. Period 2 75p

■REL 2 Pub. Anon. It. Accession of Pope Pius X, 1903. Col. UB £3

ROMAN CATHOLICISM ■REL 2

Anti-Catholicism

Various Protestant crusades incl. 'anti-Popery in Birmingham Streets' series .. .. 50p/**75p**/£1

Events

The following list does not claim to be comprehensive, but gives a typical selection of religious events for which postcards are known, in chronological order, in Periods 1 to 7.

1897. It. 19th Eucharist Congress, Venice
1898. It. Exhibition of Sacred Art
It. 20th Anniversary of Pope Leo XIII
1899. It. 800th Anniversary of St. John Baptist
1900. It. Celebrations of Holy Year
1903. It. Death of Pope Leo XIII
It. Accession of Pope Pius X
1908. Fr. Lourdes Jubilee
1914. It. Accession of Pope Benedict XV
1922. Pope Pius XI
1925. It. Celebrations of Holy Year
1939. Accession of Pope Pius XII
1958. Accession of Pope John XXIII
Price range .. .. £2/**£4**/£10
1976. 41st International Eucharist. Vatican 'Maxi' Series
1978. John Paul I. Vatican Maxi series and other issues
John Paul II. Various issues
1979. Visit of John Paul II to Ireland, Monte Cassino and other Italian locations, Poland, USA
Various Vatican 'Maxi' series
1982. Visit of John Paul II to UK
Visit of John Paul II to Argentina
1983. Visit of John Paul II to Spain
Visit of John Paul II to Poland
Price range .. .. 25p/**£1**/£3

Fund-Raising/Recruiting
Recruiting posters for priests/Vatican fund-raising, etc. .. .. 50p/**75p**/£3

General
Artist/sculpture Mastroianni religious subjects
Hospice of St. Bernard (incl. dogs)
Lourdes. Various issues
Monks (incl. liqueur making)
Pictures of angels, Biblical characters, saints
Portraits of clergy/Popes
Swiss Guard
Views of Vatican
Others
Price range 25p/**50p**/75p

SALVATION ARMY

Gen. Booth. Various .. .. £1/**£2**/£2.50
Gen. Booth memoriam card Pub. Rotary 1912 .. £1/**£3**/£6
Mrs. Booth/other members of the Booth family 50p/**75p**/£1.50
Various groups/meetings .. .. 50p/**75p**/£1.50
Period 7. International Staff Band **25p**

TEN COMMANDMENTS

Ger. Co. Period 2. Set of 10. Per set .. .. .. £7/**£10**/£12
Pub. Tuck. 2 versions: Catholic and Protestant (Nos. 163c and 163p). Per set .. .. £6/**£8**/£10
USA Pub. P.F.B. Per set .. .. £3/**£5**/£8

ROAD TRANSPORT

There is inevitable overlapping with SOCIAL HISTORY and TOPOGRAPHICAL, but here we have set out to list those themes which are more concerned with 'transporting', e.g. 'Omnibuses', than with 'activity', e.g. 'ploughing'. The highest values refer to RP cards with close-up detail. However, this is a field in which particularly good RP close-up examples can command prices beyond the valuations quoted here, especially if there is a strong social history connexion or local interest.

N.B. Values refer to Periods 1–2 unless otherwise stated.

Accidents	
Periods 1, 2	£5/**£10**/£15
Periods 3–7	£1/**£1.50**/£2
Ambulances	
Horse	£4/**£6**/£11
Motor	£4/**£5**/£9
Bicycling *see* COMPETITIONS/CRAZES	
Buses & Coaches	
Charabancs	£1/**£2**/£3.50
Horse	£7/**£12**/£25
Motor	£5/**£11**/£25
Steam	£9/**£15**/£28
Commercial Cabs/Carts ■RT 1	
(Incl. ponies and traps)	£2/**£3**/£5
Fire Engines	
Horse	£4/**£7**/£15
Motor	£4/**£6**/£15
Horse and Rider	75p/**£1**/£1.50
Lorries	
Motor	£4/**£5**/£9
Steam	£6/**£8**/£17
Motor Cars	
Periods 1, 2	£1/**£2.50**/£5
Periods 3–5	50p/**£1**/£2
Period 6	50p/**75p**/£1
Motor Cycles ■RT 2	
General	£1.50/**£3**/£5
Racing ads.	£6/**£12**/£15
Motor Racing ■RT 3	
Famous Cars	
Bluebird (Malcolm Campbell)	£2/**£2.50**/£5
Golden Arrow (Major Seagrave)	£2.50/**£3**/£5
Others	£1.50/**£2**/£4

■RT 1 Pub. Gottschalk, Dreyfus & Davis (G.D. & D.) Star Series. Local florist's delivery cart. Period 2 £3

■RT 2 Pub. H. A. Giles, Reading. WW1 army motorcyclists. RP. Period 3 £3

Fernel Series
Fernand Fernel, one of the *Collection des Cent* artists, drew a series of 10 cards *c.* 1903 called *Courses Automobiles* (Car Races). Different cards represent different races.

Price range	£3/**£4**/£5
Hill Climbs. RP. Periods 5, 6	£1.50/**£2**/£3
Motor Magazine. Portrait series	75p/**£1.50**/£3
Personalities	
Allietz	£5/**£8**/£10
Baras (Brasier)	£3/**£4**/£5
Bariller (Brasier)	£2/**£4**/£5
Boegge (Mercedes)	£3/**£5**/£6
Bonnier, Joakim	75p/**£1**/£1.50
Brabham, Jack	£2/**£2.50**/£5
Brooks, Tony	50p/**75p**/£1.50
Cagno (Itala)	£2/**£4**/£5
Duchene	£5/**£8**/£10
Fabry (Itala)	£3/**£5**/£6
Fangio, Juan	£1/**£2**/£2.50
Gabriel (Bayard-Clement)	£2/**£4**/£5
Gregory, Masten	50p/**75p**/£1.50
Hawthorne, Mike	£1/**£1.50**/£3
Lancia (Fiat)	£5/**£8**/£10
Landon (Mors)	£2/**£4**/£5

RT 3 Pub. L'Hirondelle, Paris. Seine-Inférieure Grand Prix, 1908. 'Lancia on his Fiat car' £12

Moss, Stirling	50p/**75p**/£1.50
Nazzaro (Fiat)	£3/**£5**/£6
Porsche	£5/**£8**/£10
Salvadori, Roy	50p/**75p**/£1.50
Salzer (Mercedes)	£3/**£5**/£6
Seagrave, Major H. O. D.	£2/**£3**/£4
Sisz (Renault)	£2/**£3**/£5

Races

Gordon Bennett chromo-litho	£10/**£12**/£14
Gordon Bennett photo-origin (highest for RP)	£3/**£5**/£8
Gordon Bennett course maps	£2/**£4**/£6
Indianapolis (1910)	£5/**£10**/£15
Nurburg Ring	£2/**£4**/£6
Rennen (1907). 'Kaiser Prize'	£4/**£6**/£8
Seine-Inférieure Grand Prix 1908	£4/**£8**/£12
Periods 1, 2 others	£3/**£5**/£8
Periods 3 to 6 others	50p/**£1.50**/£3

Valentine's Autocar series

Period 6	75p/**£1.50**/£3

Motor Shows *See* ADVERTISING

Royal Mail

Carts and Vans. Periods 1–6	£4/**£8**/£10
Period 7. Pub. Post Office	25p/**50p**/75p
Carts and vans	£2/**£3**/£5
Postbuses. Period 7. Pub. Post Office	25p/**50p**/£65

Traction Engines .. £4/**£8**/£15

Trams (the higher values for close-up RPs)

Electric	£3/**£8**/£10
Horse	£5/**£12**/£18
Steam	£5/**£10**/£15

Trolley Buses (the higher value for close-up RPs) £3/**£4**/£9

ROYALTY

This is a category which is inextricably bound with several others, notably:

MILITARY (In Victorian and Edwardian times Royal personages often led their countries' war efforts, at least as figureheads.)

POLITICAL (In Victorian and Edwardian times Royal personages—especially abroad—were often politically influential.)

SOCIAL HISTORY and TOPOGRAPHICAL (Royal visits were important events to the towns and cities where they took place.)

Royal cards are ideal for building up a collection throughout the 7 periods as they were amongst the first picture cards and are still being produced today.

BRITISH and FOREIGN cards are listed separately, in chronological order.

BRITISH ■ROY 1–4

Periods 1, 2, 4, 6, 7.
See Military for Periods 3 and 5.

1897. Queen Victoria's Diamond Jubilee

Pub. Dederich. Highest value for PU	£65/**£150**/£250
Pub. Preston Guardian	£15/**£20**/£25
Others	£10/**£15**/£20
Other Pre-1900 GB Royal events	£10/**£15**/£20

1900

Pub. Tuck. 'Empire' postcards Souvenir of 1900 with Queen Victoria oval portrait	£3/**£5**/£7.50
Pub. Tuck. 'Royal' postcard, ditto	£3/**£5**/£7.50

■ROY 1 Pub. Tuck. 'Empire' Postcard No. 1403. Memoriam card for Queen Victoria. 1901. UB £15

1901. Queen Victoria's Death

Pub. Faulkner, C. W. In Memoriam card produced within 15 hours of her death	..£8/**£12**/£15
Edward VII Accession commemoration	£2/**£4**/£6

Pub. Tuck. 'Empire' postcards Memoriam .. .. £6/**£8**/£15
Pub. Wrench. Memoriam cards published in Saxony and a week late in shops .. .. £6/**£8**/£15
Other Victoria mourning cards .. .. .. £5/**£7.50**/£10

1901. Voyage of the Duke and Duchess of Cornwall and York
Pub. Martin, B., Melbourne. 3 cards. Portraits of Edward VII, The Duke, The Duchess .. .. £3/**£5**/£8
Other Australian publishers .. .. £2/**£4**/£6
Pub. Tuck. 'Empire' Series 1649 .. .. .. £4/**£6**/£8
Pub. Wrench. 'Links of Empire' cards to commemorate the Royal voyage in the *Ophir*. Postcards taken on board and posted at ports of call: Series a. Ten cards. Portsmouth to Australia via Gibraltar, Malta and Port Said; Series b. Ten cards. South Africa, Canada and return to England.
Unused .. ..£8/**£10**/£12
PU from ports .. .. £10/**£12**/£15

1902. Coronation of Edward VII

Set for 26 June 1902, postponed because of the King's illness until 9 August. Cards to commemorate the coronation were published by:

Bird, Alfred & Sons (4 custard ads, UB vignettes) .. .. £10/**£15**/£25
Blum & Degen; Dobbs; Downey; Galyons; Mansell; Pasualis Moss; Rotary; Russell; Others .. .. .. £1.50/**£3**/£5
Stead, W. T. Current Event postcards. Four designs (incl. postponement) .. .. £5/**£8**/£10
Stewart & Woolf. Set of 10 col., embossed showing V.I.P.s at the coronation (note mistake 'H.R.H. Princess of Wales' on Prince of Wales card) .. .. £2/**£4**/£6
Tuck. Kings & Queens of England (*see* PUBLISHERS: Tuck). Six cards of Edward with diff. Shakespeare quote. (Date erased when coronation postponed) .. .. .. £4/**£6**/£8
Tuck. 'Coronation' series. Embossed, gilded, circular design .. .. £3/**£5**/£8
Tuck. 'Empire' postcards 1462, 1451/1453 .. .. £3/**£5**/£8
Tuck. Other designs .. .. £1.50/**£3**/£5

1902–1910. Reign of Edward VII
Many cards showing the Royal Family visiting towns, cities, seaside, races, etc. to open public buildings, review the fleet or inspect troops, sail or attend the races, etc. See SOCIAL HISTORY.

Price range .. .. 75p/**£1.50**/£6

1903
Tuck. Series of 10 cards to commemorate King's visit to Paris, issued in France .. .. £2/**£3**/£4
Voisey, Chas. Set of 15 cards to commemorate King's visit to Paris .. .. £2/**£3**/£4

1904–1907. Queen Alexandra's photographs
Pub. A. V. N. Jones. Fascinating snapshots of the British Royal Family on Royal Yacht cruises, visiting foreign royalty, celebrities, etc. Also published in book form. Over 40 cards .. .. 75p/**£1**/£2

1907
Historic meeting of Crowned Heads, Windsor Castle. Several Pubs. .. .. 75p/**£1.50**/£2

1908
Pub. Southwood. Empire Day 'Greeting from the Motherland'. Artist E. J. Walker .. .. 75p/**£1.50**/£3

1910. Edward VII's Death

Memoriam cards, many silvered, in purple or in plain black/ Coronation Souvenirs/Procession/Queen Alexandra's Message. Publishers include Beagles; Downing; East London Printing Co.; C. W. Faulkner; Hutson Bros.; Millar & Lang; Louis Levy; Lillywhite; Philco; Ritchie; Rotary and Tuck.

Price range .. .. 75p/**£1.50**/£5

1910. Proclamation of George V
Pub. Mark Cook of Chester; Judges; others 75p/**£1.50**/£2

1910. George V's First Court
Pub. Tuck. Artist Harry Payne .. .. £3/**£5**/£6

1911. Coronation of George V

The event was covered almost as thoroughly as his father's by many publishers including Davidson Bros.; Inter-Art (incl. Spurgin designs); Louis Levy; Vivian Mansell; McKenzie; Millar & Lang; Rotary; Russell; Schwerdtfeger; Taylor and Tuck.

Price range .. .. 75p/**£1.50**/£3

1911. Investiture of Prince of Wales
Various pubs. .. .. £1/**£1.50**/£3

1911. Crowning of George V as Emperor of India at Delhi Durbar
Price range .. .. 75p/**£1**/£2

1913. Marriage of Prince Arthur of Connaught and the Duchess of Fife
Various pubs. .. .. 50p/**75p**/£1

1919. Marriage of Princess Patricia of Connaught and the Hon. Alexander Ramsay
Various pubs. .. .. 50p/**75p**/£1

1922. Marriage of the Princess Royal and Viscount Lascelles
Various pubs. .. .. £1/**£1.50**/£2

1922. Marriage of Lord Louis Mountbatten and Lady Edwina Ashley
Various pubs. .. .. £1/**£1.50**/£2

1923. Marriage of Duke and Duchess of York
Price range .. .. £1/**£1.50**/£2.50

■ROY 2 Pub. Miller & Lang. King George V Coronation 1911 £3

■ROY 3 Pub. Beagles. H.R.H. The Duke of Kent with the Duchess, Princess Marina, at the coronation of HM Queen Elizabeth II, 1953. RP £2

1924. Marriage of Princess Alice and Prince Alexander of Tech
Various pubs. .. .. 50p/**75p**/£1.50

1924. Royal Family at the Wembley Exhibition
Price range .. .. 50p/**£1.50**/£3

1934. Marriage of Duke of Kent and Princess Marina
Various pubs. .. .. 75p/**£1**/£2

1935. Silver Jubilee of George V
Various pubs. .. .. £1/**£2**/£3

1935. Marriage of Duke of Gloucester and Lady Alice Montague Douglas-Scott
Various pubs. .. .. 50p/**75p**/£1.50

1936. George V's Death
Mourning and Memoriam cards by various pubs. £1/**£2**/£3

1936. Edward VIII
Various designs. Unveiling of Vimy Memorial £1.50/**£2**/£4

1937. Coronation of George VI
Various designs .. .. 75p/**£1.50**/£3

1938. Visit of George VI and Queen Elizabeth to France
Various designs .. .. 75p/**£1.50**/£2

1947. Betrothal of Princess Elizabeth and Philip Mountbatten
Various designs .. .. 50p/**75p**/£1

1947. Marriage of Princess Elizabeth and Prince Philip
Various designs . . 50p/**75p**/£1

1952. George VI's Death
Mourning cards by various pubs. . . 50p/**£1**/£2

1953. Coronation of Elizabeth II
Various Pubs. . . 50p/**75p**/£2

1960. Marriage of Princess Margaret and Antony Armstrong-Jones
Various Pubs. . . 50p/**75p**/£1

1969. Investiture of Prince of Wales
Various Pubs. . . 50p/**75p**/£1

1972. Silver Wedding of Elizabeth II and Prince Philip
Various Pubs. . . 25p/**50p**/75p

1973. Marriage of Princess Anne and Capt. Mark Phillips
Various Pubs. . . 25p/**50p**/75p
Post Office PHQ card . . **£12**

1977. Silver Jubilee of Elizabeth II
Post Office PHQ cards. Set of 5 . . **£12**
Pub. Carousel. City of Portsmouth Souvenir Postcard HMS *Victory* . . **60p**
Pub. Postcard Association of Great Britain. col. . . **40p**
Others . . 25p/**50p**/75p

1978. Silver Jubilee of Queen's Coronation
Post Office PHQ cards. Set of 4 . . **£2**

1980. 80th Birthday of Queen Elizabeth, the Queen Mother
Post Office PHQ card . . **50p**
Others . . 25p/**50p**/£2

1981. Wedding Prince of Wales
Post Office PHQ cards. Set of 2 . . **95p**
Guernsey Post Office PHQ cards. Set of 7 . . **90p**
Prescott-Pickup. Set of 60 . . **£7.50**
Others . . 25p/**50p**/£1

1982. 21st Birthday of the Princess of Wales
FAGA and others . . 25p/50p

1982. Birth of Prince William of Wales
Veldale/Carousel and others . . 25p/50p

1982. Christening of Prince William
Carousel and others . . 25p/50p

1983. 30th Anniversary of Queen's Coronation
Carousel and others . . 30p/50p

1983. Royal Tours of Australia/New Zealand and Canada
Prescott-Pickup. Australia/NZ 30 cards . . **£3.75**
Prescott-Pickup. Canada 15 cards . . **£1.85**

G.B. Royalty Portraits

Posed photographic portraits abound, in addition to those taken to commemorate the royal events listed above. Below we list cards depicting the main descendants of Queen Victoria.

Children
Victoria, The Princess Royal (*Mother of Kaiser Wilhelm II*)
Edward, Prince of Wales (*Edward VII*)
Princess Alice (*Grand Duchess of Hesse, mother of Alix, Czarina of Russia*)
Alfred, Duke of Edinburgh
Helena (*Princess Christian of Schleswig-Holstein*)
Louis (*Duchess of Argyle*)
Arthur, Duke of Connaught
Leopold, Duke of Albany
Beatrice (*Princess Henry of Battenberg, Mother of Queen Ena of Spain*)
Price range .. .. 50p/**£1**/£4

Grand-children
Children of Edward VII and Queen Alexandra:
Albert Victor, Duke of Clarence
George, Duke of York (*George V*)
Louise, Princess Royal (*Duchess of Fife*)
Victoria
Maud (*Queen of Norway*)
Price range .. .. 50p/**£1**/£3

Great-grandchildren
Children of George V and Queen Mary:
Edward Albert, Prince of Wales (*Edward VIII, later Duke of Windsor*)
Albert Frederick George, Duke of York (*George VI*)
Mary, Princess Royal (*Countess of Harewood*)
Henry, Duke of Gloucester
George, Duke of Kent
John (*died 1919, age 14*)
Price range .. .. 25p/**75p**/£2

Great-great grandchildren
Children of George VI and Queen Elizabeth:
Elizabeth (*Elizabeth II*)
Margaret Rose (*Countess of Snowdon*)
Price range .. .. 25p/**50p**/£1.50

Great-great-great grandchildren
Children of Elizabeth II and Philip, Duke of Edinburgh
Charles, Prince of Wales
Anne (*Mrs Mark Phillips*)
Andrew
Edward
Price range .. .. –/**25p**/50p

Great-great-great-great grandchildren
William of Wales (*son of Charles, Prince of Wales*)
Master Peter Phillips (*son of Princess Anne*)
Miss Zara Phillips (*daughter of Princess Anne*)
Price range 25p/50p

■ROY 4 Pub. Charles Skilton & Fry Ltd. No. 522 'The Prince and Princess of Wales and Prince William of Wales'. 1983 25p

Members of the Battenberg and Connaught families, *e.g.* Princess Ena of Battenberg, Lord Louis of Battenberg, Lord Louis Mountbatten (*Earl Mountbatten of Burma*) Duke of Connaught, Princess Patricia of Connaught, Princess Margaret of Connaught, Princess Alice of Athlone (*Queen Victoria's longest surviving grandchild, died 1981*)
Price range .. .. 50p/**£2**/£4

FOREIGN ■ROY 5–6

Period 1
Royal events postcards before the turn of the century vary from official issues (which are virtually non-pictorial) to coloured, elaborate and beautifully printed vignettes. Because of their rarity and interest, they command high prices on the Continent.

1888
Ger. Mourning card for William I.
Ger. Mourning card for Frederick III.
Price range .. ..£5/**£10**/£30

1891
Ger. Marriage of Prinz F. Augustus, Dresden .. £4/**£8**/£20

1896
Bulg. Baptism of Prince Boris.
Fr. Visit of Czar Nicholas II and the Czarina to Paris.
Ger. Visit of Czar and Czarina to the Kaiser and Kaiserin in Germany.
Ger. 70th birthday of Grand Duke Friedrich of Baden.
It. Official cards to celebrate marriage of the Prince of Naples and Princess Elena of Montenegro (5 diff. cols. exist).
It. *As above* Semi-official cards.
Price range .. ..£5/**£10**/£25

1897
Fr. Czar and Czarina's visit to Paris.
Ger. Visit of King Chulalongkorn of Siam to Germany.

Russ. Czar with Pres. Fauré of France during the latter's visit to St. Petersburg.
Price range .. ..£5/**£10**/£25

1898
Aust. Mourning card for Empress Elisabeth.
Aust. Golden Jubilee of Emperor Franz Josef.
Ger. Visit of Kaiser Wilhelm II and the Kaiserin to Jerusalem.
Price range .. ..£3/**£15**/£25

1899
Crete. Visit of Prince George of Greece to Crete.
Ger. Visit of Kaiser to Remscheid.
Price range .. ..£3/**£10**/£15

■ROY 5 Pub. 'E.B. & Cie'. Ger. Visit of Kaiser Wilhelm II and the Kaiserin to 'Doma Bagdsche', Turkey. 18 Oct. 1898 £20

■ROY 6 Pub. Anon. It. Assassination of King Umberto I, 29 July 1900 £20

Periods 2 and 4
See Military for Periods 3 and 5.
The higher valuation is for UB chromolithographed items or particularly rare items.

1900
Hol. Marriage of Queen Wilhelmina and Duke Hendrik of Mecklenburg Schwerin .. .. £2.50/**£5**/£7.50

It. Mourning cards for King Umberto I, assassinated 29 July 1900 .. .. £10/**£20**/£25
It. Accession of King Victor Emmanuel III .. ..£5/**£10**/£20

1901
Fr. Visit of Czar and Czarina to France.
Ger. 200 years of Prussian Kings.
It. Semi-official mourning card for Q. Victoria.
It. Accession of Edward VII.
It. Semi-official card to celebrate birth of Princess Yolande. Illus. by artist R. Tafuri.
Ger. Mourning card for Kaiserin Friedrich.
Price range .. ..£8/**£20**/£30

1902
Belg. Visit of Shah of Persia .. .. .. £8/**£17.50**/£25

1903
Serbia. Murder of King Alexander I and Queen Draga.
Serbia. Accession of King Peter I.
Price range .. ..£8/**£15**/£20

1905
Ger. Marriage of Crown Prince Wilhelm.
Marriage of Prince Gustavus Adolphus of Sweden.
Visit of King Alfonso XIII of Spain to Paris.
Visit of King Alfonso of Spain to Britain.
Visit of Prince & Princess of Wales to India. Pub. Tuck. Chromo-litho.
Price range .. .. £2/**£3**/£8

1906
Bavarian. 100 years of Bavarian kings.
Ger. Silver Wedding of Kaiser and Kaiserin.
Marriage of King Alfonso of Spain and Princess Ena of Battenburg.
Price range .. .. £1/**£1.50**/£3

1907
Ger. Marriage of Prinz August Wilhelm and Princess Alexandra Victoria.
Christening of heir to Spanish Throne.
Price range .. .. 75p/**£1**/£2

1908
Aust. Diamond Jubilee of Emperor Franz Josef I.
Memoriam cards for King Carlos of Portugal and Crown Prince Luis Felipe assassinated 1 Feb. 1908.
Accession of King Manoel of Portugal.
Price range .. .. £3/**£5**/£8

1911
Ger. 90th birthday of Prinz Regent Luitpold of Bavaria.
Ger. Silver wedding of Wilhelm II and his consort, Wurttemberg.
Price range .. .. £2/**£5**/£10

1912

Bulg. Coming of age of Prince Boris of Bulgaria .. £2/**£5**/£10
Ger. Mourning card for Prince Leopold of Bavaria £1/**£3**/£6

1913

Ger. Silver Jubilee of Kaiser Wilhelm II.
Ger. Marriage of Prussian Princess Victoria Louise to Duke of Brunswick.
Price range .. .. £1/**£2**/£3

1914

Aus. Reissue of 1908 Emperor Franz-Josef Jubilee card with 'United in Strength' overprint .. .. 75p/**£1**/£2

1921

Rum. Marriage of Crown Prince Carol of Rumania and Princess Helen of Greece .. .. £1/**£1.50**/£2

1922

Rum. Marriage of King Alexander of Yugoslavia and Princess Marie of Rumania and Royal gathering .. £1/**£1.50**/£5

1935

Mourning card for Queen Astrid of Belgium .. £2/**£4**/£6

Foreign Royalty Portraits of Periods 1–6

Posed photographic portraits. Highest value for Russian and obscure Balkan Royal families .. .. .. 50p/**£1.50**/£5

Hohenzollern—Gallerie

Rare Ger. series of 20 cards of monarchs up to Kaiser Wilhelm II. Period 1. Vignette. The set .. .. .. £30/**£45**/£60

SHIPPING

Many of the Period 1 and early Period 2 advertising cards were produced for shipping lines and carried chromo-litho vignettes of their ships. Sometimes these cards were sold—say at 2*d.* for 6 cards—sometimes they were given away. They often carried details of on-board menus. Andrew Reid & Co. of Newcastle-on-Tyne specialised in producing high quality chromos for shipping lines. Cards generally show the ship's name and the correct line flag or funnel. Not all postcards are concerned with the mighty transatlantic lines: shipping lines abounded around the British coastline, plying from resort to resort and from the mainland to islands. Cards showing paddle steamers, popular during the early part of Period 2, are becoming most collectable, particularly RP versions. There is overlapping here with SOCIAL HISTORY and TOPOGRAPHICAL and, as in that category, valuations can be increased by close-up details, RP printing and local interest. Additional value often attaches to cards with railway or island connexions and *Paquebot* or *Posted at Sea* postmarks and cachets.

Advertising ■S1, 2
Many early cards showing liners (in particular) are advertising cards produced by the Line concerned. General valuations are given here with more specific information on noted publishers, e.g. Andrew Reid, or artists given below.

Period 1 and early Period 2, chromo-litho vignettes, UB .. .. £3/**£6**/£8
Period 2, 3. Col. art, not vignettes, e.g. Allan Line, Blue Funnel, White Star, Cunard, Canadian Pacific, P & O, Red Star, White Star, etc. .. .. £2/**£3**/£5
Poster types .. .. £2/**£5**/£10
Other periods .. .. 50p/**£1**/£2

Artists ■S 3

Bannister, A. F. D.
Period 4 steamers, e.g. *Isle of Guernsey, Isle of Jersey,* etc. .. .. 50p/**75p**/£1
Sailing Ships. *Cutty Sark,* etc. 25p/**50p**/75p

Burgess, Arthur
Cammel Laird col. ships. HMS *Birkenhead,* HMS *Chester,* MS *La Playa,* MS *La Perla,* MS *La Marea,* etc £1/**£1.50**/£2

Cassiers, Henri†
Red Star Poster type ads. UB .. .. £4/**£7**/£10
Red Star ads. UB .. .. £4/**£5**/£6

Chilley, A.
Sailing ships. *Cutty Sark, Golden Hind,* etc. 25p/**50p**/75p

Dixon, Charles
Belfast Steam Ship Co., Red Star Line, Royal Mail Steam Packet, etc. .. .. £1/**£1.50**/£2

Eckenbrecker, T. von
Chromo detachable menu cards, e.g. Nord-Deutscher Lloyd .. .. £4/**£5**/£6

■S 1 Pub. White Star Line. R.M.S. *Oceanic*. Chromo Vignette. UB. Period 1 £6

■S 2 Pub. Allan Line. 'R.M.S. *Bavarian*' sailing from Liverpool. UB. PU 1903 £5

Forrest, A. S.
Booth Line. 'Picturesque Portugal' series .. £1/**£1.50**/£2

Mason, Frank
Merchant ships. Pub. F. T. Everard .. .. £1/**£1.50**/£2

Martino, R.
Sailing ships. Pub. H. Moss .. .. .. 50p/**75p**/£1.50

Montague, R.
Tuck 'Sea & Sky' series .. .. 50p/**75p**/£1.50

Shoesmith, Kenneth
Norwegian views .. .. £1/**£1.50**/£2

■S 3 Nippon Yusen Kaisha. S. S. *Kashima Maru*. Ship set in *Art Nouveau* design. Period 2 £5

Harbour/Shipyard Scenes
Good general detail .. .. 75p/**£1.50**/£3
Launchings .. .. £2/**£4**/£8

Hovercraft
Period 6 only **25p**

Japanese Ship Advertising
Often with Art Nouveau *borders.*
Price range .. .. £2/**£3**/£5

Life at Sea/Sailors
Oilette types, e.g. 'Britain's Bulwarks' .. 50p/**75p**/£1
Pub. Gale & Polden 25p/**50p**/75p
Others, e.g. Pub. John Walker 25p/50p

Menu/Souvenir Cards (not chromo-litho)
Periods 1 to 4 .. .. £1/**£1.50**/£2

Naval Ships (*see* MILITARY)
Period 1. Chromo-litho .. .. £5/**£6**/£8
Gale & Polden 'Wellington' series. Col. art. battleships .. .. £1/**£1.50**/£2
Tuck 'Empire' series .. ..£6/**£10**/£12
Tuck Oilettes. Our Navy, e.g. HMS *Australia*, HMS *Queen Mary*, HMAS *Sydney*, etc. .. .. .. £1.50/**£2**/£2.50

Paddle Steamers
This section is concerned with photographic origin and real photographs. RP types are most highly valued, particularly with close-up people detail. Artist-drawn cards should be valued under the *Passenger and Merchant Ships* heading.
Price range .. .. £1/**£1.50**/£3

Passenger & Merchant Ships
This section overlaps with SOCIAL HISTORY and TOPOGRAPHICAL and covers a broad spectrum of passenger and merchant vessels, e.g. ferries, trawlers, tugs, etc. Higher values are associated with clear RP cards, or where appropriate, fine chromo-litho UB examples. Local interest can raise values beyond these bands.
General Period 2 .. .. £1.50/**£2**/£2.50
General Periods 3, 4 .. .. 70p/**£1.50**/£2
Sailing ships .. .. 50p/**£1**/£1.50
Others .. .. 50p/**75p**/£1

Piccadilly Hotel (Ship Cards)
Price range .. .. 75p/**£1**/£1.50

Publishers
Most famous postcard publishers, like Salmon, Tuck and Valentine's, produced pleasing ship series. Notable series were published by the following publishers:

David MacBrayne
Glasgow & Highland Royal Mail Steamers, chromo-litho vignette. Printer McCorquodale, UB .. .. ..£8/**£12**/£20

Andrew Reid
Chromo-litho vignettes for The America Line; Belfast Steam Ship Co.; P. & O.; Pacific Steam Navigation Co. (Orient Line); Pacific Line; Ullswater Navigation & Transit Co., etc.
Ships include:
SS Arabia; SS Graphic; SS Heroic; SS Himalaya; SS India; SS Macedonia; SS Magic; SS Malwa; SS Marmord; SS Mongolia; SS Moolton; SS Moormond; SS Oravia; SS Orcana; SS Orellana; SS Oropesa; SS Oroya; SS Raven; SS Sardinia; SS Simla; SS St. Louis.
Price range .. £1.50/**£8**/£25

McCorquodale & Co.
Col. scenes for Royal Mail routes (e.g. Holyhead–Dublin).
Price range .. £2/**£3**/£4

F. G. O. Stuart
Ships series, e.g. RMS *Adriatic*, RMS *Amazon*, RMS *Aragon*, RMS *Briton*, SS *Armdale Castle*, SS *Avondale Castle*, SS *Durham*, SS *Goorkha*, SS *Kenilworth Castle*.
Price range .. £1/**£2**/£2.50

Shipwrecks ■S 4
Ship Names
Abertay (Cornwall, 1912) .. £1/**£2**/£2.50
Alaska .. 50p/**75p**/£1.50
Bardic (Lizard, 1924) RP .. £1/**£1.50**/£2
Berlin
  Pub. Hartman. Set of 12 .. £1/**£2**/£2.50
  Pub. Rotary RP .. 75p/**£1**/£2
  Pub. Philco RP .. £1/**£2**/£3
Cecile Herzogin (Salcombe, 1936) .. 75p/**£1**/£1.50
Coopland .. 50p/**75p**/£1.50
Crescent City .. 50p/**75p**/£1.50
Elizabeth (Bude, 1912) .. 50p/**£1**/£2
Gladiator, HMS (1908). Pub. Broderick .. £1/**£2**/£2.50
Hilda (St. Malo, 1905) .. 50p/**75p**/£1.25
La Gascogne (St. Nazaire) .. 75p/**£1**/£1.50
Le Chili (Bordeaux) .. 75p/**£1**/£1.25
Mahratta, SS (on Goodwins, 1909). Pub. Glencairn Craik, Deal .. 75p/**£1**/£2
Mermaris (River Tigris) .. 50p/**75p**/£1.50
Montagu, HMS (Lundy, 1906). Pub. Twiss Bros., Ilfracombe .. 75p/**£1**/£1.50
Phoenix, HMS (Kowloon, 1908). Pub. M. Sternberg .. £1/**£1.50**/£2
Pisagna (Dover, 1912) .. £1/**£1.25**/£2
Queen Elizabeth (Steamboat) (Kew, 1904). Pub. Walter Pearce, Brentford .. 75p/**£1**/£1.50
Scotia (1909). Photo S. Thorn, Bude .. £1/**£1.25**/£2
Thyra (Duncan's Bay, 1914) RP .. £2/**£2.50**/£3
Others .. 50p/**£1.50**/£3

■S 4 Pub. Thorn Photographer, Bude. 'The Elizabeth under Summerlease Point 16.2.12'. RP £2

Silks

Woven types, incl. Grant & Stevens, e.g. RMS *Adriatic*, RMS *Edinburgh Castle*, RMS *Empress of Britain*, RMS *Carmania*, RMS *Ivernia*, RMS *Mauretania*, RMS *Royal George*, RMS *Titanic*, SS *Haverford*, etc. *See* NOVELTY.

Price range .. .. £12/**£20**/£25

Titanic

Artistic

e.g. Artist W. Fred Mitchell. Pub. Salmon .. .. £2/**£3**/£4

Memoriam

Bamforth. 'Nearer my God' types .. .. .. 75p/**£2**/£3
Goodred, Cyril. Black border .. .. .. £2.50/**£3**/£5
Millar & Lang. Verse, ship and captain .. .. £3/**£5**/£8
Rotary. 'Nearer my God' types .. .. .. £2/**£3.50**/£5
Valentine's. 'Among the Icebergs' .. .. £1/**£1.50**/£2

RP Types

Price range .. .. £4/**£6**/£8

Tuck Celebrated Liners

Price range .. .. £1.50/**£2.50**/£3

As it is difficult to date a card precisely, a period system has been used in this catalogue. For a full explanation of the system see page viii.

Three Band Pricing System

Left Hand Band: The lowest price you will probably be asked to pay for this card.
Middle Band: What you will normally be asked to pay for this card: its average, reasonable price.
Right Hand Band: The highest price you will probably be asked to pay for this card.
For a full explanation of the system see page ix.

SOCIAL HISTORY

The strong interest in social history which has developed in recent years has made this one of the most popular of collecting categories. There is a clear distinction to be made between Social History and Topographical. Normally the collector of social history cards is seeking a pictorial record of a particular historical aspect—perhaps cards showing workers in particular occupational settings, buildings of a particular type (e.g. fire stations), etc. The geographical location of the subject is of less importance than the subject itself.

The collector of topographical cards on the other hand is normally only interested in cards showing people/scenes in a particular location—sometimes a county, but more usually in a particular town or even village. There is often a 'conflict' of values between the two collectors—someone interested in views of fire stations in general might be prepared to pay £1 for a particular card, but the topographical collector of the district in which that fire station is situated (if it can be identified) might pay £10. It is quite impossible in a general catalogue of this nature to cater adequately for the topographical collector, prices here refer to the subject matter of cards rather than to local interest.

AGRICULTURE/FISHING/RURAL

Included in this section are cards which show rural and fishing occupations, especially those which no longer exist (or which modern technology has completely altered), agricultural machinery and fish processing.

The higher price range applies to clear RP cards showing active scenes with good detail of people and equipment.

Agricultural Shows
RP .. .. 75p/**£1**/£2
Others .. .. 50p/**75p**/£1

Equipment/Machinery (Periods 2 to 4)
Horsedrawn carts/ploughs. RP .. .. £1/**£2**/£3
Others .. .. 50p/**75p**/£1.50
Other machinery. RP .. .. £2/**£4**/£8
Others .. .. 75p/**£1.50**/£3

Occupations
Period 1 .. .. £1/**£3**/£5

Animal-Tenders (Periods 2 to 4)
Cowherds/Pigmen/Shepherds, etc.
RP .. .. 75p/**£1.50**/£2
Others 25p/**50p**/75p

Arts/Cottage Industries/Crafts (Periods 2 to 4)
Blacksmiths/Dairy workers/Forge workers/Lace-makers/ Spinners/Weavers/Wheelwrights, etc.
RP .. .. £1/**£2**/£3
Others 25p/**50p**/75p

Fisher Folk (Periods 2 to 4)
Scenes at markets/fish halls/on board/landing the catch, coracle or Curragh fisher men, etc.

RP	£1.50/**£2**/£2.50
Others	50p/**75p**/£1
'LL'	£1/**£1.50**/£2
Pictorial Stationery Co. series	50p/**75p**/£1
Valentine's series	50p/**75p**/£1.50
Wrench series	75p/**£1**/£2

Harvesters (Periods 2 to 4)
Grain/Tobacco, etc.

RP	75p/**£1.50**/£4
Others	50p/**£1**/£2.50

Pickers (Periods 2 to 4)
Flowers/Fruit/Hops/Vegetables, etc.

RP	£1/**£1.50**/£4
Others	50p/**£1**/£3

Young & Cooper cards

Lettered cards, A to K. b & w	75p/**£1**/£2
Numbered cards, 1 to 25. col.	75p/**£1.50**/£3

Rural Scenes (Periods 2 to 4) ■SH 1

Crops/grazing herds/landscapes/views	25p/**50p**/75p
Scenes of Village Life. RP	£1/**£2**/£3
Others	25p/**50p**/75p
Tuck named series, e.g. 'Rapholette glossy'	25p/**50p**/75p

Tuck Oilettes
Series titles include 'Cottage Gardens', 'Country Charms', 'Rural England', 'The Simple Life', etc.

Price range	25p/**50p**/75p

AMUSEMENT PARKS ■SH 2

RP	£1/**£2**/£3
Others	75p/**£1**/£1.50

ARCADES

RP	£1.50/**£2.50**/£5
Others	50p/**75p**/£1.50

ASSOCIATIONS/ORGANISATIONS

See RELIGION.

Bands	50p/**75p**/£1
Boys Brigade	75p/**£1.50**/£3
Church Army	75p/**£1**/£1.25
Dr. Barnado	25p/**50p**/75p
Evangelism	£1.50/**£2**/£3
Guiding	£1.50/**£3**/£4
Jewish	£2/**£3**/£4
Political	£2/**£5**/£8
Red Cross	50p/**75p**/£1
St. John Ambulance	50p/**75p**/£1

■SH 1 Pub. Chapman & Son Dawlish (Photographers). RP. Watercress beds, Letcomb Basset. PU 1922 50p

■SH 2 Pub. Valentine's. XL Series. 'The Big Dipper. Pleasure Beach Blackpool'. RP. PU 1925 £2

Salvation Army	£1/**£1.50**/£3
Scouting	£1.50/**£3**/£4
Strikes	£4/**£7**/£10
YMCA	25p/**50p**/75p
YWCA	25p/**50p**/75p
Others	25p/**50p**/£1

BUILDINGS/STRUCTURES ■SH 3

Until recently there has been little interest in this category. Growing attention to social history has led collectors to seek picture records, particularly where demolition and other great changes have taken place. Cards in this section are essentially Period 2 with the higher values reserved for RP examples, and where appropriate, internal views with activity. Clearly there is overlapping with other sections. References are given below. Valuations are based upon the major thematic identification of the cards being to do with 'buildings' rather than 'people' although of course in some cases the presence of people identifies the building, e.g. a school. See also *'Commercial/Industrial' which follows this section.*

Bandstands	50p/**£1**/£1.50
Barracks	25p/**50p**/£1
Casinos	£1/**£2**/£4
Cinemas (*see also* ENTERTAINMENT)	£4/**£7**/£10
Factories	50p/**£1**/£1.50

■SH 3 Pub. 'A.H.J.'. 'Bandstand. Westcliff-on-Sea'. Period 2 £1

■SH 4 Pub. Wrench. No. 3740. Interior of Salt-Works, Northwich. PU 1904 £3

Fire stations (*see also* 'Uniformed Public Services' below)	£1/**£1.50**/£2
Historical buildings/structures	**50p**
Hospitals (*see also* 'Uniformed Public Services' below)	25p/**50p**/75p
Hotels	£1/**£1.50**/£2
Municipal buildings	25p/**50p**/75p
Police stations	£1/**£1.50**/£2
Post offices (*see also* 'Uniformed Public Services' below)	£2/**£4**/£6
Public houses	£1.50/**£2**/£3
Railway stations (*see also* RAILWAYS)	£2/**£4**/£7
Religious buildings	25p/50p
Restaurants	£1/**£1.50**/£2
Schools	50p/**£1**/£1.50
Skyscrapers, Chrysler Building, Flat Iron Building, New York	50p/75p
Theatres (*see also* ENTERTAINMENT)	75p/**£1**/£2
Village halls	50p/**75p**/£1
Others	25p/50p

COMMERCIAL/INDUSTRIAL ■SH 4

This section deals with picture cards which can readily be associated with a particular commercial or industrial enterprise. The highest valuations are for clear RP with good people activity.

Bridges	50p/**75p**/£1
Chimneys	25p/**50p**/75p
Coalmines. Surface scenes	£1/**£2**/£3
Coalmines. Underground scenes	£1.50/**£2**/£3
Engineering activities	£2/**£4**/£8
Factory buildings. Exterior/Interior	50p/**75p**/£1
Mills. Water	50p/**£1**/£1.50
Mills. Wind	£1/**£2**/£3
Salt works	75p/**£1.50**/£3
Shop fronts	£2.50/**£4**/£6
Shop interiors	£2/**£4**/£5
Tin mines	£2/**£3**/£4
Zinc mines	50p/**75p**/£1
Workshop scenes	£2/**£4**/£6

CRAFTS/OCCUPATIONS/SERVICES/TRADES ■SH 5

This section covers all forms of work except those included in 'Uniformed Public Services' below. All cards must have a subject contemporary to the period in which they were published, i.e. 'historical' types are not included. The major interest lies in skills or activities now out of date. See also *'Agriculture/Fishing/Rural' above. Cards showing individuals in trade situations are sometimes depicted in series such as 'London Types' published by Photochrom.* (See TOPOGRAPHICAL: *London*).

The following list of occupations does not pretend to be exhaustive but only indicative of what may be found:

Barber; Cabbie; Chauffeur; Chimney Sweep; Clerk; Deliveryman; Dentist; Doctor; Egg Seller; Errand Girl; Flower Girl; Horn Blower; Match Girl; Message Boy; Milkman; Newsvendor; Rat Catcher; Road Sweeper; Sandwichboard Man; Servants; Shoeblack; Shopkeeper; Snake Catcher; Street Trader; Town Crier; Waiter.

■SH 5 Pub. Hartmann. 'Vendor of Eggs'. Col. Period 2 £5

■SH 6 Pub. Buffalo Bill's Wild West Show. N. American Indian Squaw and Papoose. Period 2 £3

Artist drawn .. .. £1.50/**£2**/£4
Photo-origin .. .. £1.50/**£5**/£20

ETHNIC ACTIVITIES/CHARACTERS/GROUPS ■SH 6
By 'ethnic' we mean that the subject matter is directly concerned with a particular race. The reference may be humorous (the endless Irish/Scottish/Welsh jokes are of little value) or observant of activity or dress. The most highly valued cards are those of photographic origin.

Artist Drawn Cards
Cards showing national costumes, ethnic humour and general 'artistic' records of ethnic activities.
Africa .. .. 50p/**75p**/£3
Britain. Typical examples in this category are the Irish, Scots and Welsh costume cards (Welsh ladies in tall hats, etc.) and humorous cards such as those teasing the Scots about their supposed meanness 25p/50p
European Mainland. Continental collectors value these cards more highly than the equivalent cards are valued in Britain, but there are more chromo-litho examples to be found for this sub-section and hence the upper valuation is higher than average .. .. 50p/**£1**/£1.50
Far East. Early in Period 2 there was a European vogue for things Japanese and some fine artistic cards were produced such as Tucks 'Real Japanese' in the Connoisseur series 2514.
Japanese .. .. 50p/**£2**/£8
Others .. .. 50p/**75p**/£1
Gypsies .. .. 50p/**75p**/£1
India, e.g. Tuck 'Native Life in India' Series 7408 .. .. 25p/**50p**/75p
Jewish. The internationality of the Jewish race makes this a more than averagely popular theme .. .. £1/**£2**/£5
Middle East 25p/**50p**/75p
North America. American and Canadian interest in this artist drawn category is strong, and to an extent their interest is reflected in British valuations of their cards.
Artist John Innes (Can.) .. .. £1/**£1.50**/£2
Cowboys .. .. 50p/**75p**/£1
Indians .. .. 50p/**£1.50**/£3
General .. .. 25p/**50p**/£1
South America .. .. 50p/**75p**/£1

Photo Origin/RP Cards
Highest valuations for RP
Africa .. .. 50p/**£1**/£1.50
Britain 25p/**50p**/75p
European Mainland .. .. £1/**£3**/£5
Far East .. .. £1/**£1.50**/£2
Gypsies .. .. £1/**£1.50**/£2
India .. .. 50p/**75p**/£1
Jewish .. .. £2/**£3**/£5
Middle East .. .. 50p/**75p**/£1
North America .. .. 75p/**£1.50**/£2
South America .. .. 50p/**75p**/£1

HARBOURS/PORTS

See SHIPPING.

Close-up detail landward	50p/**£1**/£2
General views	25p/**50p**/75p

INLAND WATERWAYS

Bridges

Artist drawn	25p/**50p**/75p
Photo-origin with traffic detail	50p/**75p**/£1

Canals

British

Artist drawn	25p/**50p**/75p
Barge life. RP	£2/**£3.50**/£5
Photo-origin. General	£1/**£2**/£3

Foreign

Photo-origin	25p/**50p**/75p

Dams/Weirs

Price range	25p/**50p**/75p

Ferries

Price range	75p/**£1.50**/£2

Lakes

Photo-origin with boats	25p/**50p**/75p

Rivers. General Scenes with River Traffic

Artist drawn	25p/**50p**/£1
Photo-origin	50p/**75p**/£1.50

LEGEND & LORE

Many areas have their own folk history, often based on historical events. These cards are normally of non-photographic origin. However, sometimes local pageants and processions may re-enact a legend and photographic cards of that event were published. Such photographic origin examples should be valued under 'Local Events/Gatherings' below.

Customs	25p/**50p**/75p
Folk dances, Maypoles, Morris men, etc.	25p/**50p**/£1
Ghosts	50p/**75p**/£1
Gretna Green	25p/**50p**/75p
Lady Godiva (not silk)	25p/**50p**/75p
Local Legends:	
Wiltshire Moonrakers	50p/**75p**/£1
Others	25p/**50p**/75p

LOCAL EVENTS/GATHERINGS ■SH 7

The cards in this section are of photographic origin. Under 'Edwardian Life' we include all those Edwardian activities which attracted the attention of the professional or amateur photographer. Very many splendid 'posed groups' may be found—amateur theatrics, families, nurses and just people gathered together for some special occasion. Although, frequently, neither place nor person can be identified, the card can be a valuable social record.

Auctions	£1/**£1.50**/£2
Beating bounds/Crying marches	£1/**£1.50**/£2
Carnivals (mostly Continental)	75p/**£1**/£2
Edwardian life	£1/**£1.50**/£2
Elections	£1/**£2**/£4
Fairs	£5/**£8**/£10
Fêtes	£1/**£2**/£3
Flower festivals	50p/**£1**/£2
Fund-raising	£1/**£2**/£4
Goose fairs	£2/**£3**/£4
Inaugurations. (Hospitals, libraries, etc.)	£1/**£2**/£3
Markets	£1.50/**£2**/£4
Oktoberfest (Ger. Munich *Bierfest*)	75p/**£1**/£2
Ox roasts	£2/**£3**/£4
Rag days	£3/**£4**/£5
Regattas	£1/**£2**/£3
Sommerfest (Ger.)	50p/**75p**/£1
Unidentified gatherings	£1/**£2.50**/£5
Works outings	£2/**£3**/£4

■SH 7 Pub. De'Ath and Condon, Ashford. A fine Edwardian country gathering—Ploughing Match? .. Point to Point .. ? RP. Period 2 £2.50

PAGEANTS

A pageant consists of dramatic scenes enacted by local (usually amateur) performers. They are connected with local history and probably most major towns have staged one at some time. This listing does not claim to be exhaustive, but it does reflect a sampling of what might be found readily. Feasts, processions and tattoos are included in this general category. Most pageants of postcard interest were held during Period 2 and values tend to be modest unless the cards are photographic with a strong topographical content.

A list of local pageant cards was given in the third edition of this catalogue, pp. 174–175.

Price range	25p/**50p**/£1.50

SCOUTS AND GUIDES

A highly collectible theme as many collectors have fond youthful memories of their days in the organisation. The movement inspired many postcards—photographic and artist drawn—of the leaders, scout and guide groups and meetings etc. There are many comic cards by well-known artists.

Comic designs
Artists Jagger, Reg Maurice, Gilson, etc. .. 75p/**£1.50**/£3
Leaders
Baden-Powell, Prince of Wales as Chief Scout of Wales, Princess Elizabeth, Princess Margaret, Princess Mary as Girl Guides, etc.
Artist drawn .. .. 75p/**£1.50**/£3
RP .. .. £1/**£3**/£4
Pub. Millar & Lang
National series Scout designs .. .. .. 75p/**£1**/£1.50
Scouts & Guides
Jamborees, meetings, portraits of individuals, groups, etc.
Artist drawn .. .. 50p/**£1.50**/£3
RP .. .. 75p/**£2**/£4
Pub. 'SBL'
'Tommy the Tenderfoot'. Line drawings by 'The Chief Scout'. Set of 12 .. .. £3/**£4**/£5
Pub. 'The Scout'
'Lt. Gen. Baden-Powell's Boy Scouts at Work and Play'. Set of 6 by Ibbetson .. .. £3/**£4**/£5
Pub. Scout H.Q.
Official issues .. .. £1.50/**£2.50**/£4
Pub. Tuck
Empire series Baden-Powell .. .. .. £5/**£7.50**/£10
Harry Payne King's Message/Motto .. .. ..£8/**£12**/£15
'Our Boy Scout'. Rare series (No. 9950) of scouts with animal and bird heads .. .. £20/**£30**/£40

SEASIDE

Photographic origin cards with close-up detail are the most highly rates.

Bathing Beauties

Pub. Editions du Panorama de Paris. Series of coloured cards of photographic origin, UB .. .. £1/**£2**/£4

Artists

Abeille, Jack. Period 1 .. .. £10/**£15**/£20
Wennerburg, B. Period 2 UB .. .. £2/**£4**/£8
Other signed artists. Period 1 .. .. £3/**£5**/£10
Other signed artists. Periods 2, 3 .. .. .. £1/**£2**/£3
Other signed artists. Periods 4, 5 .. .. 50p/**75p**/£1
Unsigned artist drawn. Period 1 .. .. .. £1/**£2**/£3
Unsigned artist drawn. Periods 2, 3 .. .. .. 75p/**£1**/£2

Bathing Machines

Photographic Origin/R.P. Periods 1 to 3
Close-up, sharp picture with detail of people .. £1/**£2**/£4
In distance, but with detail of people .. .. .. 50p/**£1**/£2

Comic Bathing Scenes
Most of the humorous postcard artists did seasidepostcards (*see also* ARTISTS for details), e.g. Browne, 'FS', McGill, Thackeray, as well as many unknown, unsigned artists.

Periods 2 to 4	75p/**£1.50**/£3
Periods 5 to 7	25p/50p

Concert Parties on beach, pier. *See* ENTERTAINMENT
Photographic Origin/R.P. Periods 2 to 4
Pierrots

Close up, sharp detail with people	£2/**£4**/£6
As part of general beach scene	£1/**£1.50**/£3

Other Players

Close up as above	£1.50/**£3**/£5
General scene as above	75p/**£1**/£2.50

Donkeys
Artist Drawn. Periods 2 to 4

Signed	50p/**75p**/£1
Unsigned	25p/**50p**/75p
Photographic Origin/R.P. Periods 2 to 4	
Close up, sharp detail with people	75p/**£1.50**/£3
As part of general beach scene	50p/**£1**/£2

General Seaside Scenes
Photographic Origin/R.P. Periods 2 to 4

LL, with plenty of activity/people	£1/**£1.50**/£2
Others, with plenty of activity/people	50p/**£1**/£1.50
Lifeboats. Being launched	£3/**£5**/£7
Lifeboats. On shore	£2/**£3**/£5
Lifeboats. RNLI ads	£2/**£3**/£3.50
Lighthouses	50p/**75p**/£1
Piers	50p/**75p**/£1
Promenades	25p/**50p**/75p
Spas	50p/**£1**/£1.50
Photographic Origin/R.P. Periods 5 to 7	
Various	25p/**50p**/£1

UNIFORMED PUBLIC SERVICES

This section is concerned with people, and the accoutrements and equipment needed to carry out their tasks, rather than the buildings from which they may operate. Except where indicated, higher values are for clear photographic origin cards.

Customs & Excise	£3/**£4**/£5
Fire Service	£2/**£3**/£4
Nursing/Medical staff	£1/**£1.50**/£2
Police	£1/**£2**/£3
Postmen. Comic drawings. F.S., etc.	75p/**£1**/£1.25
Postmen. Photographic origin	£1/**£1.50**/£2
Postmen. Others	50p/**75p**/£1
Prison	£1/**£2**/£3
Railway (*see* RAILWAYS)	£2/**£4**/£5
Others	£1/**£1.50**/£2

SPORTS

We list below the best known artists for cards in this category, followed by alphabetical entries for each sport.

Artist Drawn. Named Artists

The Sport/Series for which they are best known is given in brackets.

Browne, Tom† .. .. £1.50/**£3**/£5
Carter, Reg† (*Sporting Chinamen. Chromo-litho series 364*)
.. .. £2/**£3**/£3.50
'Crackerjack' (*Hockey*) .. .. 75p/**£1**/£1.25
Crombie, Charles (*Golf*) .. .. £1/**£1.50**/£2
Elliott, Harry (*Horse sports*) .. .. .. £2/**£3.50**/£4.50
Hebblethwaite (*Cricket*) .. .. 75p/**£1**/£1.25
Kinsella, E. P.† (*Cricket, Cycling, Football, Tennis*) .. ..
.. .. 75p/**£1.50**/£2.50
Parett, Harry† (*Roller-skating*) .. .. .. 75p/**£1**/£1.50
Payne, Harry† .. .. £4/**£6**/£10
Pirkis, A. G.† (*Tennis*) .. .. 75p/**£1**/£1.50
Quinnell, Cecil (*Sporting glamour studies*) .. £1/**£2**/£2.50
Rowland, Ralph (*Hockey*) .. .. £1/**£1.50**/£1.75
Rowlandson, G. D. (*early chromo-lithos*) .. .. £3/**£4**/£5
Sager, Xavier† (*Bowling at le Bal Tabarin*) .. £6/**£7**/£8
Schönpflug, Fritz† (*Boxing, Football*) .. .. .. £1/**£3**/£4
Spurgin, Fred† (*Cycling*) .. .. £1/**£1.50**/£2
Thackeray, Lance† (*many sports*) .. .. .. £3/**£4**/£5
Thiele, Arthur† (*Bowling, Dancing, Tennis*) .. £3/**£5**/£8

Angling

Price range .. .. 50p/**75p**/£2.50

Archery

Price range .. .. 50p/**75p**/£1

Athletics

Athletes .. .. 50p/**75p**/£1.50
Meetings RP .. .. 75p/**£1.25**/£2

Badminton

Price range .. .. 75p/**£1**/£1.50

Ballooning

Artist drawn .. .. £1.50/**£2.50**/£4
Photo-origin (higher value for RP) .. .. .. £3/**£5**/£8

Baseball

Comic
  Baseball Illustrated. Pub. Davidson Bros. Series 2618/9. Artist Tom Browne .. .. £4/**£5**/£6
  Baseball Kidlets. Pub. Ullman Series 195 .. £2/**£3**/£4
  Others .. .. 75p/**£1.50**/£2
General
  Baseball Series. Pub. The Rose Co. .. .. 75p/**£1.50**/£2
  Baseball Terms Illustrated. Pub. Frederickson. Artist Dewey .. .. 75p/**£1.50**/£2
  Others .. .. 50p/**75p**/£2

Players
Baseball Hall of Fame. Pub. Cooperstown, N. F. .. £1/**£2**/£3
Baseball Players. Pub. Pomand. Chromolitho .. £1/**£2**/£3
Others .. .. 75p/**£1.50**/£2

Basketball/Netball
Price range .. .. 75p/**£1**/£1.50

Bicycling
See COMPETITIONS/CRAZES

Billiards/Snooker
Artwork by Tuck. Pub. J. V. A.
Caricatures .. .. £2/**£3**/£3.50
Billiards rooms .. .. 75p/**£1**/£1.50
Others .. .. 75p/**£1**/£1.50

Board Games
Price range .. .. 50p/**£1.50**/£5

Boating/Canoeing
Comic .. .. 50p/**£1**/£2
Scenes .. .. 50p/**75p**/£1

Bowls
Price range .. .. 75p/**£1.50**/£2

Boxing
Pub. Beagles. 'Famous Boxers' series .. .. £1/**£2**/£2.50
Pub. Lilywhite. 1919. Carpentier versus Joe Beckett. Twelve cards in set .. .. £2/**£2.50**/£3
Others .. .. 50p/**£1.50**/£5

Bullfighting
Price range .. .. 50p/**75p**/£1

Card Games
Price range .. .. 25p/**50p**/£1

Cricket ■SP 1
Perhaps the most documented sport on the postcard. Postcards fall into the following categories. The earlier the Period, the higher the valuation.

Players
Amateur .. .. 50p/**75p**/£1.50
Professional (County/International) .. .. £2.50/**£4**/£5

Teams
County .. .. £3/**£4**/£5
Local .. .. 50p/**£1**/£4
Touring (MCC/International) .. .. .. £2/**£3.50**/£5

Artist-drawn
Illustrated 'phrases' .. .. 75p/**£2.50**/£5
Others .. .. 50p/**£1**/£2

Publishers
Ashton & Sons, Southport. Grosvenor Series. RP
Bolland, T. Southwell, Australian Team 1905
Cambridge, S., Hove. 'Famous Cricketers'
Collins & Sons, Glasgow. 'Famous Cricketers'. Sepia. At least 5 sets
Davidson Bros. Australian Team 1909. RP
DeLittle, Fenwick & Co. Lancashire Players. B & w
Dennis, E. T. W. Dainty Series. Yorkshire Players. B & w
Dunn, Ralph, Ltd. Australian Team 1905. Series 1000–1015. B & w
Fosters of Brighton. B & w. RP
Giessen Bros. Northampton
Gottschalk, Dreyfus & Davis (G.D. & D)
Booklets sold on ground and others. Personalities incl. B. J. T. Bosanquet, Dr. W. G. Grace
Hamel & Co., Nottingham. Test Match 1905. B & w
Hart, John, Leytonstone. Essex Team 1905. B & w
Hartmann. 20 Famous Cricketers. RP. 'Very Correct'/'Whizz' Series
Henson & Co., Nottingham. Notts Test Match 1905. B & w
Melbourne Sports Dept. Col. 1907/8 English Team
Millar & Lang. National Series No. 829. Col.
Mockford, Tonbridge. Kent & Middx Players/Teams, 1906–9
Morloy, E. W., Notts Test Match 1905. B & w
Parkinson & Roy, Leeds. Yorks Players. Col.
Philco Pub. Co. Series No. 6207. RP
Rapid Photo Co. Silverprint Series 3783. RP
Rotary. Numbered Series. RP
Summers, Browne & Co. Kent/Middx Players. RP
Tuck. In the Open Series
Famous Batsmen No. 6450
Famous Bowlers No. 6451
Famous Fielders No. 6452
Others
Valentine's. Col. Series
Walker & Co. 14 Famous Cricketers/'Warner's Team' 1905. B & w
Webb Douglas. Nottingham. Notts Players/Leeds Test 1926. RP
Price range .. .. £2/**£4**/£5

Croquet
Comic .. .. 50p/**75p**/£1
Scenes .. .. 75p/**£1**/£1.50

Curling
Artist drawn 25p/**50p**/75p
Photo-origin .. .. 75p/**£1**/£1.50

■SP 1 Pub. Wrench. 'J. T. Hearne'. PU 1907 £1

■SP 2 Pub. Ettlinger. No. 4285. Artist Reg. Carter. 'The Seventh Heaven in China'. PU 1904 £3

Dancing ■SP 2

Many famous artists, e.g. Reg Carter, Mela Koehler, Thiele, Usobal, etc. did 'Dance' series.

Well-known artists	£1/**£3**/£15
Others	50p/**75p**/£1

Diabolo—*see* COMPETITIONS/CRAZES

Fencing

Comic	75p/**£1**/£1.50
Photo-origin	50p/**75p**/£1

Football—Association ■SP 3

Comic—general	50p/**75p**/£1
Comic—named artists	50p/**£1.50**/£4
Commemoratives	£3/**£5**/£6
Crowd scenes	£1/**£2**/£2.50
Grounds/scenes	75p/**£1**/£1.50
Players—amateur	75p/**£1.25**/£2
professional	25p/**£2**/£3
Teams—amateur	£1/**£2**/£3
military	50p/**75p**/£1
professional pre-1939	£3/**£4**/£5
professional post-1939	25p/**£1**/£2

Three Band Pricing System

Left Hand Band: The lowest price you will probably be asked to pay for this card.
Middle Band: What you will normally be asked to pay for this card: its average, reasonable price.
Right Hand Band: The highest price you will probably be asked to pay for this card.
For a full explanation of the system see page ix.

■SP 3 Pub. Anon. Winners of Kentish Town Challenge Cup. RP. Period 2 £1

Football—Rugby League

Players	£1/**£2**/£3
Teams—amateur	£1/**£2**/£3
professional touring	£2/**£4**/£5

Football—Rugby Union

Comic	75p/**£1**/£1.50
Grounds, scenes	£1/**£1.50**/£2
Pub. Tuck. Oilette	75p/**£1**/£1.50
Teams—city	£1/**£2**/£2.50
touring	£2/**£3**/£4
town/village	£1.50/**£3**/£4

Foxhunting—*see* ANIMALS: Horses

Gambling/Playing Cards—*see* CURIOUS/MISCELLANEOUS

Golf

Comic—general	£1/**£1.50**/£2.50
Comic—named artists	£1/**£2**/£4
Courses/Club houses	£1.50/**£2.50**/£3

Gymnastics

Price range	50p/**75p**/£1

Hockey

Comic	50p/**75p**/£1
Teams	£1/**£1.50**/£2
Others	25p/**50p**/75p

Horse racing—*see* ANIMALS: Horses

Motor Racing—*see* ROAD TRANSPORT

Mountaineering

Artist drawn. Period 1/Early Period 2	£1/**£2**/£4
Comic	50p/**75p**/£1
Pub. Abrahams, Keswick	50p/**75p**/£1
Others	25p/**50p**/75p

Olympic Games
20th Anniversary of re-establishment of the Games (1914) .. .. £6/**£10**/£12
Paris (1924). Artist Pauteuberge .. .. .. £8/**£10**/£12
Berlin (1936). Col. designs .. .. £12/**£15**/£20
Monotone officials .. .. £1.50/**£3**/£5
Garmish Partenkirchen (Winter Games) (1936) £7/**£10**/£12
Moscow (1980). Official cards. Artist drawn. Garish colour.
Printed 1978 .. .. 25p/**50p**/75p
Los Angeles (1984). Various 25p/50p
Others
Period 4 .. .. £4/**£7**/£10
Period 6 .. .. 50p/**75p**/£1

Polo
Price range .. .. 75p/**£1**/£1.50

Roller Skating—*see* COMPETITIONS: Rinking

Rowing ■SP 4
Price range .. .. 25p/**75p**/£3

■SP 4 Pub. Anon. RP. Period 2 75p

Sailing/Yachting
Crews, races, regattas, sailing ships .. .. .. £1/**£2**/£3

Shooting
Game .. .. 50p/**£1**/£1.25
Target .. .. £1/**£1.50**/£2

Show-jumping (Horse Shows)
General scenes .. .. 75p/**£1**/£1.25
Olympia Horse Show. General .. .. £1/**£2**/£4
Poster ads. .. .. £3/**£5**/£6

Skating ■SP 5
Artist-drawn .. .. 50p/**£1.50**/£5
Comic .. .. 50p/**75p**/£1
Others 25p/**50p**/75p

Sports Days & Events
Price range .. .. 50p/**75p**/£1

Swimming
Price range .. .. 25p/**£1**/£2

Table tennis (Ping Pong)

A listing of table tennis cards appeared in the third edition of this catalogue, pp. 136–137

Price range (value according to Period, Artist, etc.)	25p/**£2.50**/£12

Tennis

Artist drawn (value according to artist)	£1/**£3**/£5
Comic (value according to artists)	50p/**75p**/£3
General scenes	25p/**50p**/75p
Players. Pre-1939	£2/**£3**/£4
Periods 5–6	75p/**£1**/£1.50
Period 7	**25p**
Wimbledon scenes	25p/**£2**/£3

Tobogganing

Price range	50p/**75p**/£1

Trophies

Price range	50p/**£1**/£1.50

■SP 5 Pub. Vouga, Geneva. Artist Pellegrini. 'Wintersport in Salzburg'. Period 2 £5

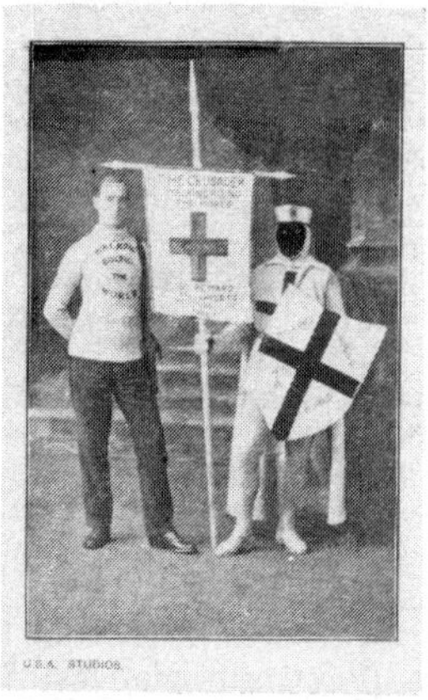

■SP 6 Pub. 'U.S.A. Studios.' 'The Crusader. Walking Round the World'. Period 2 £2

Walking ■SP 6

Racing	£1/**£1.50**/£3
Round the World	£1.50/**£2.50**/£3.50

Water Polo

Price range	75p/**£1**/£1.50

Winter Sports

Chromo-litho	£1/**£1.50**/£2
Others	25p/**50p**/75p

Wrestling

Price range	£1.50/**£2**/£3

TOPOGRAPHICAL

These cards are particularly difficult to value because they are often only of interest to people who live in a fairly small geographical area. Thus while we might pay several pounds for a view showing a deserted road through our own village of Woodnesborough, others might consider it to be well overpriced at 25p. However, it is important to be aware that apparently dull cards can command quite high values. The obvious factors which contribute to the price of a card are picture content, e.g. traffic detail and animation; and picture clarity, e.g. RP printing. Where a local publisher is named on a card that might be a reason for increased value.

London cards are perhaps more popular generally than cards showing scenes in other cities and towns. We include a London section in this listing, this follows the thematic listings—*Disasters*, *Street Scenes* and *Strikes*.

DISASTERS ■T 1

This section deals with 'Acts of God' such as epidemics, fires, floods, landslides and storms rather than obviously man-made catastrophes like rail or road accidents, except where the latter assumed disaster proportions. Probably every area of the country has had its own disaster.

Bristol. Fire (1905). Pub. Pincock Bros. RP £1.50/**£2**/£2.50
Clapham. Fire. Arding & Hobbs (1909) .. .. £2/**£3**/£4
Hampstead Colliery (1908). Pub. Nightingale .. £4/**£6**/£8
Handcross Motor Bus Fatality.
Pub. Kerhhohn & others. RP .. .. .. £1/**£1.50**/£2
Pub. Ingram Clark .. .. £2/**£4**/£6
Lincoln Typhoid outbreak (1905) .. .. £10/**£12**/£15
Louth Floods (1920). Pub. Benton, Harrison, *Yorkshire Observer* .. .. £2/**£5**/£8
Lynmouth Floods (1952). H. Barton .. .. £1/**£1.50**/£2
Messina Earthquake. It (1908). Incl. 'Before & After' Novelty cards .. .. 50p/**75p**/£1
Norwich Floods (1912). Pub. Pioneer RP .. .. £2/**£4**/£6
Paris Floods (Inondations) (1910). Over 40 pubs. Over 3000 cards .. .. 75p/**£1.50**/£3
San Francisco Earthquake (1906) 25p/**50p**/75p
Stalybridge Floods (1906). Pub. Hallas .. .. £2/**£4**/£5
Others .. .. £1/**£3**/£5

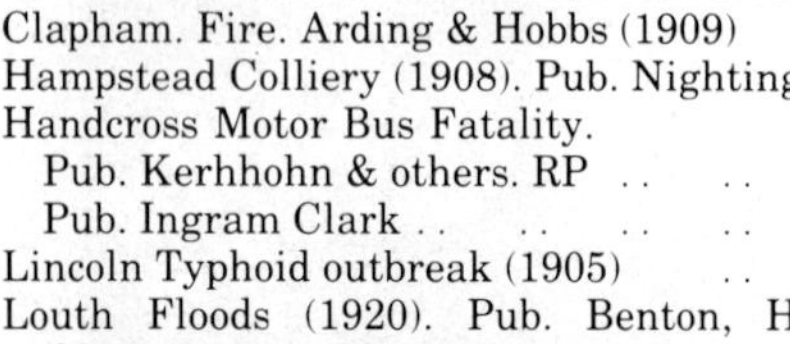

■T 1 Pub. Anon. Paris Floods, Jan. 1910. 'Saving a Paralised Lady.' RP. Period 2 £3

■T 2 Pub. Salmon. Artist A. R. Quinton. Madeira Walk, Brighton. PU 1921 £2

STREET SCENES

Artist Drawn ■T 2

Valuations depend more on calibre of the artist rather than the site depicted.

City centres	25p/**50p**/£6
City suburbs	50p/**75p**/£6
Towns, inland	50p/**75p**/£6
Towns, seaside	25p/**75p**/£6
Villages	50p/**£1**/£6

Photographic Origin

City centres—Animated	25p/**50p**/£2
Non-animated	25p/50p
City suburbs Animated	50p/**£2**/£4
Non-animated	25p/**50p**/75p
Towns, inland Animated	50p/**£2**/£4
Non-animated	25p/**50p**/75p
Towns, seaside Animated	25p/**75p**/£3
Non-animated	25p/50p
Villages Animated	50p/**£2**/£5
Non-animated	25p/**£1**/£3

Real Photographic ■T 3

City centres Animated	50p/**£1**/£3
Non-animated	25p/**75p**/£1.50
City suburbs Animated	£4/**£8**/£12
Non-animated	75p/**£1.50**/£3
Towns, inland Animated	£4/**£8**/£12
Non-animated	75p/**£1.50**/£3
Towns, seaside Animated	75p/**£1.50**/£3
Non-animated	25p/**75p**/£1
Villages, Animated	£5/**£10**/£15
Non-animated	£1/**£2**/£4

Three Band Pricing System

Left Hand Band: The lowest price you will probably be asked to pay for this card.
Middle Band: What you will normally be asked to pay for this card: its average, reasonable price.
Right Hand Band: The highest price you will probably be asked to pay for this card.
For a full explanation of the system see page ix.

■T 3 Pub. 'R.A. Postcards'. 'Albion Street, Southwick'. RP. Period 6 £5

STRIKES

Most strikes remain local issues. The upper valuations will apply where there is good photographic origin detail which identifies strongly with the locality, e.g. names of individuals involved, readable strike notices, etc.

Belfast (1907) .. .. £4/**£8**/£10
Black Country (1913) .. .. £4/**£6**/£8
General Strike (1926) .. .. £6/**£10**/£15
Ilkeston (1912) .. .. £6/**£10**/£12
Liverpool (1910) .. .. £5/**£8**/£10
Smethwick (1913) .. .. £6/**£10**/£1
Thirlwall (1910/1911) .. .. £6/**£10**/£15
Others .. .. £3/**£5**/£7

LONDON

There were literally hundreds of publishers who issued cards showing London views. Both Charles Martin and E. Gordon Smith are each said to have produced over 3000 numbered views of Greater London.

London attracts special attention as our capital city, and the home of so many postcard entrepreneurs, and provides a popular collecting theme. We are concerned in this section only with early cards, important artists and series, or cards which have a particular reason for being singled out, e.g. a London view drawn by Tom Browne, an acknowledged and well collected comic artis.

Artist Drawn ■T 5

This section lists only artists who were well known for their postcard work.

Browne, Tom.† Davidson series 2543 .. .. .. £2/**£3**/£4
Valentine's 'London Street Scene series' .. .. £2/**£3**/£4
Cassiers, H.† P. G. Huardel London views .. .. £2/**£3**/£4
Colls, H. Faulkner's first series. London views (12 cards) .. .. £1/**£2**/£3
Flower, Charles. Tuck Oilette series .. .. 50p/**75p**/£2
King, Edward. Tuck Oilettes, *e.g.* 'The Pavement Artist' .. .. 75p/**£1**/£1.25
Kyd. Pictorial Stationery Co. Peacock series. Types £2/**£3**/£5
Quinton, A. R. Pub. Salmon .. .. 50p/**75p**/£2

Sauber, R.† Pictorial Stationery Co. Familiar figures or London (12 cards) .. .. £4/**£5**/£6
Ward, Dudley, E. T. W. Dennis. London characters £1/**£2**/£3
Wheatley, F. Set of 13 'Cries of London' after originals by the artist. Various pubs. .. .. 50p/**75p**/£1.50

London Life ■T 4

In this section we list photo-origin cards. The higher values are for close-up RP pictures of events, street scenes, 'types' or views that no longer exist. Collectors will often pay more than is indicated here for an RP card that has a particular meaning for them.

Pub. Aristophot .. .. 50p/**£2**/£4
Pub. Beagles 'Real Photo' series .. .. .. 25p/**75p**/£1.50
Pub. 'LL'
Period 2. London Types .. .. £2/**£4**/£8
Period 2 pictures, published Period 4 .. £1/**£1.50**/£3
Pub. Martin, Charles
Pub. Photochrom. Celesque series. 'London Types' £3/**£4**/£5
Pub. Rotary
Photo series 10513 (over 80 cards) .. .. ..£5/**£10**/£15
Other photo series, incl. 10514 (over 40 cards), 10167, 10482, 10484 .. .. £2/**£3**/£5
Pub. Skilton. London Life .. .. £1.50/**£2**/£4
Pub. Smith, Gordon .. .. 50p/**£1.50**/£6
Sidney Street Siege (Higher value for cards showing Winston Churchill) .. .. £2/**£3**/£5
Others .. .. £1/**£2**/£3

■T 4 Pub. 'LL'. 'London Types' No. 302 'The Pavement Artist'. Period 2, republished Period 4 £3

■T 5 Pub. Tuck. 'Old London Churches' No. 6259. Artist Charles E. Flower. PU 1911 £3

Tuck ■T 5

The first Tuck cards, issued in 1899 were of London (see PUBLISHERS). *Later, in the splendid Aquarette and Oilette series, were many more views of London and its types.*

Aquarette/Oilette series .. .. 75p/**£1**/£1.50
London Life. Series 9015 .. .. 75p/**£1**/£2
Real Photograph series .. .. 50p/**75p**/£1.50
'View' series No. 1–24. UB .. .. £5/**£8**/£12

BRITISH POSTCARD CLUBS

A list of Club secretaries appears below. Details of the Club can be obtained from the Secretary. A stamped addressed envelope should be enclosed for reply.

1. National Clubs

Postcard Club of Great Britain
Mrs. Drene Brennan
34 Harper House
St James's Crescent
LONDON SW9 7DW

Irish Picture Postcard Society
S. Kearns
c/o Stamp & Coin Centre
76 Aungier Street
DUBLIN 2

2. Local Clubs

Andover Collectors Group
David Smith
66 Seville Crescent
ANDOVER
Hants. SP10 1JT

Bradford & District Postcard Society
A. E. Wood
26 Front View
Shelf
HALIFAX
West Yorkshire HX3 7JU

Brighton & District Postcard Club
R. Cairns
2 Shelley Rd.
Ringmer
BRIGHTON
E. Sussex

Bristol Postcard Club
Derek Fisher
111 Longmead Ave.
Horfield
BRISTOL BS7 8QE

Canterbury & East Kent Postcard Club
Terry Hougham
23 Hanover Place
CANTERBURY
Kent CT2 7HA

Chester & District Postcard Club
Peter Gaston
16 Westminster Green
Handbridge
CHESTER CH4 7LE

Colchester & District Card Collectors Club
Michael Napthan
17 St. Dominic Rd.
COLCHESTER
Essex CO4 4PY

Cotswold Postcard Collectors Club
Philip Griffiths
10 Smyth House
The Waterloo
CIRENCESTER
Glos. GL7 2QR

Dewsbury & District Postcard Society
A. F. Bower
Manor House
School Lane
Walton
WAKEFIELD
W. Yorkshire WF2 6PA

Doncaster Postcard Club
Sylvia Phillips
3 Main St
Cadeby
DONCASTER
S. Yorkshire DN5 7SL

Douglas Stamp & Postcard Club
18 Kingswood Grove
DOUGLAS
Isle of Man

Heart of England Postcard Club
Barry Hickman
27 Aylesford St.
LEAMINGTON SPA
Warwickshire CV31 2AH

Herefordshire Postcard Club
Tim Ward
Farm View
Upperfields
LEDBURY
Herefordshire HR8 1LE

Hertfordshire Postcard Club
R. Rundell
5 Dryden Cres.
STEVENAGE
SG2 0JG

Huddersfield & District Postcard Society
Kenneth Battye
77 Stile Common Rd.
Newsome
HUDDERSFIELD HD4 6NE

Hull & Humberside Postcard Collectors Society
C. J. Ketchell
Flat 2
105 Princes Ave.
HULL HU5 3JL

British Postcard Clubs

Leeds Postcard Club
Mrs. A. Whitelock
9 Brentwood Grove
LEEDS LS12 2DB

Lincoln Collectors Club
Peter Rowlett
32 Cliff Ave.
Nettleham
LINCOLN LN2 2PU

Llangollen & District Postcard Club
Verna Palmer
15 Bradley Fields
OSWESTRY
Shropshire SY11 1SP

Maidstone Postcard Club
Mrs. I. Hales
40 Hildenborough Cres.
MAIDSTONE
Kent ME16 0NR

Merseyside Postcard Club
P. W. Woolley
7 Patrick Ave.
BOOTLE
Merseyside L20 6EP

Moonrakers Postcard Club
A. Alexander
6 Nurstead Park
DEVIZES
Wilts SN10 3AN

Newcastle-upon-Tyne Postcard Club
Ken Brierley
41 Mallard Way
South Beach
BLYTH
Northd. NE24 3QA

Norfolk Postcard Club
P. J. Standley
63 Folly Road
WYMONDHAM
Norfolk NR18 0QR

Northamptonshire Postcard Club
G. Garner
5 Cheriton Way
NORTHAMPTON NN2 55B

North Devon Postcard Club
Marguarite Turner
19 Church Street
BRAUNTON
Devon EX33 2EL

Northern Ireland Postcard Club
W. J. Nelson
56B Willow Gdns
Dunmurry
BELFAST BT17 9QJ

North Wales Postcard Club
Michael Day
39 Links Ave.
Little Sutton
SOUTH WIRRAL L66 1QS

Nottingham Postcard Club
Pat Davies
19 Fisher Ave.
Woodthorpe
NOTTINGHAM NG5 4JE

Peterborough Postcard Club
Stephen Perry
68 Sallows Rd.
PETERBOROUGH PE1 4EU

Pickering Postcard Club
Alan Pickup
8 Cuddy Brown Close
PICKERING
North Yorkshire YO18 7EU

Potteries Postcard Club
Steve Benz
5 Queen Margarets' Rd.
Loggerheads
MARKET DRAYTON
Shropshire TF9 4EP

Reading Cigarette Card & Postcard Club
Michael Tubb
15 Wessex Gdns
Twyford
READING RG10 0BA

Rushden Collectors Circle
Mrs. Joyce Church
2 Meadow Drive
HIGHAM FERRERS
Northants NN9 8EZ

Scarborough Postcard Club
Mrs. W. L. Tindall
7 Coniston Gdns.
Crossgates
SCARBOROUGH
N. Yorkshire YO12 4JH

Somerset Postcard Club
Heather Cavell
36 Kingsway Rd.
BURNHAM-ON-SEA
Som. TA8 1ET

Southampton Postcard Club
Nigel Bachmann
Grove Lodge
Ramsey Rd.
Nursling
SOUTHAMPTON SO1 9XW

South Devon Postcard Club
Michael Dadley
Flat 3
109 Totnes Rd.
PAIGNTON
Devon TQ3 3RZ

Strathclyde Postcard Club
S. K. Hunter
34 Gray St.
GLASGOW G3 7TY

Suffolk Postcard & Cigarette Card Club
Kath Twidale
74 Western Ave.
FELIXSTONE Suffolk IP11 9NT

Surrey Postcard Club
Malcolm Covey
4 Wayside Cottages
Horsham Rd.
Holmbury St. Mary
DORKING, Surrey RH5 6NH

Postcard Club of Tayside
Jim Russell
36 Kerrington Cres.
Broughty Ferry
DUNDEE DD5 2TN

Tees Valley Collectors Club
Joan Lambert
24 Beechwood Ave.
DARLINGTON
Co. Durham DL3 7HP

Wyre Forest Postcard Club
Derek Gallimore
The Grange
30 Pinewoods Ave.
Hagley
STOURBRIDGE
West Midlands DY9 0JF

3. Specialist Postcard Clubs

Canal Card Collectors Circle
David Clough
12 Wellstead Gdns.
WESTCLIFF-ON-SEA
Essex SS0 0AY

Exhibition (Cards) Study Group
A. D. Brooks
'Fairhaven'
Sunderland Road
EAST BOLDON
Tyne & Wear NE36 0NA

Fairground Postcard Society
S. White
57 Stanley St.
Rothwell
KETTERING
Northants. NN14 2EA

Judges Collectors Club
R. Grosvenor
Yealm House
9 Brackley Rd.
TOWCESTER
Northants NN12 7DH

Lands End Postcard & Cachet Club
Mrs. J. Lawrance
83 Burgoyne Rd.
SUNBURY-ON-THAMES
Middx. TW16 7PS

Piers Postcard Collectors Circle
Nova Saunders
Yealm House
9 Brackley Rd.
TOWCESTER
Northants NN12 7DH

A. R. Quinton Society
R. Stammers
2 Tissington Ave.
Church Warsop
MANSFIELD
Notts. NG20 0RT

Royalty Postcard Collectors Club
Cindy Morris
5 Shrubbery Hill
Cookley
KIDDERMINSTER
Worcs. DY10 3UW

Southern Africa Postcard Research Group
Ms. Vivien Allen
Westcroft
The Crofts
CASTLETOWN
Isle of Man

Tuck Collectors Circle
D. Pinfold
7 Glenville
NORTHAMPTON NN3 1LZ

American and Canadian Clubs

There are at least 50 postcard clubs in the USA and Canada. A list of these can be obtained by sending a stamped addressed envelope or international reply coupon to: J. H. McClintock, Postcard Club Federation, P.O. Box 1765, Manassas, VA 22110, USA.

INDEX TO ARTISTS

For biography see page marked in bold type
For illustration see page marked in *italic* type

INDEX TO THEMES

Index to Themes